Build Your Own Macintosh® and Save a Bundle

Second Edition

Bob Brant

Windcrest®/McGraw-Hill

SECOND EDITION
FIRST PRINTING

© 1992 by **Bob Brant**.
Published by Windcrest Books, an imprint of TAB Books.
TAB Books is a division of McGraw-Hill, Inc.
The name "Windcrest" is a registered trademark of TAB Books.

Printed in the United States of America. All rights reserved. The publisher takes no responsibility for the use of any of the materials or methods described in this book, nor for the products thereof.

Library of Congress Cataloging-in-Publication Data

Brant, Bob.
   Build your own Macintosh and save a bundle / by Bob Brant.—2nd ed.
      p.   cm.
   Includes bibliographical references and index.
   ISBN 0-8306-3973-X   ISBN 0-8306-3974-8 (pbk.)
   1. Microcomputers—Design and construction—Amateurs' manuals.
2. Macintosh-compatible computers—Design and construction--Amateurs' manuals. I. Title.
TK9969.B73   1992
621.39'16—dc20   92-4783
                                                                         CIP

TAB Books offers software for sale. For information and a catalog, please contact TAB Software Department, Blue Ridge Summit, PA 17294-0850.

Supervising Editor: Sandra L. Johnson
Book Editor: Susan Bonthron
Director of Production: Katherine G. Brown
Book Design: Jaclyn J. Boone
Paperbound Cover Design: Sandra Blair Design
   and Brent Blair Photography, Harrisburg, PA.   EL1-H

Contents

Acknowledgments *xi*
Preface to the second edition *xiii*
Introduction *xv*
   A concept that has passed the test of time *xv*
   Repackage your Macintosh *xvii*
   Chapter overview *xvii*
   You can do it *xix*

1 Why build your own Macintosh 1
   Advantages of building a Cat Mac 3
      The Cat Mac concept 3
      A Ben Franklin on the Cat Mac advantages 5
   Remember, the Force is with you 7
      A little history lesson 7
      Trend one: Apple Macintosh price performance 8
      Trend two: Third-party vendor performance 10
      Trend three: Used equipment vendor performance 11
      Trend four: Mail order vendor performance 12
      One of the few guarantees in life 14
   Why build a Macintosh versus a DOS PC 15
   The future 18

2 How much you can save *19*
    The Macintosh block by block *20*
    Apple Macintosh cost overview *22*
        Macintosh real world pricing *23*
        Trends in Macintosh pricing *25*
        Macintosh logic board pricing *26*
        Logic board to system cost ratio *28*
        Macintosh upgrade pricing *29*
    Cat Mac cost overview *29*
        Cat Mac versus standard Apple Macintosh costs *29*
        Cat Mac Classic versus Apple Mac Classic *30*
        Cat Mac LC versus Apple Mac LC *31*
        Cat Mac IIsi versus Apple Mac IIsi *31*
        Cat Mac IIci versus Apple Mac IIci *32*
        Cat Mac IIfx versus Apple Mac IIfx *33*
    Cat Mac system recommendations *33*
        Recommended Cat Mac systems *34*
        Not recommended Cat Mac systems *36*

3 Macintosh logic boards *39*
    The Motorola 68000 CPU chip family *40*
    Choose your Cat Mac logic board *42*
        Obsolete Macintosh logic boards *42*
        Entry-level Macintosh logic boards *42*
        Midrange Macintosh logic boards *44*
        High-end Macintosh logic boards *45*
        Portable Macintosh logic boards *45*
        Cat Mac builder's summary *46*
    Apple Macintosh logic boards *46*
        Mac 128, 512, and Plus logic boards *46*
        Mac SE logic board *49*
        Mac SE 30 logic board *50*
        Mac Classic logic board *52*
        Mac Classic II logic board *54*
        Mac LC logic board *55*
        Mac IIsi logic board *57*
        Mac II logic board *58*
        Mac IIx logic board *60*
        Mac IIcx logic board *60*
        Mac IIci logic board *61*
        Mac IIfx logic board *63*
        Mac Quadra 700 logic board *64*
        Mac Quadra 900 logic board *66*
    Sources *67*

4 Memory and upgrades 71

How is your memory 72
    ROM, RAM, DRAM, SRAM, PRAM, cache, memory chips, SIMMs 72
    SIMM price history and trends 74

Macintosh memory upgrades 75
    Mac 128 and 512 memory upgrade 76
    Mac Classic memory upgrade 79
    SIMM memory upgrade 80
    Buying SIMMs 80
    SIMM installation and removal 82
    SIMM rules—Mac Plus and SE 85
    SIMM rules—Mac SE 30 and NuBus 86
    SIMM rules—Mac Classic, Classic II, LC, IIsi and Quadra 700 89
    SIMM rules—Mac IIfx 90

Macintosh upgrades 90
    Upgrade process 91
    Apple upgrades 91
    Accelerators 93
    Okay—accelerate me 93
    CPU/clock accelerators 95
    FPU accelerators 95
    Memory/cache accelerators 95
    SCSI bus accelerators 96
    File compression accelerators 96
    Full-function accelerators 96
    Accelerators using 68000 CPUs 97
    Accelerators using up to 40-MHz 68030 CPUs 98
    Accelerators using up to 50-MHz 68030 CPUs 101
    Accelerators using up to 55-MHz 68030 CPUs 103
    Accelerators using up to 25-MHz 68040 CPUs 104
    Accelerators using up to 33-MHz 68040 CPUs 105
    Buying accelerators 105

Sources 106

5 Storage 109

Storage definitions 110
Storage overview 113
Floppy drives 114
    Floppy drive upgrades 119
    Do not coerce your 800K floppy diskettes 119
Hard drives 120
    Why buy a hard drive 123
    Hard drive pricing and what to buy revisited 124

Who to buy from   *127*
Mounting and connecting your hard drive   *127*
Formatting your hard drive   *129*
Removable drives   *131*
Remove the hard drive   *131*
Remove the media   *131*
Optical drives   *133*
Optical drive benefits   *135*
MO drive benefits for Cat Mac builders   *136*
CD-ROM drive benefits for Cat Mac builders   *137*
WORM drive benefits for Cat Mac builders   *139*
Tape drives   *140*
Sources   *141*

6 Monitors and video cards   *149*

Monitor overview and history   *150*
The Cat Mac benefit—more video flexibility   *152*
Could you please define that   *152*
All monitors are not created equal   *154*
What to look for   *154*
Physical viewing screen   *154*
Tube   *155*
Interface   *155*
Packaging   *155*
Price performance   *156*
Monitors and video cards I have known   *156*
Low-end Cat Mac video solutions   *156*
TTL monitors and cards   *157*
The Lapis connection   *159*
Lapis 1-bit monochrome video card alternatives   *161*
Princeton MAX-15 monitor and Power R module   *162*
Midrange Cat Mac video solutions   *162*
Color Cat Mac video solutions   *163*
Apple color monitor offerings   *165*
Other color monitor offerings   *165*
The SCSI monitor connection   *166*
Combination accelerator and video cards   *167*
Build your own video interface   *167*
Sources   *169*

7 Chassis, wiring, keyboard, and mouse   *171*

Chassis   *172*
Advantages of a DOS PC chassis   *172*
PC-XT-style case   *174*
Mini-tower- or PC-AT-style case   *174*

　　　　　Low-profile PS/2-style case   *175*
　　　　　LAN-style case   *177*
　　　　　Tower-style case   *178*
　　　　　　A quick look at the back panel   *178*
　　Wiring your Cat Mac   *180*
　　　　　Power cable   *182*
　　　　　SCSI cable   *187*
　　　　　Floppy cable   *187*
　　　　　Other cables   *187*
　　Keyboard and mouse   *190*
　　　　　ADB versus non-ADB   *191*
　　　　　Keyboard alternatives   *191*
　　　　　Mouse alternatives   *195*
　　　　　Eek, a mouse invasion . . .   *197*
　　Sources   *198*

8　Putting together the original Cat Mac   *201*

　　Assembling the Cat Mac step by step   *204*
　　Before you build   *206*
　　　　　Ordering the parts   *207*
　　　　　Before you start   *208*
　　　　　Tools you will need   *208*
　　　　　Receiving your parts   *209*
　　Assembly   *209*
　　　　　Make the logic board template   *209*
　　　　　Make the rear cover plate template   *212*
　　　　　Drill the chassis case   *214*
　　　　　Drill the rear cover plate   *214*
　　　　　Drill anything else you need to drill   *215*
　　　　　Mount the power supply   *215*
　　　　　Mount the logic board   *216*
　　　　　Mount the accelerator and video cards/modules   *219*
　　　　　Mount the hard disk   *220*
　　　　　Mount the floppy disk   *222*
　　　　　Mount the speaker and cable   *224*
　　　　　Make the logic board power cable and connect it   *226*
　　　　　Connect the other cables   *230*
　　　　　Connect the case to the other parts   *233*
　　　　　Power on—Phase 1 ("Liftoff and earth orbit")   *234*
　　　　　Connect your hard disk   *234*
　　　　　Power on—Phase 2 ("Moon orbit and landing")   *236*
　　After you build   *238*
　　　　　Finishing thoughts   *239*
　　　　　New worlds to conquer   *241*
　　　　　Troubleshooting   *241*

9 New desktop Cat Macs *243*

Desktop Cat Mac *244*
- A quick course in unwelding *244*
- Mount the rear panel and logic board *246*
- Mount the power supply *248*
- Mount the speaker *249*
- Mount the accelerator/video card *251*
- Mount the hard drive *251*
- Mount the floppy drive *254*
- Cabling your Cat Mac *255*
- Mounting more than one SCSI device *256*
- Final assembly and checkout *258*

Compact desktop Cat Mac *260*
- Prepare chassis *261*
- Mount the rear panel and logic board *261*
- Mount the power supply and fan *261*
- Mount the speaker *263*
- Mount and connect the LED lamps and reset switch *264*
- Mount the video card *264*
- Mount the floppy and hard drives *266*
- Cabling your Cat Mac *268*
- Final assembly and checkout *270*

10 Upgrade kits make building easier *271*

Desktop upgrade kit *272*
- Prepare the enclosure *273*
- Prepare and install the SE 30 logic board *275*
- Reinstall the power supply and drives *277*
- Reinstall the video card *278*
- Button up the chassis *278*
- Connect the external cables and checkout *279*

Tower upgrade kits *282*
- Assembling the ATS Mac IIcx/IIci tower chassis *283*
- Open the ATS Mac IIcx/IIci tower enclosure *283*
- Mount the Mac IIcx or IIci logic board *285*
- Mount the drives and connect the cables *286*
- Button up the chassis *288*
- Finishing up steps *288*
- ATS Mac II, IIx, IIfx tower chassis *290*
- Open the ATS Mac II, IIx, IIfx tower enclosure *291*
- Mount your Mac II, IIx, or IIfx logic board *291*
- Mount the drives, connect cables, add cards *292*
- Button up the chassis *293*
- Finishing up steps *293*

Portable upgrade kit *297*

    Open the portable kit *299*
    Mount the Macintosh logic board *300*
    Mount keyboard, drives, power supply *300*
    Finishing up steps *303*
    The envelope please *305*
  Sources *305*

11 Cat Mac builder alternatives *307*

  DOS on Mac *308*
    Transfer DOS PC files *309*
    Run DOS PC programs in hardware *309*
    Run DOS PC programs in software *310*
  Mac on DOS *310*
  Mac on Mac (portable or clone) *312*
    Apple Macintosh Portable *313*
    Apple PowerBook *313*
    Other Mac portables *314*
    Clones *314*
  Mac on Atari *316*
  Mac on Unix *317*
  Sources *319*

12 The end of the beginning *321*

  Peripheral equipment you will need *322*
  Software you will need *326*
  Now that you are up and running *327*
  A few words about the future *329*
    Mail order *329*
    Magazines *330*
    Computer shows *331*
    User groups *331*
    Local dealers *332*
    Consultants *332*
    Books *332*

Glossary *335*

Index *345*

Acknowledgments

This book is dedicated to Steven Jobs and the other incredible members of the original Apple Macintosh[1] team whose vision, perseverance, and skills made it possible to introduce a better computer for "The Rest of Us;" and to John Scully whose vision carried the Macintosh forward and made it an everyday reality in corporate America. Credit must also respectfully be given to the resident genius types at Xerox Palo Alto Research Center for their STAR system, the forerunner of the Lisa (the parent to the Macintosh), even though it was not allowed to evolve to its full potential there; to the whiz kids over at Atari and Commodore, who have shown Apple, on more than one occasion, how a good idea can be "colored" and improved upon; to the individuals on the late Don Esteridge's IBM PC Boca Raton "dream team" who took an Apple idea, reinnovated it, and changed the face of the earth forever; and finally, to the hardworking individuals at all the third-party vendors, both software and hardware, for continuously pushing Apple and the "outside of the envelope" as Chuck Yeager would say.

Special acknowledgment and thanks are due to: Darwin Gross, author, musician, and wayshower to many, the most humble, creative genius anyone could ever have the good fortune to meet, for the continuing inspiration; to my wife, Bonnie Brant, for challenging the ideas, proofreading, and ensuring my written expression fell somewhat within the confines of the English language; and to my mother Mary Brant, for first sparking my interest in books, writing, and life.

---

[1] This book presumes you are already familiar, at least in passing, with Apple Computer, Inc. and the Apple Macintosh Computer. If you want additional information contact any Authorized Apple Dealer or Apple Computer, Inc. 20525 Mariani Ave., Cupertino, CA 95014, (408) 996-1010. Apple, the Apple logo, and Macintosh are registered trademarks of Apple Computer, Inc.

Preface to the second edition

I am not surprised the trends in the build-your-own-Macintosh market have moved in exactly the direction predicted by the first edition of this book (published in 1991). But I am surprised the first edition became one of Windcrest/McGraw-Hill's bestselling books. I am grateful to the numerous readers and Macintosh builders worldwide who have found it helpful, and who have also asked hundreds of questions. This second edition answers the questions asked most often, and contributes new building hints, tips, and suggestions.

While virtually every chapter of the second edition has been updated with the latest products and prices, the second edition builds on the previous book's foundation. The principles laid down in the first edition remain the same, as do the reasons why you might want to build your own Macintosh.

This book's fundamental premise—that you can easily custom-tailor your Macintosh hardware with readily available, off-the-shelf catalog parts and save money in the process—is timeless. Because no two Macintosh owners are alike, the flexibility of the Macintosh in adapting its GUI (graphical user interface) and software applications to each user's needs is what contributed to its success in the first place. Offering the same flexibility and capability with its hardware (the subject of this book) is merely a logical extension.

Watching the build-your-own-Macintosh phenomena evolve over the past several years has been interesting. Initially the activity was at the entry-level pure-price end, but Apple's late 1990 announcements closed that gap somewhat. Lately, I've noticed another reason that build-your-own-Macintosh builders do it is because of the "Burger King" phenomena—you can have it your way. You can pick and choose the options you want. You have a lot more flexibility in how you mount them, and because the case you put them in has more power, more space, and more cooling, they last a lot longer.

Lately, I've been seeing build-your-own-Macintosh builders migrate to the midrange (Mac II, Mac IIx, IIcx, and IIci logic boards) of the spectrum, and I suspect that when the 68040-based Mac Quadra logic boards become more available and Mac IIfx logic board prices come down, you'll see a lot more activity at the high end. I'm sure the fact that the price advantage of build-your-own-Macintosh solutions increases as you move toward higher-performance logic boards will help this trend along.

Watching companies jump onto the build-your-own-Macintosh bandwagon has also been interesting. Today, several companies offer products that make repackaging your Macintosh logic board even easier, while others have found economies of scale in offering their Macintosh users "standardized" packages that often share components (monitors, hard drives, chassis, and power supplies) with their DOS PC installed base.

My goal in this second edition is to expand your horizons so you can continue to apply your Macintosh to its highest and best use—making you more efficient at whatever you do. I hope you enjoy it and continue to ask questions! May the Force be with you in all your Macintosh endeavors.

Who I am

I am a full-time author and Macintosh consultant[1] who provides both software and hardware solutions for a wide range of business clients. In 1983, as Operations Manager for a publishing firm in Northern California, I became "hooked" by having one of the first $10,000 Apple Lisa systems on my desk. My initial Macintosh introduction followed a short time later, and several years in various sales and management capacities with Businessland, Nynex, Microage, and a regional reseller in the Northwest honed my experience. Prior to that, a combined 10 years with DEC and Data General in the minicomputer industry with a BSEE from the University of Denver and credits toward MSEE and MBA degrees gave me my frame of reference.

Build Your Own Macintosh and Save a Bundle—2nd Edition joins three other books I've written for Windcrest/McGraw-Hill: *Macintosh Hard Disk Management, Upgrade Your Macintosh and Save a Bundle,* and the original *Build Your Own Macintosh and Save a Bundle.*

---

[1] Books, reports, parts, and consulting services to assist you in building or upgrading your Macintosh are available from Brant Associates, P.O. Box 68708, Portland, OR 97268.

Introduction

It always intrigued me, in my contacts with various developers and system houses, that many of them "just happened" to have a custom-built Macintosh lying around, usually a Macintosh in a DOS PC[1] case. I would ask them, "What kind of a computer is that?" The answer was usually the same: "Well, we wanted to do x and we just couldn't do it in a regular Macintosh chassis."

It reinforced my own experience as a full-time computer consultant. Clients would ask: Could you mount that Macintosh in a rack? Could you fix it so that I just have one larger monitor on my desk? Could you mount it in this size space? On and on. I knew from my own experience that you could repackage a Macintosh to make it do exactly what you wanted to do and, wonder of wonders, if you could put it in a standard DOS PC case, it cost you a lot less than buying a new Macintosh.

It intrigued me that despite the wealth of information always available to all on the Apple Macintosh computer, nobody ever spoke about what was inside the box, except in hushed tones, until articles in *Computer Shopper*[2] broke the ice. I believed that it would be more helpful if all this information could be gathered together in one place. The result was the first edition of this book. The second edition that you now hold in your hand not only gathers the information together in one spot, but enlarges and updates its coverage.

A concept that has passed the test of time

My goal is to give you tools and a foundation you can build upon and use over and over again in the future. You have probably heard the saying: *Give a man a loaf of bread and he can feed his family for a day. Give him the grain and show him how to plant and harvest and he can feed his family for a lifetime.* This book builds on the same principle.

Think of it as if you were building a house. I am going to give you the tools and plans and show you the process. The exact house you build is up to you. What you learn from this book will make it easier than ever for you to upgrade your Macintosh or build a customized Apple Macintosh of your own from catalog parts (a "catalog Macintosh," or *Cat Mac*, as it's called throughout this book) at the best possible price.

Time has validated the basic premise of this book: building your own Macintosh will always be less expensive than buying a new system. Many Macintosh computer parts are less expensive today than when the first edition was published. This trend, because of existing marketing and distribution channel trends, will continue in the future.

Time has also validated the other basic premise of this book: You can repackage a Macintosh to make it do exactly what you want to do. This is not an "off-the-wall" experimental concept. Thousands of satisfied Macintosh owners around the world—members of the largest corporations as well as individual business persons—are using their Macintosh computers in configurations that Apple never dreamed of to earn their livelihood.

Apple is also positively affected, and this bodes well for the concept's future. First, it extends Apple's presence into market niches it does not directly support, and preserves a Macintosh rather than DOS PC or alternative platform solution; second, the use of used or older Macintosh equipment reinforces the sale of new Apple products, just as the used car market supports the new one; and finally, this new market provides Apple incremental revenues from products it cannot profitably manufacture itself. Third-party vendors are just as positively affected.

However, the technology is changing rapidly, so consider the products and prices you read about here only as a starting frame of reference rather than a final tally. You must do your own shopping to get the best products and prices at the time you build or upgrade.

The concept itself is also changing. New configurations are constantly being created as new needs arise, so please don't accept any design philosophy I espouse here as the last word. Besides, writing forces you to question all the things that you thought you knew. Years ago, I wrote a mail order ad for the first version of this book that began, "Build your own Macintosh, learn secrets of experts...." Today, after talking with thousands of people over several years about the subject, I am not sure there are any secrets or experts. If you look hard enough, chances are you will find someone has already done it before—maybe even better. And nothing is more sobering than to hold yourself up as an expert and then talk to someone who really knows what they are talking about. Ahhh, the sweet humility one learns from living life and writing books.

Repackage your Macintosh

Although the title says "build" you are actually going to "repackage" or "assemble" your own Macintosh from catalog parts. You won't have to build anything from scratch. No reading of schematic drawings or soldering is involved. Instead, this book's focus is on the easy way: Instructions, photographs, and illustrations assist you in repackaging or assembling your Cat Mac and getting it running in the shortest possible time so that you may enjoy the fruits of your labors—a fully operational Macintosh.

The difficult work has already been done—the parts are already available. By purchasing these identical (if not superior) parts from catalog and mail order sources and repackaging or assembling them yourself, you guarantee that the Cat Mac you build will always cost less than the equivalent standard Apple Macintosh model.

This book can help if you are a Macintosh owner and want to repackage your original vintage five-year-old Mac 128 logic board or any other Mac logic board. It can also help if you want to add more memory, a hard disk, a bigger display, or an accelerator card—all these are discussed and more. It gives tips on putting together the lowest priced, low-end Macintosh just for word processing, and on getting the newly announced, highest performance Mac Quadra 700's capabilities at the best price. If you want to upgrade your existing standard Apple Macintosh and keep the package you have, another book tells you all the tips and secrets for doing just that. (See Bob Brant, *Upgrade Your Macintosh and Save a Bundle*, Windcrest/McGraw-Hill, 1991.)

Beyond saving money, repackaging your Macintosh logic board into a different chassis gives you flexibility and performance options that you cannot get at any price from a standard Apple model. For example, a tower case allows you to package multiple hard drives and backup media into a single chassis—certainly a desirable feature for any Macintosh model intended for network server use. Apple only makes this feature available on its most expensive Quadra 900 model. You can add it to any Macintosh model you want.

Chapter overview

This book gives the exact details of how to build a Cat Mac using standard Apple Macintosh logic boards. Other Macintosh solutions are also discussed in general terms. This book will not help you if you want to build a DOS PC-compatible computer[3], although some of the concepts are similar.

In reading *Build Your Own Macintosh and Save a Bundle—2nd Edition* you will learn why building a Cat Mac could be a good idea for you, why it will always cost less than buying a new Macintosh, which are the best models to build, what upgrade options are available, how easy it is to do, how kits can make it even easier, and what the alternative building options are. Finally, you will learn about Cat Mac peripherals, software, and troubleshooting.

The book is organized into three main areas (Fig. I-1 shows the details). They include philosophy (why build your own Macintosh, how much you can save), options (how to make the best choices in Apple and third-party upgrades), and process (how to build several popular Cat Mac models, plus some alternatives).

Chapter 1 tells you why you can put a board in a box and save a bundle, points out the benefits a Cat Mac might hold for a DOS PC user, discusses the pros and cons of building a Cat Mac, and covers the market trends that guarantee that building a Cat Mac will always be less expensive than buying a new Macintosh.

Chapter 2 helps you decide which Cat Mac you should or should not build, and helps you select the best system to meet your needs from the many available options, using price and performance as your criteria.

Chapter 3 looks at the many Macintosh logic board options and suggests what choices you should make from a price/performance point of view.

Chapter 4 looks at the many memory and accelerator board upgrade options and suggests how to make the best choice.

Chapter 5 examines the world of storage options and covers floppy, hard, removable, optical, and tape drives, with recommendations.

Chapter 6 discusses monitors and video boards and how to choose the best solution for your Cat Mac.

Chapter 7 looks at keyboard, mouse, DOS PC case, and wiring/cable alternatives, with suggestions for choosing them.

Chapter 8, with the help of photographs and illustrations, explains step by step how to build the original desktop Cat Mac SE/SE 30 discussed in the first edition.

Chapter 9 describes how to build two new desktop Cat Mac SE/SE 30 models: a full-page accelerated version and a compact-chassis version.

Chapter 10 covers how ready-made compact repackaging upgrade systems from MicroMac Technology, tower repackaging upgrade systems from Atlanta Technical Specialists, and a portable repackaging upgrade from DTC Technology can help you.

Chapter 11 covers other Cat Mac alternatives you might consider and how they can help you: DOS on Mac, Mac on DOS, Mac on Mac (Portable or clone), Mac on Atari, and Mac on Unix.

Chapter 12 explores topics that might be of interest to you after you build your Cat Mac: peripheral hardware, software, "now that you are up and running" tips, and a look at the future (how you keep up-to-date).

No attempt has been made to present all the options or all the available products, because such a book would be out of date by the time it returned from the printers. This task is already performed extremely well by the excellent weekly and monthly magazines and quarterly product guides that service

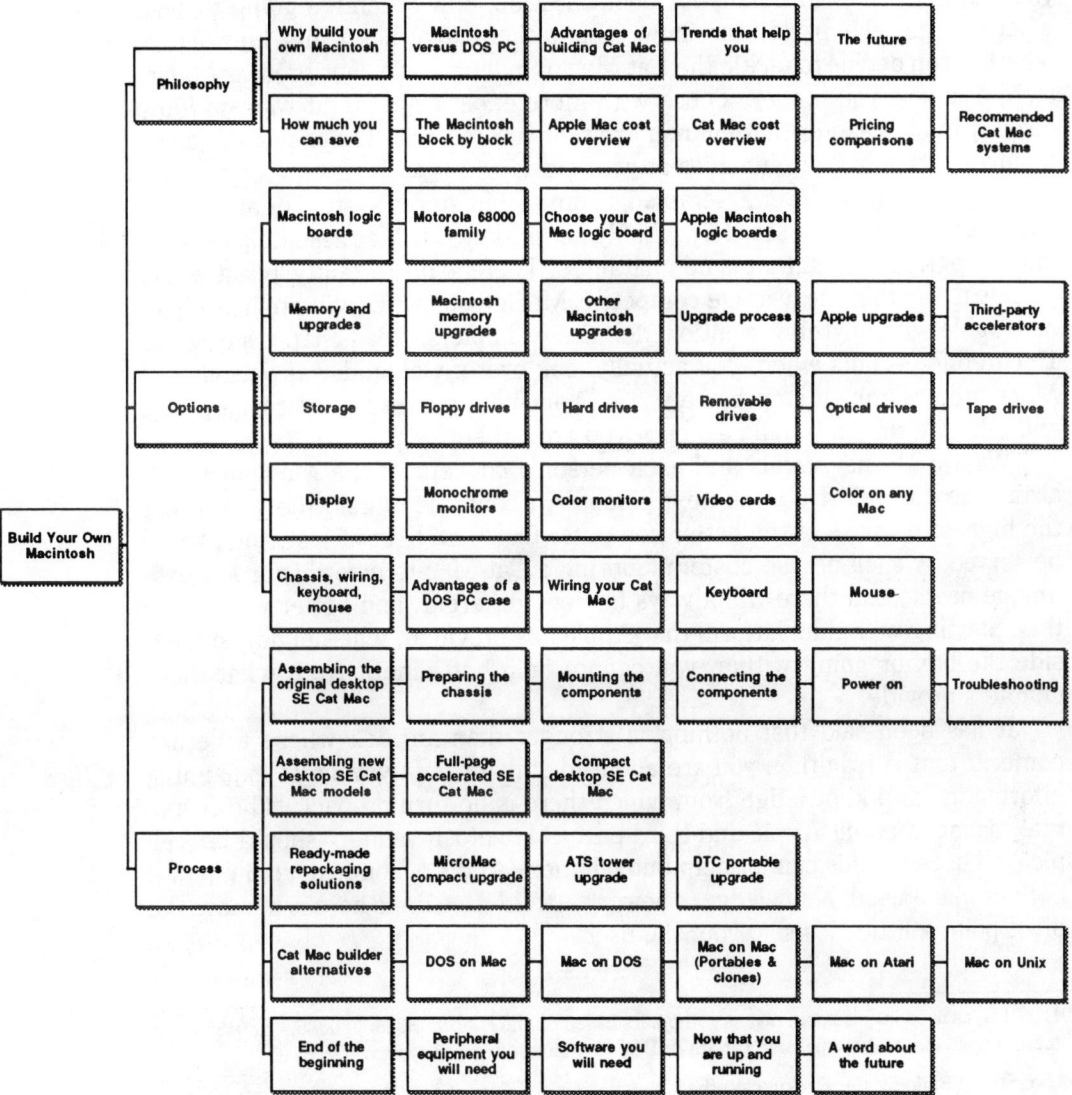

I-1 Chapter organization of *Build Your Own Macintosh—2nd Edition*.

the Macintosh community (see chapter 12 for a complete list). To make it easier for you, however, I have placed product sources in the chapters that discuss them, organized by part and manufacturer/distributor name.

You can do it

Better price performance is what the Cat Mac delivers compared to the standard Apple Macintosh offerings, and this is why it fills a market need. When

Introduction **xix**

you finish reading *Build Your Own Macintosh and Save a Bundle—2nd Edition*, you will know how to build your own Cat Mac, how much it's going to cost, where to get the parts, and how to put them together. This knowledge, whether you decide to tackle the Cat Mac or just upgrade your present Macintosh, can save you money. Those with more experience might want to jump directly into a chapter that interests you, or you can read the book from cover to cover with a bag of munchies at your side.

Anyone who has ever assembled a component stereo system or attached a video recorder to a TV set can probably handle any Cat Mac assembly or Macintosh upgrading. But that is no guarantee. There is no certainty, but it would be safe to say that the average competent Macintosh owner will probably have no trouble with anything mentioned in these chapters. Read chapters 8, 9 and 10 carefully—that's where you actually look over my shoulder as various Cat Macs are assembled step by step. Use your common sense, work carefully, and take the time to reread a step if you are not sure.

We are all individuals and each person's concept of the Macintosh will always be different from the next person's. I continue to hold the vision that the highest purpose of the better computer for "The Rest of Us" will always be served by each person custom-tailoring a Cat Mac to meet his or her own unique needs, and there will always be new, different, and better ways to do this. Starting with the platform that Apple has provided, whether staying outside the box or going within, you cannot help but benefit from what these chapters provide.

It has been said that nothing is stronger than an idea whose time has come. If that is true then you are about to embark on a voyage of expanding information and knowledge from which there is no turning back. The corporate management at Apple and third-party Macintosh vendors should be well pleased because this cannot help but sell more Apple Macintosh computers—both new and used. Knowledge is power and all I have done here is to move the pivot point a little closer to you, the user.

---

[1] DOS PC, as used in this book, means computers based on the 8086/8, 80286, 80386, or 80486 architecture that commonly runs some variant of DOS, Windows, or OS/2 system software.

[2] Max Stax, "Building the Hackintosh: the Computer for the Rest of Us," *Computer Shopper*, August 1988, was the first in a series.

[3] Aubrey Pilgrim's *Build Your Own 80286 IBM Compatible and Save a Bundle*, Windcrest/McGraw-Hill, 1989; *Build Your Own 80386 IBM Compatible and Save a Bundle*, Windcrest/McGraw-Hill, 1990; *Build Your Own 80486 IBM Compatible and Save a Bundle*, Windcrest/McGraw-Hill, 1991, and other books in the series do an outstanding job in this area.

Chapter 1
Why build your own Macintosh

Put a board in a box and save a bundle.

The original book was written on a Macintosh SE built from catalog parts—a Cat Mac SE. Like the equipment built by the lowest bidder that took the Apollo astronauts to the moon, my Cat Mac got me where I wanted to go, was very reliable, and it saved me money. Not only that, but because I built it myself, I felt a pride of ownership, particularly when I took it to shows and demonstrations. Your Cat Mac can do the same for you.

This book is being written on the 25-MHz 68030-powered Cat Mac shown in Fig. 1-1. I merely added a Mobius full-page monitor and accelerator combination to the Mac SE logic board of my earlier Cat Mac, along with an Apple 1.4Mb FDHD floppy, Quantum Pro 105Mb hard drive, Key Tronic MacPro Plus keyboard and a Mouse Systems optical Little Mouse. Later on I changed the case. Am I happy with it? You bet I am. This system (with all components from third-party vendors except the Macintosh logic board) really flies, the

1-1 A 25-MHz 68030-powered Cat Mac SE with full-page display.

Zenith-based full page display from Mobius is easy on my eyes and, best of all, the price is right. I get almost Mac IIci performance for less than 40% of the Apple list price for equivalent hardware.

This is what I mean by "put a board in a box and save a bundle." I obtained the "heart" of a Macintosh, its logic board, at the best price from the used equipment market. I surrounded it with better price performance products from third-party vendors obtained via the cost-saving mail order distribution channel. Then I put it together myself. The result is that I saved a bundle, yet I have a Macintosh as good if not better in every way than a standard Apple Macintosh model.

Other than the "thrill of victory and the agony of defeat" as they say on ABC's "Wide World of Sports," why bother to build your own Macintosh? What's in it for you? This chapter starts with the advantages and disadvantages in building your own Cat Mac versus buying a Macintosh. It then examines the prevailing marketing and distribution channel trends that will always make building your own Cat Mac less expensive than buying an equivalent new Macintosh—how a Cat Mac builder is ahead of the game no matter what future changes come along—and wraps up with the benefit to you of building a Cat Mac versus a DOS PC.

Advantages of building a Cat Mac

In the business arena, the driving marketing credo is find a need and fill it. That is why people form companies and why little companies grow into big ones. They are filling a need. That is also the driving reason for building your own Macintosh, your Cat Mac. No matter how many different Macintosh models are manufactured, no single machine will be custom tailored for you. You have to do that part yourself. You are the only one who can exactly fill your own needs. Another driving business credo is to get the most value for your money. When you build your Macintosh from catalog parts, you save money because you are providing the labor. Let's look at why the concept has been so successful.

The Cat Mac concept

The success of the Cat Mac concept is built on the foundation of the Macintosh market pricing structure. Table 1-1 tells the story at a glance. It shows the price for Macintosh whole systems and then for Macintosh logic boards (at average purchase price), grouped by discontinued (at average purchase price) and current models (at list price). No matter what Macintosh model you buy, you pay so much for it as a box, as a packaged system with Apple enclosure, power supply, logic board, memory, and drives. You pay far less for its logic board by itself. Used logic boards don't wear out, unlike the other components (power supplies, drives, etc.) of packaged systems. When you put this Macintosh logic board in a brand-new (and far lower cost) DOS PC chassis and surround it with brand-new

**Table 1-1. Price for
Macintosh system versus logic board alone.**

CPU[1]	Macintosh box	Macintosh logic board
Discontinued models		
Mac SE—1/2f	900	500
Mac II—1/1f	1900	900
Mac SE 30—1/1f	1800	1200
Mac IIcx—1/1f	2100	1200
Current models		
Mac Classic 2/40	1499	600
Mac LC 2/40	2499	1100
Mac IIsi 3/40	3769	1300
Mac IIci 5/1f	5269	1900
Mac IIfx 4/1f	7369	2900

[1]Taken from Apple's Price List for current models and used equipment vendor average prices for discontinued models and logic boards as of December 1991. Configuration with memory/number of floppy drives or memory/hard drive size appears after CPU type.

(and far lower cost) third-party drives and peripherals, you can save a lot of money and gain tremendous flexibility.

You can expect this Macintosh market pricing structure to continue in the future. As you can observe in Table 1-1, it is consistent across discontinued and current models. When newer models, such as the recently announced Mac Classic II and Mac Quadras are more widely available in the used equipment channel, they automatically appear in Table 1-1's lineup. Apple even accelerates the process by making certain logic boards available as unbundled, aggressively priced, a la carte upgrades. While the aggressive logic board pricing initially enables Apple to keep the third-party upgrade vendors at bay (no one can logically price their upgrade higher than the price of getting the genuine article from Apple), it later serves as a reference pricing point for open market transactions. (For example, the Apple SE 30 upgrade kit once cost $1499 with the SE logic board in exchange. When these kits found their way into the market via dealer liquidations, etc., they were priced at a discount from $1499 without an exchange.)

Cat Macs based on earlier Macintosh logic boards were occasionally crude and required battery holders and extra circuitry that relegated them to the province of hackers. ROMs were usually an issue as well. As Apple has continuously improved the price and performance of its newer Macintosh logic boards, more and more functions are already built in. Modern Cat Mac builders, using Mac SE and newer logic boards just need to drop them into a chassis, cable them up and go. ROMs are not a problem because they almost always come with the logic board when you buy it. If you don't want to do the legwork yourself, several vendors now provide turnkey repackaging solutions that make it even easier.

Cat Macs are hard at work by themselves and alongside their Apple Macintosh brethren in companies, governments, schools, churches, and homes around the world. Those that own them are released from the artificial obsolescence treadmill—nobody knows what you have "under the hood." And when you need more horsepower or video area, just add the appropriate board or upgrade at a fraction of the cost of buying a new Macintosh. You already know that Macintosh owners "love" their Macintoshes. It's also fact that Cat Mac owners very rarely part with their Cat Macs. It's the ultimate hardware extension of the Macintosh computer "for the rest of us" concept.

With an installed base of six million Macintoshes, used Macintosh boxes and logic boards are available from numerous sources. While you can consistently get a good deal from the major used equipment sources that make a market in used Apple Macintosh equipment, you can occasionally do even better by taking advantage of Apple dealer closeouts and overstocks, businesses upgrading or liquidating, leasing company buybacks or even private parties. And Apple supports this huge Macintosh used equipment channel because it helps sell more new Macintoshes.

A Ben Franklin on the Cat Mac advantages

Let's look at the advantages and disadvantages of the standard Apple product versus a Cat Mac. Table 1-2 shows both individual feature and overall factor comparisons. First, notice the Cat Mac solution always provides you equal or

Table 1-2. Why build your own Macintosh tradeoffs.

Comparison item	Apple Macintosh	Cat Mac
Item-for-item features comparison		
logic board	standard	identical
memory	SIMMs	identical
floppy drive	1.4Mb FDHD	identical or better
hard drive	40Mb	identical or better
video monitor	standard	always superior to 9" mono
keyboard	ADB	identical or better
mouse	ADB mechanical	identical or better
power supply	standard	always superior
case	standard	larger DOS PC case
Overall factors comparison		
price	Apple list price	typically much less
flexibility	standard options	more room, more options
resale	commodity item	harder to resell
time to build	buy it now	days to weeks
repair	Apple dealer	do it yourself

better performance on the item-by-item features. Now, let's look at the overall factors.

Price Your Cat Mac has better price performance (i.e., lower cost for the same performance or higher performance at the same price). A recent survey on computer brand-switching[1] showed that price and performance are the two main areas most important to users. Price was the main reason to switch brands chosen by 84% of the respondents, followed by performance chosen by 55% of the respondents as the second most popular reason. Other reasons were: service (40%), quality (37%), availability (24%), networking (16%), and warranty (14%). Chapter 2 shows you the details on how much you can save by building your own Macintosh.

Flexibility Beyond price, this is probably the number one reason why Cat Macs are built. You are not limited to the Apple-standard configurations. When you build your own Macintosh, you have total flexibility. You can choose from more options. You can choose from many third-party alternatives to the storage devices, displays, keyboards, and mouse you receive from Apple. There are more accelerator, video, and numerous other upgrade options that Apple doesn't offer to choose from as well. Almost all third-party solutions are more cost-effective than those from Apple. You also save money because you don't have to add them on; instead, you use them to begin with. You have the advantages of a bigger power supply, fan, and enclosure/case with fewer space and power restrictions, meaning more flexibility to accommodate additional options. On the other hand, when you purchase a new or used Apple Macintosh today, you have a wide selection but there are only so many models and options to choose from—and there will never be as many as there are people to choose them.

Resale The Macintosh is a commodity item. As a used computer it has a definite resale value. You can go out tomorrow, sell it, and have the money in your hand. On the other hand, the Cat Mac has a questionable resale value. When you go to sell your Cat Mac creation, the shoe is on the other foot. You might have difficulty in selling it because it is an unknown. The secret to selling it is to find a buyer who needs the features of the one you have to sell. Then the future buyer's choice will also be easy. From my own experience, very few Cat Mac builders ever resell their creations—they are used for years and years, upgraded as needs require and occasionally handed on down to others.

Time to build Your Cat Mac, being a unique creation, takes time to build. Even the simplest Cat Mac implementation will require time to order and receive the parts from the catalog or mail order sources before putting them together. Then you are looking at several hours to several days to put it together. While repackaging solutions from several vendors can minimize this time, you can go out and buy an Apple Macintosh today.

Repair Because your Cat Mac creation will probably be put into an oversized chassis rather than a small crowded box, with a higher capacity power supply and an industrial strength fan that dissipates much of the heat normally generated, the likelihood of your Cat Mac breaking down is much lower. But only you and a handful of others can repair it. The down side on this is less frightening than you think. By the time you finish building your Cat Mac, you will know a lot about it and will not be too intimidated by the thought of getting in and fixing it. And you will be performing the repairs at wholesale rather than retail. On the other hand, Apple has a worldwide network of repair locations to fix your Macintosh. But, you have very little control over the time it takes them to repair your Macintosh, and you might not be that giggly over the repair bill when you receive it.

There are many tradeoffs. In the final analysis, only you can determine whether it's worth it to build or to buy, but obviously building your own Macintosh has many significant advantages. Now let's look at the trends that guarantee this will continue in the future.

Remember, the Force is with you

Four prevailing marketing and distribution channel trends guarantee that building your own Cat Mac will always be less expensive than buying an equivalent new Macintosh.

A little history lesson

Digital Equipment Corp (DEC), Data General, and other primary minicomputer vendors personified the 1970s and early 1980s price performance trend in the minicomputer field. Figure 1-2 shows a typical price performance trend for a vendor's product line. Starting in time with any product (I called it product "A"), new technology and continuing development allowed the vendor to evolve new products "A1" and "B." Product A1 delivered higher performance at the same price and was usually the same generation of hardware milked or tweaked for extra performance. Product B typically defined a new generation and delivered still higher performance at a higher price. Then product B1 was introduced and the process was repeated. The A1, B1 type products defended the vendor's low-end product price. In a very price-competitive market, it would also be necessary to introduce a product "A2," which would provide the same or slightly higher performance at a lower price. Typically, same-generation product introductions took place roughly each year and there were two to five years between new generation announcements.

This was the minicomputer industry's famous price-performance curve. IBM had a similar situation with their minicomputers, and it was also true of their mainframes in that period and earlier. Third-party vendors could always offer their peripheral products, such as memory, disk drives, tape drives, and

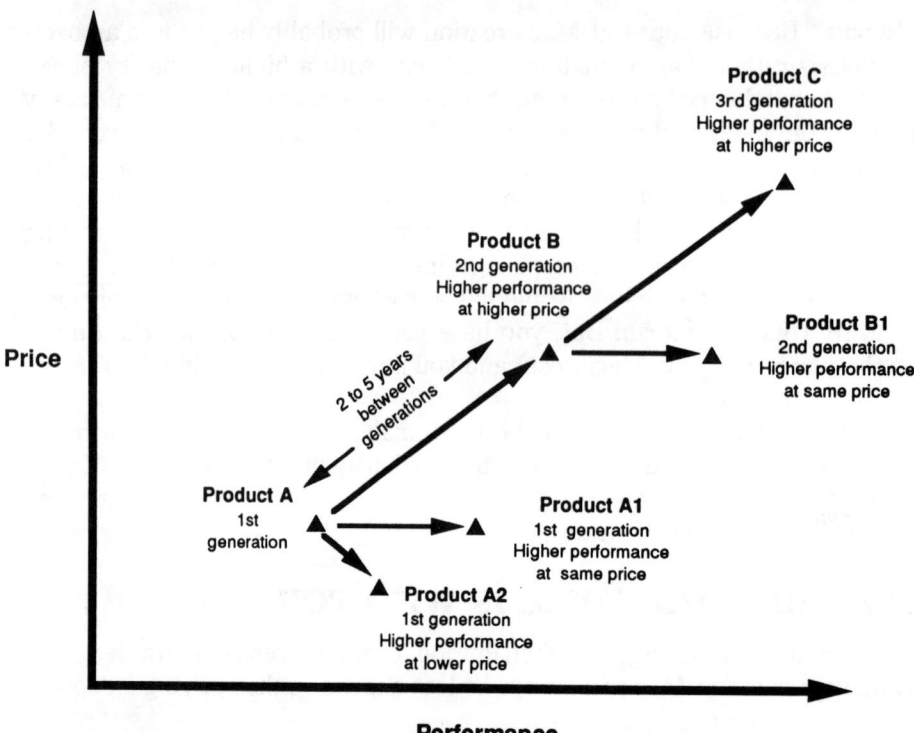

1-2 Typical computer vendor price versus performance trend.

printers at lower prices than a DEC or IBM. These vendors that wanted to attach anything to a piece of DEC or IBM gear nearly always did so at their own risk. A DEC or IBM could (and often did) suddenly change the rules by introducing a new model, bundling in more memory at a special price, or altering the microcode to handshake with the disk drive. All these held nasty financial consequences for the third-party vendors.

Yet no matter what IBM or DEC did, it was always possible to get a better priced or better performing add-on or add-in peripheral from some third-party vendor who was able to move faster in implementing the new technology and deliver it to the marketplace quicker. Although IBM and DEC always caught up (sometimes with a vengeance), and occasionally even led the third-party vendors in technology, an entire thriving cottage industry grew up around the ability of nimble, smaller companies to beat the bigger guys to market.

Trend one: Apple Macintosh price performance

Look at Fig. 1-3. You will notice a striking resemblance to Fig. 1-2. Apple is doing today exactly what earlier computer makers did, only with new chips and new technology. The strategy did not change at all—only the size of the

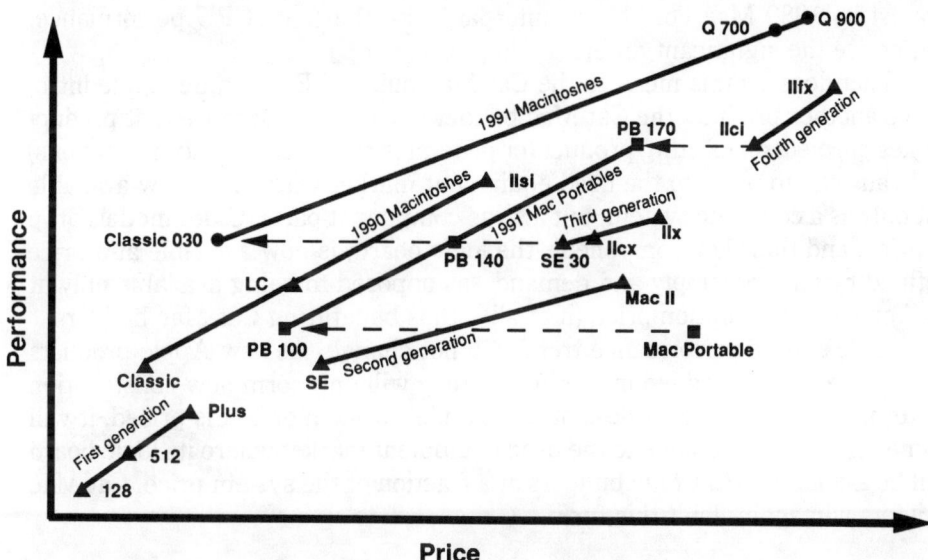

1-3 Apple Macintosh family performance versus price trend.

computers. Apple, in order to increase its market, has had to keep introducing new models whose price performance was better than those of the previous generation.

The performance versus price for seven "generations" of Apple Macintosh computers (20 models) appear as solid lines in Fig. 1-3 (the original Mac Portable stands by itself; no other Mac shared its characteristics in its time frame). Price performance on the chart gets better as you move upwards and to the left. The three dotted lines from top to bottom reflect 25-MHz 68030, 16-MHz 68030, and 16-MHz 68000 performance, respectively, and are useful for positioning the new PowerBook portable models.

The first four generations, introduced prior to 1990, include all the Mac models up through the Mac IIfx and the original Mac Portable.

The Macintoshes introduced in October 1990 (Classic, LC, IIsi) are up and to the left of all other Macintosh family members shown on the chart up until that time; they offered significantly better price performance.

The October 1991 announcements again do the same thing—offer better price performance than the other models on the chart. The 25-MHz 68040-based Quadra 700 and 900 models offer greater price performance over the 40-MHz 68030-based Mac IIfx, and the Mac Classic II (at half the price) offers greater price performance over its Mac SE 30 counterpart introduced in early 1989.

While the Mac Portable models (PowerBook 100, 140, 170) initially don't appear to measure up, keep in mind they incorporate advanced packaging, display screen, and power budgeting technologies in their cost, all of which cost

Remember, the Force is with you

extra bucks. When you measure the 1991 16-MHz PowerBook 100 model against its 1989 Mac Portable counterpart with the same CPU performance, you notice the significant difference in price.

What does all this mean to the Cat Mac builder? Every time Apple introduces another product, the Cat Mac builder wins. Why? Because that product makes obsolete an existing product (or generates ripple-down price reductions) and causes it to move to the used equipment market where it is now available not only as a complete system, but also as component parts. Older models drop in price, and their key component, the logic board, is now available at a price defined by market supply and demand—as opposed to being available only at an Apple upgrade option price (if at all)—thus benefitting Cat Mac builders.

Apple's price performance trend will not change. As new Apple products and generations are added in the future, they will only form new constellation patterns in Fig. 1-3. Regardless of how Apple's system or box is priced, it will sooner or later be available to the used equipment market where its logic board will be available to Cat Mac builders at a fraction of the system price. Cat Mac builders win again. Isn't this fun?

Trend two: Third-party vendor performance

As in the minicomputer days, today the third-party vendors offer their add-on or add-in products with better price performance than Apple. Although many of these vendors have for years been manufacturing similar types of products for the DOS PC world, they are still typified by smaller, more nimble organizations that are quicker to go to market with their products, as shown in Fig. 1-4. The third-party or "secondary" vendor either offers an "A1" product at a price significantly lower than Apple's price (i.e., memory, disks, monitors, keyboards, mice), or an "A2" product with a performance significantly greater than Apple's performance (i.e., accelerator and video cards, disks, monitors, mice). These vendors fill a market need by also offering entirely new products that Apple does not offer and, in effect, prototyping this market for Apple until the product demand builds up and it is large enough for Apple to apply its manufacturing economies of scale to and make a profit from this arena (i.e., hard disks and monitors).

Also, as in minicomputer days, third-party vendors still operate at their own risk. It is to Apple's advantage to let third-party vendors assume the technical and marketing risks during the prototyping stage as just discussed, so Apple is careful to nurture cordial relations with its third-party developers. However, as many a third-party vendor is painfully aware, Apple can change the rules of the Macintosh game at any time and has done so many times already.

Third-party accelerator board manufactures have a particularly "fun" time as Apple alternately solders and sockets its CPU chips to the board and changes its input/output interface access as its architecture evolves. In the traditional Macintosh, the third-party vendors originally had no bus to attach

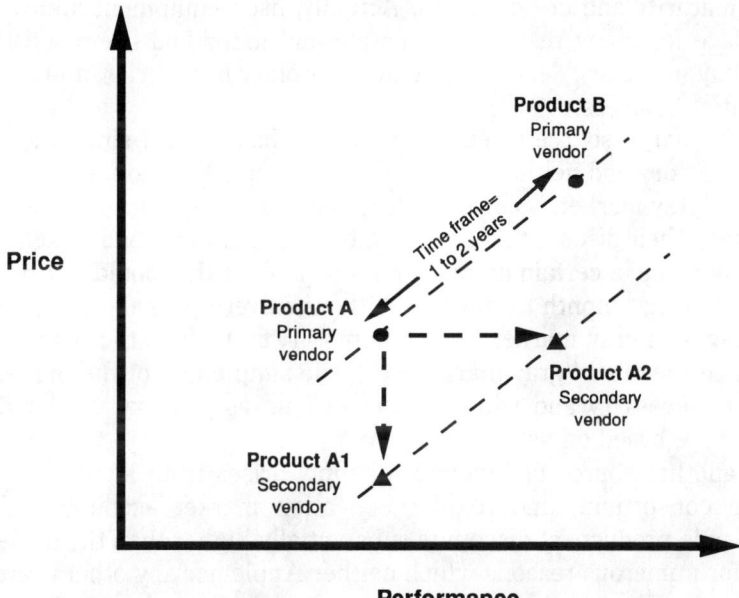

1-4 Typical third-party computer vendor price versus performance trend.

their products to—they had to attach directly to the CPU chip. Apple had a closed box. Now, the pendulum has swung back the other way with the SE models having a 96-pin direct slot, the Mac II models having multiple 96-pin NuBus slots, the SE 30 having a 120-pin direct slot, the Mac IIci and IIfx models having a cache controller slot, and the Mac IIfx having a 120-pin processor direct slot which is a superset of the SE 30s. Sometimes new and entirely different slots appear on the Mac Classics, LC, IIsi, PowerBooks, and Quadras as well. Apple's new strategy now forces third-party vendors to deploy resources and time to consider all these when they design their products.

What does all this mean to the Cat Mac builder? It is guaranteed that no matter what Apple does, it is always possible to get a better priced or better performing add-on or add-in peripheral from some faster-moving third-party vendor. It is also guaranteed that the third-party Apple Macintosh-related cottage industry will continue to thrive as clever, nimble, smaller companies take advantage of the holes in Apple's product line and get into market faster with their own products.

Trend three: Used equipment vendor performance

As older systems are replaced by new, the older systems go on to the used equipment market. This market has been in existence for decades for the mainframe and minicomputer manufacturers; for at least five years for the DOS PC makers; and for the last several years as the Macintosh market has reached maturity and critical mass. Actually, used equipment appears in the marketplace for many reasons: Corporate and individual users sell their old Macs to buy new ones; dealers liquidate their older inventories; and other dealers go out of business.

Another large source of supply exists. It has existed since the dawn of computer history and neither IBM, DEC, nor Apple likes to talk about it. It is called the "gray market." Simply stated, in order to meet primary vendor quotas and keep their discount levels, volume users had to offload or sell, without adding any value, a certain amount of their product that could not be used or resold within that month or quarter. Although every primary vendor periodically engages in gray market "witch hunts" (woe be it to the reseller who is tagged with the label "gray marketeer"), the simple fact of the matter is this practice is necessary and will continue as long as primary vendor discount structures are based on volume incentives.

Still another source of Macintosh supply arises from Apple's developer, education consortium, and regular education market accounts. All these receive Apple products at discounts substantially higher than the dealer channel, and for numerous reasons which neither Apple nor any others care to discuss, some portion of this product finds its way into the used equipment market.

Just as with automobiles, the thriving used Macintosh market supports and assists the new equipment market. By definition, used systems will always be less costly than new ones with the difference in price created by the market forces of supply and demand. Figure 1-5 illustrates that an identical product is offered at 20% to 50% discounts from its new list price in the used equipment market. The difference in price is attributed to age, condition, accessories, etc.

Macintosh computer systems on the used equipment market decline in price with time as Fig. 1-6 illustrates. It also shows that the Macintosh logic board tends to become a more significant part of the system price with time, although market supply and demand forces sometimes check and even reverse this trend. A glance back at Table 1-1 proves the point: the discontinued model logic boards are a higher percentage of the system price than the current model logic boards.

What does all this mean to the Cat Mac builder? Unlike automobiles, logic boards don't wear out, yet they decline in price with time—an absolutely wonderful situation for the Cat Mac builder. A "used" Macintosh logic board is perfect for use as the heart of your new Cat Mac system—surrounded by other, all brand-new, third-party vendor parts.

Trend four: Mail order vendor performance

Mail order evolved as a viable channel of distribution for microcomputer parts as more sophisticated users required less support but wanted better pricing. Without the need for the support overhead of the dealerships or chains, yet with the capital to obtain the same purchasing economies of scale, these mail

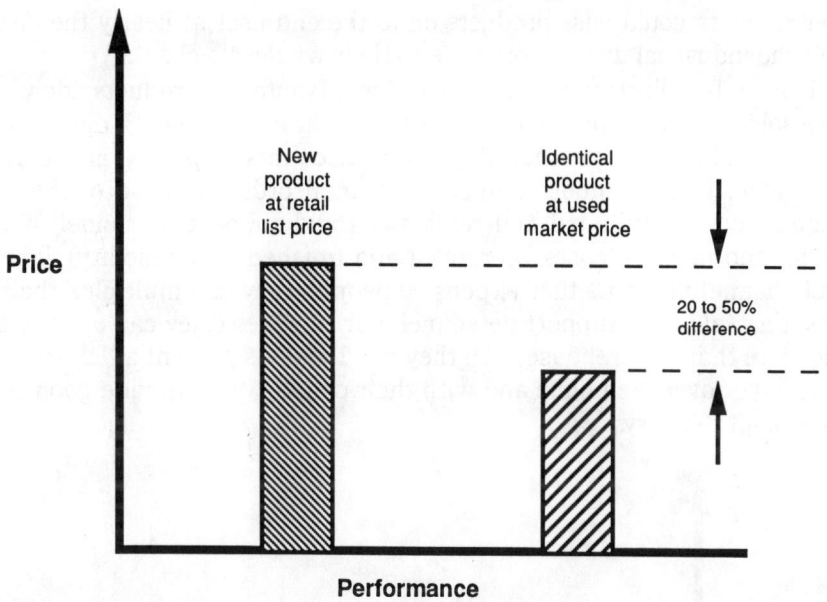

1-5 New versus used equipment pricing.

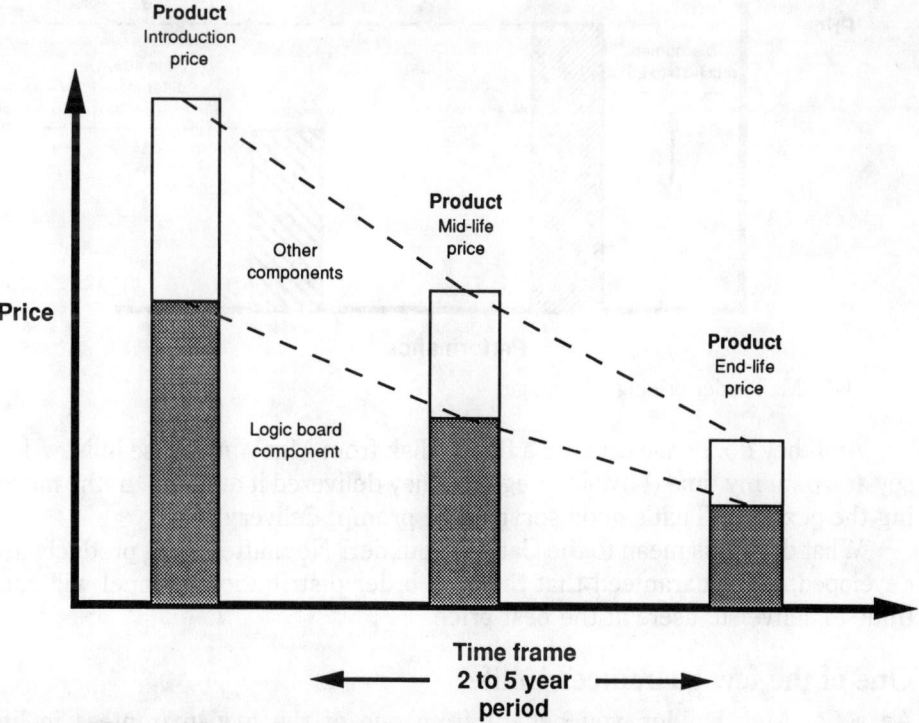

1-6 Used computer models decline in price with time.

Remember, the Force is with you

order resellers could pass products on to the end user at nearly the discount levels the industrial distributors gave to their wholesale clients.

Figure 1-7 illustrates the mail order advantage. Products identical to those sold via the retail channels are offered at a 30% to 40% discount from list price. The retail channel also offers discounts, typically in the 10% to 25% range, but it cannot compete with mail order because of the higher "people" costs (outbound and retail sales and support personnel) plus the "bricks and mortar" costs (storefront and finished office facility). The mail order channel needs neither expensive people (they can multiplex their telemarketing sales and support personnel) nor facilities (they can operate out of little more than a warehouse). All they need to do is present a "clean" image to the buyer over the phone and with their catalog, and provide good service and prompt delivery.

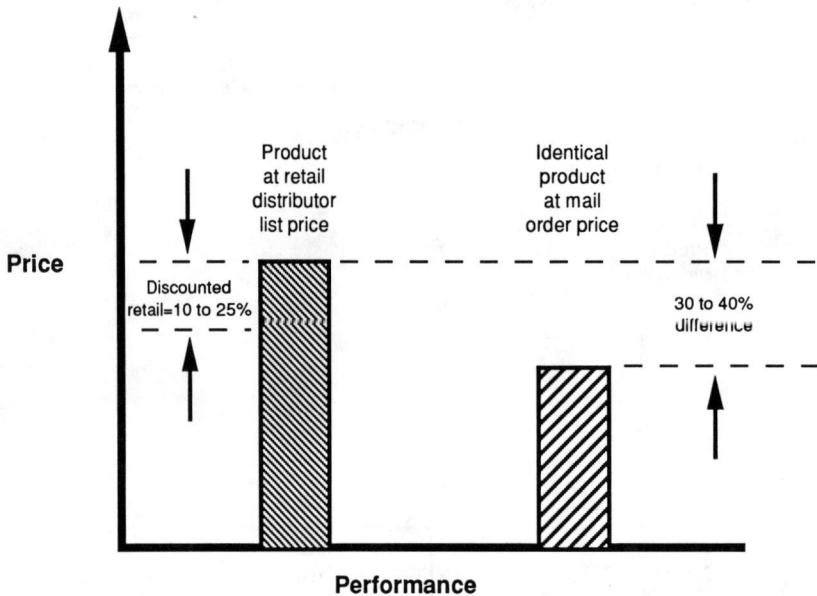

1-7 Mail order pricing advantage.

And they do. I once ordered a floppy disk from MacWarehouse in New Jersey at 4 p.m. my time (I live in Oregon). They delivered it at 9 a.m. in the morning the next day. That's good service and prompt delivery!

What does this mean to the Cat Mac builder? No matter what products are developed, it is guaranteed that the mail order distribution channel will continue to deliver to users at the best price.

One of the few guarantees in life

As a Cat Mac builder, you benefit from one of the few guarantees in life because of these four trends I just discussed. Building your Cat Mac will always be less expensive than buying a discounted new system. And unless some other market forces change the rules, you can expect these trends will continue indefinitely into the future. To summarize them again:

- Primary vendors such as IBM, DEC, and Apple must always provide increased price performance in their new models, thus making the old obsolete and driving them to the used equipment market.
- Third-party vendors must always provide cheaper and/or faster add-on or add-in products than the primary vendors.
- Used equipment must always cost less than the same equipment purchased new, and used equipment prices decline with time. Logic boards also decline in price with time yet they don't wear out.
- Mail order vendors must always be the least expensive distribution channel from which products can be purchased.

Why build a Macintosh versus a DOS PC

Stewart Alsop[2] once observed that the Macintosh, using Apple's A/UX (Apple's Unix software) and Insignia Solutions' Soft PC DOS PC emulator software, is the only computer that can simultaneously run Macintosh, DOS, Windows, and Unix software. This capability is also available on a Cat Mac. But there are so many more DOS PC machines. While there were more than six million Macs in the world at the end of 1991, there were over 60 million DOS PCs installed. So let me first answer the question: "Why build a Macintosh instead of a DOS PC?"

From my own DOS and Macintosh computer consulting business experience, I have learned that there are definite applications that each type of system is best suited to perform. I can pass either system solution on to a client; sometimes both working together is the answer.

I have also learned that DOS PC users typically have four main objections about a Macintosh: It's a toy, not DOS compatible, too slow, and too expensive. There are as many, if not more, DOS PC users who are adamant and gung-ho that their DOS PC's are the best as there are Macintosh users who feel the same way about their Macs. These hardcore users are not even interested in trying a Macintosh under any circumstances. I've learned through experience not even to attempt to tell this class of DOS PC user anything about the Macintosh. However, the majority of PC DOS users that I encounter in my business are a bit more open-minded.

I also know it is impossible to convey in words, written or spoken, the difference a Macintosh environment, with its totally integrated graphical user interface (GUI), makes in working with a personal computer. So I simply tell them that nothing I can say can possibly change their opinion of a Macintosh until they actually use one and then compare it application by application with the DOS PC they are now using.

I tell them to be fair though, and don't ask to see a Mac 128. Ask to see a Mac Classic, Mac SE, Mac SE 30, Mac IIsi, Mac IIci, or Mac IIfx (ho, ho, ho!). Go up to a friend who also happens to own a Mac and ask them for a demo of their Mac. Tell them the ground rules are they are to shut up during the demo—no Mac proselytizing. All they can do is answer any question you might have—briefly. Help them out a little bit though, give them a hint, tell them what you might be interested in doing with a Mac, such as word processing, spreadsheet, graphics, database, etc., so they demo in your interest area. If you have no Mac friends, have a salesperson at a computer store reproduce the process.

No matter who did the demo, you should at least have gone away with the following impressions:

- The Mac is different—especially that, what do they call that funny little thing you hold in your hand—a mouse? After I got the hang of it, it saved me a lot of time . . ..
- The Mac is graphic. Well I remember all I had to do to delete a file was to put its "icon" in the "trash." Hey, look at me, I'm talking Macintosh!
- The Mac might be easy to use; those icons and pull-down menus that I just clicked on with the mouse, they couldn't be that hard to learn . . ..

Guess what? Your instincts served you well. You are correct in your perceptions. Some say that Apple employed the "Trojan Horse" strategy to bring Macintoshes into corporate America. The simple fact is the Macintosh has sold itself.

Initially, the Macintosh was positioned squarely against IBM PCs and their clones. Now it is "the second standard." How quickly we forget. Why, despite its overwhelming disadvantage in numbers, price, and marketing has the Mac succeeded? What is it about Apple's Macintosh interface that has IBM and others running, not walking, to copy it?

In company after company around the world, when PC users tried a Mac and then tried out the identical application on their DOS PC, and later were asked to choose between a Mac and a DOS PC machine when price was removed from the equation, they overwhelmingly chose the Mac. Study after study conducted in these corporations proved what you already know from a brief exposure to it. The Mac is easier to learn and easier to use.[3]

So let me go back to the four initial objections. It's a toy, not DOS compatible, too slow, and too expensive. The first three objections are today untrue. The fourth one is solved uniquely by the Cat Mac.

A toy You don't compromise software power on the Macintosh. Some of the most powerful software programs made for any computer run on the Macintosh and, in fact, were ported back to the PC: Aldus PageMaker and Microsoft Excel are two examples that come to mind. If a software application is not available for the Macintosh, it's usually because it has not been developed yet—not because it cannot be. The Mac is not a toy.

Not DOS compatible Apple's 1.4Mb FDHD floppy drive reads and writes DOS PC 3½" floppies. Third-party vendors make products to read DOS PC 5¼" floppies in a Macintosh. DOS word-processing, spreadsheet, and database programs are all accessible via Apple File Exchange software and third-party software such as Mac Link Plus from Dataviz. You can run DOS software on a Mac using a software emulator and, if you need better performance, you can even put a hardware board like Orange Micro's Orange 386 into your Macintosh to make it emulate a DOS PC. Of course, without an emulator, you cannot run DOS programs on a Mac—but that was never the issue. The data is the issue. And there is no DOS PC text data, that I am aware of, that you cannot pull over into a Macintosh and operate on. Graphical data is a little trickier to play with between DOS and Mac platforms but there are ways around this also. I would say the Mac is DOS compatible.

Too slow Apple's early 1990 offering, the Macintosh IIfx, significantly outperformed IBM's top of the line 80486 PS/2 Model 70 and Compaq's 33-MHz 80386 in independent testing company equivalent cross-platform Aldus PageMaker and Microsoft Excel benchmarks. Apple's late 1991 Quadra 68040-based Quadra models extend the lead. Basically, you can add accelerator cards to any Macintosh to obtain this performance. And DOS machines are now also adopting the SCSI interface standard because it performs so well on the Mac. Nope, the Mac is not too slow.

That leaves price The DOS PC environment is an open one. Multiple vendors competing on a somewhat level playing field to make the best product drive the prices down. Not so with Apple. Until the October 1990 Macintosh announcements, Apple's proprietary Mac environment kept high prices to amortize engineering and development costs and keep their stockholders happy. Even with the success of the Mac Classic model (over one million sold), Macintoshes are still more expensive than DOS PC machines.

Enter the Cat Mac. If you build it in a PC case, as most people do, it even looks like a DOS PC. But it does everything the Macintosh does. It is a Macintosh. And because you build it yourself, you save money no matter what model you choose.

Since the first edition of this book was written, IBM has announced OS/2 version 2, Microsoft has delivered Windows 3 in volume, Apple has delivered System 7 in volume, and IBM and Apple have entered into a historical, precedent-shattering agreement. What do these mean for do-it-yourself Macintosh builders?

If imitation is the sincerest form of flattery, the emergence of OS/2, Windows, GeoWorks (from Ensemble), NewWave (from HP) and numerous other GUI-based operating system software products has to make Apple proud indeed. Yet none of these is the equal of Apple's Macintosh operating system software: System 7 in its latest incarnation.[4]

The benefit of buying a Macintosh is the proven productivity gains of using it. IBM itself has recognized this as shown by its historical agreement with Apple to use the Apple Macintosh core technology for development of future IBM-platform products. The benefit of building your own Macintosh is that you get this capability at the best possible price with the greatest flexibility.

The future

Whatever Macintosh you are now using or plan to use, it is virtually certain that a slicker, faster, cheaper, or lighter one will be developed in the future. Just as new models roll off the Detroit auto assembly lines each year, the marketplace in its quest for better price performance and Apple's stockholders in their quest for profits, demand continued Macintosh improvement and innovation. The third-party vendors, whose product cycles are even shorter than Apple's, are even more intensely driven by change to excel.

You, the astute Cat Mac builder and Macintosh user, are the real beneficiary of this change because you can work it to your advantage. Just as you wouldn't necessarily buy a new auto each year, unless the price of a new car represents only a week's allowance or is merely pocket change to you, it isn't necessary to always buy the latest Macintosh model either. You can add enhancements to the Cat Mac or Macintosh model you have, get the maximum value out of it, and save your big outlays for those times when there have been major changes (improvements!) made to the Macintosh product line. Keeping in mind, of course, the XIVth corollary of Murphy's Law, which loosely translated states, "Never buy serial number 0001 of anything—wait for others to test the new, improved model to verify that it is improved and continues to work after it is new."

---

[1] Taken from CRN PC Expo attendees poll data provided in Susan Tito and Merilee Gale, "Inside the mind of the buyer," *Computer Reseller News*, 1 July 1991, p. 3.

[2] Stewart Alsop, "Apple's A/UX, Version 2.0 Will Give the Mac a Leg Up on DOS, Unix," *Infoworld*, 2 February 1990, p. 106.

[3] One Minute Manager, "Apple and Peat Marwick & Main prove Mac Productivity," *MacWEEK*, 12 September 1989, p. 40, and Marketwatch, "What justifies a Mac purchase?," *MacWEEK*, 13 February 1990, p. 76.

[4] Susan Tito, "MIS managers rate Macs higher than Windows 3.0," *Computer Reseller News*, 29 July 1991, and numerous other trade press articles make this point abundantly clear.

Chapter 2
How much you can save

When you take a trip, you usually decide on your destination first. Same with building your own Cat Mac. Normally, you are starting from someplace. You have no Macintosh, you have a Mac 128, a Mac SE, etc. You have a destination, a goal, an objective. You want to build a Cat Mac from the ground up but keep it under $2000. You want to get the best price performance and money is no object. (Please call me. My daytime number is . . ..) You want to add a video monitor or hard disk to your existing Macintosh. Regardless of what you want to do, it helps to first list your options. Then you can narrow down your list to home in on your objective.

Of course, just about everyone's final objective is different. That's the beauty of building your own Cat Mac. You control the outcome—you're in control of your own destiny. If you want a larger disk, put one in. A bigger monitor, add it on. Don't want to spend as much—scrounge for better prices on parts or go the used or bartered parts route. In any event, the choices are practically limitless and totally up to you. Besides, once you have your own expertise, you can add enhancements neither Apple nor anyone else has thought of and be able to market it for a few bucks, thus reducing the cost of your machine even further!

The availability of newer products might mean you change what you build and how you build it. But the approach outlined in *Build Your Own Macintosh and Save a Bundle* has stood the test of time and will be useful to you regardless of what you do or how you do it.

In other words, you will always be able to begin with a standard Macintosh logic board[1] available in the used marketplace from a number of sources at a worthwhile price, put it into the chassis of your choosing, cable it up to a power supply and add the other components to finish your Cat Mac as you choose. It will always be possible to do this at a price that is lower than buying a new Macintosh.

How much can you save by building your own Macintosh? You determine that by deciding what kind of Macintosh you want to build. That, in turn, is determined by the costs of the "parts" or "building blocks" or "modules" you put into your Cat Mac. This chapter will focus on costs; chapter 3 focuses on the performance aspects.

Once you build your Cat Mac, it only gets better. Each step you take opens you up to more future possibilities. You also gain the knowledge and experience to do more innovative things. And think of all the fun you will have. Plus learning. Plus your wife or husband, friends or business associates will think you're a genius when you say, "Why, yes I built it myself."

The Macintosh block by block

To assist you, the Cat Mac builder, in evaluating the cost alternatives of any decision you make, let's take a look at the "modules" that make up every

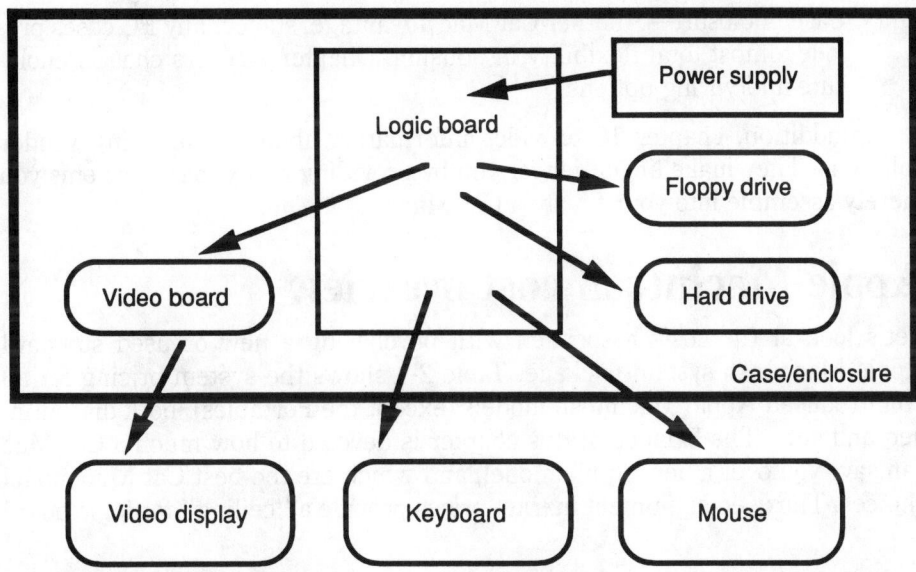

2-1 Macintosh block diagram.

Macintosh model, including your Cat Mac. Later chapters will cover each one of these in detail. The block diagram in Fig. 2-1 shows the relationship between the modules:

- Logic board and memory—The heart of your Cat Mac and almost always the most expensive part. Logic boards and memory are discussed in chapter 3. All other decisions are subordinate to and dependent upon your choice here. Accelerator cards would also logically be grouped with this module, but to keep the comparisons focused and simple, they have been left out of this chapter's cost tradeoffs and they are discussed in chapter 4.
- Hard drive—The second most important and expensive part after the logic board. Your Cat Mac's performance is mainly determined by your hard drive and logic board choices. Chapter 5 discusses hard drives.
- Floppy drive—The main input/output and archival storage device for your Cat Mac. Floppy drives are also discussed in chapter 5.
- Video display/board—The visual interface to your Cat Mac. Every Cat Mac builder enjoys the advantage of selecting exactly the type of monitor needed. Monitors and video options are discussed in chapter 6.
- Keyboard and mouse—The main user interface for your Cat Mac. Keyboard and mouse options are discussed in chapter 7.
- Power supply—Another Cat Mac advantage, since almost all DOS PC power supplies provide more than enough power. Power supplies are discussed in chapter 7.

- Case/enclosure—Another Cat Mac advantage, since many PC cases provide almost total flexibility in housing. Chapter 7 covers chassis/enclosure and wiring options.

In addition, chapter 10 provides information about repackaging vendor solutions. They make life easier for you by providing ready-made systems you merely assemble into your finished Cat Mac.

Apple Macintosh cost overview

Let's look at the costs associated with purchasing a new or used standard Apple Macintosh system package. Table 2-1 shows the system pricing for all 16 introduced Apple Macintosh models (except the Portables), both discontinued and new. The balance of this chapter is devoted to how much a Cat Mac can save you over a new Apple model, and which are the best Cat Mac model choices. The used equipment market prices provide a "ceiling" for logic board

Table 2-1. New or (used) price for Apple Macintosh system.

CPU type[1]	68000	68020	68030	68040
Discontinued models				
Mac 128 - 128/1f	(200)	—	—	—
Mac 512 - 512/1f	(400)	—	—	—
Mac Plus - 1/1f	(600)	—	—	—
Mac SE - 1/2f	(900)	—	—	—
Mac II - 1/1f	—	(1900)	—	—
Mac SE 30 - 1/1f	—	—	(1800)	—
Mac IIcx - 1/1f	—	—	(2100)	—
Mac IIx - 1/1f	—	—	(2500)	—
Current models				
Mac Classic 2/40	1499	—	—	—
Mac LC 2/40	—	2499	—	—
Mac Classic II 2/40	—	—	1899	—
Mac IIsi 3/40	—	—	3769	—
Mac IIci 5/1f	—	—	5269	—
Mac IIfx 4/1f	—	—	7369	—
Mac Quadra 700 4/1f	—	—	—	5699
Mac Quadra 900 4/1f	—	—	—	7199

[1]Taken from Apple's Price List for current models and used equipment vendor average prices for discontinued models as of December 1991. Discontinued model used equipment prices appear in parentheses. Configuration with memory/hard drive size or number of floppy drives appears after CPU type.

prices and this will also be covered. First, let's examine the Apple list prices in Table 2-1—the numbers might seem "low" to some readers, "high" to others. Let me depart briefly into the subject of "real world" prices to clear up the confusion.

Macintosh real world pricing

In some parts of the world, the Apple US dollar list prices quoted in Table 2-1 would be low. Export "uplifted" prices seem to average about 35% above list. On the other hand, in some parts of the United States, New York City and Los Angeles, for example, typical "street" price discounted prices seem to average 25% below list. In addition, Apple is continuously playing with its dealer costs via various incentive programs and outright adjustments. Beyond that, there is the used Macintosh local and mail order market to consider. An "overhang" of used models in any particular geographic area or in the national mail order channel tends to depress the "street" value of new models even further. This typically occurs several months after a new model is introduced, when Apple Developers, Value Added Resellers, Apple Education and Consortium accounts, dealers (all who purchase at 25% to 50% off list), and Apple itself liquidate older inventory to free up capital and make room for the new models.

Trends in Macintosh pricing

In addition to geographic and situational variance, Macintosh pricing components are also variously interrelated with the time. Figure 2-2 shows a snapshot of the different pricing activity during a several month period from August 1989 through March 1990 for a popular model of that time period, the Macintosh SE 20 with an extended keyboard. Although the prices are dated, the example is just as valid today. There are five separate price lines in the figure to follow in Fig. 2-2. Let's look at each one:

Apple SE 20 list price This started out at $3998. Apple dropped their list price by $300 in August 1989. When Apple did this, the "street" price and "used" price, which are tied directly to it, also immediately dropped. In other words, when you woke up the next day and read in the morning paper of the price reduction, your own personal Macintosh SE 20 Model had also dropped in price (and of course numerous dealer inventories with that model in it—but dealers receive "price protection"). In March 1990 Apple dropped the list price again, this time by $500 to $3198. Again it had immediate impact on the "street" and "used" prices.

Apple SE 20 street price This averaged roughly 25% off list so it started out at about $3000 and at the end was about $2400. This price is tied to the Apple list price but is usually a "whatever the traffic will bear" phenomenon driven by supply and demand in a given geographic area. The simple fact of

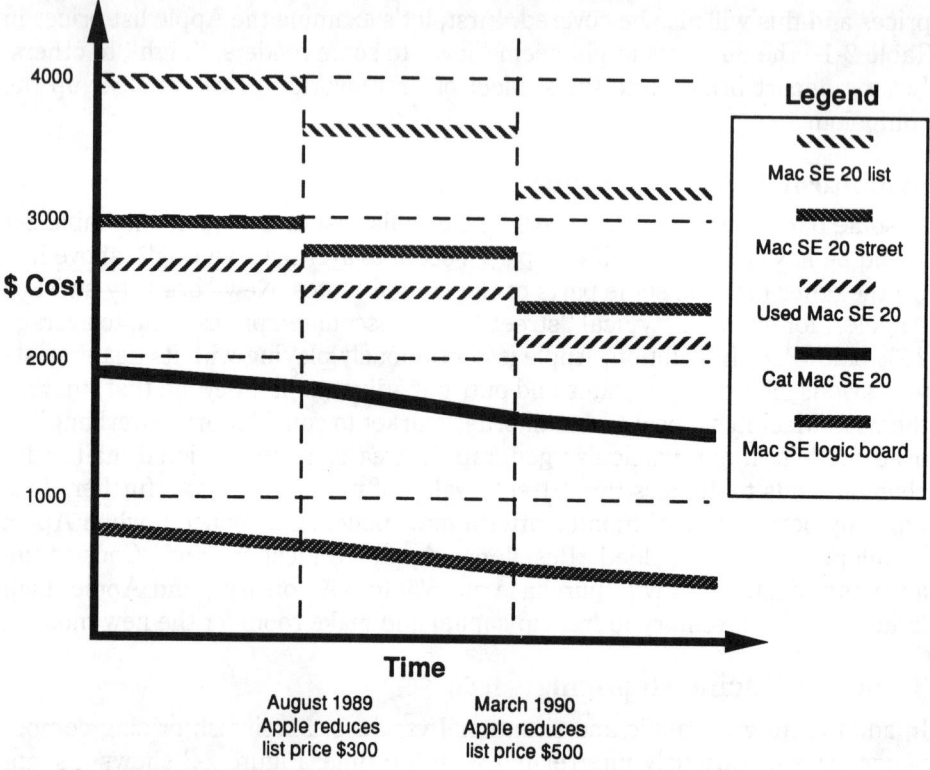

2-2 Macintosh real world pricing.

life is that buyers in a city with many dealers and alternate sources pay less than buyers in cities with fewer dealers.

Used Apple SE 20 price This was $300 lower than the street price so it started out at about $2700 and at the end was about $2100. This price is also tied to the Apple list price and also a "whatever the traffic will bear" phenomenon but it is driven by supply and demand in the new and used equipment distribution channel, a much broader geographic market. In any given "spot" market, the price can vary widely. Do you need to sell your Mac SE 20 today for a down payment on your new car? You might take a lot less for it, etc. Or the converse. Mr. Smith, I can get you those ten used SE 20s today but you're going to have to pay a little extra for them, etc.

Cat Mac SE 20 price This price is driven by the cost of the SE logic board, typically the most expensive module, to which all of the other third-party vendor module costs are then added. It started out at about $1900 and at the end was $1650. It is tied only indirectly to the Apple list price and tends always to go downward as more cost-effective third-party modules are introduced and the logic board declines in price with time.

Mac SE logic board This price is only a composite of what it could be obtained for on the used equipment marketplace. At any given time, its "spot" price can vary widely and is more dependent on its availability on a given reseller's shelves than any Apple list price or price reduction. To the delight of the Cat Mac builder, its price slowly but relentlessly decreases with time. It started out at $800 and at the end was $600.

Okay. That was the real world of prices. Notice how the passage of time validated the main premise of this book. Apple dropped their SE prices twice but logic board prices also dropped and the ratios stayed the same. You still save by building your own Cat Mac.

Macintosh logic board pricing

Apple Macintosh logic boards—the part that saves Cat Mac builders money—are manufactured with state of the art, automated, robotic, assembly machines using the highest quality reliable components. A Macintosh logic board—especially the most recent models—are truly a work of art in addition to being an engineering and manufacturing marvel. After your Macintosh logic board has faithfully served you in your Cat Mac chassis, you can mount it on your wall!

Unlike used automobiles, used Macintosh logic boards don't wear out. As a Cat Mac builder you are in the incredible position of being able to purchase a logic board whose price has declined with time but whose capability to perform for you has not changed at all.

Logic board costs are definitely a moving target varying almost daily with supply and demand, new product introductions, Apple policies, who you buy from, and where they are located. That is why a range of values—taken from reliable used equipment sources—appears in Table 2-2. Your personal negotiation skills and scrounging abilities might enable you to do much better. While the overall trend in Macintosh logic board prices is always downward over time, you are cautioned to beware of spot situations and mini-trends which might cause prices for certain boards to rise. Here's where the Cat Mac builder's flexibility really shines: nothing forces you to go with the temporarily more expensive logic board—you can always choose the most cost-effective one and just be innovative with your design.

A few words of caution. All the major vendors stand behind the used Macintosh logic boards they resell to you and offer warranty (the logic boards are tested before shipment and you know you are getting a quality, working product). The same cannot be said of all second- and third-tier vendors.

The higher price you pay to first-tier vendors might be thought of as peace-of-mind insurance. Occasionally some of them are guilty of "low-balling:" you are quoted an unbelievably good price on a logic board but find out it is not in stock. Over time, you find out it is never in stock. Yup, sad but true. The payback is simple. Go with those vendors who stock the product and deal honestly.

Table 2-2. Macintosh logic board prices.

Apple part number	Logic board[1]	Price range
Discontinued models		
661-96152	Mac 128	50 – 100
661-96236	Mac 512	100 – 200
661-0525	Mac Plus	300 – 500
661-0526	Mac SE	179[2] – 600
661-0528	Mac II	575[3] – 1100
661-0527	Mac SE 30	950 – 1300[4]
661-0537	Mac IIcx	1100 – 1400
661-1813	Mac IIx	1400 – 1700
661-1610	Mac Portable	600 – 900
Current models[5] (except PowerBooks)		
661-0596	Mac Classic	300 – 600
661-0672	Mac Classic II	600 – 800
661-0593	Mac LC	700 – 1200
661-1615	Mac IIsi	1200 – 1400
661-0532	Mac IIci	1500 – 2000
661-0522	Mac IIfx	2400 – 3000
661-0666	Mac Quadra 700	3000 – 3600
661-0665	Mac Quadra 900	3400 – 4200

[1] Used equipment vendor average prices for logic boards as of December 1991.

[2] Throughout 1991, Shreve literature offered SE logic boards without ROM chips at $179. SE Logic board with FDHD ROMs is Apple part 661-0536.

[3] Throughout 1991, Maya literature offered Mac II logic boards at $575.

[4] Price rose after Classic II announced.

[5] Not all models are widely available yet in reseller market.

One final word: Prices change, usually down, sometimes up. Please do not go to your friendly Macintosh used equipment provider on any item of used hardware and tell them that, "Bob Brant said I could get it for this price." After stifling a laugh, they will tell you today's asking price followed by a mini-lecture on the economics of supply and demand. Please emblazon this on your mind: The price for any used Macintosh equipment is determined by what you are actually willing to pay a supplier *at the time you buy it*. What it sold for in the past was history. What it will sell for in the future is still in the future. From my own experience, I can tell you that how good a price you can get is limited only by your own creativity and your willingness to shop around.

Logic board to system cost ratio

An important ingredient to help you evaluate the "goodness" of your logic board purchase price is the logic board to system price cost ratio:

$$\text{Ratio} = \frac{\text{Logic board cost}}{\text{Mac system cost}}$$

Table 2-3 applies the formula to the Macintosh system prices in Table 2-1 and logic board prices in Table 2-2 to arrive at a list of the high and low ratios for all models. In addition to proving chapter 1s postulate that "logic boards tend to become a higher percentage of the system price with time," here's what else Table 2-3 tells you:

- No absolute values, but current model logic boards average about one-third of system list price and discontinued model logic boards about one-half of used system market price—try not to pay more than these values.
- Better values are pointed out by lower ratios in Table 2-3. The SE, Mac II discontinued models, and Classic, LC, and IIci current models are examples.
- Less advantageous to Cat Mac builder models (due to strong market demand or limited supply) are pointed out by higher ratios in Table 2-3. The discontinued Mac IIx and the new Quadra models are examples.

Table 2-3. Cat Mac ratios for system versus logic board prices.

CPU[1]	Low ratio	High ratio
Discontinued models		
Mac 128 - 128/1f	0.25	0.50
Mac 512 - 512/1f	0.25	0.50
Mac Plus - 1/1f	0.50	0.83
Mac SE - 1/2f	0.20	0.67
Mac II - 1/1f	0.30	0.58
Mac SE 30 - 1/1f	0.53	0.72
Mac IIcx - 1/1f	0.52	0.67
Mac IIx - 1/1f	0.56	0.68
Current models		
Mac Classic 2/40	0.20	0.40
Mac Classic II 2/40	0.32	0.42
Mac LC 2/40	0.28	0.48
Mac IIsi 3/40	0.32	0.37
Mac IIci 5/1f	0.28	0.53
Mac IIfx 4/1f	0.32	0.41
Mac Quadra 700 4/1f	0.52	0.63
Mac Quadra 900 4/1f	0.47	0.58

[1] Taken from Apple's Price List for current models and used equipment vendor average prices for discontinued models and logic boards as of December 1991. Configuration with memory/hard drive size or number of floppy drives appears after CPU type.

Macintosh upgrade pricing

Apple is one of the few major manufacturers that provides upgrades to its products. While it provides them across a broad spectrum of upgrade option categories—memory, logic board, floppy drive, hard drive, monitors, printers, keyboard, mouse, coprocessor, and networking—the categories of interest to Cat Mac builders are logic boards and floppy drive upgrades. Table 2-4 shows their prices.

Table 2-4. Apple Macintosh upgrade prices.

Apple part number	Upgrade	Price[1]
Logic boards		
M2518	Mac 128 to Mac Plus	799
M2518	Mac 512 to Mac Plus	599
M1545LL/A	Mac Classic to Mac Classic II	599
M1102LL/A	Mac SE to Mac SE 30	999[2]
M5816LL/A	Mac IIcx to Mac IIci	1499[3]
M0375LL/B	Mac II/IIx to Mac IIfx	2599[4]
M5950LL/A	Mac IIcx/IIci to Mac Quadra 700	3499
Floppy drives		
M2516	Mac Plus 800K drive + ROMs	299
M6052/B	Mac SE 1.4Mb drive + ROMs	449
M6051/C	Mac II 1.4Mb drive + ROMs	449

[1] Apple's List Price. Discontinued models also available through used equipment vendors.

[2] Old price $1699 before May 1991.

[3] Old price $2399 before May 1991.

[4] Old price $2999 before May 1991.

The importance of the Apple Macintosh logic board upgrades is that they make logic boards available to the used equipment market (via dealer overstock, liquidations, and closeouts, etc.) and help set the selling price. Depending on the seller's circumstances, you can occasionally get a logic board without having to provide another in exchange. For example if, due to a distress sale, you are able to pick up the Mac IIci logic board upgrade at its $1499 price without an exchange, you've just saved yourself $400 over what it would cost you at one of the major used equipment dealers.

Another pricing implication is that they also set the price umbrella under which all the third-party accelerator vendors must operate. If Apple's Mac IIfx upgrade is offered for $2599, it is probably unwise to price your 40- to 50-MHz 68030-based accelerator board for much beyond that.

Finally, the obvious benefit is that they are the genuine Apple article (totally compatible with all other upgrades), have a definite resale value, etc.

The importance of the Apple Macintosh floppy drive upgrades is that they make floppy drives and the ROMs needed to support them available to the used equipment market, and provide Cat Mac builders with additional flexibility in their system designs.

Cat Mac cost overview

How much your Cat Mac can benefit you—in direct cost savings as well as other tangible ways will be covered next. First, let's do a fair apples to apples comparison (ho, ho, ho!) . . ..

Cat Mac versus standard Apple Macintosh costs

Table 2-5 shows a comparison of Apple Macintosh systems cost versus the equivalent Cat Mac model. The Apple Macintosh system costs are based on a system with logic board, memory, floppy/hard drives, power supply and case/enclosure. The built-in 9" video monitor is also part of the package on the Mac Classic. The costs for the feature-for-feature comparable Cat Mac model are separately itemized. Here are my exact assumptions for Table 2-5:

- Logic board—The best price from Table 2-2 was used.
- RAM—Memory was built up to the equivalent Apple models requiring a memory card with 1Mb for the Classic, four 512K SIMMs for the IIsi, and four 1Mb SIMMs each for the IIci and IIfx.
- Floppy drive—The Apple internal 1.4Mb FDHD drive was used, discounted from its $349 list price.
- Hard drive—The Quantum LPS52 hard drive was used.
- Power supply & case—The PS/2-style case was used for the Classic, LC, and IIsi; tower case for the IIci and IIfx. Mounting hardware/cables are included in cost.
- Keyboard—Apple standard keyboard was used, discounted from its $129 list price.
- Optical mouse—Mouse Systems Little Mouse was used.
- Video monitor/board—Samsung 14" paperwhite monitor and video card was used.
- Apple model—The model and price from Table 2-1 was used.

You can see I did nothing magic in Table 2-5—only repackaged the logic board with a superior chassis/power supply and third-party peripherals—yet the savings ranged from 5% on the Mac Classic model and 39% to 58% on all the other models. In general, savings increased as performance increased. Why are such savings possible? Easy. You take a logic board (whose cost averages one-third of the Apple Macintosh System price) and add a very low cost chassis/hard drive/floppy drive combination (whose cost is relatively fixed for all logic board models). Let's use the Mac LC as an example. You are adding a $700 logic board (28% of system cost) to a chassis/hard drive/floppy drive combination that costs you $650. Even if you build a top-of-the-line Cat Mac IIfx

Table 2-5. Cat Mac versus Apple Macintosh systems cost comparison.

Component	Classic	LC	IIsi	IIci	IIfx
logic board	300	700	1200	1500	2400
RAM	150	—	100	160	200
floppy drive	250	250	250	250	250
hard drive	240	240	240	—	—
power supply/case	160	160	160	240	240
keyboard	90	90	—	—	—
optical mouse	80	80	80	80	80
video monitor/board	150	—	—	—	—
Cat Mac total	1420	1520	2030	2230	3170
Apple model	1499	2499	3769	5269	7369
Cat Mac savings	79	979	1739	3039	4199
percentage savings	5%	39%	46%	58%	57%

with the same hard drive, this combination only costs you $930 (factoring in the cost for more memory and the tower chassis).

Now that you've seen how the Cat Mac concept works for just the boxes, let's build up some actual complete Cat Mac systems and see how they compare with their Apple Macintosh counterparts. The same assumptions will be used as in Table 2-5—only this time memory, hard drive, monitor, and keyboard will be added and compared to an equivalent complete Apple Macintosh system.

Cat Mac Classic versus Apple Mac Classic

Table 2-6 shows the Cat Mac Classic system. You already met this model in column one of Table 2-5 (it was the only Apple Macintosh model that came

Table 2-6. Cat Mac Classic versus Apple Mac Classic cost.

Item	Apple Mac Classic	Cost	Cat Mac Classic	Cost
logic board	standard Classic 2/40	—	identical	300
memory	2Mb RAM	—	memory card	150
hard drive	40Mb	—	Quantum LPS52	240
floppy drive	1.4Mb FDHD	—	identical	300
keyboard	Apple std Classic	—	Apple standard ADB	90
mouse	Apple std Classic	—	Little Mouse optical	80
video display	9" monochrome	—	Samsung 14" paperwhite	100
video board	Located with P.S.	—	video card/cable	50
power supply/case	Apple std Classic	—	230 watts—PS/2-style	70
miscellaneous	Apple std Classic	—	cables, flppy brkt, panel	90
total price		$1499		$1420

How much you can save

complete with a monitor). The information is repeated here in more detail. With the Cat Mac model, you save $79 ($1499 – $1420), or 5%, over the cost of Apple's Classic offering. But the Cat Mac Classic is identical in every department and offers superior hard drive, keyboard, monitor, and chassis/power supply solutions for a lower cost. Part of the reason the Cat Mac Classic is not more cost-effective is that its Classic memory card must be purchased as a separate a la carte item and requires a special cable/bracket to lay flat in the Cat Mac chassis, as opposed to just expanding with memory SIMMs alone as with the other logic boards. Let's move up the line into an entry-level color system.

Cat Mac LC versus Apple Mac LC

In the case of the Cat Mac LC, you are adding Apple's RGB Hi Res color monitor and the 512K VRAM SIMM it takes to support it to the Cat Mac LC system you already met in column two of Table 2-5. Table 2-7 shows the results. With the Cat Mac LC, you save $1423 ($3673 – $2250), or 39%. But the Cat Mac LC is identical in every department and offers superior hard drive, keyboard, and chassis/power supply solutions for a lower cost. Let's move further up the line into a more powerful 68030-based color system.

Table 2-7. Cat Mac LC versus Apple Mac LC cost.

Item	Apple Mac LC	Cost	Cat Mac LC	Cost
logic board	standard LC 2/40	2499	identical	700
memory	2ea 1Mb SIMMs	—	identical	incl
hard drive	40Mb	—	Quantum LPS52	240
floppy drive	1.4Mb FDHD	—	identical	250
keyboard	Apple std LC	—	Apple standard	90
mouse	Apple std LC	—	Little Mouse optical	80
video display	Apple 14" RGB Hi Res	999	identical	650
video board	LC 512K VRAM upgd	175	identical	80
power supply/case	Apple std LC	—	230 watts—PS/2-style	70
miscellaneous	Apple std LC	—	cables, flppy brkt, panel	90
total price	—	$3673	—	$2250

Cat Mac IIsi versus Apple Mac IIsi

With the Cat Mac IIsi, you are adding more memory, an extended keyboard, and Apple's RGB Hi Res color monitor to the Cat Mac IIsi system you already met in column three of Table 2-5. Table 2-8 tells the story. With the Cat Mac IIsi, you save $2137 ($4997 – $2860, or 43%. Once again you are better off in more than just price. You have the identical Apple IIsi logic board, 1.4Mb floppy drive, and Apple RGB color 14" monitor. Plus you have slightly more memory (4Mb versus 3Mb RAM), a larger, faster hard drive, equivalent extended ADB keyboard, a better ADB optical mouse, a heftier 230-watt

Table 2-8. Cat Mac IIsi versus Apple Mac IIsi cost.

Item	Apple Mac IIsi	Cost	Cat Mac IIsi	Cost
logic board	standard Mac IIsi 3/40	3769	Mac IIsi logic board	1200
memory	3Mb RAM	—	4ea 1Mb SIMMs	160
hard drive	40Mb	—	Quantum LPS52	240
floppy drive	1.4Mb FDHD	—	identical	250
keyboard	Apple extended	229	MacPro Plus extended	120
Mouse	Apple std IIsi	—	Little Mouse optical	80
video display	Apple 14" RGB Hi Res	999	identical	650
video board	not required	—	not required	—
power supply/case	Apple std IIsi	—	230 watts—PS/2-style	70
miscellaneous	Apple std IIsi	—	cables, flppy brkt, panel	90
total price	—	$4997	—	$2860

power supply and fan, and more chassis expansion room. Now you can definitely begin to see the pattern. Let's move still farther up the line.

Cat Mac IIci versus Apple Mac IIci

With the Cat Mac IIci, you are adding more memory, a hard drive, a cache card, an extended keyboard, and Apple's RGB Hi Res color monitor to the Cat Mac IIci system you already met in column four of Table 2-5. Table 2-9 tells the story. By repackaging the Cat Mac IIci, you save $3657 ($7197 – $3540), or 51%. Again you are better off even beyond price. You have the identical Apple IIci logic board, RAM memory, 1.4Mb floppy drive, and Apple RGB color 14" monitor. Plus you have a much larger, faster hard drive (105Mb versus 80Mb), equivalent cache card, equivalent extended ADB keyboard, a better ADB optical mouse, a heftier 250-W power supply, and a far more expandable tower

Table 2-9. Cat Mac IIci versus Apple Mac IIci cost.

Item	Apple Mac IIci	Cost	Cat Mac IIci	Cost
logic board	standard Mac IIci 5/80	5969	Mac IIci logic board	1500
memory	5Mb RAM	—	identical	200
hard drive	80Mb	—	Quantum LPS105	350
floppy drive	1.4Mb FDHD	—	identical	250
keyboard	Apple extended	229	MacPro Plus extended	120
mouse	Apple std IIci	—	Little Mouse optical	80
video display	Apple 14" RGB Hi Res	999	identical	650
video board	not required	—	cache card	150
power supply/case	Apple std IIci	—	250 watts—tower-style	150
miscellaneous	Apple std IIci	—	cables, flppy brkt, panel	90
total price	—	$7197	—	$3540

chassis. It kind of makes your mouth water doesn't it? Let's go to the top of the mountain.

Cat Mac IIfx versus Apple Mac IIfx

With the Cat Mac IIfx, you are adding a hard drive, an extended keyboard, and Apple's RGB Hi Res color monitor and video card to the Cat Mac IIfx system you already met in column five of Table 2-5. A glance at Table 2-10 gives you the picture. By repackaging the Cat Mac IIfx you save $5457 ($9997 − $4540), or 55%. Again you are better off even beyond price. You have the identical Apple IIfx logic board, RAM memory, 1.4Mb floppy drive, and Apple RGB color 14" monitor. Plus you have a much larger, faster hard drive (105Mb versus 80Mb), equivalent video card (you pay less for your used 8-bit Apple video card than the 8/24-bit video card Apple currently offers), equivalent extended ADB keyboard, a better ADB optical mouse, a heftier 250-W power supply, and a far more expandable tower chassis. And once again, as a Cat Mac builder, you enjoy enormous flexibility and room for growth. Apple only offers a tower chassis in its Quadra 900 model, but you can have one with any model you choose. The Cat Mac IIfx configuration in a tower chassis is a particularly logical combination. Needless to say, it makes an excellent choice as a server.

What more can I say? Your Cat Mac solution will always have greater flexibility and cost you less than the equivalent Apple Macintosh model. Plus it only gets better as you move up the line into more powerful models.

Table 2-10. Cat Mac IIfx versus Apple Mac IIfx cost.

Item	Apple Mac IIfx	Cost	Cat Mac IIfx	Cost
logic board	standard Mac IIfx 4/80	8069	Mac IIfx logic board	2400
memory	4Mb RAM	—	identical	200
hard drive	80Mb	—	Quantum LPS105	350
floppy drive	1.4Mb FDHD	—	identical	250
keyboard	Apple extended	229	MacPro Plus extended	120
mouse	Apple std IIfx	—	Little Mouse optical	80
video display	Apple 14" RGB Hi Res	999	identical	650
video board	Apple 8/24-bit video card	699	Apple 8-bit video card	250
power supply/case	Apple std IIfx	—	250 watts—tower-style	150
miscellaneous	Apple std IIfx	—	cables, flppy brkt, panel	90
total price	—	$9996	—	$4540

Cat Mac system recommendations

Time to recap what you have just learned. Figure 2-3 does just that. It summarizes the message of Tables 2-6 through 2-10—your Cat Mac can save you 5% to 55% over an equivalent Apple Macintosh system. And the Cat Mac benefit

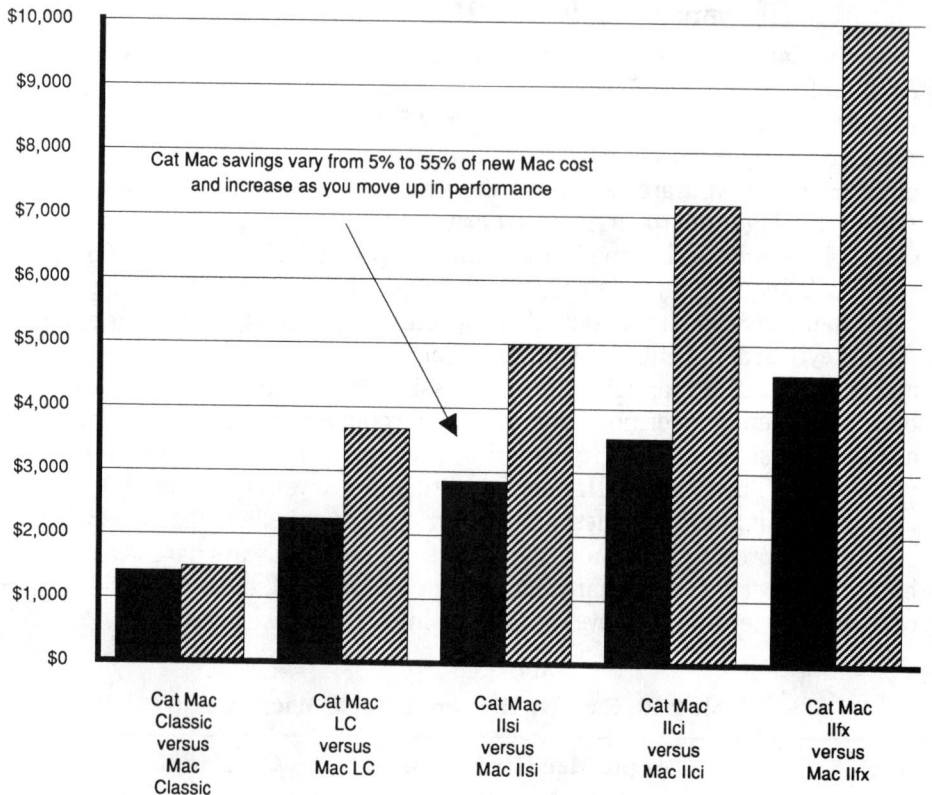

2-3 Summary of Cat Mac cost savings.

increases as you move up in performance. Thus far the Cat Mac has been compared to the respective Apple Macintosh models. Now let's move ahead and compare the different Cat Mac options among themselves and give you some recommendations.

Recommended Cat Mac systems

While the previous sections have focused on building Cat Mac models using current model Macintosh logic boards, you can occasionally obtain even better values by starting with discontinued model Macintosh logic boards. The main point to observe is, in order to run Apple's System 7 and several popular Macintosh application software programs concurrently, you shouldn't start with anything less than an SE logic board (which has built-in SCSI plus ADB), 2Mb of RAM (4Mb preferred), a 1.4Mb floppy drive, a 40Mb hard drive, and a 14"

Table 2-11. Recommended Cat Mac systems cost comparison.

Component(s)	CatMac SE	Accelerated SE	CatMac II	CatMac IIcx
Mac SE logic board	179	179	—	—
Mac II logic board	—	—	575	—
Mac IIcx logic board	—	—	—	1100
Mobius accelerator/video	—	1100	—	—
4Mb memory	160	160	160	160
Quantum LPS52 hard drive	240	240	240	240
Apple 1.4Mb floppy drive[1]	350	350	350	250
Key Tronics extended keyboard	120	120	120	120
Mouse Systems optical mouse	80	80	80	80
Amdek 14" monochrome	350	—	—	—
Mobius full-page display	—	included	—	—
Apple 14" RGB Hi Res color	—	—	650	650
Lapis video (color) card	included	—	—	—
Apple 8-bit video card	—	—	250	250
power supply/case	70	70	150	150
Miscellaneous	90	90	90	90
Cat Mac totals	1639	2389	2665	3090

[1]CatMac SE and Mac II models use Apple 1.4Mb FDHD upgrade kits with ROMs.

or larger video monitor (preferably full page or greater and color). In other words, the Cat Mac models shown in Table 2-11. Let's look at the candidates:

- Entry-level Cat Mac SE featuring a 640×480 monochrome display driven by a Lapis video card.
- Accelerated Cat Mac SE featuring a Mobius full-page display and 25-MHz 68030 (Mac IIci performance) accelerator/video card combination.
- Mac II and Mac IIcx Cat Macs featuring Apple's timeless and ever-popular 14" RGB Hi Res color monitor.

The special situation on the Cat Mac SE logic board price (identified in Table 2-2) should leap out at you as an outstanding value. The entry-level Cat Mac SE is easier to build (SIMMs and video just plug in—no special cables to build) than the Classic-based Cat Mac shown in Table 2-6 with more memory (4Mb versus 2Mb) and better video (a 640×480 monochrome display driven by a Lapis video card versus the 512×348 standard Macintosh video). All at little more than the cost of a Cat Mac Classic. Plus it offers more expansion options—although the Mac Classic is rapidly catching up.

If you utilize the Mac SE as a starting platform and add the unique Mobius accelerator/video board/full-page display combination, you can enjoy Mobius' superb Zenith-based full-page display and Mac IIci performance while maximizing your savings.

The Mac II is an outstanding platform for the Cat Mac builder to start with—particularly for color systems. The special situation on the Mac II logic board price (identified in Table 2-2) allows you to build a Cat Mac II at only slightly more than the cost of a Cat Mac LC. Yet it delivers vastly superior initial performance (having both 68020 CPU and FPU chips versus the LC's 68020 CPU only), more SIMM sockets (eight versus two) and greater expansion potential (six NuBus slots in a tower chassis versus the LC's one PDS expansion slot). Want more performance? Add a top-of-the-line DayStar 50-MHz 68030 accelerator to it at $1300 and enjoy Cat Mac IIfx performance for a total system cost of only $3965 ($575 less than the Cat Mac built up from the Mac IIfx logic board shown in Table 2-10), underscoring the point that it is usually possible to save money accelerating an existing Apple logic board rather than buying the next higher performance model.

The Cat Mac IIcx is another outstanding color platform for the Cat Mac builder. It provides only slightly less performance than a Cat Mac IIsi, yet its three NuBus slots and tower chassis provide greatly enhanced expansion potential at only slightly over a Cat Mac IIsi's cost. Plus you can add a 400-MHz DayStar 68030 PowerCache accelerator at $900, a 25-MHz 68040-based Radius Rocket at $1800, or another accelerator to enjoy higher performance. Without the color monitor, either the accelerated Cat Mac II or Cat Mac IIcx in the tower chassis gives you an excellent server in the $3000 price range.

Not recommended Cat Mac systems

While you can still build an entry-level Cat Mac based on a Mac 128, 512, or Plus logic board (as shown in the first edition of this book), there is little point in doing it today. Today's Macintosh software applications require more memory, speed, and (floppy and hard drive) capacity to run. You severely limit yourself by choosing any of these Macintosh logic board models as your starting platform. Not only are these logic boards less powerful, but the ROM chips they require are less available today (Outbound and other vendors are using them in Macintosh portables!), you are limited to 800K floppy drives (unless you go to more expensive third-party SCSI products), and your accelerator, memory expansion, video, and keyboard/mouse options are decreasing over time. Finally, from the pure cost point of view shown in Table 2-1, it is difficult to justify anyone building a Mac 128, 512, or Plus when you can buy a used one for $200, $400, or $600, respectively.

However, having said all that, if you received one of these models as a gift (i.e., your starting cost is zero), plus if you don't mind working with an 800K floppy drive, scrounging for 128K ROM chips, keyboard, mouse, and mounting either an upgrade or an accelerator board on it—by all means proceed.

Also not recommended, but for different reasons, are the Mac Classic, Classic II, Mac IIx, and Mac Quadra logic boards. At this time, the Mac Classic logic board does not do anything more for Cat Mac builders than the Mac SE and Mac LC logic boards that bracket it in price and performance, respectively. Plus its memory slot card expansion is just more difficult to work with. The Mac IIx logic board is not recommended unless you happen to acquire it at a good price. The Mac II combined with an accelerator board gives you the six NuBus slots for less and the Mac IIfx gives you six NuBus slots plus a lot more for only a slightly greater investment. The Mac Classic II and Mac Quadra logic boards are just not widely available yet, and you are paying an unnecessary premium for their performance versus equivalent alternatives. In the future however, as they become more readily available, each of these logic boards should become the Cat Mac builder's vehicle of choice in their respective performance niches.

[1]Logic boards in existence at the end of 1991—Mac 128 through Mac Quadra logic boards—are covered in this book. You will have to research future not-yet-released logic boards yourself.

Chapter 3
Macintosh logic boards

The heart of your Cat Mac and usually its most expensive part is the Apple Macintosh logic board. Once you have selected your logic board, you have your Cat Mac. The rest of the items are just peripherals to support it. All you need to do is connect power to it, add the disk drives, video display, keyboard and mouse, put it in a pretty enclosure, and presto, you are in business.

Chapter 2 focused on costs. This chapter's focus is performance. It positions the Macintosh logic boards to help you make the best decision on which one to use in your Cat Mac.

The Motorola 68000 CPU chip family

If the logic board is the heart of your Macintosh, then the Motorola 68xxx CPU (central processing unit) chip is the soul of it. This microcomputer chip is the engine that makes your Macintosh go. Although encased in a larger protective housing, the chip itself is no larger than your thumbnail. Yet, it offers more capability than the room full of electronics required by the IBM mainframes of the 1960s or the rack full of electronics required by the Digital minicomputers of the 1970s.

Thanks to the lessons learned from Digital and other minicomputer makers of the 1970s, Motorola has chosen a path that ensures your Macintosh software investment will not be obsoleted. Each newer chip is fully instruction-set-compatible with the one before it, yet contains significant performance improvements. Because of this strategy, you can replace an older chip with a newer one in your CPU line and everything still runs—only faster. Of course, there are hardware technical details to work out (such as how you talk to the chip, etc.) but your software code still works.

This is good news for the Cat Mac builder. You can remove your Mac SE logic board from your Cat Mac chassis and pop in your Mac SE 30 or Mac IIsi logic board and everything works. It also works for Mac Classic to Mac Classic II, Mac II to Mac IIx or Mac IIfx, Mac IIcx or Mac IIci to Quadra 700. Even the older Macintosh models had a compatible upward migration path: Mac 128 to Mac 512 to Mac Plus. On the down side, any logic board you have today will be superceded by newer models in the Apple Macintosh logic board family.

Figure 3-1 shows the trends in the Motorola 68xxx chip family on which the Macintosh is based. It took five years to go from 68,000 to 195,000 circuits on a chip in the early 1980s; it only took two years to go from the 68030 chip with its 300,000 circuits to the 68040 chip with its 1,200,000 circuits. There is a lot of optimized and parallel processing going on in the new 68040 chip. As a result, the 68040 can execute the average instruction in only 1.3 clock cycles versus the 3.4 clock cycles required for the 68030 chip. Motorola says its 25-MHz 68040 offers three times the performance of a 25-MHz 68030; its integral on-chip floating-point unit—no separate 68882 style chip needed—allows it to perform floating-point operations ten times faster.

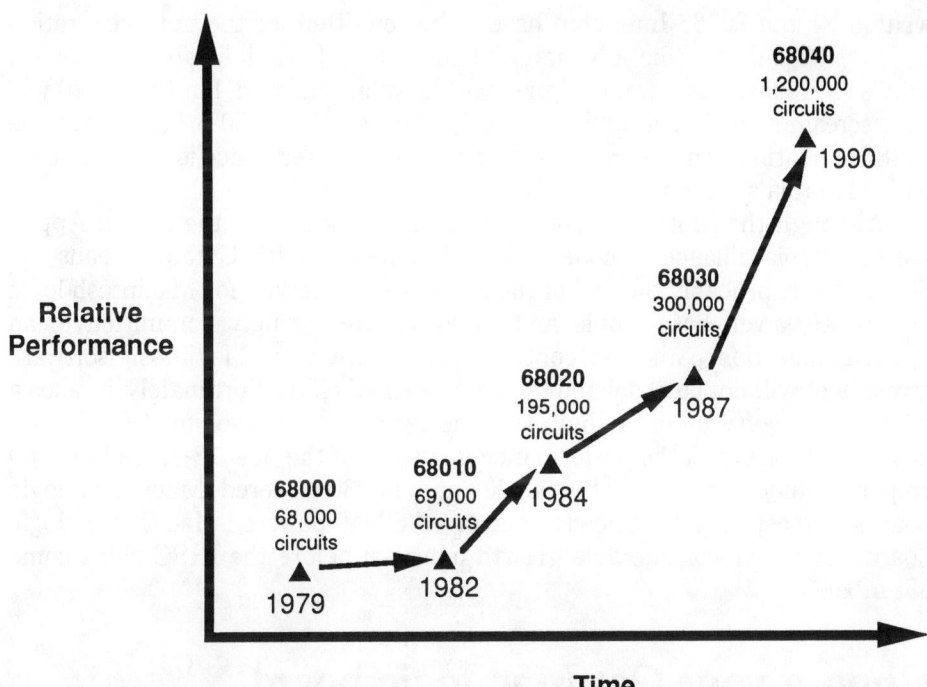

3-1 Motorola 68xxx chip family trends.

What this means to you is that you can replace your 68030 chip with a 68040 chip and your software will run faster. Before you get too ecstatic, however, not all applications will be able to fully exploit the 68040 when it first comes out because of the chip's architectural differences (it handles floating-point operations and memory management differently from the 68030s, as the early Apple Quadra models proved). Like anything new, you can expect a period of adjustment as software patches are developed to catch up with the hardware capabilities. Another subtle corollary here is that you shouldn't pass up your currently compatible 40- and 50-MHz 68030 accelerator cards—they will still be faster than the 25-MHz version of the 68040. Plus, until the 68040 software patches are completed, you will be more likely to be able to use them at full speed.

There is more good news when you compare the Motorola chips with their Intel counterparts in the DOS PC world. Motorola released performance results showing its 68040 chip delivered 20 Mips versus the Intel 80486 chip's 15 Mips. Each chip was running at 25 MHz during the measurement. So the 68040 chip has a 33% performance advantage in throughput over the 80486 chip, and Mac users can take heart that with the 68040, they are absolutely getting a hotter chip than their current generation DOS PC counterparts. Raw speed doesn't tell the whole story though. As just mentioned, all chips are upward compatible in the Motorola 68000 family, whereas the applications written for the 80386 Intel chip have to be rewritten for the next generation Intel 80486 chip to take advantage of its power. Let's talk about graphics. Intel's entire line was never designed with graphics in mind, but the 68040 will be a screamer for 3-D graphics and CAD because it is 350% faster than the 80486 in floating-point operations. In fact, 68040 performance is right up there with Motorola's current 88000 RISC-based chip set.

Although the Motorola 68060 chip is in development, the recent Apple/IBM/Motorola alliance to codevelop new generation RISC chips means the 68040 chip is probably the end of the line to be earmarked for Macintosh logic boards. However, both Apple and Motorola are strongly committed to an upward migration path that continues to ensure your Macintosh software investment will not be obsoleted by the new RISC chips. Fortunately, it takes a while for the software to catch up with the hardware, and even the Mac Classic has not yet wrung all the performance gains out of the now 12-year-old 68000 chip technology it uses. The 68020- and 68030-powered Macintosh logic boards, and especially the newly announced 68040-powered Mac Quadra logic boards, still have considerable growth potential before the RISC chips come out in 1993.

Choose your Cat Mac logic board

You were introduced to the price performance comparison of the 20 different Macintosh logic boards back in chapter 1 with Fig. 1-4. Figure 3-2 lays these same models out by category: obsolete, entry-level, midrange, high-end, and portable. Let's look at your individual choices.

Obsolete Macintosh logic boards

While you can use the Mac 128, 512, and Plus logic boards for your Cat Mac, they don't measure up. You have to upgrade them just to get what you already have in place on the Mac SE and newer logic board models. From a building point of view, the performance you get for the assembly labor and time you expend is simply not worth it. I will briefly cover them for current "owners" who might have a special need (e.g., an individual who just obtained a "free" Mac 512 logic board or school district that must utilize the Mac 128, 512, Plus hardware it owns) but please understand if you are starting from scratch you have less costly, less time consuming, and more functional alternatives.

Entry-level Macintosh logic boards

Here's where Cat Mac builders should start. Macintosh logic boards in this category are typically purchased for dedicated use. Depending on your need—low to high performance, color, immediate or future, etc.—there will be a logic

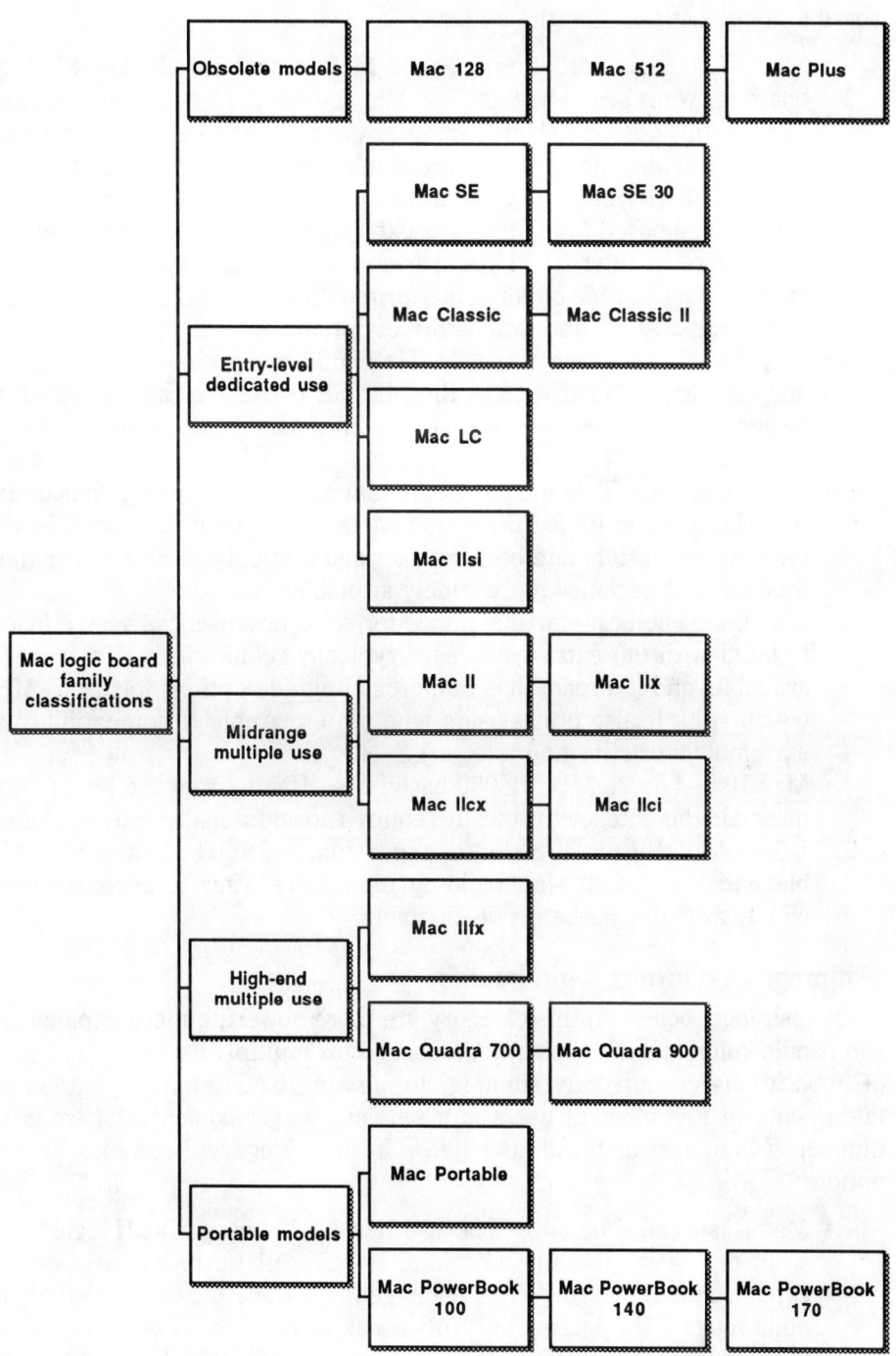

3-2 Macintosh logic board categories.

Choose your Cat Mac logic board

board to fill it. Let's look at the options:

- Mac SE (special situation)—The 8-MHz 68000-based Mac SE logic board is your best low-end Cat Mac building platform at this time because (in addition to being aggressively priced) it is easy to build with, readily available, and has numerous upgrade options available.
- Mac SE 30—If you need color or more performance, start with the 16-MHz 68030-based Mac SE 30 (its external connectors are identical with Mac SE's—its internal PDS expansion connector is not). It is another exceptional Cat Mac building platform with speed plus widespread software compatibility and availability of options.
- Mac Classic—Another good 8-MHz 68000-based choice, but it is not quite as easy to build with as the Mac SE because of its memory card design. In time, it will be the most readily available model with the most options.
- Mac Classic II—This model will be an even better starting choice than the Mac Classic (it features a 16-MHz 68030 chip, on-board SIMM memory expansion, and both speaker and microphone external connectors) when it becomes more widely available.
- Mac LC—The best starting choice for color because it is very efficient to build with (no extra video card typically required), it is reasonably available, and it already has numerous upgrade options for its 16-MHz 68020 chip. It also offers users who require Apple II compatibility an extremely attractive upgrade path.
- Mac IIsi—The 20-MHz 68030-based Mac IIsi delivers the best performance in this category, typically requires no additional video card, offers a flexible NuBus or PDS slot for expansion, and will become a more viable entry-level Cat Mac building alternative after it becomes more widely available in the resale channel.

Midrange Macintosh logic boards

Macintosh logic boards in this category are more powerful, more expandable, can handle color, and are typically purchased for multiple use, e.g., a number of applications concurrently running, foreground/background operation, or taking care of a number of users in a network server capacity. There are a number of logic boards to fill your needs in this category. Let's look at your options:

- Mac II (special situation)—The 16-MHz 68020-based Mac II logic board is an excellent midrange Cat Mac building platform when color and expansion is required. When packaged in a Cat Mac tower chassis, its numerous CPU upgrade and NuBus (six slots) expansion options mean it could be the last Macintosh logic board you ever have to buy. Its aggressive special situation pricing makes it an exceptional value at this time.

- Mac IIx—The 16-MHz 68030-based "big brother" to the Mac II offers all its advantages plus performance at a higher price.
- Mac IIcx—A 16-MHz 68030-based solution with three NuBus expansion slots that is usually a great value because of its wider availability. Its slots, widespread software compatibility, and numerous CPU upgrade and NuBus expansion options make it an exceptional Cat Mac building platform.
- Mac IIci—Identical to the Mac IIcx logic board in size, only slightly above it in cost (consider yourself among the truly fortunate if you have been able to pick one up at its $1499 upgrade cost without having to trade in), and adding only one extra video output to its external connector lineup, the 25-MHz 68030-based Mac IIci is an ideal Cat Mac building platform. You get speed, slots, cache expansion slot, and no video card required until you need to push larger mono/color monitors.

High-end Macintosh logic boards

Macintosh logic boards in this category will give you years of service as top-of-the-line blazing performance color systems, network servers, database engines, CAD/CAM platforms, scientific workstations, or anything else requiring loads of brute horsepower and speed. Let's look at your options:

- Mac IIfx—Today's ultimate Cat Mac building platform. Although the priciest of today's logic boards, the Mac IIfx gives you everything (speed, slots, and color). Identical in size to the Mac II and Mac IIx logic boards, it retains their external connector lineup. You get six NuBus slots, widespread software compatibility, and enhancement potential now that accelerator boards have even been announced for it!
- Mac Quadra 700—Tomorrow's ultimate Cat Mac building platform. Available also as an Apple upgrade, when the general availability of the 25-MHz 68040-based Quadra 700 logic board becomes reality and the software bugs are ironed out, it will replace the Mac IIfx logic board as king-of-the-hill because it offers even greater SCSI and NuBus speed (although only two NuBus slots) and direct on-board video support at a better price performance point.
- Mac Quadra 900—Even further in the future (because no Apple upgrade kit is available and Macintosh owners aren't likely to part with theirs soon) lies the 25-MHz 68040-based Quadra 900 logic board. It offers all the advantages of the Mac Quadra 700 logic board plus five NuBus slots, and allows you to have 64Mb on the board using 4Mb SIMMs. Cat Mac builders can put this one in their dreams.

Portable Macintosh logic boards

The Macintosh portable logic boards appear for information only. They are either not available at all (PowerBooks) or not cost-effective (Mac Portable) alternatives for Cat Mac builders at this time.

Cat Mac builder's summary

Here is my logic board buying advice to the Cat Mac builder: Avoid the Mac 128, 512, and Plus models. Also avoid the Mac IIx. Wait on buying the Classic or Classic II models. Go with a Mac SE board at the low end, a Mac IIfx at the high end. Buy a Mac LC if you need color. Buy a Mac II if you need color plus slots and lots of upgrade potential. Buy a Mac SE 30 or IIsi if you need performance and color in less space. Buy a Mac IIcx or IIci logic board if you need performance, color, and slots. If you just need the latest and greatest, stand in line to plunk down your money for the Mac Quadra 700 logic board. Dream about the Mac Quadra 900.

Whatever Cat Mac you want to build will be found in one of the boxes on this chart. But you must make the decision based on what you want to do! As a general rule of thumb, you can expand or upgrade any Macintosh logic board model into the next higher capability category without any problem. But if you are thinking of going from the lowest to the highest category, you are better off starting with another Macintosh of higher capability. Yes, you can expand your Mac SE to have almost the performance capability of a Mac IIfx—but after all is said and done you would be better served by buying a Mac II or Mac IIcx or Mac IIci and upgrading into it via Apple or third-party upgrades. Or just buy the Mac IIfx to begin with. One of the great benefits of the Macintosh is that virtually any software will run on a lower capability model—just not as fast. So you can buy as much as your pocketbook allows and upgrade later.

Apple Macintosh logic boards

Now let's take a look at the individual logic boards in the Macintosh family in more detail. For four of the five categories of Macintosh logic boards, we'll look at the characteristics of its members and the pros and cons of using them: obsolete Macs (Mac 128, 512 and Plus); entry-level Macs (Mac SE, SE 30, Classic, Classic II, LC and IIsi); midrange Macs (Mac II, IIx, IIcx and IIci); and finally, high-end Macs (Mac IIfx and Quadras). The Portable category will not be covered.

Mac 128, 512, and Plus logic boards

The Mac 128 was state-of-the-art when first introduced back in early 1984.[1] The Mac 512—or the "Fat Mac" as it was known—was a giant step forward when announced a few months later.[2] Much has happened since then, but the elegance and simplicity of the vision Steve Jobs and the "team" created has not been dimmed by the passage of time. Yet the 128 and 512 Macs clearly have been passed over in time. There are no benefits to them and their down side is considerable.

If you own a Mac 128 or 512, there is no logical rationale for keeping it, especially in nonupgraded form, rather than opting for one of today's Macintosh offerings. You can play with MacWrite and MacPaint programs in MFS format on your Mac 128/512 and enjoy yourself immensely, but the 400K floppy drives, limited memory, older 64K ROMs, and lack of a SCSI hard disk interface, lock you out of all but the most rudimentary current software, and limit you to the earliest versions of powerful software programs such as Word, Excel, or Pagemaker. To take advantage of the HFS System and Finder, high speed SCSI Hard Disks, 800K Floppy Drives, and the wealth of Macintosh software available today for which these are a prerequisite, it takes the equivalent of Mac Plus or more to do it. While your Mac 128/512 can be made the equal of the Mac Plus logic board via a daughterboard upgrade (with 1Mb of memory plus SCSI port) or you can take it all the way up to 68030 performance and 4Mb of memory by the addition of a full-fledged accelerator card, it still cannot directly support a 1.4Mb FDHD floppy drive, more convenient ADB keyboard and mouse options, and the latest storage and video offerings. Plus the Cat Mac builder still has to add batteries and additional components to use them. Figure 3-3 shows a Mac 512 logic board (the Mac 128 is virtually identical except for its RAM chips), and identifies some of its key components. Notice the floppy connector (the pen-

3-3 Mac 512 logic board.

Apple Macintosh logic boards **47**

cil points to it). It is the only internal signal connector on the board; anything else to be attached must be connected via the 68000 chip. Also notice the soldered-in memory RAM chips on the front of the board—much harder to upgrade than using SIMMs.

The Mac Plus, announced in early 1986, is the minimally acceptable logic board for doing useful work today.[3] Figure 3-4 shows a Mac Plus logic board and identifies its key components. Just beyond the back of the board, you can see a 40 pin Killy clip—the kind you would attach to the NCR 5380 SCSI chip (indicated by the pencil) to have internal case access to the SCSI bus. The other pencil again points to the internal floppy connector. In this case the 68000 chip has a Killy connector clip on it, waiting for a third-party device to be attached. The four rows of SIMM memory chips in their sockets are clearly visible at the front. The Mac Plus logic board's two main benefits are its SCSI port and SIMM sockets. The addition of the NCR 5380 SCSI chip brought out to an

3-4   Mac Plus logic board.

48   *Macintosh logic boards*

external connector lets you attach external SCSI hard disks mounted in their own cases. The addition of four snap-in SIMM memory sockets rather than soldered-on memory RAM chips enables you to easily expand your memory to 4Mb using 1Mb SIMMs. While the Mac Plus logic board opens up additional possibilities for the Cat Mac builder, and can also be taken up to 4Mb 68030 performance with the addition of an accelerator card, it still cannot directly support an Apple 1.4Mb FDHD floppy drive, ADB options, or the latest storage and video offerings, and it also requires the addition of batteries plus supporting components. All these drawbacks combine to make the Mac Plus logic board an unsuitable foundation for a Cat Mac project.

Mac SE logic board

While the Mac SE, introduced back in early 1987,[4] appeared at first glance to be nothing more than a repackaged Mac Plus, a look inside revealed the only parts shared in common were the CRT screen and its 800K floppy drive mechanism. Figure 3-5 shows the Mac SE logic board and identifies its key components. Notice it has four SIMM sockets like the Mac Plus but they are now at

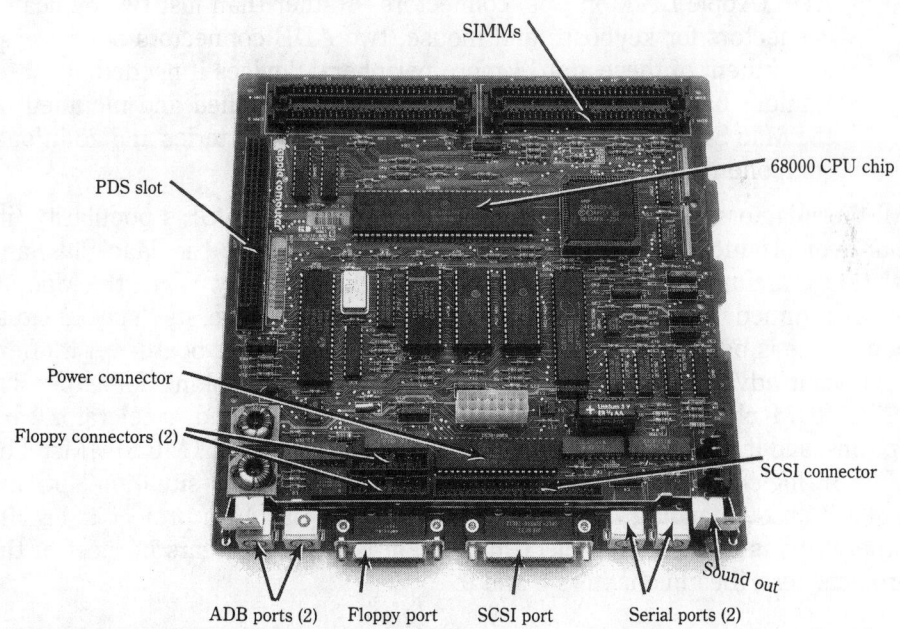

3-5 Mac SE logic board.

the front of the board in two parallel rows. For Cat Mac builders, the additional benefits of the Mac SE logic board over the Mac Plus make it the ideal platform for use in your entry-level Cat Mac project:

- 256K ROM chips—Gives you 20% greater performance than the Mac Plus with its 128K ROM chips.

Apple Macintosh logic boards **49**

- Two internal floppy drives—Two internal floppy drive connectors allow two internal floppy drives to be accommodated—a tremendous flexibility.
- SWIM chip—Later versions of the Mac SE logic board and Apple 1.4Mb upgrade contain newer ROM chips and a SWIM chip that allows the Mac SE logic board to directly support 1.4Mb FDHD floppy drives. This is a tremendous advantage over the Mac Plus and earlier logic boards, and gives the much older SE logic board the same ability as current Mac logic boards.
- Internal hard drive—In addition to an external SCSI connector port like the Mac Plus, the Mac SE has an SCSI connector on its logic board that allows it to accommodate an internal hard drive.
- Expansion slot—The Mac SE's 96-pin PDS (Processor Direct Slot) was a first for any Mac model. It allowed vendors to custom-tailor a wide variety of accelerator, video, and upgrade option cards without the need for clipping onto the 68000 chip, and really "opened up" the Mac SE to the world.
- ADB (Apple Desktop Bus) connectors—Rather than just two dedicated connectors for keyboard and mouse, two ADB connectors permit easy attachment of these and 14 more peripheral devices if needed.
- Lithium battery (7-year)—A battery already attached and mounted on the Mac SE logic board eliminates the need for batteries and additional components to be added by Cat Mac builders.

All these factors taken together probably account for the SE's popularity (its four year production run was second in longevity only to the Mac Plus) and why there are many upgrade options you can add to it today. While the Mac SE is discontinued, the Mac SE logic board is readily available, its "special situation" price is below even that of the Mac Plus or 512 logic board, yet it offers significant advantages. You don't have to run around looking for expensive 128K ROM chips, you have numerous video monitor and accelerator card options, and it is easily expandable to 4Mb of memory with 1Mb SIMMs. The Mac SE logic board's tremendous flexibility and "special situation" pricing make it an outstanding choice for an entry-level Cat Mac project today. Its superiority as a Cat Mac project foundation is why it appears in most of the projects described in chapters 8 and 9.

Mac SE 30 logic board

The Mac SE 30 logic board—first introduced in early 1989[5]—is exactly identical to the Mac SE logic board in size, mounting holes, and power connector pinouts. Figure 3-6 shows the Mac SE 30 logic board and identifies its key components. The eight SIMM sockets are all in a row at the front left of the board. The Mac SE 30 ROMs are also socketed and appear on the right front of the board opposite the front row of SIMMs. The Mac SE 30 logic board

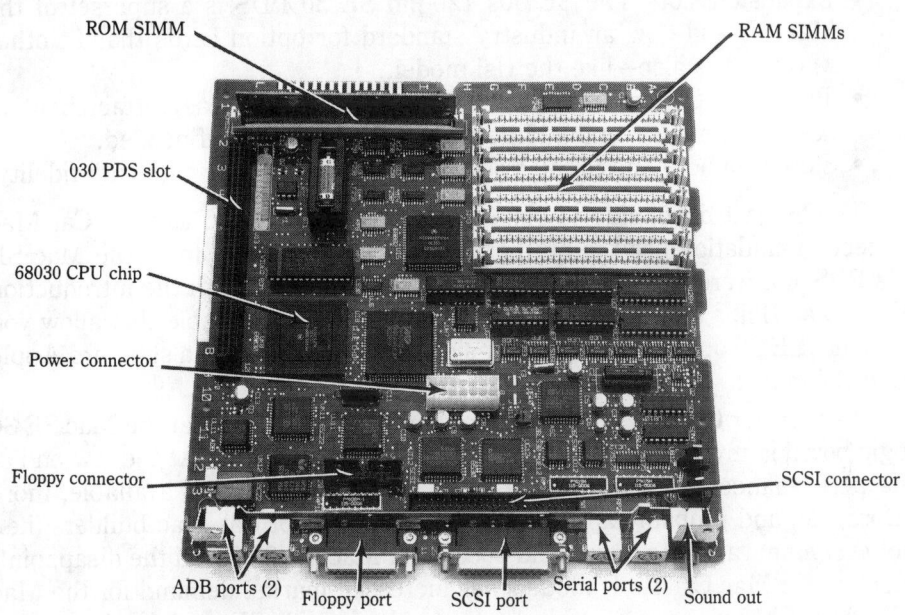

3-6 Mac SE 30 logic board.

might even be a better choice than the Mac SE logic board for your Cat Mac project—if your budget allows it. Apple made it slightly easier for Cat Mac builders by reducing the SE 30 logic board upgrade price to $999 (as you recall from Table 2-4 of chapter 2) before it discontinued the SE 30 model. There are many benefits to starting with the Mac SE 30 logic board:

- 68030 CPU chip running at 16 MHz—Faster and better in technology than the Mac SE's 68000 chip, it will probably be around for a while because it handily runs Apple's new System 7.0 software. Plus no accelerators are needed unless you want a 25-MHz, 33-MHz, or 50-MHz 68030 screamer.
- 68882 FPU chip running at 16 MHz—Hardware floating-point capability at speeds far beyond the software-only execution possible on a Mac SE.
- 256K ROM SIMMs—Supporting color, gray scale graphics, and video.
- Eight RAM SIMM sockets—Like those on the Mac II family boards, supporting a total of up to 32Mb of on-board RAM when 4-Meg SIMMs are used.
- FDHD floppy—Its benefits are many: speed, more storage (1.4Mb per diskette), convenience, and compatibility with DOS PC media. The Mac SE 30 logic board will also work perfectly well with 800K floppy drives.

Apple Macintosh logic boards **51**

- Expansion slot—The SE 30s 120-pin SE 30 PDS is a superset of the Mac SE and now an industry standard for option cards that fit other Mac models also—like the IIsi model.
- Two ADB Connectors—Two ADB connectors for easy attachment of keyboard, mouse, and additional peripheral devices if needed.
- Stereo sound—The SE 30 brings it home to both your ears with fidelity!

The biggest down side to using the SE 30 logic board as your Cat Mac project's foundation used to be that option cards designed to fit the Mac SE 30s PDS slot were all vertically mounted. Not so today. With the introduction of the Mac IIsi, a slew of 90 degree adapter cards are available that allow you to mount SE 30 option cards on their sides—just as you do in a standard Apple Mac IIsi model.

As a former Cat Mac SE 30 owner, there is no question that the Mac SE 30 logic board is my engine of choice. However, times change. At the low end of the performance spectrum, the Mac SE logic board is more available, more affordable, and probably appeals to a broader class of Cat Mac builders (i.e., not everyone wants the power and speed of a Mac SE 30). And the disappointment of the Mac Classic II models has increased market demand for the Mac SE 30 logic boards as pure upgrades to standard Apple SE models—increasing the Mac SE 30 logic board's price. At the higher end of the spectrum, you can choose either the Mac IIsi logic board, which gives more performance and more convenience (built-in video) than the Mac SE 30, or the Mac IIcx logic board, which gives you everything the Mac SE 30 does plus more slots (three NuBus slots)—at the same or better pricing than the Mac SE 30.

Mac Classic logic board

In October 1990, Apple announced the Mac Classic,[6] a 68000-based Macintosh optimized for the lowest cost. Figure 3-7 shows the Mac Classic logic board and identifies its key components. The eight 1Mb RAM chips soldered to the board are clearly visible at the left. The 44-pin socket just to the left of the RAM chips mounts the optional memory expansion card. Think of the Mac Classic logic board as a re-engineered Mac SE logic board at $8^{3/4}'' \times 5''$ in size with components on both sides, compared with the Mac SE logic board's $8^{3/4}'' \times 8''$ footprint with components on one side. Here are its benefits:

- 68000 CPU chip running at 8 MHz—Same as found in the Mac SE. Accelerators and high performance options can be added via direct attachment to the CPU chip.
- 1Mb RAM soldered on board, additional SIMM sockets on memory expansion card support up to 4Mb total.
- 256K ROM—Same size as in the Mac SE—gives about 20% greater performance than the Mac Plus with its 128K ROM chips.
- FDHD floppy drive—Supports one internal 1.4Mb floppy drive and one external 1.4Mb floppy drive.

- Internal hard drive—Features both external and internal SCSI connectors that allow it to accommodate an internal hard drive.
- Expansion slot—The Mac Classic's 44-pin memory expansion card slot has allowed vendors to custom-tailor a wide variety of memory and video upgrade cards.
- ADB (Apple Desktop Bus) connector—A single connector for keyboard, mouse, and other ADB peripheral devices as needed.
- Lithium battery (7-year)—Battery already mounted on logic board.

While there is no question of the utility of the Classic logic board to Cat Mac builders in the long term (when it becomes more available and its price comes down), its memory card expansion and clip-on-to-the-CPU-chip accelerator option makes it harder for Cat Mac builders than starting with a Mac SE logic board. The problem is that the Mac Classic logic board locks you into a nonstandard memory and video expansion card. Available cards are only designed to mount *vertically* inside the standard Apple Mac Classic case. This is a great design feature of the Classic but a nuisance for the CAT Mac builder using a low-profile PC style case who must make a special 44-pin cable or connector bracket. While third-party vendors make accelerator board options with memory SIMM sockets that allow you to get around the memory expansion problem because they attach directly to the 68000 CPU chip, Mac Classic expansion options are simply not as convenient as the universe of expansion products available today to fit the Mac SE and Mac SE 30 PDS expansion connector slots.

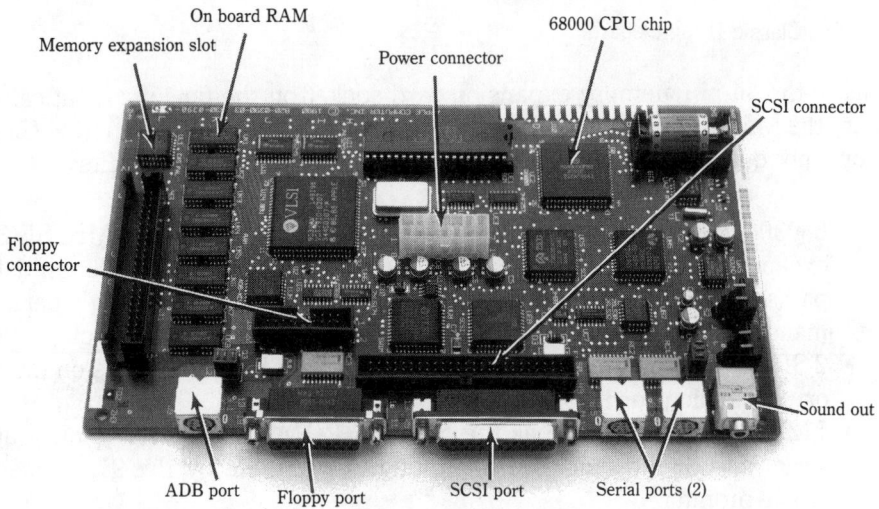

3-7 Mac Classic logic board.

Apple Macintosh logic boards 53

Mac Classic II logic board

Apple announced the Mac Classic II[7] in October 1991, a 68030-based Macintosh optimized for the lowest cost. Figure 3-8 shows the Mac Classic II logic board and identifies its key components. The two SIMM sockets are clearly visible at the upper right, as is the additional microphone input connector just

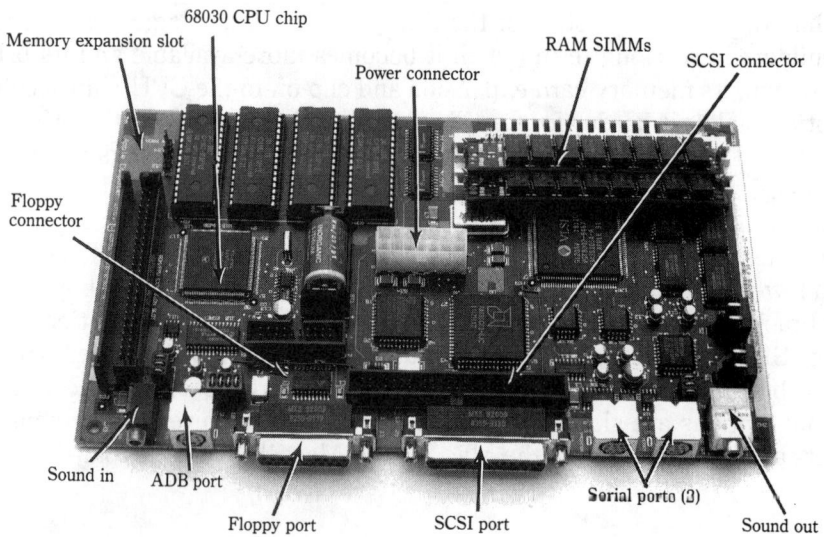

3-8 Mac Classic II logic board.

beneath the 44-pin memory expansion card socket on the far left. Identical in size to the Mac Classic logic board, think of it either as a souped-up Mac Classic or a not quite as powerful SE 30 logic board. Here are its benefits:

- 68030 CPU chip running at 16 MHz—Same as found in the Mac SE 30 except with 16-bit data paths to memory instead of the faster 32-bit data paths found in the SE 30 logic board. Accelerators and high performance options can be added by direct attachment to its CPU chip.
- 2 SIMM sockets on logic board plus additional SIMM sockets on memory expansion card can support up to 10Mb total.
- 512K ROM—Same size as the Mac LC ROM, it supports color, grayscale, and 32-bit QuickDraw, although not usable by the 9" standard Apple monitor.
- FDHD floppy drive—Supports one internal 1.4Mb floppy drive and one external 1.4Mb floppy drive.

- Internal hard drive—Features both external and internal SCSI connectors that allow it to accommodate an internal hard drive.
- Expansion slot—Like the Mac Classic's 44-pin memory expansion card slot, it allows vendors to custom-tailor a wide variety of memory and video upgrade cards.
- ADB (Apple Desktop Bus) connector—A single connector for keyboard, mouse, and other ADB peripheral devices as needed.
- Lithium battery (7-year)—Battery already mounted on logic board.
- Microphone input—The only additional external connector added over the Mac Classic.

The same comments on nonstandard expansion attachment made for the Mac Classic also apply to the Mac Classic II. While the Mac Classic II logic board is an even better starting point than the Mac Classic for Cat Mac builders in the long term (when it becomes more available and its price comes down), today you are better off starting with a Mac SE (if you don't need color) or with a Mac SE 30, LC, or IIsi logic board if color is needed.

Mac LC logic board

Apple announced the Mac LC[8] in October 1990, a 16-MHz 68020-based Macintosh optimized for both low cost and on-board color. Figure 3-9 shows the

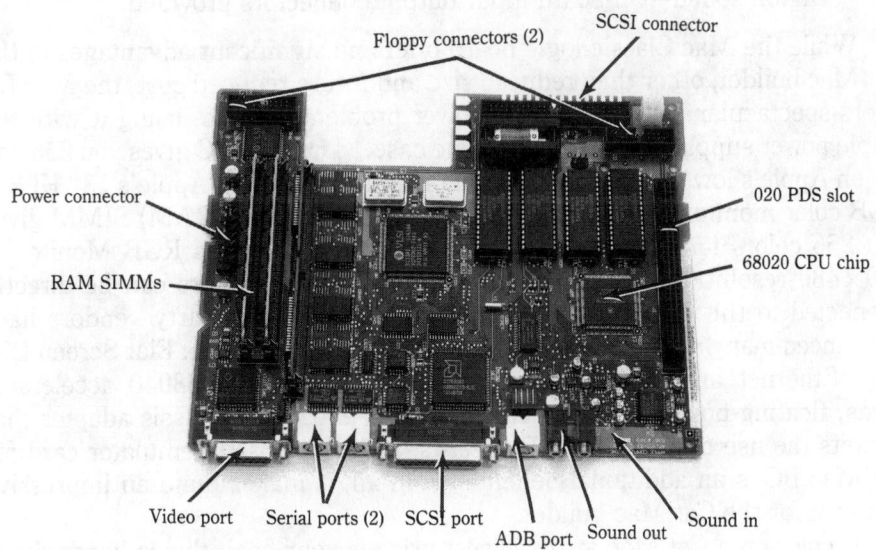

3-9 Mac LC logic board.

Mac LC logic board and identifies its key components. There are many benefits to starting with the Mac LC logic board:

- 68020 CPU chip running at 16 MHz—Same as found in the Mac II. Handily runs Apple's new System 7 software, plus 68030 accelerators and optional hardware floating-point capability can be added via PDS cards.
- 2Mb RAM soldered on board, two additional SIMM sockets support a total of up to 10Mb of on-board RAM when 4Mb SIMMs are used.
- 512K ROM SIMM—Gives you 20% greater performance than the Mac Plus with its 128K ROM chips.
- Two internal FDHD floppy drives—The only logic board (other than the Mac SE and Mac II) with connectors that allow two internal floppy drives.
- Internal hard drive—Features both external and internal SCSI connectors that allow it to accommodate an internal hard drive.
- Internal video support—256K of video RAM (expandable to 512K) supports various Apple color monitors directly plus many VGA monitors.
- Expansion slot—The Mac LC's 96-pin 020 PDS allows vendors to custom-tailor a wide variety of FPU, accelerator, video, and upgrade option cards.
- ADB (Apple Desktop Bus) connector—A single connector for keyboard, mouse, and other ADB peripheral devices as needed.
- Lithium battery (7-year)—Battery already mounted on logic board.
- Digital sound—On-board input/output connectors provided.

While the Mac Classic logic board offers no significant advantages to the Cat Mac builder, other than reduced size and future reduced cost, the Mac LC offers spectacular benefits plus no power problems—unlike using it with the Apple power supply in the standard Mac case.[9] The Mac LC gives you 256 colors on Apple's low-cost 12" color monitor, and 16 colors on Apple's 13" Hi Res RGB color monitor. Adding another 256K, VRAM (video RAM) SIMM gives you 256 colors (or shades of gray) on Apple's 13" Hi Res RGB Monitor at 640×480 resolution. In addition, third-party VGA monitors can be directly connected to the LC if you build the right cable. Third-party vendors have announced many new products to fit the LC's PDS connector: Flat Screen Display, Ethernet and IBM connectivity cards, 68030 and 68040 accelerator cards, floating-point expansion cards, and an expansion chassis adapter that permits the use of multiple NuBus cards. Plus Apple's IIe emulator card for the Mac LC is an additional benefit. All in all, it makes quite an impressive platform for the Cat Mac builder.

If color on a Cat Mac at the lowest price is your goal, this is hands down the logic board for you. Although the "special situation" pricing on the Mac II logic board makes it exceptionally attractive at this time, Cat Mac builders get all the benefits of the original 16-MHz 68020-based Mac II (except NuBus slots). In time the Mac LC logic board will be more available, more affordable, and probably appeal to a broader class of Cat Mac builders because of its compact $8^{3}/_{4}''$ wide $\times 7''$ deep dimensions versus the Mac II's $15'' \times 12''$ footprint.

Mac IIsi logic board

Apple rounded out its October 1990 announcements with the Mac IIsi.[10] Figure 3-10 shows the Mac IIsi logic board and identifies its key components. The

3-10 Mac IIsi logic board.

Mac IIsi is an even better deal for Cat Mac builders than the Mac LC. It provides everything the Mac LC does—except an Apple IIe emulator card—with more speed and greater flexibility. The Mac IIsi also has additional capabilities that the Mac SE 30 doesn't. Here are the Mac IIsi benefits:

- 68030 CPU chip running at 20 MHz—Faster than an SE 30. Handily runs Apple's new System 7 software plus accelerators and optional 68882 floating-point chip can be added using either PDS or NuBus cards.
- 1Mb RAM soldered on board, four additional SIMM sockets support up to 17Mb of on-board RAM total when 4Mb SIMMs are used.
- 512K ROM—Like the Mac IIci's versus the 256K Mac SE 30 ROM.
- FDHD floppy drive—Supports one internal 1.4Mb floppy drive and one external 1.4Mb floppy drive.

- Internal hard drive—Features both external and internal SCSI connectors that allow it to accommodate an internal hard drive.
- On-board video monitor support—identical to that of the Mac IIci—uses any Apple monitor and doesn't waste a slot.
- Expansion slot—The Mac IIsi's 120-pin PDS allows either standard SE 30 or NuBus option cards to be used.
- ADB (Apple Desktop Bus) connector—A single connector for keyboard, mouse and other ADB peripheral devices as needed.
- Lithium battery (7-year)—Battery already mounted on logic board.
- Stereo digital sound—On-board input/output sound connectors provided.

The Mac IIsi logic board gives Cat Mac builders a 20-MHz 68030 CPU, instant, full-fledged System 7 software compatibility, "32-bit clean" 512K ROMs and on-board video just like the Mac IIci, and either NuBus or SE 30 PDS card single-slot expansion capability—all on a $10\frac{1}{2}''$ wide × 8" deep logic board only slightly larger than the Mac LC's.

Regarding the Mac IIsi's two different Apple adapter cards: one allows you to use NuBus expansion cards in it, and the other allows you to use SE 30 PDS expansion cards in it. Both adapter cards come with a 68882 FPU chip plus supporting chips on them and extend the base-level capability of the Mac IIsi (the theory is that you do not add the FPU expansion capability until you need it). Third-party adapter cards occasionally even provide a second slot in addition to the 68882 FPU chip. These adapters make the Mac IIsi logic board ideal for use in low profile PS/2 style Cat Mac cases. Plus Cat Mac builders can be very comfortable plugging any Mac SE 30 or NuBus card ever built into a Mac IIsi logic board—there is no such thing as a power budget in the build-your-own Macintosh world.

The Mac IIsi logic board is positioned very close in price to the Mac SE 30 logic board and occasionally can be obtained for less. Many of the reasons that would make you choose a Mac SE 30 logic board should make you take a close look at the Mac IIsi. The Mac IIsi logic board is perhaps the better choice because of its greater flexibility in monitor and expansion options, and because it's still being manufactured, it should be more available and affordable with time.

Mac II logic board

Introduced in early 1987 along with the Mac SE, the Mac II[11]—the first open architecture Macintosh—was an instant success. The Mac II logic board, far from being a dinosaur, is an outstanding Cat Mac builder platform today. Figure 3-11 shows the Mac II logic board and identifies its key components. It offers the following benefits:

- 68020 CPU chip running at 16 MHz—Identical to the Mac LC, it has four times the throughput of the 68000 chip used by the Mac SE and

Mac Classic (the 68020 chip runs at twice the 68000 chip's clock speed—16 MHz versus 8 MHz—and moves twice as much data per cycle—32 bits versus 16 bits).
- 68881 FPU chip—Allows faster floating-point calculation—far beyond that possible with Mac SE or Mac Classic.
- 256K ROM—Mac II was the first Macintosh to support color monitors—it only required using the appropriate video card in a NuBus slot.
- PMMU option—Addition of this inexpensive memory management chip allows Mac II to run A/UX and Apple's System 7.
- Eight SIMM Sockets—Mac II supports up to 32Mb total of on-board RAM (with 4Mb SIMMs) compared with the SE's four SIMM sockets.
- Two internal FDHD floppy drives—Like the Mac SE and Mac LC, its two connectors allow two internal floppy drives to be accommodated.
- Internal hard drive—Features both external and internal SCSI connectors that allow it to accommodate an internal hard drive.
- Six NuBus expansion slots—The most on any Macintosh (it shares this distinction with the Mac IIx and Mac IIfx). In addition, its NuBus slots are self-configuring—unlike a DOS PC, you don't have to tell it what card was in what slot and set jumper switches, etc.
- Two ADB connectors—For easy attachment of keyboard, mouse and additional peripheral devices if needed.
- Stereo sound—Versus monaural sound output of Mac SE and Classic.

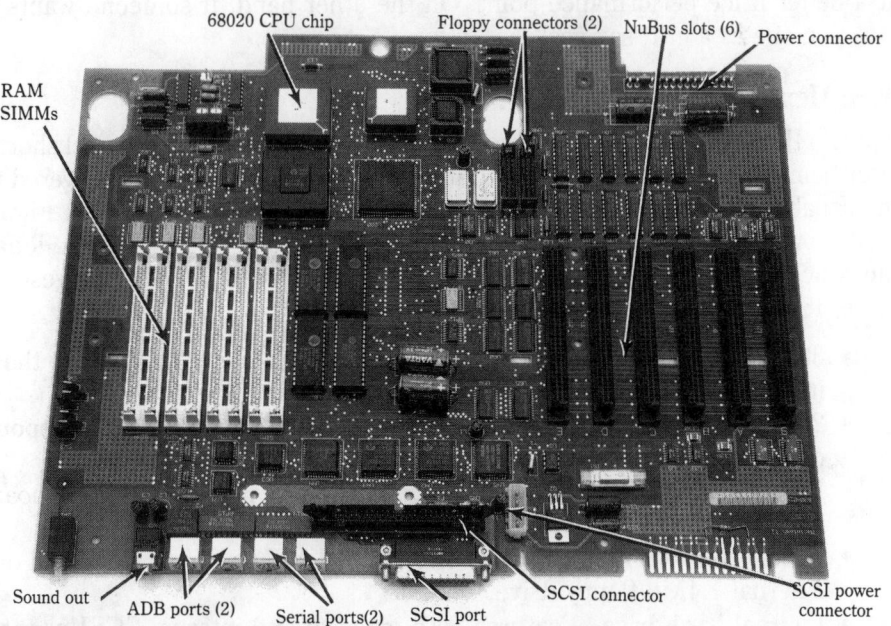

3-11 Mac II logic board.

Apple Macintosh logic boards 59

The Mac II logic board has a larger footprint area (15″ wide × 12″ deep, identical with the Mac IIx and Mac IIfx) than any other Macintosh logic board but, mounted in a tower chassis, it gives the Cat Mac builder enormous future flexibility and expansion potential while being highly cost-effective today. Although it offers speed, slots, expansion, and color benefits compared to a Mac SE or Mac Classic logic board, today's "special situation" pricing makes a Mac II logic board available at nearly the same price. Plus the birth of the Mac IIfx logic board (it gives the Mac II logic board a direct replacement upgrade path) makes the Mac II logic board even more valuable. You can buy a Mac II logic board today at a very attractive price, enjoy its many benefits, and upgrade it to a Mac IIfx logic board when your needs require it.

Mac IIx logic board

The Mac IIx,[12] quietly announced in late 1988, was actually Apple's first 68030-based Macintosh. It offers Cat Mac builders the same basic capabilities as the Mac II logic board while extending its performance via a 16-MHz 68030 CPU chip and 1.4Mb FDHD floppy drive support. Although it makes an even better midrange logic board platform for Cat Mac builders when mounted in a tower chassis, the fact that relatively few were manufactured combined with the fact that few users part with them to the used equipment market has kept their price artificially high. For the money, you are better off with a Mac II logic board at the low price end, Mac IIcx or Mac IIci logic at about the same price, or a Mac IIfx logic board at the high end—any are more readily available at a better price performance point. On the other hand, if someone wants to give you one as a gift, say yes!

Mac IIcx logic board

Apple's IIcx[13] immediately became the most popular Macintosh model shortly after being introduced in early 1989. It wasn't hard to see why—it delivered all the capabilities of the Mac IIx (only three fewer slots) at a lower price. Figure 3-12 shows the Mac IIcx logic board and identifies its key components. Today, the Mac IIcx logic board brings Cat Mac builders the same advantages and more. It offers the following benefits:

- 68030 CPU and 68882 FPU chip running at 16 MHz—Identical to those in the Mac SE 30 and Mac IIx.
- 256K ROM—Similar to those in Mac SE 30 and Mac IIx, it supports color monitors using the appropriate video card in a NuBus slot.
- Eight SIMM sockets—Mac IIcx supports up to 32Mb total of on-board RAM with 4Mb SIMMs.
- FDHD floppy drive—Supports one internal 1.4Mb floppy drive and one external 1.4Mb floppy drive.
- Internal hard drive—Features both external and internal SCSI connectors that allow it to accommodate an internal hard drive.

- Three NuBus expansion slots—Three self-configuring NuBus slots, a distinction it shares with the Mac IIci.
- Two ADB connectors.
- Stereo sound.

What does a Mac IIcx logic board do for you as a Cat Mac builder? Plenty. The Mac IIcx logic board's 11" wide × 12" deep footprint gives you more mounting flexibility compared to the larger-footprint Mac II, IIx, IIfx models (put it into an AT size DOS PC case or into a tower chassis). Although the Apple Mac IIcx's one-screw snap-apart construction plastic case and power

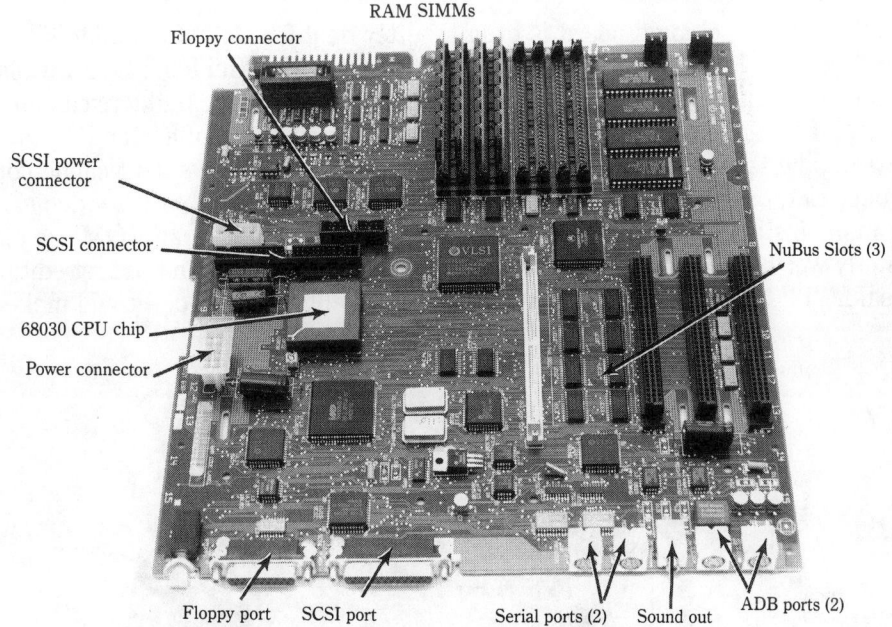

3-12 Mac IIcx logic board.

supply is an exceptional design, Cat Mac builders pick up an instant $500 savings (versus a used Apple Macintosh IIcx) and far more expansion and drive-mounting options, merely by repackaging the Mac IIcx logic board in a standard DOS PC case with a bigger power supply. Plus, for some reason that I have yet to fathom, the market has decided to price the Mac IIcx logic board at parity with or even less than the Mac SE 30 logic board!

Mac IIci logic board

When the Mac IIci[14] was announced by Apple in late 1989, it improved upon the Mac IIcx in several dimensions. Cat Mac builders receive these advantages today at greatly reduced cost. Figure 3-13 shows the Mac IIci logic board and identifies its key components. The Mac IIci logic board offers the following additional benefits over the Mac IIcx logic board:

- 68030 CPU and 68882 FPU chips running at 25 MHz—60% faster than the Mac IIcx.
- 512K ROM—Supports built-in color video, 32-bit QuickDraw, virtual memory, and parity memory.
- 120-pin cache controller slot—Allows you to add third-party cache cards to crank up the speed even more.
- On-board video connector—Allows you to deliver 8-bit color to an attached monitor without using a NuBus card slot to do it and uses the Mac IIci's 80-ns RAM memory as a video screen buffer.

The Mac IIci logic board is even a better deal for Cat Mac builders than the Mac IIcx logic board. Due to the fact that the Mac IIci logic board is also available as an upgrade option at a $1499 list price, Cat Mac builders can often obtain it for only a few hundred dollars more than the cost of a Mac IIcx logic board. The faster 25-MHz 68030 chip, expansion via a convenient cache controller slot, on-board video alleviating the need for an extra NuBus video card in many instances, and the added capabilities in its 32-bit clean ROM are distinctly worthwhile advantages for the slight increase in cost. In the first edition I said, "I'll keep my eye on the price and availability of the IIci—it will make a

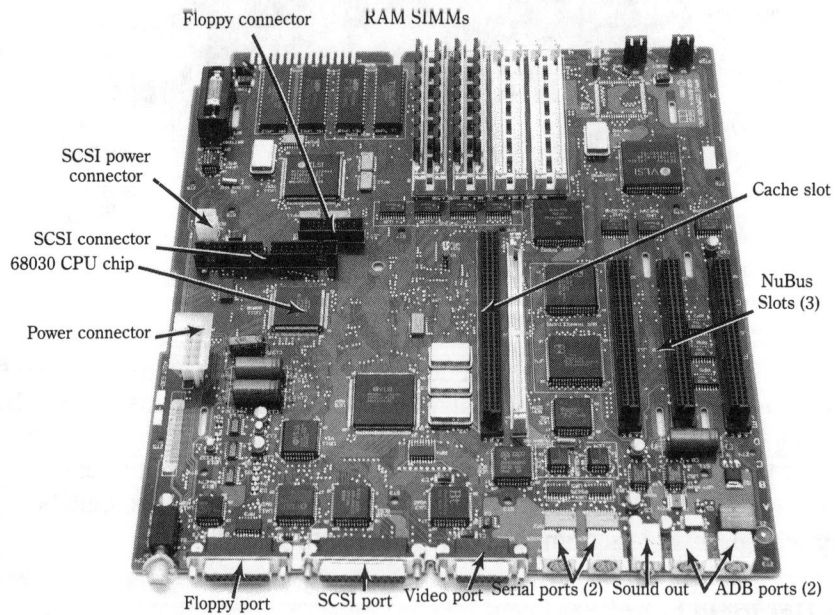

3-13 Mac IIci logic board.

great platform for a future Cat Mac project when the price is right." Well folks, the price *is* right today.

Mac IIfx logic board

Apple's highest performance 68030-based Macintosh, the Mac IIfx,[15] was introduced in early 1990. Figure 3-14 shows the Mac IIfx logic board and identifies its key components. A true workstation-class machine, the Mac IIfx is

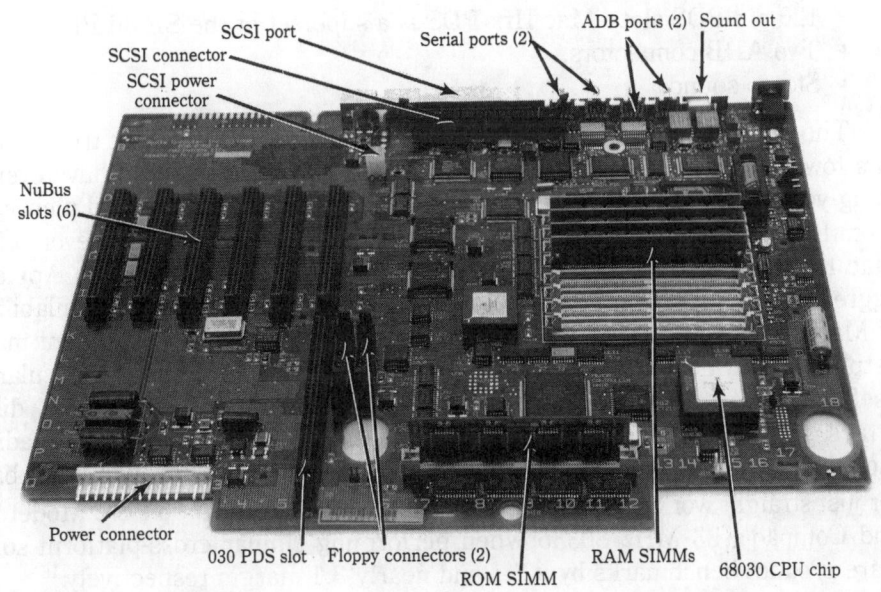

3-14 Mac IIfx logic board.

approximately 60% faster than a Mac IIci. Everything on the Mac IIfx logic board is optimized for speed (the "move more data and move it faster" theme). Here are its benefits:

- 68030 CPU and 68882 FPU chips running at 40 MHz—The Mac IIfx features much optimization, including fewer wait states (the CPU does not have to wait for faster memory).
- 512K ROM—A superset of the 512K ROM introduced in the Mac IIci that supports Apple's 24-bit video cards.
- Cache memory—32K of 25-ns static RAM—CPU thinks it is looking at faster memory.
- DMA (direct memory access) SCSI controller chip—CPU gets hard drive and other SCSI data faster.
- Custom IOPs (input/output processors)—CPU gets serial, floppy, and ADB port data faster.

- Eight SIMM sockets—Holds up to 32Mb RAM total on-board (with 4Mb SIMMs) and uses special 64-pin wide SIMMs that support overlapped RAM read/writes for faster speed.
- Two internal FDHD floppy drives—Like the Mac II and Mac IIx, its two connectors allow two internal floppy drives to be accommodated.
- Internal hard drive—Features both external and internal SCSI connectors that allow it to accommodate an internal hard drive.
- Six NuBus expansion slots—Like the Mac II and Mac IIx, it offers six NuBus slots.
- 120-pin PDS slot—Mac IIfx PDS is a superset of the SE 30 PDS.
- Two ADB connectors.
- Stereo sound.

The Mac IIfx logic board is the Cat Mac builder's dream come true. Put it in a tower case (its has a 15" wide × 12" deep footprint) and you have everything you would ever need: speed, slots (both NuBus and PDS), and plenty of room for expansion. And if it's not fast enough, third-party vendors even offer Mac IIfx accelerators! The best news of all for Cat Mac builders is Apple's aggressive Mac IIfx upgrade price of $2599—it translates to ready availability of Mac IIfx logic boards at very attractive prices in the used equipment marketplace. Cat Mac builders find tower-based Mac IIfx logic boards particularly useful as network servers (they can readily mount larger hard drives, disk arrays, and backup devices) and as cross-platform workstations (they readily mount coprocessor boards and emulators). The Mac IIfx is probably not bad for just straight workstation use either: it blew away IBM's 486 PS/2 Model 70 and Compaq's 33 MHz 80386 when performing similar cross-platform software product benchmarks by a 2:1 and nearly 3:1 margin respectively.[16]

Mac Quadra 700 logic board

Announced in October 1991, the Mac Quadras[17] are Apple's latest and greatest high-end Macintoshes, replacing the Mac IIfx as king-of-the-hill. The Mac Quadra 700 logic board, thanks to being offered by Apple as a direct replacement for the Mac IIcx or Mac IIci logic boards as a $3499 upgrade, is available to Cat Mac builders. The Mac Quadra 900 logic board, buried in the middle of Apple's only tower Macintosh case and not likely to be soon parted with by users, is not available unless you get lucky. So I will focus on the Mac Quadra 700 here. Although the Mac Quadra 700 logic board delivers true workstation-class performance approximately 20% greater than the Mac IIfx, it most closely resembles the Mac IIci logic board. Figure 3-15 shows the Mac Quadra 700 logic board and identifies its key components. Here are its benefits:

- 68040 CPU chip running at 25 MHz—It features integral memory management, math coprocessor, and 8K of memory cache—all of which combine to make it faster and more efficient than 68030-based Macintoshes.

- 1Mb ROM—Supports 68040 chip, on-board video, digital sound, Ethernet, functions, plus bootable RAM disk and SANE (standard Apple numerics environment) floating point in addition to 68040 floating point.
- Two internal data bus paths—System bus running at 25 MHz connects between 68040 CPU and main/video memory, NuBus/SCSI controllers, and 68040 PDS slot. I/O bus running at 16 MHz connects between Ethernet, floppy drive, ADB, serial I/O, and audio I/O ports. Advantage is maximum speed and performance independently allowed in each area.
- 4Mb RAM soldered-on logic board plus four SIMM sockets—Holds up to 20Mb RAM with 4Mb SIMMs or 68Mb RAM with 16Mb SIMMs.
- Internal video support—512K of video RAM (expandable to 2Mb) supports various Apple color monitors directly plus many VGA monitors.
- Internal FDHD floppy drive—Internal connector supports 1.4Mb FDHD floppy drive.
- SCSI-2 controller chip (53C96)—Compatibility with new, faster SCSI-2 standard (up to 4Mb/second—roughly twice Mac IIfx speed), while supporting both external and internal SCSI connectors as on earlier models.
- Two NuBus 90 expansion slots—Redesigned NuBus architecture is compatible with new, faster NuBus 90 standard and current NuBus cards (block transfers up to 9Mb/second).
- 140-pin 68040 PDS slot—Mac Quadra PDS is a superset of 68030 and earlier expansion PDS.
- Ethernet connector—On-board Ethernet available directly.
- Two serial connectors.
- Two ADB connectors.
- Sound input and stereo sound output ports—Features three new chips: ESAC (enhanced Apple sound chip), ASIC (application specific integrated circuit), and DFAC (digitally filtered audio chip) that provide high-performance buffered 16-bit stereo output, 8-bit sound input at low noise and distortion levels.

The Apple Mac Quadra 700 upgrade gives Cat Mac builders early access to a latest generation 68040-based 11″ wide × 12″ deep logic board that, when repackaged into a tower chassis, delivers highest performance and flexibility at the lowest price. It will deliver years of high end performance for you and will also have high end accelerators and expansion options available for it. It will also be relatively scarce. Consider yourself fortunate should you be able to acquire a Mac Quadra 700 logic board as a foundation for your Cat Mac project.

A word about Mac Quadra 68040 software "incompatibility." Don't worry about it. Spend your time getting your own programs running smoothly. Because the 68040 incorporates so much functionality on the chip, particularly

3-15 Mac Quadra 700 logic board.

in its cache and floating-point circuitry, it wasn't as easily made backward compatible as the 68030 chips were. As a result, many mainstream popular Macintosh programs simply didn't run on the Macintosh Quadras at announcement time (this was really nothing new, it was also true of the Mac IIci at its announcement). Vendors moved quickly to cure this situation as the Mac Quadras moved into the mainstream. While the 68040-based Macintoshes might evolve a totally new family of software quirks uniquely their own, you can rest assured that all mainstream software past and future will run on any Macintosh 68040-based platform.

Mac Quadra 900 logic board

The Apple versions of the Mac Quadra 900 and 700 differ in more than their logic boards. The main differences for the Mac Quadra 900 logic board are:

- 4Mb RAM soldered-on logic board plus twelve SIMM sockets—Holds up to 64Mb RAM on-board with 4Mb SIMMs.
- Five NuBus 90 expansion slots—Two 25-W NuBus slots (oversize) and three 15-W NuBus slots (standard height cards).
- Two SCSI-2 controller chips (53C96)—Supports dual SCSI architecture: one controller supports internal devices (single SCSI internal connector); the other controller supports external devices (with two SCSI connectors—internal and external).

66   Macintosh logic boards

- Two line-input connectors—for auxiliary audio inputs (e.g., from CD-ROM, audio tape, or VCR audio outputs).
- One ADB connector.

While the Mac Quadra 700 logic boards are likely to be scarce, the Mac Quadra 900 logic boards will definitely be scarce or simply unavailable. The Mac Quadra 900 is a great box from Apple, but Cat Mac builders are unlikely to get a Mac Quadra 900 logic board from any reseller at any price for some time.

Sources

Logic boards are available new and as upgrade replacements through Apple dealers. Used boards are available through the Apple used equipment dealers and, occasionally, through other distribution channels.

Manufacturers—Apple

Apple dealers will stock logic boards under the following part numbers:

661-96152	Mac 128
661-96236	Mac 512
661-0525	Mac Plus
661-0526	Mac SE 800K
661-05236	Mac SE FDHD
661-0527	Mac SE 30
661-0528	Mac II
661-0529	Mac IIx
661-0537	Mac IIcx
661-0532	Mac IIci

Mail Order—used Apple Macintosh equipment dealers

Boston Computer Exchange
55 Temple Pl.
Boston, MA 02111
(800) 262-6399

Compu-D
6471 Van Nuys Blvd.
Van Nuys, CA 91405
(800) 783-5783

Computer Brokerage Services
New York, NY
(212) 947-7848

CRA
700 S. University Parks Dr., #600
Waco, TX 76706
(800) 950-8212

ESD Electro Rent Div.
200 West Mark St.
Wood Dale, IL 60191
(800) 222-2870

Exsel Inc.
2200 Brighton-Henrietta Twnln. Rd.
Rochester, NY 14623
(800) 624-2001

Interstate Computer Bank
Mountain View, CA
(415) 968-8733

MacHeaven
Chantilly, VA
(703) 263-2527

Mac Sale International
3828 Quakerbridge Rd.
Mercerville, NJ
(800) 729-7031

Maya Computer
P.O. Box 680
Waitsfield, VT 05673
(800) 541-2318

Micro Exchange
682 Passaic Ave.
Nutley, NJ 07110
(201) 284-1200

National Inventory Exchange
3901 E. LaSalle
Phoenix, AZ 85025
(800) 633-2869

North Shore Computers
Milwaukee, WI
(414) 963-9700

Peripheral Outlet
314 S. Broadway
Ada, OK 74280
(405) 332-6581

Pre-Owned Electronics
205 Burlington Rd.
Bedford, MA 01730
(800) 274-5343

Shreve Systems
3804 Karen Ln.
Bossier City, LA 71112
(800) 227-3971

Sun Remarketing
P.O. Box 4059
Logan, UT 84321
(801) 752-7631

---

[1] Matthew Douglas, "Inside the Mac," *Macworld*, May/June 1984, p. 34. This was the Volume 1, Number 1 issue of *Macworld* with Steve Jobs standing over a row of Mac 128s on its cover.

[2] Danny Goodman, "The Macintosh Deluxe," *Macworld*, November 1984, p. 56. The cover lead was the 512K Fat Mac Arrives!

[3] Michael D. Wesley, "Macintosh Plus! Packed With Power," *MacUser*, March 1986, p. 38; David Ushijima, "A Change for the Plus," *Macworld*, April 1986, p. 86; and Steven Bobker, "The Macintosh Maze," *MacUser*, May 1986, p. 42 all talk about the capabilities/features and expanding of the Mac Plus.

[4] Lon Poole, "More than a Plus," *Macworld*, April 1987, p. 140; Jerry Borrell, "SE Close-up," *Macworld*, May 1987, p. 112.

[5] Henry Bortman, "Much Ado About Something," *MacUser*, March 1989, p. 174; Bruce F. Webster, "The Mac SE Turns 030," *Macworld*, March 1989, p. 112.

[6] Daniel Farber and Henry Norr, "They're here: Classic, LC, and IIsi," *MacWEEK*, 10/16/90, p. 1; Ric Ford, "Hands on the new Macs: Meet the Classic," *MacWEEK*, 30 October 1990, p. 1; Rik Myslewski with Editors and Staff of MacUser and its Labs, "Three Cheers For Three New Macs," *MacUser*, December 1990, p. 90.

[7] Lon Poole, "Macintosh Classic II, Improving on a theme," *Macworld*, December 1991, p. 148.

[8] Cheryl Spencer, "Mac LC," *Macworld*, December 1990, p. 180; Doug and Denise Green, "Inexpensive Color Makes LC The Mac II For The Rest of Us," *Infoworld*, 26 November 1990, p. 96.

[9] Andrew Gore, "Power trips up new Macs," *MacWEEK*, 6 November 1990, p. 1.

[10] Jim Heid, "Mac IIsi," *Macworld*, December 1990, p. 188.

[11] David Ushijima, "Macintosh II: Opening to the Future," *Macworld*, April 1987, p. 126; Michael D. Wesley, "For the Best of Us," *MacUser*, April 1987, p. 74.

[12] Gil Davis, "Meet the Mac IIx," *MacUser*, November 1988, p. 34; David Ushijima, "68030 at Last," *Macworld*, December 1988, p. 83.

[13] Lon Poole, "The Compact Mac," *Macworld*, April 1989, p. 130; Russell Ito, "Introducing the Mac IIcx," *MacUser*, May 1989, p. 30; and John J. Anderson, "Apple Mac IIcx: The Modular Macintosh," *MacUser*, June 1989, p. 120.

[14] Dan Littman and Tom Moran, "Apple Introduces a High Performance IIcx," *Macworld*, November 1989, p. 114; Russell Ito, "Macintosh IIci: New Speed Champ," *MacUser*, November 1989, p. 46.

[15] Jim Heid, "Power At A Price," *Macworld*, May 1990, p. 280; Russell Ito and John Rizzo, "The Mac IIfx: Fast Times at Apple Computer," *MacUser*, May 1990, p. 114; Nick Baran, "Apple's Special fx," *Byte*, April 1990, p. 111.

[16] John Batelle, "IIfx puts Apple at head of performance pack," *MacWEEK*, 20 March 1990, p. 1. National Software Testing Laboratories of Philadelphia, an independent organization, did the testing.

[17] Russell Ito, "Dual Dynamos: The Macintosh Quadra 700 and 900," *MacUser*, December 1991, p. 114; Bruce F. Webster, "Macintosh Quadras, Power but No Pizzazz," *Macworld*, December 1991, p. 140.

Chapter 4
Memory and upgrades

As a Cat Mac builder, you have numerous choices. After choosing your Macintosh logic board, you must choose how much memory to add and how to add it. Some logic boards require that memory cards be added before you can add the memory itself. This chapter will help you make these choices.

Beyond adding memory is the broad subject of upgrades. Upgrade boards are the Cat Mac builder's customizing tool—they come in all sizes, speeds, option configurations, and prices. They can be used to take your Mac 512 to a 4Mb 68030-based screamer, convert your Mac SE to the equivalent of a 25-MHz 68030 Mac IIci, give you 40-MHz Mac IIfx performance from a Mac IIcx, or boost your Mac II all the way up to the capabilities of a 25-MHz 68040-based Quadra. My objective in this chapter is not to discuss the pros and cons of every upgrade—only to introduce those relevant to you as a Cat Mac builder. I will discuss what they are, what they do for you, and several types you might consider for your Cat Mac project.

How is your memory

The memory issue is relatively straightforward. More memory is always better. Since memory prices have dropped drastically from their late 1988 peak, there is no excuse for you not to have at least 2Mb (4Mb is a more realistic minimum) in your Cat Mac to run today's high-performance Apple System 6 Multifinder or System 7 Macintosh software with one or more applications opened. Let's take a brief detour for some definitions, then get into the details.

ROM, RAM, DRAM, SRAM, PRAM, cache, memory chips, SIMMs

No, you didn't just get a briefing from the military. However, before reading about memory, you should have a few definitions and a little history under your belt.

Binary numbers Computers "think" in binary language (1s and 0s). The circuit is either "on" or "off." In computer terms, each individual 1 or 0 is called a *bit*. In mathematical terms, the number *2* raised to a power is a *binary number*. Three bits in a row (111) represent binary numbers with values of 2^0, 2^1, and 2^2, so their base ten values (the numbers we think in) would be 1, 2, 4, and the three bits together represent the number 7. By changing the 1s and 0s pattern, the sum of their digits could represent any number from 0 to 7, or eight different values. In this way, computer values are changed to those we understand and vice versa.

Byte The smallest computer "word" or "character" consists of 8 bits and is called a *byte*. The 8 binary bit positions can be arranged to define 256 different characters or symbols. This is how your computer keyboard works.

K, Mb, Gb "K" usually means a thousand, "M" a million, and "G" a billion. However, a *K* (or kilobyte) isn't a thousand bytes because computers think in binary numbers. Their counting system is based on the number two, not on the number ten, and 2^{10} or two multiplied by itself ten times equals 1024. So 1K is really 1024 bytes. Similarly, 1Mb equals 2^{20} equals 1,048,576 bytes, and 1Gb equals 2^{30} equals 1,073,741,824 bytes. Today, shorthand notation has proliferated and become more in vogue in the computer industry. Depending on who you are talking to, either 1024K or 1000K equals 1Mb and 1024Mb or 1000Mb equals 1Gb.

Word length Earlier computers and chips "thought" in word lengths of 8, 12, 16, and 24 bits. They defined and moved data in chunks of that size. Two raised to that number defined the limit of memory they could directly address. Most of today's computers and chips use 32 bits and are able to directly address four billion address locations—2^{32} or 4Gb.

ROM (read only memory) This is a permanent storage medium that is uniquely "programmed" with data. Think of it as a chip with thousands and thousands of tiny fuses on it that are either blown or intact, in accordance with the instructions. You give any computer its unique personality by telling it how it will execute certain instructions. This is done by storing its programming instructions in ROM. The Motorola 68xxx processor chip at the heart of the Macintosh is also used in the Atari, Amiga, NeXT, and numerous other computers. The major difference between them (physical architecture aside) is the instructions stored in their ROM chips. When Apple first introduced the Mac 128, the 64K of instructions optimized and crammed into its ROM is what really made it a Macintosh. It represented countless thousands of man-hours, was the engineering marvel of its day (1982 – 1983), and still is very impressive by today's standards. The 128K ROMs in the Mac Plus, 256K ROMs in the Mac SE and later models, 512K ROMs in the Mac IIci and later models, and 1Mb ROMs in the Mac Quadras each required successively more work. Yet put the tiny Apple Mac ROM chips into a clone computer and you have a Macintosh—not Apple's idea of a good time. Now you have at least a small idea of why Apple covets its code so zealously.

RAM (random access memory) Memory is also called DRAM (dynamic RAM, which must be constantly refreshed), SRAM (static RAM, which does not need constant refreshing, and consumes less power), and PRAM (parameter RAM, which is a small amount of RAM powered by the Mac's internal battery, and set aside to store a few user-definable settings so they are not lost each time the Mac is turned off). Today's semiconductor computer memory, like the processor chips, is very fast but volatile—when you turn the power off you erase memory. So RAM memory only temporarily stores your data. No power, no data. Mid-1970s minicomputer memory used magnetic cores and was slower but nonvolatile. It permanently stored your data but was extremely expensive compared to today's semiconductor memory. It was also less dense. In those days, 32K of memory was a lot—top of the line minicomputers had 256K. Computers used 4K memory chips, then 16K, then 64K, then 256K, then 1Mb, and now 4Mb. Soon they will use 16Mb chips, and 64Mb chips are in the labs already. More powerful and less expensive memory and CPU chips have fueled the personal computer explosion.

Cache Cache is like a small pocket or purse (e.g., the change purse in a woman's handbag). You look in it first to get your change. Mainframe and minicomputer manufacturers have for years used high speed memory in front of regular processor memory to speed up their computers. Here's how it works: When your computer writes data in main memory, it leaves a copy of it in cache memory too. When your computer goes to read data, it looks first in cache memory. If it finds the data there, it doesn't bother with looking in main memory. If your cache and your program loops are of the right size, your computer hardly ever looks in main memory. Result: everything runs a lot faster. Motorola, Apple, and a host of Macintosh third-party vendors have integrated these concepts into their products for higher performance.

RAM chips Apple soldered 64K RAM memory chips directly onto the Mac 128 logic boards and 256K RAM memory chips onto the Mac 512 logic boards. Repairing or upgrading them was very difficult.

SIMM (single inline memory module) A SIMM typically consists of two or eight individual RAM chips attached to a small printed circuit card. Some IIci and IIfx SIMMs use nine chips—the extra one is for parity—a quick way of checking your memory's health. Memory was revolutionized by the use of SIMMs. First introduced with the Mac Plus in 1986, SIMMs made it possible to add additional memory easily to the Macintosh Plus logic board and to any Macintosh developed since then.

SIMM price history and trends

Good news for Macintosh users: SIMM memory prices continue to slide downward. Look at Fig. 4-1 showing the 30 month price trends of 1Mb and 4Mb SIMMs between June 1989 and December 1991. I took this data straight out of the advertising pages of MacWEEK for one mail order vendor. The mail order price for 1Mb SIMMs has temporarily stabilized at under $40 and that of 4Mb SIMMs at $125—the same as 1Mb SIMMs were 24 months earlier. Activity in the composite or built-up SIMMs area has picked up significantly, with a number of vendors also providing 512K, 2Mb, 8Mb, and 16Mb SIMMs built up from standard-sized RAM chip parts. Even obsolete 256K SIMMs continue to prove useful when repackaged into 1Mb SIMM form using third-party vendor's 4:1 cards. You can expect further SIMM price declines after the 16Mb RAM chip parts enter the market in volume. At that point (roughly in 1993) you can watch a replay of Fig. 4-1, this time with 4Mb and 16Mb SIMMs.

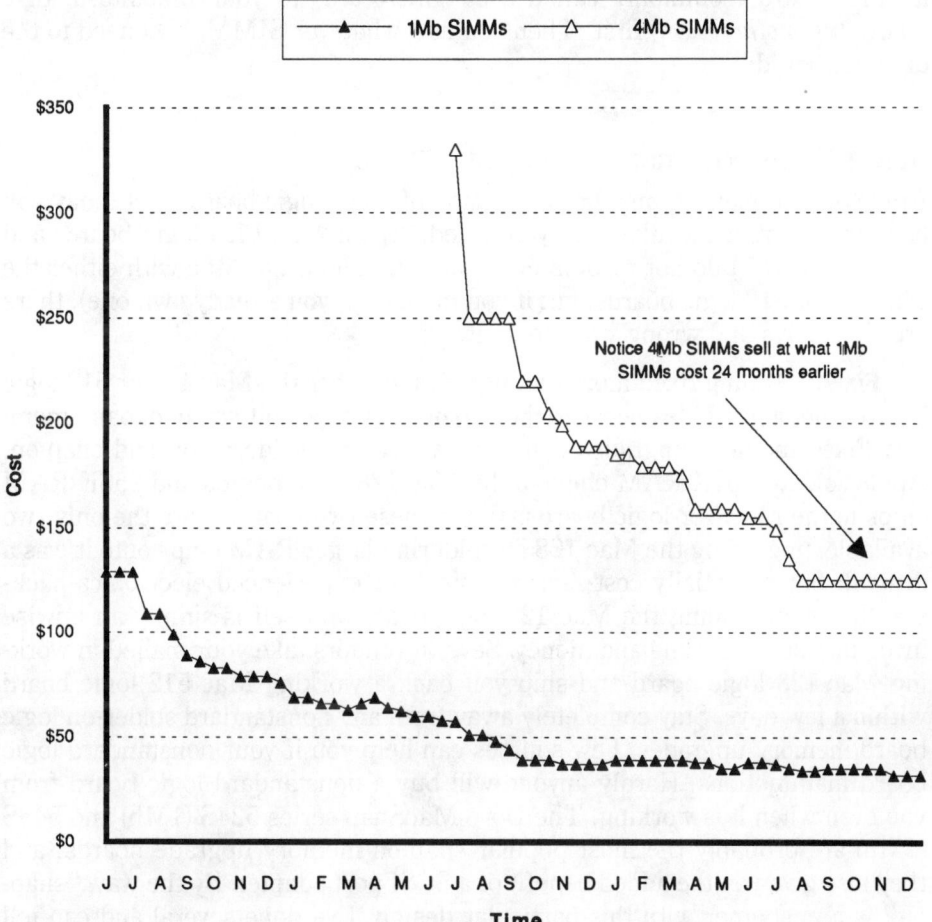

4-1 30-month price trends for 1Mb and 4Mb SIMMs.

Beyond that the 64Mb RAM chips, now in the pure prototyping stage, will arrive to reenact the same scene with different players. This repeating pattern of RAM memory price performance quadrupling roughly every three years prompted one semiconductor analyst to say that with the coming generations of chips, "memory will be almost free compared to the other things you can buy in a computer."

Macintosh memory upgrades

With only two exceptions, all Macintosh logic boards (and the upgrade boards themselves) can be upgraded in memory capacity by substituting larger-capacity SIMMs for smaller ones. The two exceptions are the original Mac 128 and 512 logic boards and today's Mac Classic logic board. In each case, you attach another board (commonly called a *daughterboard*) to your Macintosh logic board (the *motherboard*) first. Then you add whatever SIMMs you need to the daughterboard.

Mac 128 and 512 memory upgrade

Apple did not plan for memory expansion of these logic boards, yet today you have three options available to you: fixed, Apple Mac Plus logic board, and daughterboard. I do not recommend that you build a Cat Mac with either the Mac 128 or 512 logic boards, but if you must (i.e., you already own one), there are right ways and wrong ways to do it.

Fixed Adding fixed memory upgrades to either the Mac 128 or 512 logic board is not a good idea because they do not easily permit you to expand memory. Fixed memory upgrades come in two flavors: soldered-on and snap-on. Apple soldered 64K RAM chips to the Mac 128 logic boards and 256K RAM chips to the Mac 512 logic boards. When these two boards were the only two available, upgrading the Mac 128 by soldering larger RAM chips onto it was a difficult but potentially cost-saving project for experienced electronics hackers. Today, upgrading the Mac 128 logic board yourself is simply an unwise investment of your time and money. Several vendors take your mailed-in working Mac 128 logic board and ship you back a working Mac 512 logic board within a few days. Stay completely away from any nonstandard solder-on logic board memory upgrades. Few sources can help you if your nonstandard logic board malfunctions. Hardly anyone will buy a nonstandard logic board from you even when it is working. The Dove MacSnap series 524S (1Mb) and 548S (2Mb) are probably the most popular snap-on memory upgrade boards, and they also give you the added benefit of a SCSI port adapter. By the way, "snap-on" is a misnomer with this particular design. I've done several and can tell you that a small hydraulic press would be useful during installation. With both the fixed soldered-on upgrade and the snap-on upgrade (which at least you can remove, though you waste the cost of the upgrade and its RAM chips), what you have the first time you upgrade is what you get forever. If future expansion is important to you—you need to do something else.

Apple The Apple Mac 128/512 to Mac Plus logic board upgrade is expandable. But it is an unnecessarily expensive solution for Cat Mac builders. The Apple Mac 128 and Mac 512 upgrades take you to a 1Mb Mac Plus for a list price of $799 and $599, respectively. As a prerequisite to either one of these, you need to add the Apple 800K floppy upgrade (it includes the all-important 128K ROM chips) at a list price of $299. Whatever you pay, you wind up with a Mac Plus logic board—the genuine Apple article—to which you can add SIMM memory upgrades later on. While you can undoubtedly do better than list price, Cat Mac builders must carefully weigh these costs versus those of newer logic boards (plus their other advantages).

Daughterboards to the rescue Computer Care and NewLife Computer have introduced a better way to expand a Mac 128 or 512 logic board: Use a daughterboard that clips onto the 68000 CPU chip on the Macintosh logic board. Both vendor solutions include the daughterboard with new 68000 chip, SCSI chip, and SIMM sockets, plus Killy clip[1] and SCSI cable. Both, in addition, offer video options that drive monitors up to 640 × 480 in resolution. First, you attach the Killy clip to the Mac logic board's 68000 chip as shown in Fig. 4-2. Then you plug the daughterboard into the Killy clip, add memory chips, set a DIP switch or move jumper settings, and you are in business. NewLife Computer's Newlife 1 board with 8 SIMM sockets that allows you to mix and match 256K and 1Mb SIMMs with settings controlled by jumper blocks is shown installed on a Mac 512 logic board in Fig. 4-3 (pencils point to SCSI cable and memory jumpers). Computer Care's MacRescue board with 6 SIMM sockets that allows you to use either 256K or 1Mb SIMMs with settings controlled by a DIP switch (my finger points to SCSI connector and cable—video cables are above video output pins at top edge of board) is shown in Fig. 4-4, and installed on a Mac 512 logic board inside a Cat Mac chassis in Fig. 4-5. Either board lets you expand all the way to 4Mb of SIMM memory. You still

4-2 Attaching a Killy clip to a Mac 512 logic board.

Macintosh memory upgrades 77

4-3 NewLife Computer NewLife 1 board installed on a Mac 512 logic board.

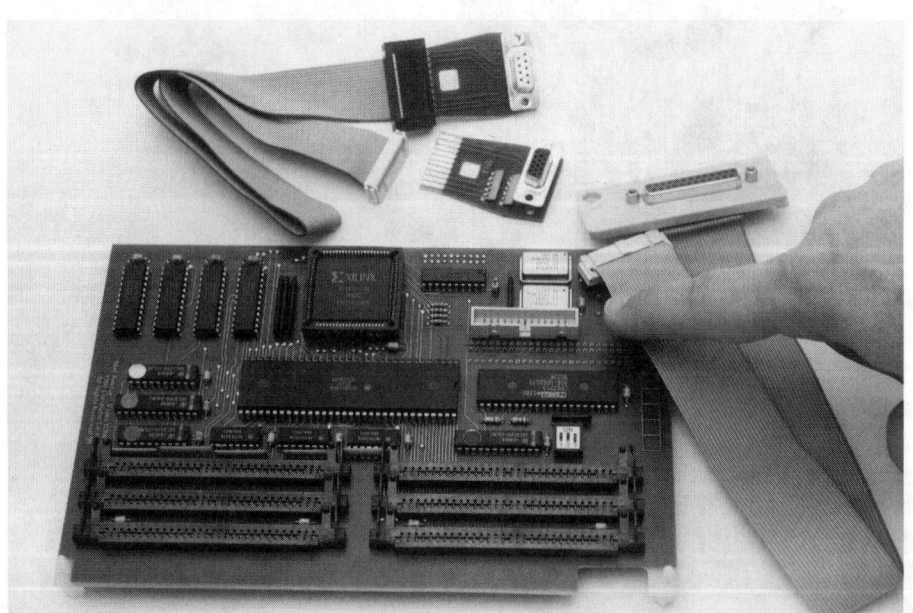

4-4 Computer Care MacRescue board with video option.

4-5 Computer Care MacRescue board installed on Mac 512 logic board in Cat Mac chassis.

need to add the Apple 800K floppy upgrade with its 128K ROMs, but you get a 20% performance improvement and save quite a few dollars versus the Apple Mac Plus logic board upgrade cost.

Don't do a fixed upgrade—go with either a daughterboard or an Apple upgrade to your Mac 128/512—because you can take your SIMMs with you when you later get an accelerator. On balance, the daughterboard is probably the most cost-effective solution.

Mac Classic memory upgrade

Apple did plan for memory expansion of the Mac Classic logic board, but in a manner that would minimize its manufacturing cost, not in a manner that would be convenient for the Cat Mac builder. Both Apple and numerous third-party vendors make daughterboards for memory/video expansion that plug into a 44-pin socket provided for exactly this purpose on the Mac Classic logic board. The Mac Classic logic board comes with 1Mb RAM soldered-on. Most Mac Classic memory upgrade daughterboards, like the ones from Apple (on left) and Computer Care (on right) shown beneath a Mac Classic logic board in Fig. 4-6, also have 1Mb RAM soldered-on plus two SIMM sockets. Populating these sockets with 1Mb SIMMs gives you 3Mb on the memory card and brings you up to 4Mb of total memory when plugged into the Mac Classic.

4-6 Memory cards for the Mac Classic logic board (top), Apple (left), and Computer Care (right).

SIMM memory upgrade

Cat Mac builders using Mac Plus logic boards on up through the Mac IIfx and latest Mac Quadra logic boards have a much simpler memory upgrade task. Upgrade your memory capacity just by adding SIMMs. Unlike Mac 128/512 owners, you don't have to worry about upgrading your floppy disk drive ROMs along with memory. Everything you need is already there—just add the SIMMs. Many of the 1990 and later Macintosh logic boards already have 1Mb, 2Mb, or 4Mb permanently soldered onto the board. Let's briefly cover how you buy SIMMs before getting into the installation details by model.

Buying SIMMs

You need to concern yourself with the following areas when buying SIMMs (numerous articles have been written that expand on this area more):[2]

SIMM types SIMMs come in two flavors: DIP (dual inline package) and SOJ (surface mount). The RAM memory chip pins on DIP SIMMs are soldered on through holes, require a larger width SIMM circuit card, sit higher in their logic board socket, and cannot be used in height critical Plus or SE boards—but cost less. SOJ SIMMs are shorter in length than DIP SIMMs and their pins are soldered onto the surface of the SIMM circuit card. They can be used in any SIMM socket and typically cost more.

SIMM sizes Today's SIMMs come in three standard sizes: 256K, 1Mb, and 4Mb plus several more composite or built up sizes: 512K, 2Mb, 8Mb, and 16Mb. They can be mixed and matched, but you have to follow certain rules—slightly different for each Mac model—regarding size and speed. Figure 4-7 shows three different kinds of SOJ, or surface mount SIMMs. In the front is 1Mb SIMM with eight 80-ns RAM chips on it; in the middle is a 256K SIMM with two 80-ns RAM chips on it; and at the rear is a 256K SIMM with eight 120-ns RAM chips on it.

SIMM speeds The suffix numbers on RAM chips mounted on the SIMM are important. They tell you the chip's speed. The "–15" means you have a 150-ns chip, "–12" denotes a 120-ns chip, "–10" denotes a 100-ns chip, "–80" means an 80-ns chip, "–70" means a 70-ns chip, etc. There is no advantage in using chips faster than your logic board needs because its clock speed and wait states are fixed and cannot take advantage of faster chips. So don't spend money on faster SIMMs than you need—unless you plan on taking your SIMMs with you to a higher performance Mac model later. Anything faster than 150-ns on your Mac Plus or SE, and faster than 120 ns on your Mac II or SE 30 is wasted. On the other hand, the Mac SE 30, Mac IIx, and Mac IIcx will take 100 ns, and your accelerator board might need 100 ns or better

4-7 Three 30-pin SIMM types.

SIMMs to perform well. The Mac IIci and IIsi use SIMMs for video RAM and require at least 80 ns chips. On the other hand, you cannot run slower SIMMs than your particular Mac requires and you must exactly match the speed of all SIMMs used in any given Mac's memory bank if you wish to avoid erratic and intermittent operation of your Mac that results in data loss. Table 4-1 summarizes your memory speed options across all Mac models.

SIMM prices You can save greatly if you buy wisely. Identical SIMM parts can vary in price by 200%—depending on who you buy them from. With virtually all vendors offering warranties and some offering lifetime guarantees—there is no need for you to pay full retail list price. Use Fig. 4-1 as a guideline when you shop around.

Table 4-1. SIMM speed options for various Macintosh models.

Model	150 ns	120 ns	100 ns	>80 ns	Comments
Mac Plus	yes	yes	yes	yes	no 4Mb SIMMs
Mac SE	no	yes	yes	yes	no 4Mb SIMMs
Mac Classic	no	yes	yes	yes	no 4Mb SIMMs
Mac Classic II	no	yes	yes	yes	
Mac SE 30	no	yes	yes	yes	
Mac II	no	yes	yes	yes	
Mac IIx	no	yes	yes	yes	
Mac IIcx	no	yes	yes	yes	
Mac LC	no	no	yes	yes	
Mac IIsi	no	no	yes	yes	Apple ships 80 ns SIMMs!
Mac IIci	no	no	no	yes	requires 80 ns SIMMs
Mac IIfx	no	no	no	yes	64-pin SIMMs only
Mac Quadra 700	no	no	no	yes	requires 80 ns SIMMs

SIMM amounts Today, you should not have less than 2Mb of memory in your Macintosh. Why? Because 2Mb is the minimum amount of memory that will allow you to run Apple's System 6.0 Multifinder, and 4Mb is really required to run System 7 software. With 1Mb SIMM prices under $40, there is no excuse for you not to have at least 2Mb to 4Mb or more of memory in your Macintosh. All the new Apple Macintosh models come with 2Mb already installed (except the bare-bones Mac Classic), so perhaps Apple is telling us something. My recommendation here is very straightforward. Buy the most memory your pocketbook will allow.

SIMM installation and removal

Adding or removing SIMMs is literally a snap. Figures 4-8 through 4-11 show the steps in removing a SIMM from a Mac Plus logic board. Installing a SIMM is just the reverse—but even easier because it just snaps in place. Whether the

4-8 SIMM removal: screwdriver points to "finger" on socket.

4-9 SIMM removal: screwdriver moves "finger" to edge of SIMM.

Macintosh memory upgrades **83**

4-10 SIMM removal: screwdriver behind SIMM (now free of socket).

4-11 SIMM removal: fingers remove SIMM—handle by edge only please!

SIMMs mount at an angle (as shown here) or vertically (as on Mac II-family logic boards), the basic procedure is the same.

Notice that the SIMM is held in place by clips at either end. If you carefully use a flat-bladed screwdriver or your fingernail you can in most cases easily remove the SIMM chip. The screwdriver points to the little black plastic "finger" at the edge of the SIMM socket holding it in place in Fig. 4-8. The object of the game is to use either your screwdriver or a fingernail to move the "finger" off to the edge of the SIMM circuit board, working one end at a time as shown in Fig. 4-9. So the process is to pry one edge loose halfway, go back to the other side of the SIMM chip and pry it loose halfway, go back to the other side of the SIMM chip and pry it loose the rest of the way, and finally, go back to the other end of the SIMM chip and pry it loose the rest of the way as shown in Fig. 4-10. Then just use finger pressure to push the SIMM chip out of the socket and—when the edge connectors no longer restrain it—lift it up and out of its socket as shown in Fig. 4-11.

The most important thing to remember in the care and handling of SIMMs is static. When removing or installing any SIMM—be careful to handle it by its edge only! Be sure to thoroughly ground yourself before handling your SIMMs, and if you feel the least bit unsure, use the antistatic wrist strap.

I have never had a problem using a small, flat-bladed screwdriver to remove SIMMs. The screwdriver is a lot easier to use than my fingers—I am always able to remove the SIMM after a few moments of effort. My secret is I use the screwdriver gently and never force anything. The process might be a little tedious, but it is quite satisfactory. I have never met anyone who has damaged a SIMM or a socket using this technique if they were careful of what they were doing.

SIMM rules—Mac Plus and SE

There are four SIMM sockets on both the Mac Plus and SE logic board. As you look down on the Mac Plus board with the front edge toward you as shown (refer back to Fig. 3-4 in chapter 3 if you like), the SIMM sockets are numbered 1, 2, 3, 4 starting with the SIMM socket closest to the CPU chip. On the Mac SE board with its front edge toward you (refer back to Fig. 3-5), there are two rows of SIMM sockets: number 1 (upper left) and number 2 (upper right) are in the row closest to the CPU, number 3 (lower left) and number 4 (lower right) are in the row closest to the front edge of the logic board. Although the four sockets are physically arranged differently in the Mac Plus and Mac SE, there are four identical allowable memory configurations using the 256K and 1Mb memory chips. Table 4-2 summarizes them.

Apple has laid down some simple rules[3] that, if followed, make life much simpler. Here are the SIMMs guidelines for either a Plus or an SE:

- Each SIMM must use 150 ns or faster RAM chips.
- All RAM chips in a row must be the same speed and size.

- Each SIMM must be filled with eight RAM chips. The nine RAM chip SIMMs used in IBM PC chips will not work.
- All rows must either be empty or contain two SIMMs.
- The SIMMs with the larger RAM chips must always be installed in row 1.

There is also a corresponding need to modify the SIMM resistor on the Mac Plus logic board, as shown in Fig. 4-12, and the resistor or jumper the Mac SE logic board—a newer logic board with jumpers is shown in Fig. 4-13. Table 4-3 summarizes the options.

SIMM rules—Mac SE 30 and NuBus

On the Mac SE 30, Mac II, IIx, IIcx, IIci, and IIfx logic boards, socketed SIMMs allow you to expand memory to 32Mb. There are eight SIMM sockets on all these logic boards. As you look down at these logic boards, with the front edge toward you and connectors away from you, the four SIMM sockets in Bank B are: closest to the front of the logic board for the Mac SE 30 (refer back to Fig. 3-6), closest to the left of the logic board for the Mac IIcx or IIci (refer back to Fig. 3-12 or Fig. 3-13), closest to the center of the logic board for

Table 4-2. SIMM configuration options for Mac Plus and Mac SE.

Configuration	1Mb	2Mb	2.5Mb	4Mb
SIMM #1 (old SE & Plus)	256K	1Mb	1Mb	1Mb
SIMM #2 (old SE & Plus)	256K	1Mb	1Mb	1Mb
SIMM #3 (old SE & Plus)	256K	—	256K	1Mb
SIMM #4 (old SE & Plus)	256K	—	256K	1Mb
SIMM #1 (new SE Board)	256K	—	1Mb	1Mb
SIMM #2 (new SE Board)	256K	—	1Mb	1Mb
SIMM #3 (new SE Board)	256K	1Mb	256K	1Mb
SIMM #4 (new SE Board)	256K	1Mb	256K	1Mb

Table 4-3. Resistor/jumper options for Mac Plus and Mac SE.

Configuration	2 SIMMs	4 SIMMs	All 256K	All 1Mb
Plus: resistor R9 "one row"	installed	removed	—	—
Plus: resistor R8 "256K bit"	—	—	installed	removed
SE: resistor R36 "one row"	installed	removed	—	—
SE: resistor R35 "256K bit"	—	—	installed	removed
New SE: jumper on "1Mb"	—	—	1Mb installed	—
New SE: jumper on "2/4Mb"	—	—	—	2Mb installed
New SE: jumper off	—	2.5Mb installed	—	—
New SE: jumper off	—	—	—	4Mb installed

4-12 RAM-size resistors R8 and R9 on Mac Plus logic board.

the Mac II or IIx (refer back to Fig. 3-11) and closest to the rear of the logic board for the Mac IIfx (refer back to Fig. 3-14). Each "bank" consists of four SIMM sockets and must always be either all filled or all empty. There are five allowable memory configurations using the 256K, 1Mb, and 4Mb SIMMs, and these are summarized in Table 4-4. The Bank A "4B1" nomenclature shown in Table 4-4 means "SIMM #4, Byte #1."

Apple's rules changed slightly for the Mac SE 30, Mac II, IIx, IIcx, IIci, and IIfx logic boards, but there are no resistor changes to worry about. Here are their SIMM guidelines:

- Each SIMM must use 120 ns or faster RAM chips (80 ns or faster for the IIci or IIfx plus it must have fast page mode for the IIci).
- All RAM chips in a row must be the same speed and size.
- Each SIMM must be filled with eight RAM chips. Nine RAM chip

Macintosh memory upgrades **87**

SIMMs to enable parity checking can be used in IIci and IIfx models when equipped with custom PGC (Parity Checker and Generator) IC on the IIci and custom RPU (RAM Parity Unit) IC on the IIfx model.
- All rows in a bank must either be empty or contain four SIMMs.
- The SIMMs with the larger RAM chips must always be installed in bank B.
- RAM SIMM pinouts are different for the IIfx and not interchangeable with other model SIMMs.

4-13 SIMM jumpers on Mac SE logic board.

Table 4-4. SIMM options for Mac SE 30 and NuBus Macs.

Configuration	1Mb	2Mb	4Mb	5Mb	8Mb	16Mb	17Mb	32Mb
SIMM 4B1 (bank A)	256K	256K	1Mb	1Mb	1Mb	4Mb	4Mb	4Mb
SIMM 4B0 (bank A)	256K	256K	1Mb	1Mb	1Mb	4Mb	4Mb	4Mb
SIMM 3B3 (bank A)	256K	256K	1Mb	1Mb	1Mb	4Mb	4Mb	4Mb
SIMM 3B2 (bank A)	256K	256K	1Mb	1Mb	1Mb	4Mb	4Mb	4Mb
SIMM 2B1 (bank B)	—	256K	—	256K	1Mb	—	1Mb	4Mb
SIMM 2B0 (bank B)	—	256K	—	256K	1Mb	—	1Mb	4Mb
SIMM 1B3 (bank B)	—	256K	—	256K	1Mb	—	1Mb	4Mb
SIMM 1B2 (bank B)	—	256K	—	256K	1Mb	—	1Mb	4Mb

SIMM rules—Mac Classic, Classic II, LC, IIsi and Quadra 700

The rules change again for the Mac Classic, Classic II, LC, IIsi, and Quadra 700 models. The allowable memory configurations for them using 1Mb and 4Mb SIMMs are summarized in Table 4-5. Each model is a little different.

The Mac Classic special case was already mentioned earlier. It comes with 1Mb RAM soldered to the logic board. You expand memory by adding the optional memory card. The Apple optional memory card comes with 1Mb already soldered to the card and a bank of two SIMM sockets. You get the various possible expanded memory combinations (2.5Mb is also possible using two 256K SIMMs) by adding the card and two 1Mb SIMMs. You cannot use 4Mb SIMMs.

On the Mac Classic II and LC, 2Mb are already soldered to the logic board and you have a bank of two SIMM sockets for expansion. You get the various possible combinations of 2, 4, or 10Mb of RAM by adding either none or two 1Mb SIMMs or two 4Mb SIMMs to the logic board.

On the Mac IIsi, 1Mb is already soldered to the logic board and you have a bank of four SIMM sockets on the logic board for add-in memory (Apple normally ships its newest Mac IIsi models with 3Mb using 512K SIMMs). You get the various possible combinations of 1, 5, or 17Mb of RAM by adding either none or four 1Mb, or four 4Mb SIMMs to the logic board.

On the Mac Quadra 700, 4Mb is already soldered to the logic board and you have a bank of four SIMM sockets on the logic board for add-in memory.

Table 4-5. SIMM options for Mac Classic, Classic II, LC, IIsi and Quadra 700.

Configuration	2Mb	3Mb	4Mb	5Mb	8Mb	10Mb	17Mb	20Mb
SIMM #1 (Classic)[1]	Mem Bd	—	1Mb	—	—	—	—	—
SIMM #2 (Classic)	Mem Bd	—	1Mb	—	—	—	—	—
SIMM #1 (Classic II)[2]	Std	—	1Mb	—	—	4Mb	—	—
SIMM #2 (Classic II)	Std	—	1Mb	—	—	4Mb	—	—
SIMM #1 (LC)	Std	—	1Mb	—	—	4Mb	—	—
SIMM #2 (LC)	Std	—	1Mb	—	—	4Mb	—	—
SIMM #1 (IIsi bank B)[3]	—	512Kb	—	1Mb	—	—	4Mb	—
SIMM #2 (IIsi bank B)	—	512Kb	—	1Mb	—	—	4Mb	—
SIMM #3 (IIsi bank B)	—	512Kb	—	1Mb	—	—	4Mb	—
SIMM #4 (IIsi bank B)	—	512Kb	—	1Mb	—	—	4Mb	—
SIMM #1 (Quadra bank B)[4]	—	—	Std	—	1Mb	—	—	4Mb
SIMM #2 (Quadra bank B)	—	—	Std	—	1Mb	—	—	4Mb
SIMM #3 (Quadra bank B)	—	—	Std	—	1Mb	—	—	4Mb
SIMM #4 (Quadra bank B)	—	—	Std	—	1Mb	—	—	4Mb

[1] Mac Classic memory expansion is all via memory card; first 1Mb RAM is soldered on memory card.

[2] Mac Classic II and Mac LC come standard with 2Mb RAM soldered on logic board.

[3] New Apple Mac IIsi models come with 3Mb: 1Mb RAM soldered on logic board plus 2Mb via SIMMs.

[4] Mac Quadra 700 comes standard with 4Mb RAM soldered on logic board.

You get the various possible combinations of 4, 8 or 20Mb of RAM by adding either none or four 1Mb, or four 4Mb SIMMs to the logic board.

SIMM rules—Mac IIfx

The rules don't change for the IIfx as much as the physical appearance of its SIMMs, memory slots, and memory slot orientation in the chassis.

The big difference is shown in Fig. 4-14. Notice the IIfx 1Mb SIMM in the foreground is a 64-pin wide unit rather than a standard off-the-shelf 30-pin 1Mb SIMM for other Mac models shown in the rear. Apple improved the performance of its IIfx system by going to an overlapping read/write technique. Apple calls it "latched read/write" where even though the IIfx's 68030 only supports 32-bit data paths, you grab data in the form of 64-bit words because your read and write accesses can overlap. The improved performance 64-pin SIMMs command a higher price than their standard cousins, but performance conscious IIfx owners gladly pay the difference. The metal clips on the IIfx SIMM sockets are a tremendous improvement over the standard plastic ones that are hard on your fingernails and easy to break. All Apple 1991 models incorporated them.

4-14   Mac IIfx 64-pin SIMM in foreground versus 30-pin SIMM at rear.

Macintosh upgrades

While Macintosh upgrades are unquestionably even more useful to Cat Mac builders—no space or size or power budget limitations—the upgrade issue must be approached in stages. Your primary need is always the driving factor. Do you want better performance and a full-page monitor? Or color and top speed? Or something else? Your possible options are enormous. While a more powerful Apple Macintosh logic board is always the best solution—it might not fit in your budget. If you already own your logic board, the objective is to get more performance out of it at less than the cost of a newer, more powerful logic board. In addition to your performance needs, any upgrade must also be compatible with your video requirements. Maybe you just need to increase performance in a specific area—like the SCSI bus. This section will sort out the upgrade options and issues so you can make the best choice.

Apple announcements and technology advances have caused this section to be totally rewritten from the first edition of the book. Aggressively priced, new Apple Macintosh logic board upgrades cause third-party vendors to move rapidly to adjust their prices and reposition their products. Plus technology has enabled third-party vendors to create newer upgrade boards which are less expensive, easier to install, and provide a higher compatibility with existing software than did their predecessors of just a few years ago. Upgrade board performance levels have drifted higher as increasingly hotter chips became available, and this trend will continue.

Upgrade process

The upgrade process itself is quite simple. You start with the logic board you have. You can elect to swap it for a more powerful Apple Macintosh logic board upgrade. Certain swaps also require that you upgrade the floppy drive and ROM. Or you might just add an accelerator board. Figure 4-15 shows the upgrade paths at a glance for 14 Macintosh logic boards (the Mac Quadra 900 and the four Mac portable models are not covered; the Mac 128 is combined with the Mac 512). Eight Macintosh logic boards can be upgraded further via six Apple logic board upgrades. One upgrade, the Mac IIci, can be upgraded further. Three require a prior floppy drive and ROM upgrade. All can be accelerated further. For the moment, all 68000-based logic boards can be accelerated to 40-MHz 68030-based models, and all 68020/68030-based models can be accelerated to at least 50-MHz 68030-based or 25-MHz 68040-based models. The Quadra 700 can be accelerated to a 33-MHz 68040 model. The Mac IIfx can be accelerated to a 55-MHz 68030 model. That's it in a nutshell. Now let's look at the Apple upgrades and third-party vendors' accelerators in more detail.

Apple upgrades

As already mentioned in chapter 2, Apple is one of the few major manufacturers that provides upgrades to its products. Its logic board and floppy drive upgrades, the categories of interest here, were summarized in Table 2-4 along with their prices. The point of Fig. 4-15 is that they are just another alternative to take you, as a Cat Mac builder, where you want to go. You need to weigh their value—in terms of both price and performance—to your Cat Mac project compared to other alternatives. Obviously, if you are able to pick up an Apple upgrade at a good price without exchange, you've not only equalled or saved yourself money over a third-party vendor solution but you also own the genuine Apple article with all its attendant benefits.

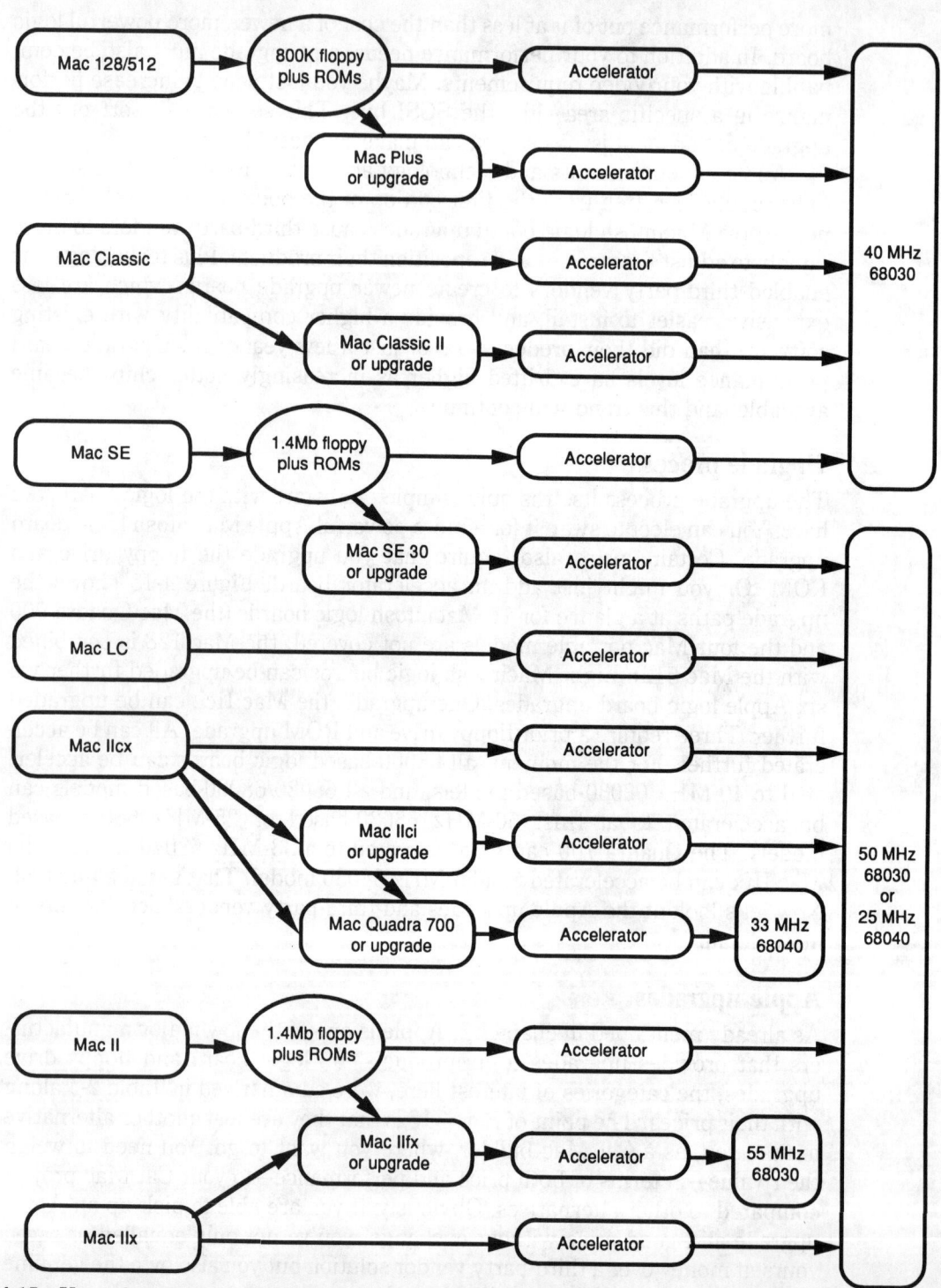

4-15 Upgrade paths for 14 Macintosh logic boards.

Accelerators

In your car, you can take out the four or six cylinder engine and replace it with a more powerful eight cylinder one. The car body and everything else stays the same. The same principle applies to adding an accelerator board to your Cat Mac. You take a new board with a more powerful CPU chip and either clip it on to your Macintosh logic board's existing CPU chip, or remove the old CPU chip entirely and plug the new board in its place. Everything else stays the same. Well, not exactly. You also need some additional software, and you might even want to reformat your hard disk for better performance. Most of your programs, including all of the major ones—word processors, spreadsheets, etc.—run exactly as before only faster.

Your goal is simple: Save yourself money by upgrading with an accelerator board rather than buying a more powerful and expensive Macintosh logic board. There are a wide variety of accelerator boards to help you but not all are created equal as far as the Cat Mac builder is concerned. Here's the lineup:

- CPU/clock cards that merely speed up the CPU clock or bus.
- FPU chips/cards that speed up the processing of math intensive tasks.
- Memory cache cards that speed up your cache memory.
- SCSI bus accelerator cards that increase the speed with which your NuBus Mac can talk to SCSI peripherals.
- File compression cards that increase the speed of compressing and decompressing files.
- Full-function accelerator cards with memory and CPU chips that provide significant increases in performance.

Full-function accelerator cards are definitely useful to Cat Mac builders. Cat Mac builders might or might not find other cards useful on a case-by-case basis. My objective in this section is to introduce you to the broad subject of accelerator boards. I'll briefly cover some definitions and introduce you to the several types of accelerator boards, then spend time on the full-function types that can help you in upgrading your Macintosh, including comparative positioning/pricing and suggestions for a strategy for you.

While many good articles on accelerator boards have been written,[4] there is little point in reading any but the most recent ones because third-party accelerator vendor offerings and prices change so rapidly.

Okay—accelerate me

Here are some definitions for terms you are likely to encounter in discussing accelerator boards:

- CPU Chip—Accelerators come in the four chip flavors you already met in chapter 3: 68000, 68020, 68030, and 68040. Today, your best accelerator performance is provided by 68030-based products. The 68040 will obviously supplant it in the future. The 68000 and 68020-based products provide the best values under specific circumstances.

- Clock speed—Given the identical say 68000 CPU chips running at 16-MHz and 8-MHz clock speed—two times the operating frequency means that twice as many operations are performed each second. Today, accelerator boards are available that run at up to 55 MHz.
- Throughput—The 68030 chip has internal 32-bit data paths—twice as wide as the internal 16-bit data paths in the 68000 chip. Two times the path width means that twice as much data is transferred in each operation. Twice as much data moving at twice the previous speed means the 68030 chips have four times the throughput of the 68000 chip.
- Cache—As explained earlier, this is a small amount of faster memory in front of main memory. The CPU only has to look at it for the next instruction or piece of data. On-chip instruction and data cache added in the 68030 improves its performance, especially of looping, iterative programs.
- FPU (floating-point unit)—An optional 68881 or 68882 FPU chip (68882 is twice as fast as 68881) used in conjunction with the CPU chip can accelerate math-intensive applications such as spreadsheets, graphics, and CAD programs by performing the calculations in hardware.
- PMMU (paged memory management unit)—An optional 68851 chip used in conjunction with the 68020 (already on the 68030 chip). This chip or function must be present to run the "virtual" software operating systems such as A/UX (Apple's Unix Software), Connectix's Virtual, and Apple's System 7.
- Memory options—Not all accelerator boards are created equal in this department. Some require their own extra fast SIMMs, some use your logic board's RAM, while some use both. Most specify that you must use faster SIMM chips than the 150-ns SIMMS that came with your Mac Plus or SE.
- Control software—The most essential function of the control software packaged with each third-party vendor's product is to allow you to disable the accelerator board or its cache so that you can keep using programs that work only in your logic board's native mode. It also provides other "nice to have" features, such as copying ROM into high speed RAM at startup, configuring FPU options, setting speeds, and sizing memory.
- Expansion options—It is important that you know which video monitor and other option cards can be driven from your accelerator card before you buy it! Today, most accelerator board manufacturers support their own video monitors and those of other third-party vendors—verify that the model you want is supported.

CPU/clock accelerators

At the opposite end of the spectrum from the full-function accelerators' boards are the CPU/clock speedup cards. These boards have no memory on them, only a faster CPU and optionally, a faster FPU chip. All you are doing is working with one of the performance elements—a higher CPU clock rate—and optionally a higher performance FPU. But the good news is that these little goodies are easy on your pocketbook and sometimes provide just the speedup you need to make the difference between happiness and drudgery in running programs on your Cat Mac.

The performance of the 8-MHz 68000-based Mac Plus, Classic, and SE logic boards can only be enhanced approximately 50% by the addition of a CPU/clock board with a 16-MHz 68000 CPU on it (some offer an optional 16-MHz 68881 FPU chip). These are available at prices around $200 to $400 from AOX, Brainstorm, Dove, and Newer Technology.

Dove also offers a similar solution for the 16-MHz 68030-based Mac SE 30 logic board—a 32-MHz 68030-based CPU/clock board that improves the performance of the Mac SE 30 logic board approximately 40%. On the down side, this particular board doesn't let you format FDHD floppies at speed—you have to turn off the acceleration function—but it is an inexpensive way to pump up your SE 30 at around $500.

FPU accelerators

As you learned in the definitions, the FPU or floating-point unit is a chip used in conjunction with the CPU chip to accelerate math-intensive calculations. Actually, they offload the CPU by doing the math processing in parallel—they are coprocessor chips. On Mac LC and IIsi logic board models, Apple unbundled the FPU chip to save cost—and created a robust market for add-on FPU chips/boards. Applied Engineering, DayStar, PSI, and numerous others provide plug-in board solutions in the $100 to $200 range. Virtually all third-party accelerator vendors (except those providing 68040 solutions where the FPU feature is already included in the CPU chip) also provide chip/board FPU upgrade options to their products. Cat Mac builders are well-advised to take advantage of the FPU option in either case. Not only will you will find most software gives much more satisfactory performance with the FPU present but some software products (Microsoft's Excel version 2.2 on the Mac IIsi was a notorious example) didn't run at all without it.

Memory/cache accelerators

Apple created an entire new market almost overnight with the cache slot in its Mac IIci model. The premise is simple. If a little amount of faster static RAM in front of your main RAM gives increased performance—then a lot more still faster SRAM should do even better. Apple validated the market even further by introducing its own aggressively-priced 32K Mac IIci Cache Card and eventually bundling it with all new Mac IIci models after a several month delay to iron out all the bugs. Third-party vendors responded by offering cache cards with 64K (or more) of 25-ns SRAM at $200 or less. Adding a cache card gives the Cat Mac IIci builder a nice performance boost for little more than the cost of a 4Mb memory upgrade. Cache card vendors include: DayStar Digital, Micron, Technology Works, Total Systems, and UR Micro among others.

SCSI bus accelerators

Although the Mac IIfx SCSI/DMA controller chip enhances the SCSI bus by providing devices on the bus with direct access to memory, the Mac SCSI bus is still a bottleneck—particularly to the faster peripherals. Intelligent NuBus boards from DayStar Digital (SCSI Power Card) and Storage Dimensions (Data Cannon) change this picture. Both boards use an on-board coprocessor (acting as an independent background I/O processor) that relieves the Macintosh CPU from dealing with SCSI transactions and also speeds up burst transfers. Of course, to obtain either card's full benefits, you have to use it with high capacity, high transfer rate disk drives such as the 400, 600, or 1200Mb drives with 2Mb to 3Mb per second transfer rates from the Seagate/Imprimis Wren family. If your applications need this capability, around $1000 added to the cost of a high performance disk drive puts one into your NuBus Cat Mac.

File compression accelerators

Sigma Designs Double Up NuBus card uses its Stac 9703 40-MHz data compression coprocessor to boost data compression speeds to 1Mb per second and data decompression speeds to 5Mb per second. It comes bundled with Disk Doubler software that gives you compression capabilities of 2:1 on average with up to 15:1 possible. It provides no-loss, real-time file compression that means data, images, and applications can be compressed and decompressed at speeds that are virtually unnoticeable and no data is ever lost or altered. A painless way to optimize your NuBus Cat Mac—particularly if you do a lot of handling of graphics and database files.

Full-function accelerators

As a Cat Mac builder, full-function accelerators are your best investment. An added benefit is that you have even more flexibility in using them because (unlike conventional Apple Macintosh owners) you have no power budget, space, or size restrictions. As opposed to the single-function accelerators just reviewed, full-function accelerators give you far more dramatic gains in immediate performance, and position you better for future growth—all for only a nominal additional investment. Let's take a look at the design techniques that enable full-function accelerators to achieve their superior performance:

- Use a "hotter" CPU chip running at a higher clock speed.
- Usually install a "hotter" FPU chip on-board.
- Put SIMM memory sockets right on the accelerator board so the accelerator board's CPU chip can access it faster.
- Add high-speed cache memory to further increase its performance.
- Provide faster SCSI "handshaking."
- Provide intelligent software to adapt/accommodate the accelerator to the logic board.
- Provide flexible software to maximize accelerator board user options.

While none of these steps is earth-shattering in itself, using all of them together produces significant performance gains—you are usually quite satisfied with the results. That is why I strongly recommend full-function accelerators: you notice the difference and are happy with your investment when a full-function accelerator board gives you a 100% performance improvement. The same cannot always be said for a single-function accelerator board that only gives you a 20% to 40% performance improvement.

Table 4-6 summarizes the recommendations. It adds specific vendor solutions to the upgrade path goals shown in Fig. 4-15. Notice that, with the exception of a single 68000-based accelerator board recommendation, everything else is 68030- or 68040-based. Today's full-function accelerator solutions can take your low-end Macintosh logic board up to a 40-MHz 68030, a midrange Macintosh logic board up to a 50-MHz 68030 model or a 25-MHz 68040, a Mac IIfx logic board up to a 55-MHz 68030, and a Mac Quadra up to a 25-MHz 68040. Let's examine the different categories more closely.

A brief note on accelerator board pricing. I included pricing in Table 4-6 (only with the greatest reluctance) for comparison purposes. I guarantee some prices (and even some products) will be out of date by the time you read this. Such is life in the "fast lane" of accelerator board vendors. In addition to vendors directly adjusting the "suggested retail price" of their products, product "street prices" can vary over a broad range in the mail order channel—particularly if distributed widely or in a hotly contested area of the market. You can routinely expect to pay 20% to 30% less on a widely distributed product. In the hotly contested 25-MHz 68040 accelerator market, vendors and resellers cut prices nearly every other month as 68040 chips come into the market in volume. Please don't pay full retail when numerous resellers are clamoring to offer you a better deal—just shop around a bit!

Accelerators using 68000 CPUs

There is only one in this category. Harris Laboratories has innovated a unique product for upgrading a Mac Classic logic board. It's called the Performer and it does just that. The entire accelerator is contained on a board that slips over the Mac Classic logic board and clips onto its CPU. Figure 4-16 shows the board (the hole in the center fits over the power connector and adds stability

Table 4-6. Mac full-function accelerator board recommendations.

Manufacturer/accelerator	Logic board(s)	CPU speed(MHz)	Price
Accelerators using 68000 CPU			
Harris Laboratories Performer	Classic	16	300
Accelerators using up to 40 MHz 68030 CPUs			
Total Systems Mercury	128, 512, Plus, SE	16	500 – 900
Novy Quik 30	128, 512, Plus, SE	16,25,33	500 – 1200
NewLife Computer 25	128, 512, Plus, SE	16,25	600 – 900
NewLife Computer 33	SE	33	1900
Applied Engineering Transwarp	SE	16,25,40	1200 – 2200
Accelerators using up to 50 MHz 68030 CPUs			
Total Systems Classic	Classic	20,33,50	800 – 1300
Total Systems Ultra	128, 512, Plus, SE	20,33,50	800 – 1300
Applied Engineering Transwarp	LC	33,40,50	1500 – 2200
DayStar PowerCache	LC, SE30, Mac IIs	33,40,50	1000 – 2000
Accelerators Using up to 55 MHz 68030 CPUs			
TechNoir Nexus fx	IIfx	55	1100
TechNoir Nexus fx	II, IIx	55	3000
Newer Technology fx/Overdrive	IIfx	55	2000
Accelerators using 25 MHz 68040 CPUs			
Applied Engineering Transwarp 040	NuBus	25	3100
Total Systems Magellan 040 PDS	LC, SE30, IIsi, IIci	25	2000 – 2500
Fusion Data Systems TokaMac	LC, SE30, IIsi, IIci	25	2800 – 3200
IIR Performance/040	NuBus	25	2500
Radius Rocket 25i (uses 68LC040)	NuBus	25	1500
Radius Rocket 040	NuBus, Quadra	25	2000
Accelerators using 33 MHz 68040 CPUs			
Newer Technology Quadra/Overdrive	Quadra	33	350

and rigidity to the mounting). The Performer features a 68000 CPU chip running at 16 MHz, 64K of SRAM, and uses 25-ns PAL chips for speed. It comes with its own init software for sound and cache, supports an optional 68881 FPU chip, and is 100% compatible with all Macintosh software and Apple's System 7. Using it gives you a Mac Classic that runs 90% faster than the standard model with 70% faster math (80% if you elect the FPU option) and even gives you a 15% faster SCSI port. All for a fraction of the cost of the Apple Mac Classic II upgrade.

Accelerators using up to 40-MHz 68030 CPUs

Full-function accelerators in this category boost your Mac 128, 512, Plus, or SE logic board to 16 MHz or all the way up to 40 MHz for an investment of from $500 to $1500.

The Novy 16, 25, and 33-MHz 68030 solutions for Mac 128, 512, Plus, or

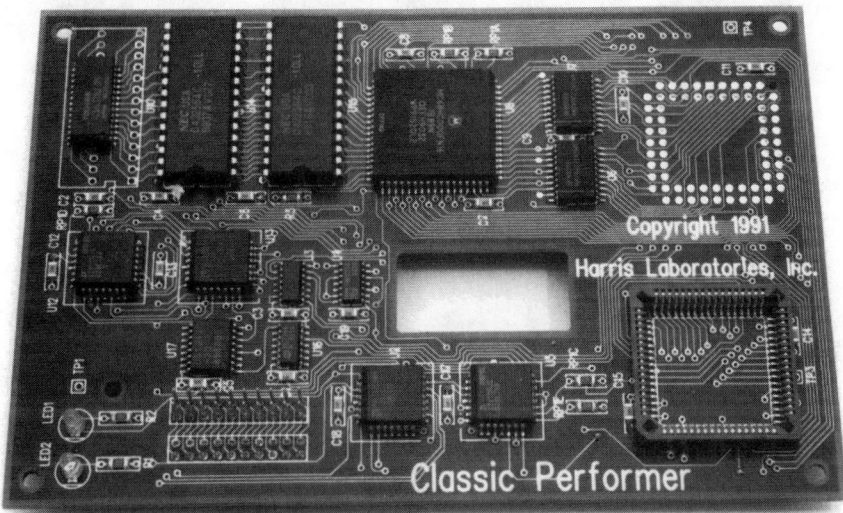

4-16 Harris Laboratories Performer accelerator for Mac Classic logic board.

SE logic boards are marketed directly by its System Technology Corp. division and licensed to other vendors who add enhancements and remarket them under other brands. The Novy Quik 30 solutions (shown in Fig. 4-17) feature complete kits with ease of clip-on installation, flexibility of expansion via SIMM and FPU sockets, enhanced control software, Apple System 7 compatibility, and full warranty. Novy's ImagePro combination accelerator/video cards give you accelerated one-page or two-page video monitor solutions. I'll talk more about them in chapter 6.

NewLife Computer's 25/33c solutions (its basic accelerator technology is licensed from Novy) are available in two versions: one for clip-on to the Mac 128, 512, and Plus logic boards (a SCSI port is optional), and the other for plugging in to the Mac SE logic board. Either gives you a full-function 68030/68882 combination. NewLife Computer adds flexibility by offering video expansion options compatible with a wide range of monitors to its full-function accelerator products. Figure 4-18 shows the New Life 25 accelerator card on the left and video card on the right. Performance of the NewLife (or Novy) 25-MHz accelerator boards is about the same—zoom! The NewLife 33, available only for the Mac SE logic board, is a still hotter solution featuring 256K of 25-ns static RAM (it offers zero-wait-state performance with 70 ns SIMMs). You get near Mac IIfx performance, usable on-board memory to 16Mb using Virtual 3.0, System 7 compatibility, plus video expansion options—all at a very attractive price.

Total Systems 16-MHz 68030 Mercury accelerator board provides an a la carte solution for this category. You can buy less to start with (for a lower cost) and expand it as your needs grow. The accelerator board is in the upper right of Fig. 4-19, the high-speed SCSI expansion card is in the upper left, and the

4-17 Novy Systems Quik 30 accelerator boards for Mac Plus and SE.

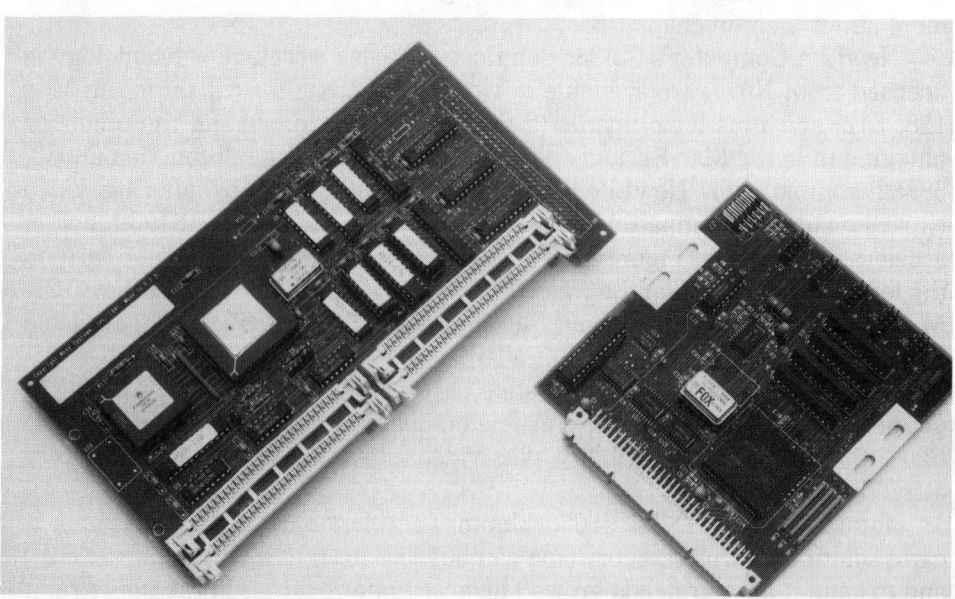

4-18 NewLife Computer NewLife 25 accelerator with companion video card on right.

4-19 Total Systems Mercury accelerator card lets you add only what you need.

32-bit RAM expansion card is beneath them both. All this capability is already on a full-function accelerator board; giving you the a la carte option merely makes it easier on your budget.

Applied Engineering's TransWarp SE accelerator for Mac SE logic boards, available in 16-, 25-, or 40-MHz 68030 flavors, rounds out the offerings in this category. Figure 4-20 shows the TransWarp LC above the TransWarp SE. It comes with 4 SIMM and 68882 sockets for expansion, features 32K of 25-ns SRAM cache, a video expansion connector, full System 7 compatibility, control software, and a SANE software patch ('882 Express) that improves math function processing by up to 500%. I've seen the TransWarp SE with 68882 offered mail order under $750 for the 25-MHz (near Mac IIci performance) version and under $1400 for the 40-MHz (near Mac IIfx performance) version. Cat Mac SE builders have never had it so good!

Accelerators using up to 50-MHz 68030 CPUs

Total Systems full-function Classic and Ultra 68030-based full-function accelerator board offerings boost performance all the way to 50 MHz on the Mac Classic, 128, 512, Plus, and SE logic boards. Mama mia!

Applied Engineering's TransWarp LC is a still more "tricked-up" version

Macintosh upgrades **101**

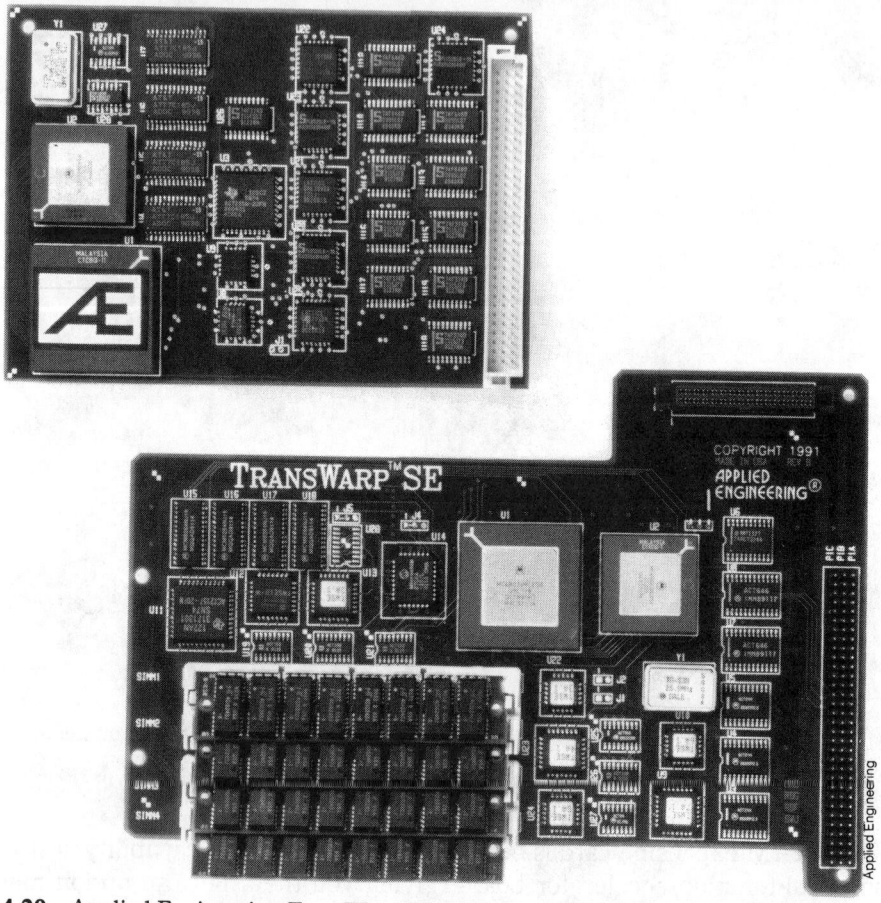

4-20 Applied Engineering TransWarp SE (lower) and TransWarp LC accelerators.

of the product introduced in the previous category available for the Mac LC logic board in 33-, 40-, and 50-MHz flavors. I've seen the TransWarp LC offered mail order under $750 for the 33-MHz version and under $1000 for the 40 MHz version. Obviously, at these prices, any of these are outstanding values for Cat Mac SE builders.

DayStar Digital has developed adapters for its popular, proven, and powerful PowerCache card, so the same board (with a different adapter) can run across the entire midrange of the Macintosh logic board line: Mac LC, Mac SE 30, Mac II, IIx, IIcx, IIci and IIsi. Its 33-, 40-, and 50-MHz PowerCache cards are high-performance logical alternatives to purchasing Mac IIci and IIfx logic boards for owners of other midrange Macintosh logic boards. And for flexibility, the DayStar Mac IIsi dual port adapter card includes a pass-through connector, allowing another PDS card (video, Ethernet, etc.) to be used in addition

102 *Memory and upgrades*

4-21 DayStar Digital PowerCache accelerator card and adapter for Mac IIsi on right.

to the PowerCache on the Mac IIsi logic board. Other Mac II adapters leave all your NuBus slots open. Figure 4-21 shows the PowerCache card on the left with the Mac IIsi dual port adapter on the right. DayStar Digital's performance testing has proven its Power Cache cards with 32K of 25-ns SRAM, a 40-MHz or 50-MHz 68030 CPU chip, and matching 68882 FPU chip can more than hold their own versus the new breed of 25-MHz 68040-powered accelerator cards. In addition they offer System 7 software compatibility and (unlike the 68040 accelerators) no incompatibility with existing Macintosh software. Plus the price is right: PowerCache 40- and 50-MHz models are available mail order for under $900 and $1300, respectively (about $150 more for FPU versions).

Accelerators using up to 55 MHz 68030 CPUs

You are no longer at a performance dead end as a Mac IIfx logic board owner. Newer Technology offers the fx/Overdrive accelerator that plugs into the Mac IIfx (all NuBus slots are still accessible) and pumps you up to 55 MHz of 68030 performance, including the 68882 FPU chip. You can select from 40-, 45-, 50-, 55-MHz modes via software. After installation, you benefit not only from speed improvements over the Mac Quadra and third-party vendor 25-MHz 68040 products, but also retain full software compatibility with Macintosh application programs. Your expenditure is under $2000.

TechNoir's Nexus fx product offers the identical 55-MHz 68030 performance to Mac IIfx logic board owners via a 128K 15-ns cache and other clever performance enhancements. Your tradeoff is a slightly more difficult installation (it requires soldering) versus a lower cost (in the $1100 ballpark). TechNoir also offers Mac II and IIx owners the same upgrade at under $3000.

Accelerators using 25-MHz 68040 CPUs

This is where the action is today. Fueled and given legimacy by Apple's Mac Quadra logic board introductions, five vendors have superb System 7-compatible solutions in this area. I'll position them for you.

Total Systems Magellan 040 offers Mac LC, SE 30, IIsi, and IIci logic board owners a solution via their PDS slot. PDS cards offer inherently faster execution over NuBus cards. Plus "smart" control software can be instructed to bypass incompatible software programs on the fly and switch into a non-copyback cache mode (the major source of the 68040 Macintosh software incompatibility problems).

Fusion Data Systems, maker of the first Macintosh 68040 accelerator, also offers solutions for Mac LC, SE 30, IIsi, and IIci logic board owners via the PDS or cache PDS (Mac IIci) slot. Its control software enhances application compatibility in two ways—either by turning off the 68040 caches when an incompatible application is run or by patching incompatible applications to run with the 68040 caches turned on. Slick.

The IIR Performance/040, a NuBus card solution marketed directly by its Impulse Technology Sales division, was recently reintroduced after the company regained the licensing rights it had sold to Sigma Designs. The card includes eight SIMM sockets (accommodates 4Mb to 128Mb of on-board RAM), control software that automatically disables the 68040s copyback and writethrough caches, and customizable software that allows maximum math-intensive software execution.

Applied Engineering's TransWarp 040 accelerator, shown in Fig. 4-22 (notice the giant 68040 chip!), utilizes technology acquired from now-defunct Siclone to achieve very fast performance on a NuBus card. It features eight SIMM sockets (up to 128Mb of on-board memory), offers block mode master/slave capabilities for peak SCSI and video performance, an on-board 040 PDS, and intelligent control panel software that recognizes the presence of incompatible software programs and turns accelerator and caches on or off as desired.

4-22 Applied Engineering TransWarp 040 accelerator—notice huge 68040 chip on left side of board.

Radius' Rocket 68040 family of accelerator products for NuBus Macintosh logic boards offers solutions at both ends of the spectrum. Its economy version, the Rocket 25i priced at under $1500, uses the lower-cost 68LC040 CPU chip to deliver nearly all the performance of a full-fledged 68040 chip except floating point. The original Radius Rocket 040 was optimized for graphics performance, so owners of this accelerator get the benefits of block mode NuBus video transfer support, built in QuickDraw, QuickColor and QuickCAD, plus the flexibility of eight SIMM sockets—a combination that delivers 25 mips (peak) and 3.6 Mflops according to Radius performance benchmarks. But the real story is software. Radius control panel software—RocketWare—is already the most innovative and flexible among all the accelerator vendor offerings in its class. Radius' Saturn 5 software expected in 1992 will allow the Radius Rocket accelerator to operate as an independent coprocessor on Mac Quadra logic boards—effectively giving Cat Mac builders two 68040 processors for the price of one in a single chassis. How sweet it is.

Accelerators using up to 33-MHz 68040 CPUs

Just so Mac Quadra logic boards have something to look forward to, Newer Technology offers the Quadra/Overdrive accelerator at under $350. While not really a full-function accelerator in the same class as other products in this category, it offers a daughterboard that replaces the 25-MHz 68040 chip with a hotter Motorola 33-MHz 68040 chip, giving you at least a third more performance out of your Mac Quadra logic board—again pushing the 68040 to king-of-the-hill performance status (even over the 55-MHz 68030 models).

Buying accelerators

You have learned that entry-level 68030 full-function accelerators cost under $500 via mail order, and that you can get a top-of-the-line model in the range of $1500 to $2000; that Mac IIfx owners can enjoy speedier performance for only $1100 more, and Mac Quadra owners for only $350 more; and that virtually any midrange Mac owner can enjoy all the functionality of a 68040 solution for an investment in the $1500 to $2500 price range. That about covers it. Although Table 4-6 summarized my recommendations, you must ultimately choose the best one for you based on your budget and how much performance you want. Now you have to go out and actually buy one. As a Cat Mac builder, the key in buying your accelerator board is keeping your future expansion options as open-ended as possible for the direction you want to go. Here are some pointers.

Buying checklist Figure out what your needs are and rank them in order of importance before you buy. Your buying checklist should contain at least the following:

- Video needs—This should be at the top of your list. Do you need color, size, or compatibility with a specific monitor? What does the accelerator

board provide now? What other video expansion options does it provide? If you are thinking of adding a bigger monitor later on, it pays to think now of what kind of monitor that is going to be, and make sure that the accelerator board you choose now supports it. Better still, buy them both now if you can afford to.
- Performance needs—Do you need a full-function accelerator, a boost in only one specific area, or both? Do you need FPU, more on-board memory for speed, PDS or NuBus compatibility? Make your list.
- Budget needs—Do you need it all now or can you stretch out your purchases over time? You can start with a Macintosh logic board, add an accelerator card, and later upgrade it to a hotter accelerator or better monitor. The installment approach means you pay more money overall but each step costs you less. You need to have your plan worked out before you do your shopping.

Software/hardware compatibility Make sure your accelerator works with the applications software you're using now and that it has Apple System 7 compatibility. Make sure it doesn't bomb or otherwise wipe out the use of a system function that you're presently enjoying or utilizing quite heavily. A software example of this might be a spreadsheet program that no longer functions when the accelerator is operating. Hardware examples might be the ability to read and write 1.4Mb Macintosh or DOS PC floppies, or to access high-speed I/O data. Make sure the accelerator you're considering doesn't require you to turn off its accelerated mode every time you need these functions. If it does, choose another accelerator.

Quality vendor Because the accelerator card and your Macintosh are almost inseparable, it behooves you to go with a brand name product from a reputable reseller or vendor-direct. You want to get quality, warranty, support, and a trial or test period during which it can be returned if it doesn't meet your needs. None of these are a problem with any of the quality vendors. If you do have problems, choose another vendor.

Sources

Apple upgrades are available through Apple dealers. New and used Apple upgrades are also available through the Apple used equipment dealers. Memory and accelerator boards are available directly from the manufacturer and through the mail order distributors.

Memory and upgrade suppliers

Chip Merchant
9541 Ridgehaven Ct., #A
San Diego, CA 92123
(800) 426-6375

Computer Care Inc.
Suite 1180, 420 N. 5th St.
Minneapolis, MN 55401
(800) 950-2273

Delta Research Labs
26802 Vista Terrace Dr.
El Toro, CA 92630
(800) 999-1593

Digi Graphics
764 E. Village Wy.
Kaysville, UT 84037
(801) 544-2009

Dove Computer Corp.
1200 N. 23rd St.
Wilmington, NC 28405
(919) 763-7913

LLB Company
300-120 Ave. NE., Bldg 7, #108
Bellevue, WA 99800
(800) 848-8967

MacProducts USA
8303 Mopac Expwy., #218
Austin, TX 78759
(800) 622-3475

Memory Masters
2023 O'Toole Ave.
San Jose, CA 95131
(800) 726-2897

Microtech International
29 Business Park Dr.
Branford, CT 06405
(800) 325-1895

NewLife Computer Corp.
20 Edgewater St.
Kanata, ON K2L 1V8 Canada
(800) 267-7231

Peripheral Outlet
327 E. 14th
Ada, OK 74820
(800) 256-6581

PSI
2005 Hamilton Ave., #200
San Jose, CA 95125
(800) 622-1722

Technology Works
4030 Baker Ln. W.
Austin, TX 78759
(800) 622-2210

Accelerator board suppliers

Applied Engineering
3210 Beltline
Dallas, TX 75234
(800) 554-6227

Daystar Digital
5556 Atlanta Hwy.
Flowerey Branch, GA 30542
(800) 962-2077

Dove Computer Corp.
1200 N. 23rd St.
Wilmington, NC 28405
(800) 622-7627

Fusion Data Systems
8920 Business Park Dr., #350
Austin, TX 78759
(512) 338-5326

Harris Laboratories
7379C Washington Ave. S.
Edina, MN 55439
(800) 783-3726

Impulse Technology Sales (div. IIR)
210 Dahlonega St., #205
Cummin, GA 30130
(404) 889-8294

New Life Computer Corp.
603 March Rd.
Kanata, ON K2K 2M5 Canada
(800) 663-6395

Newer Technology
1117 S. Rock Rd., #4
Wichita, KS 67207
(800) 678-3726

Novy Systems
1860 Fern Palm Dr.
Edgewater, FL 32141
(800) 638-4784

Radius
1710 Fortune Dr.
San Jose, CA 95131
(408) 434-1010

Second Wave Inc.
9430 Research Blvd., Echelon II, Suite 260
Austin, TX 78759
(512) 343-9661

TechNoir (div. Tyrell Corp)
150 Aviation Way
Watsonville, CA 95076
(408) 763-0250

Total Systems Integration
1720 Willow Creek Circle
Eugene, OR 97402
(800) 874-2288

---

[1] The Killy clip has its positive features and its drawbacks. On the plus side, it is quick and easy to connect or disconnect, positive contact is made, and no soldering is required. On the down side, clip-equipped Macs occasionally experience intermittent operation, with expansion/contraction of the logic board due to heating/cooling and oxidation/moisture being the most frequent reasons given for contact loss on pins.

[2] If you only have time to read a few, choose: Victoria van Biel, "How to buy memory," *MacUser*, February 1992, p. 259; Owen W. Linzmayer, "SIMMple Pleasures," *MacUser*, April 1991, p. 194; Bob LeVitus, "Memory-Upgrade Options," *MacUser*, June 1990, p. 299; Jim Heid, "Getting Started With Memory," *Macworld*, April 1990, p. 235; and Russell Ito, "The Persistence of Memory," *MacUser*, February 1989, p. 140. If you receive *MacWEEK*, David Ramsey's biweekly "Help Desk" articles are invaluable.

[3] Apple, *Guide to the Macintosh Family Hardware—2nd Edition*, Addison Wesley, 1990, chapter 5.

[4] If you only have time to read a few, choose: Adrian Mello, "The Accelerated Course," *Macworld*, July 1991, p. 211; Winn L. Rosch and *MacUser* Labs staff, "Chasing the IIfx: Accelerators," *MacUser*, August 1990, p. 84; and Cheryl England Spencer, "Full Speed Ahead," *Macworld*, August 1990, p. 134.

Chapter 5
Storage

Do you see the recurring theme for Cat Mac builders yet? If not, then this chapter will very clearly make the point.

What is the theme? Chapters 2 and 3 showed how Cat Mac builders got the most flexibility out of any given Macintosh logic board at the lowest cost. Chapter 4 showed how Cat Mac builders benefitted likewise from memory and accelerators—the most for the least. Ditto for storage devices in this chapter. Regardless of the Cat Mac project you build, you have far more ability to do exactly what you want with the storage device(s) you need at a lower cost than the average Apple Macintosh owner.

Why? Easy—Cat Mac builders have more chassis options. Do you anticipate needing a lot of different storage devices, like a Macintosh used in a network server application? Get a big tower chassis. Stuff it with a couple of full-height 1.2Gb hard drives, DAT backup drive plus 1.4Mb floppy drive and have lots of room left over. Even the smallest Cat Mac projects are likely to be put into DOS PC PS/2-sized chassis that have plenty of "cubbyholes" for adding an extra drive or two when you need it. Plus you save space (everything is inside one case); you add convenience (everything is powered from one on/off switch); and you save money (you can buy internal versions of the storage devices without the extra cost of external housings and power supplies).

There's more. Just like logic boards, memory, and accelerator boards covered in the previous chapters, the good news here is that prices have dropped on the basic storage devices you need (floppy and hard drives) since the first edition of the book. And new technology devices have replaced the old.

Wait, there's still more. Today, you have far more types of storage devices available to you at better prices than just a few years ago. Floppy drives, hard drives, removable drives, optical drives, and even tape drives are available to you.

Which storage devices do you choose for your Cat Mac project? How much capacity do you need? What are the pros and cons? This chapter will cover the topic for you. Of course, everything cannot be covered in one chapter. To learn more, read my book[1] plus the most recent articles on storage that appeared in *Macworld* and *MacUser*. Here, my objective is to give you the framework to make your own choices. Of course, you must still make the final decision yourself. To get started, I'll discuss some definitions and background, then cover the storage options, show you some products, make a few recommendations, and leave you with guidelines to make your own decisions.

Storage definitions

To begin with, you need to know something about the terms you are likely to encounter. Let's take a brief detour for a few definitions:

- Platters—Also called the *media*. This is the flexible disk medium in a floppy diskette (typically made of thin plastic with an even thinner magnetic coating on both sides of it) or the rigid disk medium in a hard disk (made of a metallic alloy or glass and magnetically coated).

- Drive—A floppy, hard, removable, or optical *disk* (or tape) mechanism is the physical disk itself. A controller is the device used to make it interact with your computer. In the SCSI-standardized Macintosh world, regardless of the type of storage being discussed, these two devices are usually found integrated together into one physically inseparable unit. The term *drive* (i.e., hard drive, floppy drive, optical drive, tape drive) will be used in this book to mean the *disk plus controller unit*.

- Cylinders, tracks, sectors—Like a phonograph record, floppy and hard disk platters have information stored on each side. Unlike a phonograph record's spiral, a computer disk's platter is recorded in concentric circles. Each side of a platter is called a *cylinder*. *Tracks* are the pattern of concentric circles or rings on the disk's surfaces established by the formatting software onto which the data is written. Frequently, cylinders and tracks are interchanged in usage. *Sectors* are the subdivided portions of the tracks. They are also called *blocks* and refer to a specific location on a given track onto which data is written. A Macintosh diskette might be formatted with 512 bytes of data in a sector or block. The interface reads or writes one sector at a time regardless of the amount of data actually being read from or written into the sector.

- Heads—Also called *read/write heads*. Almost, but not quite, like the tone arm of a record player. It would have to be a tone arm with no weight at its needle end that could go to any spot on the record instantly and transfer information at an almost unbelievable rate once it got there. On a floppy drive, heads on opposite sides of the media press it between them and the tiny electromagnets at the tip of the heads either read or write data. A hard disk functions the same way except the heads float on a cushion of air and never touch the platter's incredibly flat surface. A particle of dust is a giant boulder to a hard disk's heads, so all hard drives are sealed to prevent contamination.

- Formatting—When you first obtain a floppy, hard, or optical drive, although it has been tested at the factory, it is a clean slate to you as far as your purpose is concerned. Much like you would build sorting bins into the blank wall of a post office, the formatting step puts these specific track and sector "pockets" into your hard disk—it builds exact locations where you can later find data. To quickly move data on and off the disk, it identifies certain tracks as directory tracks. These contain information tags (flags or pointers) that point to or identify the location of data on the disk. When you delete data on a PC-DOS machine or throw an icon into the trash on a Macintosh, all you are doing is deleting its entry from the directory. The data is still there—until you write over it.

- Capacity—This refers to the amount of binary data in 8-bit bytes that can be stored on the disk platter's surface. Raw capacity is greater than when formatted—sections set aside for directory and housekeeping usage are not available for data. Formatted disk capacities depend on the computer, disk controller, and formatting software used.

- Average access time—Refers to the amount of time it takes, on average, to position the read/write heads over the track that holds the data. Be aware that not all disk average access times are "stated equal." Technically, it is defined as seek time (time to find the track) plus settling time (time to stabilize over the track) plus latency time (time to bring the sector data on the track under the head). Some manufacturers ignore both the average consideration and the latency factor to publish better times.
- Interleave—Depending on the speed of the computer attached to the hard disk, the computer might not be fast enough to read all the data from one sector transferred by the disk interface or to write it in one rotation of the disk. To avoid this problem, hard drives initially being formatted to work with slower Macintoshes have their sectors interleaved. A slow Mac Plus requires a 3:1 interleave. That means the next logical sector that the controller reads or writes data on actually skips two sectors over from the last "physical" sector located on the disk. A faster Mac SE requires a 2:1 interleave. The next logical sector read or written actually skips one sector over from the last physical sector located on the disk. Mac II's, Mac SE 30s, and up use a 1:1 interleave. The next logical sector read or written by the controller is identical with the physical sector located on the disk. Newer hard drives with internal buffering (such as those from Quantum) are shipped with fixed 1:1 interleave and automatically adjust to whatever Macintosh they are attached to.
- Fragmentation—On a freshly formatted hard drive, files are written to continuous and connected (i.e., *contiguous*) sectors and tracks. As you use the hard drive (erasing files, writing new ones, etc.) all the contiguous space eventually gets used up and new files are then written in pieces or "fragments" all over it. This is called *fragmentation* and greatly reduces hard drive performance.
- SCSI Interface (small computer system interface)—Refers to a high-speed bus that transfers data at 1.5Mb per second and allows you to daisy chain up to seven devices (disk drives, CD-ROM drives, tape drives, scanners, printers, etc.) each generating its own input and output traffic on the bus. SCSI hard drives contain an *embedded controller*, meaning an intelligent controller board is part of the disk drive package.
- Size and Height—Size refers to the diameter of the disk inside the enclosure—to its width—5 1/4" and increasingly 3 1/2" today. Height is a carry-over from early IBM DOS PC days. *Full-height* refers to a disk that takes up the entire height of the original PC front bezel opening designed to fit 5 1/4" wide disk cases. *Half-height* means half that dimension—you

stack two drives in that space. For today's new hard drives, the one-third height (approximately 1" high) 3½" size is the norm.
- MTBF (mean time between failures)—An MTBF rating of 50,000 hours does not mean each hard disk will last that long before needing repair. It means that in a population of 50,000 hard drives, one will fail every hour, 24 hours per day, or about 18% of the drives will have to be repaired before year's end. Over a three-year period, more than one-half (54%) of the original 50,000 hard drives will require some amount of service.

Storage overview

Storage affects your Cat Mac project in three forms: short-term, working, and long-term. The respective products that address these requirements today are floppy drives, hard drives, and backup devices (floppy, hard, removable, optical, and tape drives).

Short-term For short-term storage, all you really need is a device for getting data in and out of your Cat Mac. Floppy drives do this job nicely and are commonly used today. Early Macintoshes used only two 400K floppy drives—one had the system software on it; the other, applications and data. Today's standard is the 1.4Mb FDHD floppy, and larger capacities are now entering the market. Given the cost-performance benefits of hard drives today, a floppy drive should never be the only storage device on your Cat Mac project.

Working For working storage, you want the device for storing and using your Cat Mac's data on a day-to-day basis to have speed and capacity. Hard drives fit these criteria perfectly and offer the additional benefit of low price. During the Macintosh's brief lifetime, they have overwhelmingly improved in performance and dropped in price. The earliest 20Mb Macintosh hard drives were slow, attached to the Macintosh's serial port, and cost you at least $2000. Today's low-end 40Mb hard drives are faster, quieter, attach to the Macintosh's SCSI port, and cost you only slightly more than $200 mail order. Today, all new Apple Macintosh models are equipped with 40Mb or larger hard drives. You should follow the same guidance for your Cat Mac project.

Long-term For your long-term storage you want a device to back up your data for safety and/or preserve your data for archiving. In this area, low-end Cat Mac builders are (today and into the foreseeable future) thoroughly taken care of using floppy drives. As you increase the amount of data you want to store, removable cartridge or read/write optical drives typically come into play, with tape drives as a lower cost alternative.

For backup, when floppy drives no longer do the job for you, my experience suggests you next consider a removable cartridge or read/write optical drives. Both are quicker than a tape unit in storage/retrieval. Plus, with a removable or optical drive you go directly to the data you need to retrieve versus having to look serially through an entire tape. On the other hand, you get a lot more tape drive and media for your money.

For archival storage, optical wins over magnetic media. No matter what you do—dehumidifiers, air conditioning, etc.—your valuable data will gradually fade from its magnetic media. You also need to select a vendor and a drive mechanism that will be around as long as the media—so you can read your data![2]

Floppy drives

The performance of floppy drives used for getting data into and out of your Cat Mac has steadily improved over time. Owners of the original 1984-vintage Mac 128 that pioneered the use of 3½" diskette media had life easy—no choice was involved. Early Macintoshes could only use 400K floppy drives and you needed two of them—one had the system software on it, the other, applications and data. Today's Cat Mac builders can choose from five different floppy drive capacities:

400K floppy drive This is now obsolete. Although you can pick one up for $25 to $50, it is slower, offers the least storage capacity, and at this point is a solution only if you are contemplating a hobbyist or low-utilization word-processing use on your Cat Mac 128 or 512 system.

800K floppy drive This is still the most commonly found model. It is offered in two flavors: the Sony drive that Apple sells and the Fujitsu drive sold by everyone else. Either drive also reads and writes 400K diskettes. Street price on replacement Apple drives averages $175, and Fujitsu drives are available mail order for $99 from Cutting Edge and MacDirect. The reason for the lingering popularity of this model is twofold: the drive mechanism is most commonplace (five years of Apple Macintosh production included them), and the diskette media is the least costly—an 800K floppy diskette costs you less than $0.50. In the first edition of the book, the 800K Fujitsu drive was a mainstream product in plentiful supply and came with its own integrated front bezel—making life easy for Cat Mac builders. Today, Fujitsu is ramping down production, lower cost versions are packaged inside plastic housings that eliminate the need for a front bezel entirely, and the 800K drive itself is no longer that desirable. Cat Mac builders should only use 800K drives in special situations—must fit in a special package, lowest cost, etc. Figure 5-1 shows the Apple Sony 800K drive (plus the bracket it normally is packaged in) on the left, and the Fujitsu model and its typical Cat Mac mounting brackets on the right.

1.4Mb floppy drive Today's de facto standard is the Sony drive used in Apple's FDHD (floppy drive high density) and by other repackagers. Apple's FDHD (also called the SuperDrive) reads and writes 400K, 800K, and 1.4Mb

5-1 Comparison of 800K floppy drives and mounting brackets: Apple on left, Cutting Edge (Fujitsu) on right.

Macintosh 3¹/₂" diskettes, and also reads and writes DOS PC 3¹/₂" diskettes formatted at 720K and 1.4Mb. Street price on replacement Apple internal 1.4Mb drives averages $250 ($350 for the drive and ROM/SWIM upgrade kit). The reasons for all Cat Mac builders to use 1.4Mb floppy drives in any project today are compelling (if not overwhelming): Macintosh media compatibility—backward compatible with all older Macintosh diskette media formats plus compatible with current standard shipped on all of today's Apple Macintosh systems; DOS PC media compatibility—cross-compatible with current DOS PC 3¹/₂" 720K and 1.4Mb formats; higher capacity—the convenience of being able to store more data in the same physical space; and low additional cost versus the 800K drive—a 1.4Mb drive costs only $75 more ($250 versus $175), and a 1.4Mb diskette costs only $0.50 more ($1.00 versus $0.50). Figure 5-2 shows the Apple Sony 1.4Mb drive (plus the bracket it normally is packaged in) on the left, and ATS mounting bracket and integral faceplate bezel on the right.

Physically, the Apple Sony 1.4Mb floppy drive looks almost identical to the Apple Sony 800K floppy drive. You can tell them apart in two ways. One way is by turning them upside down as shown in Fig. 5-3 where my finger points to the Apple Sony 1.4Mb floppy drive on the right. You'll notice both of them have the word Sony prominently displayed on the flywheel label, but one of them indicates it is a Sony 1Mb drive and the other indicates it is a Sony 2Mb

5-2 Apple 1.4Mb floppy drive on left with ATS 5¼" mounting bracket on right.

5-3 Tell Apple Sony 800K from 1.4Mb floppy drives by reading label underneath—1.4Mb floppy on right.

drive (2Mb translates to 1.4Mb FDHD after formatting). The other way you can tell them apart is from the front. Figure 5-4 shows the front of a 1.4Mb floppy drive that has three microswitches on it (one on the left, two on the right side). My finger points to the two microswitches on its right side. The 800K floppy drive only has two microswitches in the front (one on each side).

Other 1.4Mb floppy drive solutions are also available to Cat Mac builders. External Sony-based floppy drives are available from Applied Engineering and

5-4 Apple Sony 1.4Mb floppy drive also has two microswitches at right front.

Quadmation for $229. PLI's external floppy drives, which utilize the Macintosh SCSI port for greater performance, include its Superfloppy (1.4Mb/ 800K), available mail order for $449, and its Turbofloppy (1.4Mb only) available mail order for $309. Kennect Technology's Rapport/Drive 2.4 gives the functionality of Apple's 1.4Mb floppy to all Cat Mac models and provides data compression—up to 2.4Mb (4Mb with Fastback II) can be stored on a standard high density 1.4Mb diskette. Mail order pricing for Rapport (the adapter) is $189 and for Drive 2.4 is $319. Dayna Communication's DaynaFile II is available at $449 mail order, for those who need to add the ability to read/write DOS PC 1.4Mb (or 720K) diskettes onto any existing 800K floppy-based Cat Mac.

2.8Mb floppy drive The newest standard. This drive offers increased speed as well as increased capacity because its new barium ferrite technology records data bits vertically rather than longitudinally in the track, so bit densities are higher—yielding higher bit data rates. The 2.8Mb floppy drive is positioned squarely as the 1.4Mb drive replacement (a 20 million drives per year market). While current drive and media prices are initially higher, there is no question that both will become competitive with 1.4Mb pricing in the future as volumes increase. IBM and NeXT have designed 2.8Mb floppy drives—downward compatible with 1.4Mb and 720K drives—into their newest products, making it certain that this technology will begin appearing in other manufacturer's products. Can Apple be far behind?

20.8Mb floptical drive The newest replacement market offering, this drive targets the 800,000 drives per year niche backup market. Its name is derived from its construction—an indelible servo track optical pattern is stamped into its $3^1/2''$ floppy diskette media surface. It is offered in two flavors:

Insite Peripherals' Floptical and Brier Technology's Flextra. Each product employs the same idea but a different approach. Each has licensed a number of vendors. Insite's drive is available from several third-party Macintosh drive vendors at around $600 mail order. Media costs approximately $30 per diskette. The Insite drive also reads and writes 720K and 1.4Mb diskettes, but not older Apple Macintosh 800K and 400K formats. The drive itself is of the one-third height 3½" size with integral controller—easily mounted in Cat Mac project chassis. So Cat Mac builders have an interesting alternative here—ten times as much storage on the same physical media size.

Figure 5-5 summarizes Cat Mac builder's floppy drive options and costs. The Apple Sony 1.4Mb floppy drive is recommended for all Cat Mac projects today. Don't build any Cat Mac project with 400K floppy drives. Build with the 800K floppy drive only under special circumstances and certainly consider augmenting or replacing those drives in existing Cat Mac models with a 1.4Mb floppy drive if the opportunity presents itself. Don't get too complacent with your 1.4Mb floppy drives because the 2.8Mb floppy drive will, in turn, replace it in a few years. Take a look at floptical drives if carrying a $30 20Mb floppy diskette in your shirt pocket makes sense to you.

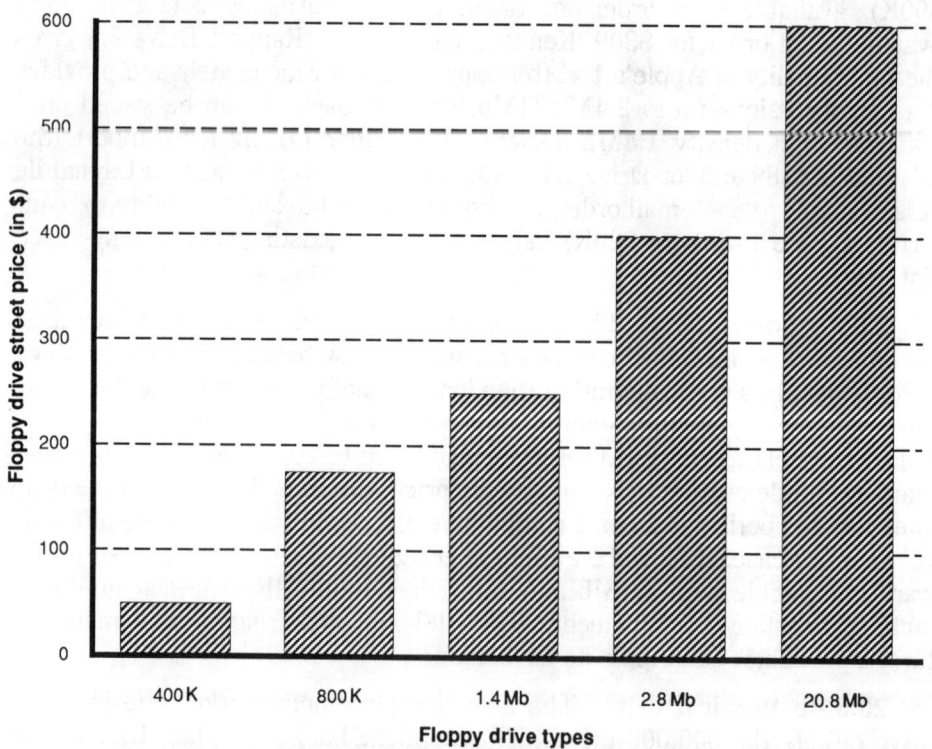

5-5 Cat Mac builder's floppy drive options.

Floppy drive upgrades

Usually, adding a new floppy drive to your Cat Mac involves nothing more than unplugging the old and replacing it with the newer model. Occasionally, third-party vendors require that software be changed, but their instructions are very explicit and you will have no trouble with the changes. Apple has only three floppy drive upgrades that also involve changing the ROM chips on your logic board (Table 2-4 of chapter 2 summarized them): adding 800K floppy drive to the Mac 512 logic board, and adding a 1.4Mb floppy drive to older Mac SE or Mac II logic boards. Table 5-1 summarizes the ROM and SWIM chip part numbers and locations for the three upgrades. Figure 5-6 shows the ROM locations on the Mac 512 logic board and the low ROM chip being removed using a chip puller. The ROM locations for the Mac SE logic board and Mac II logic boards are shown in Fig. 5-7 and Fig. 5-8, respectively. The process could not be simpler:

- Thoroughly ground or discharge yourself first and use an antistatic wrist strap.
- Remove old ROM (IWM) chip.
- Reinstall new ROM (SWIM) chip.
- Don't mix old and new ROMs.
- Reinstall new chips with same orientation—dimple in same direction—as removed chips.

Do not coerce your 800K floppy diskettes

Although 800K floppy diskettes resemble 1.4Mb floppy diskettes—differing only by an extra hole punched in the plastic protective housing—you cannot make 1.4Mb Macintosh floppy diskettes from your 800K ones by just punching another hole in the corner. I know you've read it in the first edition, there are tools available to help you and a lot of you have already tried it, just like myself. It can work for you for awhile and then Murphy's law will come into play—exactly at the time when you don't want it to happen! My advice to you today is don't do it.

There are two reasons why it cannot work dependably: the media and the drives. The 800K diskettes coercivity specification is 600 Oersteds, the 1.4Mb

Table 5-1. Macintosh floppy drive upgrades ROM chip part numbers.

IC chip/number & location	Mac 512	Mac SE	Mac II
ROM, high	342-0341-C	342-0701 D6	661-0639 U6
ROM, medium high	—	—	661-0640 U5
ROM, medium low	—	—	661-0641 U4
ROM, low	342-0342-B	342-0702 D7	661-0642 U3
SWIM	—	344-0062 D8	344S0062 U66

5-6 Two ROMs to upgrade a Mac 512 logic board.

diskette's is 720 Oersteds. Their respective drive mechanisms are obviously set up accordingly. What this means to you is the 1.4Mb media is more sensitive to magnetism, the 800K media less. If you punch a hole in it and use the 800K media in your 1.4Mb drive, because its weaker write head is not set up to magnetize the less magnetically sensitive 800K media correctly every time, you are flirting with disaster. Conversely, if you should happen to load your 1.4Mb media in an 800K drive and format it as an 800K floppy, the blast you give the 1.4Mb diskette's magnetic surface with the much stronger 800K drive's write head makes the 1.4Mb diskette unusable as a 1.4Mb floppy ever again—you can't go back and reformat it.

What should you do? Use Stuffit, Disk Doubler, Fastback with compression—a number of products let you quickly and safely put more data onto your 800K diskettes. And you don't have to spend time cutting extra holes in them. The final choice is yours, but I believe you'll sleep better at night.

Hard drives

For your working storage, you want the device for storing and using your Mac's data on a day-to-day basis to have speed and capacity. Hard drives fit the

5-7 Three chips (two ROMs plus IWM) to upgrade a Mac SE logic board.

5-8 Five chips (four ROMs plus IWM not shown) to upgrade a Mac II logic board.

bill nicely. But hard drives come in fixed and removable flavors and with magnetic, optical, and combination media. Which type should you use? Although there are exceptions, your working storage needs are best met today by fixed magnetic media hard drives. Because hard drives fit the speed and capacity criteria perfectly and offer the additional benefit of low price, I will deal with them first. The sections that follow cover removable and optical drives.

Magnetic media hard drives have changed drastically since their first introduction in the 1950s—this technology trend continues today. Next to memory and CPU chips, hard drives are the number one reason for the increase in the number of personal computers currently installed. Today, 2Gb $5^{1}/_{4}''$, 600Mb $3^{1}/_{2}''$ and 240Mb $2^{1}/_{2}''$ hard drives are a fact of life. And there is no end in sight—over the next ten years, the ability to store information on a given size hard disk is expected to increase tenfold. Their increased storage capacity, smaller size, reduced access time, and much lower cost has brought their benefits within reach of every personal computer user.

Remember the old-time music jukebox in the corner restaurant? Its 78- or 45-rpm record platters were stored in a stack or bin. When you made your selection, the record with your music on it would be moved into place and the pickup arm with the needle in it would be moved over the starting groove on the record. While the Quantum Q250 40Mb $5^{1}/_{4}''$ hard drive shown in Fig. 5-9 works in a similar fashion, its technology is a universe away (only mid-1980s technology—Apple first used it in the Mac II model introduced in 1987). Its

5-9 Inside a Quantum $5^{1}/_{4}''$ half-height drive.

platter is a perfectly flat, highly polished metal disk rather than a vinyl plastic one, with a thin magnetic oxide layer deposited on it to a high tolerance of purity and uniformity rather than grooves. Like the jukebox, multiple platters and read/write heads can be stacked for higher capacities. Its read/write head is a tiny electromagnet at the end of an arm that has been optimized for minimum mass rather than a pickup arm with a phonograph needle in it. This read/write head goes directly to the location on the disk it wants—moved in precise increments using servo feedback technology—rather than waiting for the record to spiral around to it. Digital data going to and from its read/write heads is moving at 5Mb/second rates rather than the analog audio data collected by the needle at up to 20 KHz/second rates. And, unlike the jukebox, every hard drive is sealed from the surrounding air—a tiny particle of dust is like a giant boulder to its delicate read/write heads.

Why buy a hard drive

Anyone building a Cat Mac today with the intention of doing serious work on it should add a hard drive. Why? Three reasons: speed, cost, and convenience. All new Apple Macintosh models (except the PowerBook 100 2/20 and PowerBook 140 2/20) are equipped with 40Mb or larger hard drives. You should follow the same guidance. Today, you can buy a new Quantum LPS 52Mb internal hard drive through a mail order reseller for under $250—equal to the street price of an Apple 1.4Mb internal FDHD floppy drive. The floppy rotates at 300 rpm. The hard drive rotates at 3600 rpm. Bottom line, you get over ten times faster retrieval speed and over 35 times more storage capacity for the same cost outlay. Not only that, but all your applications and data are on your desktop, and you can take advantage of Apple's new System 7—which doesn't run off a floppy.

When you build your own Cat Mac, you can save even more. Many standard Apple Macintosh models can only be expanded by adding an external hard drive. This means you have another chassis case housing plus another power supply—more money. One of the byproducts of building your own Macintosh in a DOS PC case is that the power supply and case you need for the hard drive are already there. The DOS PC case is already set up to power and mount your Macintosh hard drive (it's designed to do the same task for DOS PC hard drives), with no need for a separate case.

When you build your own Cat Mac, you also have more flexibility. You can be bold, brave, adventuresome. Put a full-height, $5^{1}/_{4}"$ 2Gb hard drive alongside your Mac SE logic board! You can reap the greatest rewards from your Cat Mac project in this area. The inside of almost any Cat Mac chassis gives you space that the original Macintosh designers at Apple could only dream about. You can easily mount multiple $3^{1}/_{2}"$ or $5^{1}/_{4}"$ drives in this space and maybe even several of each if you have opted for the tower configuration chassis.

Now that you know you need a hard drive, let's address the topics of what to buy, who to buy it from and how much to spend. Since Cat Mac builders are a cost-conscious lot, I'll start with the last subject first.

Hard drive pricing and what to buy revisited

Today, the 40Mb hard drive is rapidly being superseded by larger capacity models as the most popular choice. Your choice really depends on your individual needs—current and projected. With Word, Excel, Pagemaker, and a couple of other graphics and business programs loaded, 20Mb of your hard drive is already filled—how much more space you need for data is up to you. As a rule of thumb, remember Parkinson's Law about data expanding to fill the space available on your hard drive, and buy more than you need. Today, 40Mb would be an absolute minimum, 80Mb to 105Mb probably about right. A byproduct of buying a larger hard drive is that speed usually increases (or access times go down) as hard drive capacity rises. Your larger hard drive will be faster than your smaller hard drive. Don't let anyone tell you different—faster is always better.

In the first edition, I included a table in this section comparing hard drive prices from Apple and others and said, "please consider this information subject to change early and often." I didn't know how right I was. To say that hard drive prices have dropped drastically since then would be an understatement. Apple dropped all hard drives except an 80Mb model in 1991 due to the fierce competitive pricing pressure. And several other vendors have just gone out of or left the business (Crate, Jasmine, Rodime). For this edition, I've included a price trends chart which I believe you will find more valuable.

Figure 5-10 tells the story, current as of the end of 1991. It shows the decline in pricing for popular Quantum internally mounted hard drive models available from one mail order hard drive vendor (taken from its *MacWEEK* advertisement). What can you glean from it? First, notice that hard drive prices declined by almost 50% in the 24 months covered by the chart! The 210Mb and 105Mb models were selling below the cost of the 105Mb and 40Mb models, respectively, of only 24 months earlier. If you extrapolate Fig. 5-10 through the end of 1992, the LPS 52 should drop below $200, the LPS 105 drop to the LPS 52's price, and the Pro 210 drop into the $400 region.

There are two messages for you here. First, more costs less. Comparing the 52Mb to the 105Mb situation, you get twice the capacity for only one-third more. Buy the bigger drive if your budget allows it. Second, don't buy a lot more capacity than you need because tomorrow it will cost you less.

For most Cat Mac builders, the Quantum LPS 105 at $339 or Pro 210 at $629 hard drives would be good high-capacity choices, with the LPS 52 hard drive at $229 as a light-utilization alternative. Frankly, as you've already noticed, I simply cannot say enough about the Quantum LPS 52 shown in Fig. 5-11—it's a fast, rock-solid workhorse and the price is certainly right. Quantum's newest 425Mb model at $1299 would be a cost-effective heavy-utilization alternative. Add $80 to $100 for external models with "zero-footprint"

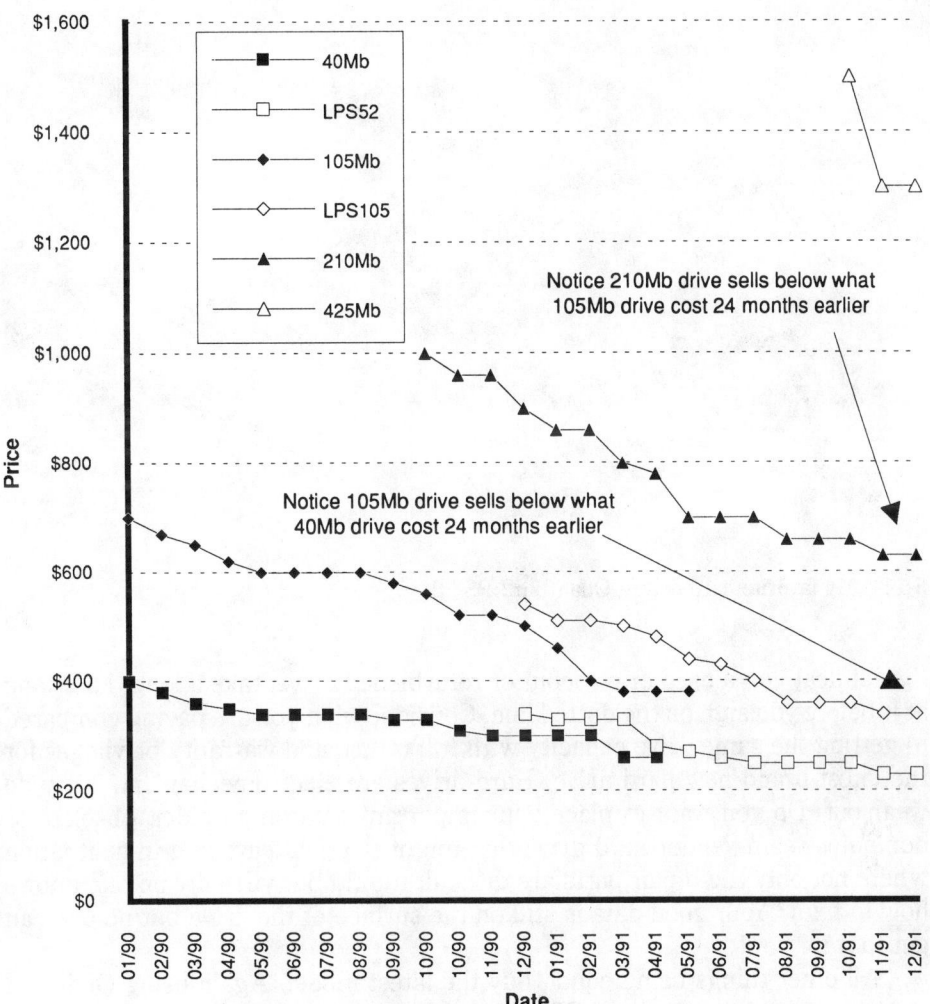

5-10 Hard drive pricing trends for one reseller over 24 month period.

housings. If you are paying significantly more than the prices mentioned here from Fig. 5-10, make sure what you are buying and who you are buying it from justifies your additional outlay.

Notice that new model introductions heavily lowered the cost of existing drives as the vendor moved to clear out its inventory. This is a buying opportunity for you. There is nothing wrong with buying the identical new 105Mb hard drive that cost $699 in January 1990 for $379 in June 1991. You can still expect to obtain three to five years of performance from it while saving almost half your investment! Do take advantage of closeouts on mainstream, proven-reliable new hard drives from established vendors.

One other little tidbit. Do not buy a used hard drive. If you are offered a

5-11 My favorite hard drive—Quantum LPS 52.

"great deal" on a used or closeout or refurbished drive, take a long, hard look at it before you sign on the dotted line. Consider what you are paying compared to getting the same drive capacity with full return and warranty privileges for the latest brand new hard drive. Hard drives are electromechanical. They do wear out. Do you want to place your important data on an older, obsolete or nonmainstream vendor hard drive that might fail and leave you in a situation where not only the repair parts are difficult to find but virtually no one knows how to fix it? Your good data is still on the surface of the drive but no one can get to it for you!

All other things being equal, buy the latest model. Again using Quantum as the example, its newest LPS series drive (e.g., LPS 105 versus ProDrive 105) is superior in every way to its predecessor: speed, reliability, cost, size, and weight. The same holds true for other vendors. The reason is better technology, and there is no end in sight. Hard drive capacity will be increased by increasing the number of tracks per inch; performance by increasing the number of bits per track. These will both occur because of technological improvements in media. Platters will be made even smoother (flatter), and metallic thin-film cobalt-nickel alloys will replace iron oxides so that more bits can be packed closer together on the media (and be easier to magnetize by the head) yet more resistant to magnetization by their neighboring bits. Read/write Heads will fly closer to the media, head gaps will be made smaller, and newer thin-film heads will use magneto-resistive technology. Still more sophisticated electronics techniques will be developed to obtain faster data throughputs via more use of caching, error detection/correction encoding, and array/mirroring.

Who to buy from

Hard drives involve three levels of vendor functions: manufacture, repackaging, and distribution. The hard drive manufacturers list has undergone some consolidation recently, but the main Macintosh market players include Quantum, Seagate, Connor, Maxtor, Micropolis, Fujitsu, IBM, Hewlett-Packard and Sony—to name a few. All the other vendors repackage these manufacturers' drives. The distinction between vendors who package versus those who distribute hard drives has become increasingly blurred because the market has become lowest cost driven as more purchases are made through the mail order channel. In a sense these vendors are also victim to today's better quality products. The quality of the raw drives along with that of external drive enclosures, power supplies, internal mounting brackets, SCSI/power cables, and formatting software has somewhat eliminated the need for a middleman. And it always pays to shop around. Not only do you learn a lot, but the same hard drive can vary widely in price among the different suppliers—reflecting their own supply/demand and competitive situation at any given point in time—and you can save a lot too.

So my "who you buy from" advice has to be somewhat generalized. Buy a quality product—a mainstream hard drive with a good reputation and specifications—from a high-profile, quality vendor—someone you asked around about and who has checked out. Then be sure you are getting at least a one-year warranty (some vendors offer more) and a full return privilege if the product for any reason doesn't meet your specifications. None of the quality distributors would hesitate to honor these terms. By taking these steps, even if this is your first attempt, you can sleep nights!

To be honest with you about my biases, I have been buying Quantum drive mechanisms repackaged by Alliance Peripheral Systems in both internal and external flavors with brackets, cables, terminators, software, and manuals for the past several years with total satisfaction. It's hard to top Quantum drives for reliability and performance. And you'd have to get up pretty early in the morning to beat Alliance Peripheral Systems in price, attention to detail, and overall customer satisfaction. But there are hundreds of hard drive manufacturers, distributors, and resellers not mentioned here. You might want to check out the advertising pages of *Macworld*, *MacUser* or *MacWEEK* and also the *Macintosh Product Registry* before making your purchase.

Mounting and connecting your hard drive

Now that you have purchased your hard drive, all that remains is for you to install it into your Cat Mac chassis and hook it up. Installing your hard drive is no more difficult than hooking up your stereo, if you observe a few simple rules:

- Always connect and disconnect your hard drive cables and/or SCSI jumpers with the power off.

- Make sure you have discharged yourself of static electricity before you handle your hard drive. Don't grab it like you would a ham and cheese sandwich—handle it only by its edges and keep your fingers away from the controller board and connector pins.
- Heat, static electricity, lack of adequate air circulation, and an inadequate or unstable power source are the only real hard drive killers. If you don't store it in the icebox or oven, or shuffle across the rug with it before installation, or drop, bump, or bang it during installation, and you operate it from the same power outlets the elevator motors use after installation, chances are it will live a long and healthy life.

With those instructions emblazoned on your mind, there are really only five steps involved in hooking up your hard drive.

Physical mounting The good news is that not only were you able to purchase the least expensive "internal" mount model, but installing it into your Cat Mac chassis is a snap. Figure 5-12 shows three generations of SCSI hard drives from Quantum. From left to right you are looking at a 5¼" half-height model (1987 vintage), a 3½" half-height model (1988 vintage) and a 3½" third-height model (1990 vintage). Notice the almost identical location of the 4-pin power connectors, SCSI 50-pin drive connectors, and SCSI ID jumpers on each. My experience has shown that well over 90% of the time, Cat Mac builders are dealing with one of these sizes. To mount them, merely bolt them into the appropriate opening of your chassis. You can also mount a 3½" hard drive in a 5¼" opening—using a special mounting adapter—you'll see how it's done in chapter 9.

The power connector Hooking up your hard drive is equally simple. The hard drive requires a source of +5 V and +12 Vdc power and a solid ground. Your hard drive's industry-standard 4-pin power socket is keyed to accept the mating industry-standard 4-pin power plug from any DOS PC-style Cat Mac

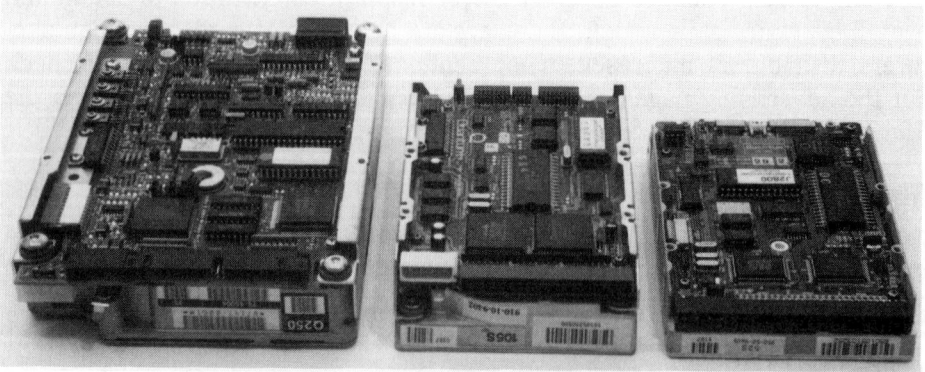

5-12 Three generations of Quantum hard drives.

chassis (all will have one or more plugs from the power supply available). Just plug it in.

The SCSI cable SCSI hookup is equally simple. In most instances, you are directly connecting the 50-pin SCSI socket on the back of the hard drive to the 50-pin SCSI connector socket on your Cat Mac logic board. All it takes is a 50-pin SCSI ribbon cable with two 50-pin plugs on it.

The SCSI ID jumpers SCSI ID jumpers are equally simple. Up to seven devices can be connected to a Mac logic board's SCSI port(s). Each device therefore has an address between 0 and 6. You set the address you want your hard drive to have by adjusting the shorting blocks on its SCSI jumper connector. Table 5-2 shows your choices. Figure 5-13 shows you the six SCSI jumper pins A0, A1, A2 just to the right and behind the 50-pin SCSI connector on the back of a Quantum Pro 105Mb half-height $3^1/2''$ hard drive.

Table 5-2. Hard drive SCSI jumpers.
A "1" means jumper is in,
a "0" means jumper is out.

SCSI Address	A2[1]	A1	A0
0	0	0	0
1	0	0	1
2	0	1	0
3	0	1	1
4	1	0	0
5	1	0	1
6	1	1	0
7	reserved for Macintosh		

[1]Quantum uses this A2, A1, A0 designation for their on-drive jumper pins. Conner uses E3, E2, E1 instead. Find your vendor's SCSI ID jumper designations and location from the installation manual.

SCSI termination All internal Macintosh hard drives are shipped with internal terminating resistor "packs" already in place. You don't have to do anything except make a quick visual check. If, for some reason, they are not installed (i.e., you removed the drive from an external case, etc.), Fig. 5-13 also shows how easy it is to do. The three termination resistor packs just plug into the matching holes directly behind the SCSI connector. Just match the polarity dot on the resistor pack with the arrow on the circuit board and insert it into the circuit board's holes.

Formatting your hard drive

It used to be that you needed a resident software genius to format your hard drive and install your driver software on it. But not today. This is another area

5-13 SCSI ID jumper pins and resistor terminator packs for Quantum half-height 3½" hard drive.

that has changed substantially since the first edition of this book. Every Macintosh hard drive reseller or repackager now ships its hard drive to you preformatted with Apple Macintosh System software already installed. In addition, at no extra cost, they all provide software that allows you to reformat your hard drive and even repartition it into separate volumes at the click of a mouse. Anyone can use today's hard drive formatting software.

Every reseller's or repackager's formatting program will work on their own hard drives, but not necessarily on any others. If you are working with multiple drives and/or need to do something that basic formatting software doesn't provide, I recommend you take a look at any of these products:

- FWB's 8-module Hard Disk Tool Kit—This kit does it all, the best of any power HD utility.
- La Cie's Silverlining—Close behind the Hard Disk Tool Kit, good for formatting and partitioning.
- Casa Blanca Works Drive 7—Nearly all the features of Silverlining at a lower price.

- MacPeak's Spot On—Uniquely optimizes your drive for speed plus formatting, etc.
- Software Architect's Formatter 5—Flexibility with DOS partitions and other media.

Removable drives

Removable drives enter the picture when you want to back up your primary hard drive and you have more data than fits on a floppy; or you need to protect data for security reasons; or you need to ship a large amount of data over a distance. Removable drives come from two schools of thought—each has multiple variants within it. The first school says make the external housing and power supply stationary and add a bracket to make a standard hard drive removable so you can take it with you. The second school says just make the media itself removable. Each school has its pros and cons. Cat Mac builders win in either case because again—as was the case with hard drives—only the internal mechanism needs to be purchased; no external case and power supply is necessary.

Remove the hard drive

The housing, bracket, and hard drive school was pioneered by Tandon in 1987 for DOS PCs. The newest Macintosh entrant is none other than Quantum with its Passport XL line in late 1991. I have found it useful for high-reliability, high-security environments and individuals who need to take their data back and forth between office and home and don't want to carry their CAT Mac back and forth too.

Wetex International makes a frame and adapter combination at roughly $120 that allows Cat Mac builders the further flexibility of mounting whatever $3^{1}/_{2}''$ hard drive they choose in it. Figure 5-14 shows a Quantum $3^{1}/_{2}''$ hard drive mounted in the Wetex removable slide in adapter pack, pulled halfway out of its mounting frame—with everything resting on its plastic carrying case. As an example of real life operation, you install an adapter into both your home and office Cat Mac. Then each day at closing time, you shut down your office Cat Mac, unlock the hard drive pack, put it in the plastic and foam carrying case that comes with it, take it home with you, and plug it into your home Cat Mac adapter. The newest Macintosh $3^{1}/_{2}''$ hard drives accommodate 425Mb and more, and the tiny carrying case beats the heck out of carrying around a whole computer (even a laptop) and your precious data never leaves your sight. Slick.

Remove the media

The remove-the-media school has three divisions: overall market leader Iomega; Macintosh market leader SyQuest; and newcomer Ricoh a far distant third. SyQuest and Ricoh package hard drive technology in a removable car-

5-14 Wetex removable hard drive frame and adapter, carrying case, and Quantum 3 1/2" hard drive.

tridge. Iomega's Bernoulli design resembles a large floppy. While offering the same performance as some hard drives—none of these removable cartridge drives is suitable as your main system drive—in the Bernoulli case it is particularly not advisable because you just wear the media out and expose yourself to data loss in the process.

SyQuest is the de facto leader in the Macintosh 44Mb removable cartridge media market with an installed base of over 500,000 drives. This tremendous installed base—one out of every ten Macintosh users—directly maps to convenience and security. Chances are the typesetter across the country you want to ship your large graphics file to also has access to a SyQuest drive. Or if you go down, you know of another SyQuest owner nearby who can help you out in a pinch. Plus the SyQuest SQ555 44Mb price—under $500 for the drive and under $70 for the media—is an overwhelming advantage over the alternative removable cartridges. Plus there are numerous sources for both the drives and the cartridges. The new SyQuest SQ5110 88Mb drive can read from, but not write to, its 44Mb predecessor and is universally available from mail order sources at $650. The 88Mb media goes for $120.

Ricoh took SyQuest's design one step further and redesigned the cartridge (making it user-proof!) so that it can no longer be inserted backwards, and at the same time sealed it better—providing its rigid media with an environment more closely resembling a real hard drive. But the 50Mb Ricoh drive is new, its installed base is very small, both the drive (at $900) and media (at $100) are relatively expensive compared to SyQuest and there are far fewer sources for product.

Iomega's Bernoulli design employs flexible media inside its rigid cartridge—it resembles a large floppy. The "Bernoulli" principle—the air flow that pulls the flexible media toward the heads in operation—results in a drive media whose surfaces are virtually immune to head crashes. But the thin plastic flexible media also has its down side: it wears out with use due to the continual flexing, and it's more susceptible to heat. Storing a SyQuest or Ricoh removable cartridge in your car trunk on a hot summer's day is no big deal—doing the same with an Iomega cartridge would probably destroy it. Iomega was the first to arrive in the Macintosh market, but kept its distribution channel small, its 44Mb drive and media prices high (these were $1200 and $120 respectively), and focused on selling to the DOS PC world. Thus, its Macintosh installed base is small. Apparently, the more sophisticated Macintosh market perceived the Iomega drive and media to be overpriced, bulkier, and noisier relative to competitive offerings, and few Macintosh owners had ever experienced hard drive head crashes—the primary Iomega benefit. Like the new SyQuest drives, new generation Iomega 90Mb drives can read from but not write to lower capacity Bernoulli cartridges. They are available from a limited number of mail order sources at $800, and the 90Mb media goes for $150.

Removable cartridge-media drives offer Cat Mac builders significant benefits. They are cost-effective as your storage needs expand (additional cartridges are less expensive than additional hard drives), and you can offload your less-used data to a cartridge drive yet have it instantly available at your fingertips. The "instant" aspect also makes them more popular than tape drives as backup devices for users who want to accomplish backup or retrieval quickly. Finally, they offer the security of removable hard drives but the convenience of only having to store the media. Figure 5-15 shows an APS SyQuest SQ555 44Mb drive ready for installation in a Cat Mac chassis $5^1/_4''$ opening.

Optical drives

When asked in the movie *Officer and a Gentleman* what he wanted to fly, Richard Gere answered, "Jets—all the way, sir." If you asked me my first choice for a backup device, the answer would be, "Optical—all the way," delivered in the same tone of voice used by Mr. Gere. Optical drives are the jet planes of the storage business.

Notice I said backup device. Some optical media evangelists would have you believe that optical drives are quickly going to replace hard drives (and all

5-15 APS SyQuest SQ555 44Mb drive ready for installation in Cat Mac 5¼" chassis opening.

other media!). With all deference and respect to these learned people, that is simply not going to happen. The same technology that guarantees you can write tremendous amounts of data in a small space, is impervious to stray magnetic fields and head crashes, and whose media life is measured in decades, also guarantees that current optical drives will never be as fast as most current hard drives. But this has never really been an issue. As a general rule of thumb, you buy hard drives to give you performance, and back them up with optical drives whose removable cartridge media give you access to unlimited volumes of data storage. Once again Cat Mac builders win because (as was the case with hard drives) only the internal mechanism needs to be purchased; no external case and power supply is necessary.

For your long-term storage you want a device to back up your data for safety and/or preserve your data for archiving. While optical drives might never compete successfully with hard drives in read/write speed, there are many sound reasons why, in their three different flavors, each type holds the most promise for future dominance of its market niche:

- Magneto Optical (MO) or Erasable Optical (EO)—Read and Write. Backup device with 600Mb per cartridge (5¼") or 128Mb per cartridge (3½"). Widespread use for backup, archiving, and transport of larger files required by scientific, database, and CAD/CAM applications.
- Write Once Read Many (WORM)—Read only after writing once. Archi-

val device with 600 to 800Mbs per cartridge. Niche use for computer-age replacement of microfiche.
- CD-ROM—Read only, just like those in your stereo system. Distribution device with 400Mb to 500Mb per disk. Widespread use for distribution of computer software and information because of the convenience of the media.

Optical drive benefits

Because a laser can accurately focus its beam in an extremely small spot, optical drives can store more information in less space than hard drives can. Also, because they use a laser, the read/write heads of an optical drive don't need to be as close to the surface of the media, and as a result optical drives are not subject to surface wear and head crashes. Optical drives are also impervious to external magnetic fields or radiation (even the MO drive, which uses magnetic media, is virtually impervious to external magnetic fields because you would have to heat the media to 300 degrees centigrade to change the magnetic state of its bits). The protective outer layers of any optical diskette protect it from fingerprints and dust, and further protection is provided by its plastic cartridge or CD-ROM caddy. Unlike magnetic media, surface dirt and scratches are ignored by the laser when it reads the data. Because of its sealed construction and protective layers, optical media is not subject to oxidation or corrosion and has a shelf life of 10 to 20 years—several times that of magnetic media.

For the last several years, MO and WORM drives have labored under the stigma of high price ($3000 to $4000 for the drive), slower access times than hard drives, bulky drive electronics, and $5^{1}/_{4}''$ media. CD-ROM drives have been hampered by the "chicken or the egg" phenomenon—not enough of the right types of programs to justify their purchase. As the graph of MO, WORM, and CD-ROM shipments over time in Fig. 5-16 shows, the optical drive market is about to change rapidly and drastically.[3] CD-ROM drives (at today's average unit price of $500 to $700) dominate the current installed-base picture. Their use will simply become more widespread as applications proliferate and drive prices decline. MO drive use (at today's average unit price of $2500 to $3000) becomes increasingly significant over time as $3^{1}/_{2}''$ drives enter the market at lower prices and increasing media storage capacities. WORM drive use (at today's average unit price of $3000 to $3500) actually declines slightly as they lose market share to both CD-ROM and more cost-effective MO devices. While Sony, Ricoh, and Canon dominate the picture, the manufacturing community for the optical drive market is made up of some of the largest electronics companies in the world. Each has invested substantially in this market and you can bet that they will continue to pour resources into it as it grows. What this means is you can expect both quality and technical excellence in the products that evolve. Let's look at MO, CD-ROM, and WORM devices and what they hold in store for Cat Mac builders.

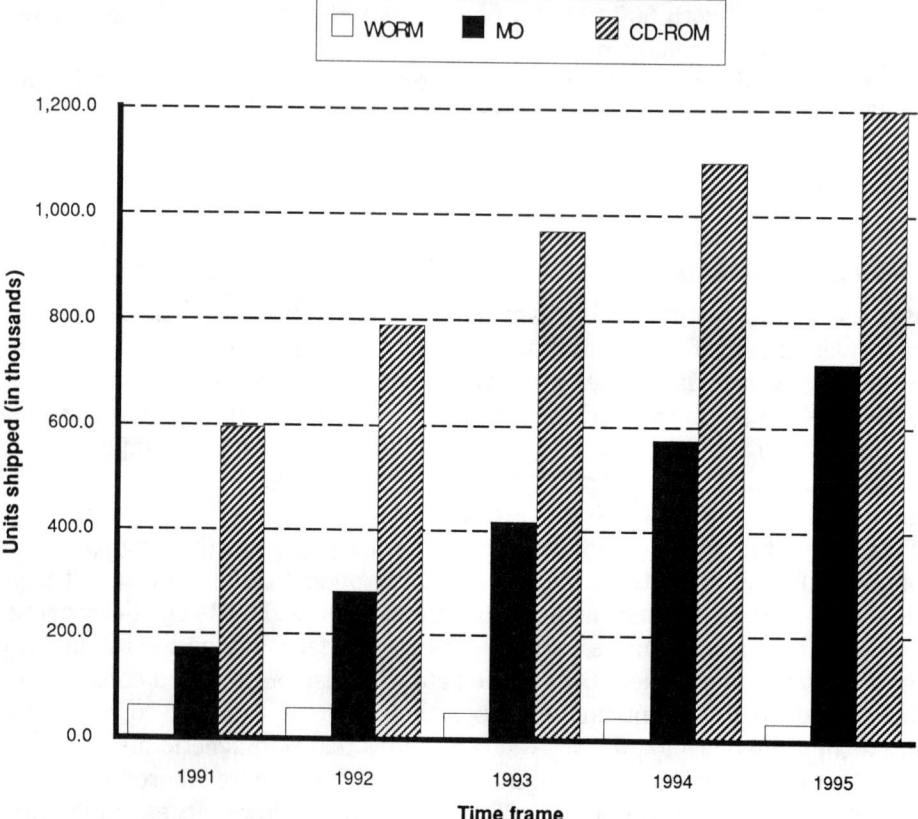

5-16 Optical drive market trends.

MO drive benefits for Cat Mac builders

At the low-capacity end of the storage spectrum, the 3½" 128Mb removable-media MO drive has to be today's hottest new item. Repackagers are advertising drives in the back pages of Mac User for $1499 and media for $99. By the end of 1992, these prices should drop even further. The 3½", 128Mb media resembles an 800K floppy diskette (it's only slightly thicker), meets ANSI and ISO standards ensuring compatibility, is likely to outlive your Cat Mac, yet fits in your shirt pocket. What more could you ask for? Table 5-3 tells the story. The handwriting is on the wall for removable magnetic media manufacturers. Frankly, even the new floptical vendors should be worried. What this means to Cat Mac builders, however, is that you are now entering a new era of flexibility, price performance, convenience, and portability that can make you even more productive. Shipping files on media across the country to a service bureau will cost far less, you need far less space for storage of your backup files, and all the files you need for an important Macintosh multimedia presentation or to gener-

Table 5-3. 1/2" MO drive versus removable and floptical.

Comparison	3 1/2" MO	5 1/4" removable	3 1/2" floptical
performance	hard drive	hard drive	floppy drive
access time	25 ms	25 ms	50 ms
capacity	128Mb	88Mb	20Mb
media reliability	optical	hard drive	floppy drive
media convenience	3 1/2" diskette	5 1/4" cartridge	3 1/2" diskette
drive cost (street price)	$1500	$650	$600
media cost (street price)	$100	$120	$30

ate an A/UX system fit in your shirt pocket. It gets even better as 3 1/2" optical media rapidly evolves to 256Mb and beyond.

At the high-capacity end of the storage spectrum, the 5 1/4" 600Mb removable-media MO drive has advantages of its own compared to hard drives and removable magnetic media. Figure 5-17 shows a comparison of hard drives, SyQuest cartridge drives, and MO cartridge drives at today's street prices. My assumptions for it are:

- Hard drives—A 1.2Gb hard drive costs you about $2100 today. To get to 2.4Gb, add a second hard drive.
- SyQuest cartridge drives—The 88Mb SyQuest drive costs $650. 88Mb cartridges are $120. To store 2.4Gb, you need 28 of them.
- MO cartridge drives—5 1/4" MO drive street prices are around $3000. 600Mb cartridges are $200. Four 600Mb cartridges store 2.4Gb.

As you can see, we have a clear winner here. The lower slope of the MO line in Fig. 5-17 versus the other two tells the whole story. Above 2.4Gb, where high volume storage users (CAD, scientific data acquisition, 24-bit color work, digital music, electronic publishing professionals) must have large contiguous storage space, MO cartridges not only provide a more cost-effective solution, but are more convenient, easily transported and offer unlimited storage expansion potential. To put it into perspective for you compared with today's popular 800K floppy, $200 per 600Mb MO cartridge works out to be 33 cents per megabyte, or less than the cost of an 800K diskette. Nobody would contest the convenience of one 5 1/4" MO cartridge compared with handling 600 floppy diskettes, and the MO cartridge will also outlive the floppy diskettes (or any other magnetic media).

CD-ROM drive benefits for Cat Mac builders

Figure 5-16 showed CD-ROMs leading all optical devices in units shipped, but this is a small installed base compared to the 45 million audio-CD players. There is only a small bridge left to cross in terms of gaining consumer mindshare for the benefits of CD-ROM, and it is becoming more indispensable

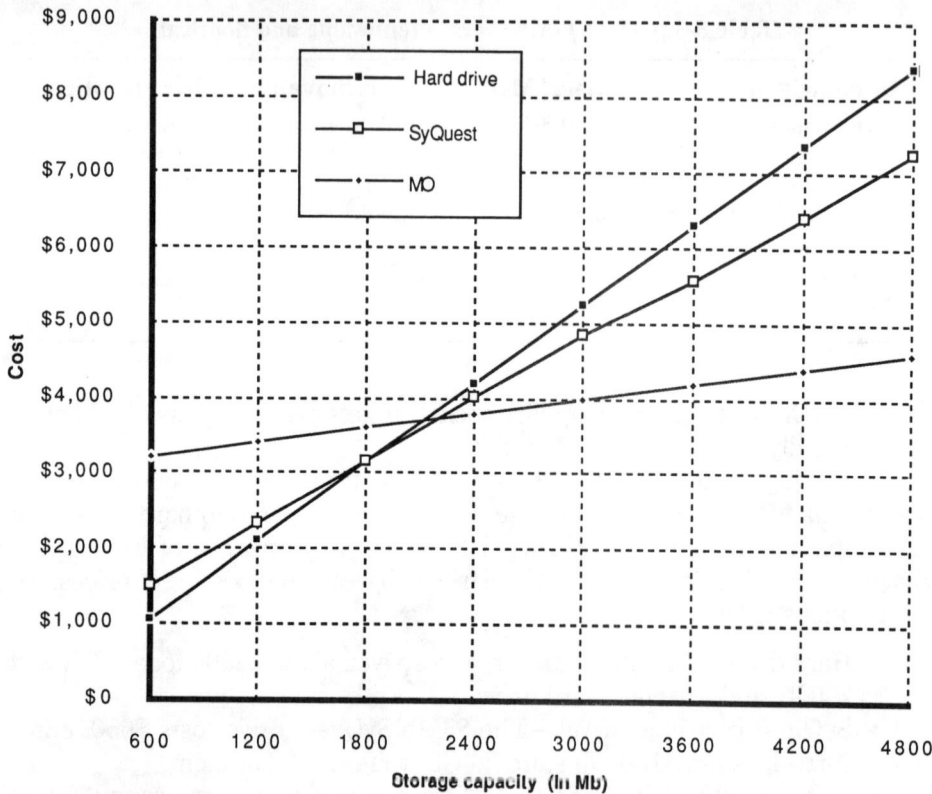

5-17 Benefits of MO cartridge drives over SyQuest removable drives and hard drives.

every day as software vendors turn to electronic publishing; more useful large reference volumes are published, and prices decline with increased activity. CD-ROM drive prices now hover around $500, and typical diskettes go for $50 to $200 (although you can still pay $10,000 for annual subscriptions to special interest databases). While not competitive with audio-CD drives at $200 and diskettes at $20, you can expect CD-ROM cost to approach these levels as its future use becomes more widespread.

CD-ROM offers Cat Mac builders a unique opportunity today. While multimedia "workstations"—a CD-ROM unit inside a standard DOS PC chassis with hard drive, color monitor, keyboard, and mouse—proliferate on the DOS PC side, popularized by vendors such as Tandy and others, no counterpart exists in the Macintosh world. Why? Apple doesn't provide room in its standard Apple Macintosh chassis. Enter the Cat Mac. Once again the Cat Mac offers a superior solution. You can really have it all. Not only can you mount a CD-ROM drive as an integral part of your Cat Mac chassis but you can couple it with a monster hard drive in the same Cat Mac case to take maximum advantage of it. The possibilities are endless and mouth-watering. Figure 5-18 shows

5-18 APS Toshiba XM3301 CD-ROM drive ready for use with Cat Mac.

an APS Toshiba XM3301 CD-ROM drive in an external case ready for use or for installation in a Cat Mac chassis.

WORM drive benefits for Cat Mac builders

As Fig. 5-16 suggested, WORM drive growth is expected to be limited. The reason is simple: standardization. The multiplicity of incompatible WORM formats has allowed the more standardized MO drive market to encroach on its turf. That factor combined with the increased flexibility of MO drives (its ability to both read and write), the much lower cost of the $3^1/_2"$ MO format, and overlap with O-ROM and WO CD-ROM technology will limit WORM use to niche markets.

- Sony is pushing its new $3^1/_2"$ format "O-ROM" (optical read-only-memory) technology—a single drive that uses conventional MO media or CD-ROM style O-ROM media. The advantages are that once you've got what you want on the MO media you can quickly and inexpensively master O-ROM copies of it for smaller, dedicated-purpose, CD-ROM style distributions. Unlike CD-ROM, you don't need 10,000 or even 1000 copies to justify your mastering costs. With O-ROM, you can easily justify delivering 100 or only 50 copies of a large volume of data.
- WO CD-ROM—JVC Information Products is pushing its new "write-once" CD-ROM. Disks written in the ISO 9660 file format meet the

Optical drives **139**

industry's Orange Book standard and can be read by any CD-ROM drive. JVC expects the drive to be especially useful to multimedia VARs and developers who need to show a few copies of an application before sending it out to a mastering house.

However, if you are a Cat Mac builder who works with documents that need to have every change ever made recorded (e.g., book publishers, screenwriters, banking, real estate, insurance, medical, and legal applications); or are automating your microfilm and microfiche storage; or need to permanently store extremely large contiguous graphics and text files, WORM media might provide new applications and solutions for you not possible with the earlier technology.

Tape drives

Early reports of magnetic tape's death on the Macintosh have been greatly exaggerated. Here are my Cat Mac builder tape drive recommendations. Focus your search on two devices. TEAC mechanisms take care of your low- and midrange needs. DAT takes care of you at the upper end. TEAC/DAT tape drives combined with Dantz's Retrospect, a world-class archiving and backup software package, make tape backups or restores fast, reliable, and painless. Either mechanism, easily mounted inside a DOS PC style chassis, gives Cat Mac builders a convenience and ease of operation simply not available to standard Apple Macintosh owners.

A TEAC mechanism is a Cat Mac builder's best backup choice for Macintosh hard drives to 150Mb in size. TEAC data cassettes (they look like a standard audio cassette but are very different inside), originally available in 60Mb flavors, now have given way to the 150Mb variety. The TEAC 155 tape drive is considerably faster than the DC 2000 (first popularized by Apple's Tape Backup 40SC) or DC 6000. Today, compared to other tape alternatives, most DC 2000 drives are slow. If you do find a faster one, the extra money you spend on it is better spent on another tape alternative. DC 6000 tape drives are the DC 2000s bigger brother. Although the DC 6000 is a good midrange tape drive—its media holds 150Mb (newer extended length DC 6000 tapes offer 320Mb or 525Mb capacity) and works 60% faster—it is higher in price and not as fast as the comparable TEAC 150Mb offering that goes for around $600 mail order (150Mb cartridges are around $30). With the TEAC you get a proven cartridge design, a fast and reliable tape drive, plus most vendors typically package it with Retrospect. Figure 5-19 shows an APS TEAC 155 tape drive ready for installation in a Cat Mac chassis $5^{1}/_{4}"$ opening.

A DAT mechanism is a Cat Mac builder's best backup choice above 150Mb—both for personal and network backup. DAT tape drives—based on 4-millimeter tape—hold 1.2Gb on 60-meter tape and 2Gb on 90-meter tape. A 1.2Gb DAT drive costs $1500 mail order and its 1.2Gb cartridge costs $20.

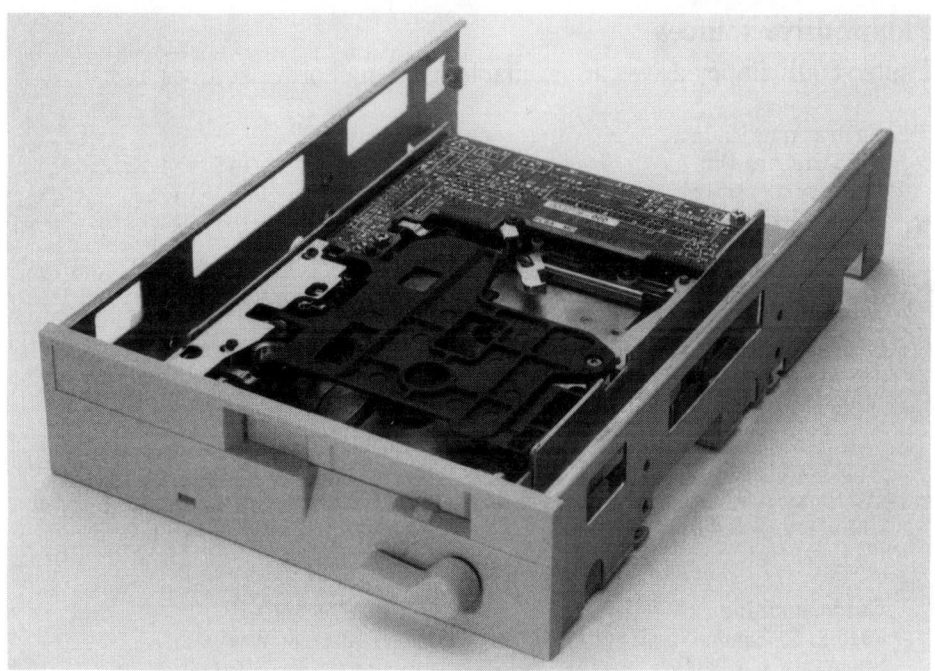

5-19 APS Teac 155 tape drive ready for installation in Cat Mac 5¼" chassis opening.

While the larger capacity 8-millimeter format (based on videotape) holds 2.2Gb, when you jump to DAT, you are going from the analog to the digital world—you get a higher level of reliability and data integrity than with 8-millimeter analog tape. You also get multiple sourcing (Exabyte is the sole manufacturer of 8 millimeter drives—its 2.2Gb drive is available for $2100 mail order and you can get cartridges for $10). In addition, DAT's smaller 3½" size, near 8-millimeter capacity on 90-meter tapes, and multiple-source availability make it a superior choice over 8-millimeter. At the low end, the TEAC 155 is great, but if my need was for heavy duty backing up of networks, my choice would be the DAT—both for cost and performance. You're spending a little more for the drive ($1500 versus $600), actually spending less for the media ($20 versus $30) and you can rest easier nights knowing that DAT is probably providing a more reliable tape backup for you and giving you longer tape life.

Sources

Apple floppy, hard and tape drives are available new and as upgrade replacements through Apple dealers. New and used Apple drives are also available through the Apple used equipment dealers. All other hard drives are available directly from the manufacturer and through the mail order distributors.

Floppy drive sources

Fujitsu 800K floppy drives are available from mail order sources and:

Fujitsu America Inc.
3055 Orchard Dr.
San Jose, CA 95134
(800) 626-4686

MacDirect
60 E. Chestnut, #145
Chicago, IL 60611
(800) 621-8461

Cutting Edge Inc.
97 S. Willow Rd.
Evanston, WY 82930
(800) 443-5199

The 1.4Mb floppy drives are available from mail order sources and:

Applied Engineering
P.O. Box 5100
Carrollton, TX 75011
(214) 241-6060

Peripheral Land Inc.
47421 Bayside Pkwy.
Fremont, CA 94538
(800) 288-8754

Quadmation Inc.
1016 E. El Camino Real, Suite 160
Sunnyvale, CA 94087
(408) 733-5557

Kennect Technology
120-A Albright Way
Los Gatos, CA 95030
(800) 552-1232

Mirror Technologies Inc.
2644 Patton Rd.
Roseville, MN 55113
(612) 633-4450

Dayna Communications
50 S. Main St., 5th Fl.
Salt Lake City, UT 84144
(801) 531-0203

Floptical drives are available from mail order sources and:

Insite Peripherals Inc.
4433 Fortran Dr.
San Jose, CA 95134
(408) 946-8080

Brier Technology
25 Meca Dr.
Norcross, GA 30093
(404) 564-5550

Peripheral Land Inc.
47421 Bayside Pkwy.
Fremont, CA 94538
(800) 288-8754

Quadram
1 Quad Wy.
Norcross, GA 30093
(404) 923-6666

Hard drive sources

Hard drives are available from the following mail order drive specialists and other mail order sources:

Alliance Peripheral Systems
2900 S. 291 Hwy.
Independence, MO 64057
(800) 645-5401

Club Mac
3 Musick
Irvine, CA 92718
(800) 258-2622

Hard Drives International
1912 W. 4th St.
Tempe, AZ 85281
(800) 767-3475

Wholesale 54
2415 S. Roosevelt Ave.
Tempe, AZ 85282
(800) 927-3179

Hard drive manufacturers are:

Connor Peripherals
3081 Zanker Rd.
San Jose, CA 95134
(408) 456-4500

Micropolis Corp.
21211 Nordhoff St.
Chatsworth, CA 91311
(818) 718-7777

Core International
7171 N. Federal Hwy.
Boca Raton, FL 33487
(407) 997-6055

NEC Technologies Inc.
1414 Massachusetts Ave.
Boxborough, MA 01719
(508) 264-8000

Fujitsu America Inc.
3055 Orchard Dr.
San Jose, CA 95134
(408) 432-1300

Quantum Corp.
500 McCarthy Blvd.
Milpitas, CA 95035
(800) 624-5545

Hewlett-Packard
19310 Pruneridge Ave.
Cupertino, CA 95014
(800) 752-0900

Seagate Technology
920 Disc Dr.
Scotts Valley, CA 95066
(408) 438-6550

Hitachi America Ltd.
2000 Sierra Point Pkwy.
Brisbane, CA 94005
(415) 539-8300

Sony Corp. of America
655 River Oaks Pkwy.
San Jose, CA 95134
(408) 432-0190

Maxtor Corp.
211 River Oaks Pkwy.
San Jose, CA 95134
(408) 432-1700

Toshiba America Information Systems Inc.
9740 Irvine Blvd.
Irvine, CA 92718
(800) 456-3475

IBM/OEM
1133 Westchester Ave.
White Plains, NY 10604
(914) 642-6049

Western Digital
8105 Irvine Center Dr.
Irvine, CA 92718
(714) 932-5000

Hard drive repackagers are:

Apple Computer
20525 Mariani Ave.
Cupertino, CA 95014
(408) 996-1010

CMS Enhancements
2722 Michelson Dr.
Irvine, CA 92714
(714) 222-6000

Bay Microsystems Inc.
210 Columbus Ave., Ste. 108
San Francisco, CA 94133
(415) 563-8392

Deltaic Systems
1701 Junction Ct., Ste. 302
San Jose, CA 95112
(800) 745-1240

Ehman Engineering Inc.
P.O. Box 2126
Evanston, WY 89231
(800) 257-1666

EMAC Div Everex
48431 Milmont Dr.
Fremont, CA 94538
(800) 821-0806

FWB Inc.
2040 Polk St., Ste. 215
San Francisco, CA 94109
(415) 474-8055

GCC Technologies Inc.
580 Winter St.
Waltham, MA 02154
(800) 422-7777

IDS Systems Inc.
2107 N. First St., Ste. 280
San Jose, CA 95131
(408) 441-0500

LaCie Ltd.
19552 SW. 90th Ct.
Tulatin, OR 97062
(503) 691 0771

Liberty Systems Inc.
120 Saratoga Ave., Ste. 82
Santa Clara, CA 95051
(408) 983-1127

MicroNet Technology Inc.
20 Mason
Irvine, CA 92718
(714) 837-0633

Microtech International Inc.
158 Commerce St.
E. Haven, CT 06512
(800) 626-4276

Mirror Technologies Inc.
2644 Patton Rd.
Roseville, MN 55113
(612) 633-4450

Optima Technology Inc.
17526 Von Karmen
Irvine, CA 92714
(714) 476-0515

Peripheral Land Inc.
47421 Bayside Pkwy.
Fremont, CA 94538
(800) 288-8754

PCPC
4710 Eisenhower Blvd., Bldg. A4
Tampa, FL 33634
(800) 622-2888

Procom Technology Inc.
200 McCormick Ave.
Costa Mesa, CA 92626
(714) 549-9449

Relax Technology Inc.
3101 Whipple Rd., Ste. 22
Union City, CA 94587
(415) 471 6112

Ruby Systems Inc.
930 Thompson Pl.
Sunnyvale, CA 94086
(408) 735-8668

Storage Dimensions
2145 Hamilton Ave.
San Jose, CA 95125
(408) 879-0300

Tulin Corp.
2156H O'Toole Ave.
San Jose, CA 95131
(408) 432-9025

Removable drive sources

Removable hard drive manufacturers/repackagers include:

Bering Industries
240 Hacienda Ave.
Campbell, CA 95008
(800) 237-4641

CD Technology Inc.
780 Montague Expwy., Ste. 407
San Jose, CA 95131
(408) 432-8698

Deltaic Systems
1701 Junction Ct, Ste. 302
San Jose, CA 95112
(800) 745-1240

EMAC Div. Everex
48431 Milmont Dr.
Fremont, CA 94538
(800) 821-0806

ETC Peripherals
5426 Beaumont Center Blvd., Ste. 300
Tampa, FL 33634
(800) 882-2863

Mass Microsystems
810 W. Maude Ave.
Sunnyvale, CA 94086
(408) 522-1200

Quantum Corp.
500 McCarthy Blvd.
Milpitas, CA 95035
(800) 624-5545

Tradewinds Peripherals Inc.
2633 E. 28th St., Ste. 612
Signal Hill, CA 90806
(213) 595-7272

Wetex Int'l Corp.
1122 W. Washington Blvd., Ste. D
Montebello, CA 90640
(213) 728-3119

Syquest-mechanism removable drives are available from the following mail order drive specialists and numerous other mail order sources:

Alliance Peripheral Systems
2900 S. 291 Hwy.
Independence, MO 64057
(800) 645-5401

Club Mac
3 Musick
Irvine, CA 92718
(800) 258-2622

Hard Drives International
1912 W. 4th St.
Tempe, AZ 85281
(800) 767-3475

Wholesale 54
2415 S. Roosevelt Ave.
Tempe, AZ 85282
(800) 927-3179

Ricoh-mechanism removable drives are available from the following repackager:

GCC Technologies
580 Winter St.
Waltham, MA 02154
(800) 422-7777

Microtech International Inc.
158 Commerce St.
E. Haven, CT 06512
(800) 626-4276

Bernoulli-mechanism removable drives are available from the following:

Iomega Corp.
1821 W. 4000 S.
Roy, UT 84067
(800) 456-5522

Optical drive sources

Optical drive products are obtainable from:

Cannon USA Inc.
One Cannon Plaza
Lake Success, NY 11042
(516) 488-6700

CD Technology Inc.
780 Montague Expwy., Ste. 407
San Jose, CA 95131
(408) 432-8698

DGR Technologies
1800 Rio Grande, Ste. 205
Austin, TX 78701
(800) 235-9748

FWB Inc.
2040 Polk St., Ste. 215
San Francisco, CA 94109
(415) 474-8055

Hitachi America Ltd
2000 Sierra Point Pkwy.
Brisbane, CA 94005
(415) 539-8300

Iomega Corp.
1821 W. 4000 S.
Roy, UT 84067
(800) 456-5522

Liberty Systems Inc.
120 Saratoga Ave., Ste. 82
Santa Clara, CA 95051
(408) 983-1127

MacProducts USA
608 W. 22nd St.
Austin, TX 78705
(800) 622-3475

Mass Microsystems
810 W. Maude Ave.
Sunnyvale, CA 94086
(408) 522-1200

Maxoptix Corp.
2520 Junction Ave.
San Jose, CA 95134
(408) 954-9700

MicroNet Technology Inc.
20 Mason
Irvine, CA 92718
(714) 837-0633

Microtech International Inc.
158 Commerce St.
E. Haven, CT 06512
(800) 626-4276

Mitsubishi Electronics America Inc.
991 Knox St.
Torrance, CA 90502
(213) 217-5732

MOST Inc.
11205 Knott Ave., Ste. B
Cypress, CA 90630
(714) 898-9400

O.C.E.A.N. Microsystems Inc.
246 E. Hacienda Ave.
Campbell, CA 95008
(408) 374-8300

Optical Access International
36 Commerce Wy.
Woburn, MA 01801
(617) 935-2679

Optimem div. Archive Co.
297 N. Bernardo Ave.
Mountain View, CA 94043
(415) 961-1800

Panasonic Communications & Systems Co.
2 Panasonic Wy.
Secaucus, NJ 07094
(201) 348-7000

Peripheral Land Inc.
47421 Bayside Pkwy.
Fremont, CA 94538
(800) 288-8754

Pinnacle Micro
19 Technology
Irvine, CA 92718
(800) 555-7070

Pioneer Communications
600 E. Crescent Ave.
Upper Saddle River, NJ 07458
(800) 527-3766

Procom Technology Inc.
200 McCormick Ave.
Costa Mesa, CA 92626
(714) 549-9449

Relax Technology Inc.
3101 Whipple Rd., Ste. 22
Union City, CA 94587
(415) 471-6112

Ricoh Corp.
3001 Orchard Pkwy.
San Jose, CA 95134
(408) 432-8800

Sony Corp. of America
655 River Oaks Pkwy.
San Jose, CA 95134
(408) 432-0190

Storage Dimensions
2145 Hamilton Ave.
San Jose, CA 95125
(408) 879-0300

Tape drive sources

Tape drive products are obtainable from:

ADIC
P.O. Box 2996
Redmond, WA 98073
(800) 336-1233

Alliance Peripheral Systems
2900 S. 291 Hwy.
Independence, MO 64057
(800) 645-5401

Apple Computer
20525 Mariani Ave.
Cupertino, CA 95014
(408) 996-1010

Bering Industries
240 Hacienda Ave.
Campbell, CA 95008
(800) 237-4641

Blackhole Technology Inc.
225 East St.
Winchester, MA 01890
(800) 227-1688

CMS Enhancements
2722 Michelson Dr.
Irvine, CA 92714
(714) 222-6000

Deltaic Systems
1701 Junction Ct., Ste. 302
San Jose, CA 95112
(800) 745-1240

EMAC Div. Everex
48431 Milmont Dr.
Fremont, CA 94538
(800) 821-0806

Exabyte Corp.
1685 38th St.
Boulder, CO 80301
(303) 447-7359

FWB Inc.
2040 Polk St., Ste. 215
San Francisco, CA 94109
(415) 474-8055

Irwin Magnetic Systems Inc.
2101 Commonwealth Blvd.
Ann Arbor, MI 48105
(313) 930-9000

Maynard Electronics (an Archive Co.)
36 Skyline Dr.
Lake Mary, FL 32746
(800) 821-8782

MicroNet Technology Inc.
20 Mason
Irvine, CA 92718
(714) 837-0633

Microtech International Inc.
158 Commerce St.
E. Haven, CT 06512
(800) 626-4276

Mirror Technologies Inc.
2644 Patton Rd.
Roseville, MN 55113
(800) 654-5294

Optima Technology Inc.
17526 Von Karmen
Irvine, CA 92714
(714) 476-0515

Peripheral Land Inc.
47421 Bayside Pkwy.
Fremont, CA 94538
(800) 288-8754

Personal Computer Peripherals Corp.
4710 Eisenhower Blvd., Bldg. A4
Tampa, FL 33634

Procom Technology Inc.
200 McCormick Ave.
Costa Mesa, CA 92626
(714) 549-9449

Qualstar Corp.
9621 Irondale Ave.
Chatsworth, CA 91311
(818) 882-5822

Relax Technology Inc.
3101 Whipple Rd., Ste. 22
Union City, CA 94587
(415) 471-6112

Techmar Inc.
6225 Cochran Rd.
Solon, OH 44139
(216) 349-0600

---

[1]Bob Brant, *Macintosh Hard Disk Management*, Windcrest/McGraw-Hill, 1992.

[2]Paul Hyman, "Poof! Into Thin Air," *Electronic Buyers' News*, 11 March 1991, p. 31. Paul observes that the government recently noticed it might be losing its 1960 to 1980 Census Data and its NASA Space Programs Data from 1958 onward—all carefully stored on reels of low-density magnetic tape—for this very reason. But look at the bright side, the IRS is gradually losing all your earlier tax return data for the same reason!

[3]Taken from table provided by Freeman Associates Inc., *Computer Reseller News*, 25 November 1991, p. 87.

Chapter 6
Monitors and video cards

T his chapter extends the recurring theme for Cat Mac builders—the most for the least—into monitors and video cards. At the low end, chances are your monitor selection will always be superior to (and cost less than) the standard Apple Macintosh 9" monitor. Not that there is anything wrong with the Apple offering, but in video monitors, bigger is almost always better. As you go up in performance, Cat Mac builders enjoy a tremendous flexibility and optimizing edge regardless of the monitor solution being implemented. You don't need two monitors on your desk when one will do nicely (the result when an expanded screen is added to a Classic-style Apple Macintosh) nor do you need to suffer the indignities of not being able to use the monitor you want with the logic board you have (the result of power supply limitations in Apple Mac LC and IIsi models).

Cat Mac builders can have it all—your way—in monitors and video cards. Your video monitor and its interface adapter can be the most rewarding area of your Cat Mac project, and you can admire the sagaciousness of your choice every time you turn it on. And if you either don't like or have outgrown your choice, you can change it—without having to sell your Cat Mac to do so!

This chapter will give you a framework to make your own monitor and video card decisions. I'll start again with a few definitions, take a look at the monitor and video interface options available to Cat Mac builders today, and give you my recommendations. First a little overview and history.

Monitor overview and history

Monitors are the most visible choice of your Cat Mac builder options. I don't mean this as an oxymoron. The fact is, you have to live with your selection everyday. If you made a good one, you'll love yourself, forget about it, and go on more efficiently than ever. If you made a bad choice, you're going to be kicking yourself about it and hoping the product you got came with a 30-day return privilege. More than in any other area (except the keyboard and mouse) your decision here is important and not just aesthetic.

Originally, there was no decision to make. You got the monitor that came with your Macintosh—the 9" screen. Before there were larger monitors (yes, there was such a time—how quickly we forget) nobody complained about the size of the screen they had on their Macintosh. It was the only screen you got, it was the only screen you could get.

However, a trickle of complaints started and eventually became an avalanche. Customers would come into a computer store and complain about the Macintosh screen. Sophisticated corporate users complained about their loss of productivity, unsophisticated users just complained about its small physical size. In 1988, this shortcoming was addressed by Radius, E-Machines, and then a multitude of other companies with full-page and two-page monochrome monitor offerings in the 15" to 19" and up range. SuperMac and others added color a short while later. Gray scale monitor capability became available about that same time. In 1989, Apple legitimized the market by introducing its own big screen monitors.

The original Macintoshes had their video contained onboard. But it was closed to use from outside the chassis and there was nothing else you could add. With the introduction of Apple's Mac II in 1987, a video interface card was introduced that had the ability to be either 4-bit video—to drive Apple's Monochrome monitor—or 8-bit video—to drive Apple's 13" RGB Hi-Res color monitor—depending upon the number of video RAM chips you put in it. Apple's Mac II family NuBus logic board design gave Macintosh monitor and video interface vendors the same opportunity to provide the wide variety of choices the DOS PC world had, with two important differences: simplicity and graphics.

Simplicity Just pick the monitor you like and plug its video interface card into a Mac II NuBus slot. NuBus slots let you have as many monitors attached to your Mac II as you want—limited only by your imagination and your slots. On a Mac II, you plug a card into a slot, click a screen with a mouse, and have your monitor set up and running within five minutes. I dare you to even put a second monitor on your DOS PC machine!

Graphics Designed from the chips up to be a graphics machine, the Mac has always had better graphics than DOS PC machines, first with monochrome video and later with color. The newest offerings just extend its lead. The original Mac color capability at eight bits per pixel was pretty impressive in 1987. The newer color monitor and video card offerings that display 24 and 32 bits of color information are nothing short of phenomenal. Looking at a 19" or 21" Macintosh monitor driven by a 24-bit color card is like looking at a photographic slide. Plus newer video offerings are being introduced in ever increasing numbers and very sophisticated multimedia video cards are coming.

After addressing the high end of the market and monitor products that delivered full-page, two-page, gray-scale, and color capability, vendors turned their attention to the low end. Today, you can put a relatively inexpensive monitor identical to those used on DOS PCs on any Macintosh and enjoy all the benefits of a larger screen. A few third-party vendors have raised adding video to existing Macintosh logic boards (even the enclosed Classic-style models) into an art form. The newest trend is to put accelerator and video functionality on the same add-in board, because they usually have mutually dependent needs.

Today's newest Macintosh logic boards, the Mac LC, IIsi, IIci and Quadras again offer video capability on the logic board—but this time it is open to the world and has all the capabilities once contained solely on the Apple NuBus video cards. Plus one third-party video vendor (recently joined by several more) has innovated a clever video add-on available totally through the SCSI port, and another third-party vendor has placed the Macintosh video monitor interface inside the monitor itself.

The Cat Mac benefit—more video flexibility

Owners of enclosed Classic-style Apple Macintoshes (the Mac 128 through the Plus, Mac SE, SE 30, Classic, and Classic II) have two choices: to stick with what they have, or use two monitors—the Mac's plus a much larger one—on their desk.

Enter the Cat Mac—it definitely changes the monitor picture for the better. As a Cat Mac builder, you can choose the larger monitor you want to begin with. You can now put a relatively inexpensive monitor, identical to those used on DOS PCs, on your Cat Mac and enjoy all the benefits of a larger screen. Even if you originally started with a Classic-style Apple Macintosh. Merely plug in or clip on your video card to your Macintosh logic board, then plug the monitor into this video card. And you only have one monitor—exactly the one you have chosen—on your Cat Mac.

Builders of Mac II, NuBus-style Cat Macs have it even easier. Plug in your NuBus card to the Mac II logic board of your choice (or use the existing on-board video). You have no restrictions due to power-supply capacity or chassis size. Build exactly what you want to begin with and add as many readily available NuBus cards as you like.

The first time I opened up my Apple Mac SE and found a Samsung label on its video monitor tube, my American as Apple Pie notions were all destroyed in a glance. On the other hand, I now have no hesitancy at all in recommending a larger Samsung (or any other third-party monitor) for your Cat Mac project. Neither should Apple. After all, it's just a larger version of the same type of tube they use in a different case with slightly different video drive electronics. Today, as a Cat Mac builder, you have numerous truly excellent monitor choices from Apple and other vendors. Your biggest task is to make the best choice for you.

Could you please define that

First, a brief detour for a few definitions to get our basic vocabulary straight.

- Video monitor—Somewhat redundant in usage but refers to the monitor reproducing a visual image on a television or computer screen. This is as opposed to an audio monitor that would monitor sound frequencies.
- Pixel—Short for "picture element." It's the smallest dot that a monitor can display.
- Pixel density—The number of dots per inch (dpi) on the screen.
- WYSIWYG—"What you see is what you get." One of the benefits of the Macintosh interface is that what you see on the screen is reproduced faithfully by the printed output. To accomplish it, Apple specified that Macintosh-compatible displays have a one-to-one ratio between the 72 dots per inch on the display and the 72 dots per inch at which the Apple

ImageWriter prints. Third-party monitor vendors bent this rule to suit their needs. The tradeoff is that more than 72 dpi fits more information on the screen, but shrinks it—it's harder to read; less than 72 dpi fits less information on the screen, but enlarges it—it's easier to read.

- Size—Monitor size, sometimes called viewing area, is measured diagonally from corner to corner. The 9" Macintosh screen is actually $7^{1}/_{2}"$ wide $\times$ $5^{1}/_{2}"$ high.
- Resolution—The number of pixels across and down (sometimes called *pixel dimensions*) is the amount of information displayed. The 9" Macintosh screen paints a picture that has a resolution of 512 pixels across $\times$ 342 pixels down—a total of 175,104 pixels.
- Size versus resolution—The size of the monitor does not determine its resolution. By just hooking up a larger 14" monitor to your Cat Mac and not changing the amount of information fed to it, you make the viewing area larger, but you don't increase the amount of information displayed. To state it in another way, you are making your 512×342 image viewing area larger, but not increasing your productivity, since it takes the same scrolling time to view information on the screen. On the other hand, you can hook up the same monitor through a video card to get resolutions of: 720×350 pixels (252,000 total, or an increase of 144%), or 640×480 pixels (307,200 total, or an increase of 175%). At the high end, an E-Machines Big Picture 17" 1024×808 monitor increases the pixels by 473%, or adding a full two-page 21" 1280×960 monitor increases the pixels by 702%. You get the picture?
- Full-page or portrait monitor—Reproduces the familiar vertical format $8^{1}/_{2}" \times 11"$ (or A4 European) page you are used to working with on the screen. This is good for heavy word-processing work where it is helpful to see the entire page at a glance.
- Two-page or landscape—Gives you two full side-by-side pages and is useful for doing page-layout work. It is also useful for working with spreadsheets, because it can either show many cells of a spreadsheet at one time or enlarge a few cells at a time for better viewing in group presentations.
- TTL (transistor transistor logic)—Although, strictly speaking, this definition applies to a type of electronic interface, this label has also come to apply to the whole universe of the simplest and least expensive (under $100) monitors you can buy, because they use that interface.
- Multisync—The ability of a more expensive than TTL monitor to adjust itself to a wide range of video input signal frequencies and thus be usable for a large variety of applications implemented over numerous computer platforms.
- Gray scale—Each pixel can display up to 256 shades of gray as opposed to just black or white available in a standard monitor. Many monitors

can be converted into gray scale just by changing the interface card driving them. This is useful for working with scanned photographs—you can see much more of the tonal range.

All monitors are not created equal

One of the principal Cat Mac monitor benefits is the wide range of options you can choose from—but it is a highly subjective decision. There are monitors and there are monitors. You can compare all you want with pencil and paper, but buying a monitor is one area where seeing is believing. If possible, I would encourage you always to look at the results on the screen of the monitor you are thinking of buying before you make your final decision.

What to look for

There are certain selection criteria that can help you regardless of whether you are looking at the lowest priced TTL solution, a large screen color monitor at the other end of the price scale, or something in between.

Let me give you a few items to consider when shopping for a monitor. Some might be more important to you than others—it's your choice—but you should at least be aware of all of them. I divided my list into five sections: the physical viewing screen, the tube itself, the interface, the packaging, and price performance.

Physical viewing screen

This section is concerned with the overall characteristics of your monitor:

- Resolution—One of the most important decisions. Yes, a 640 x 480 monitor is a nice size, but if you are working mostly with full-page text, 640 x 860—one full page—would be a better choice.
- Pixel density (dpi)—Are you getting 72 dpi? If not, do you know why you are getting more or less, and agree that it's the best choice?
- Refresh rate and flicker—Excessive flicker is a strain on the eyes; no flicker is best. A high refresh rate reduces flicker. At 60 Hz (the screen image is redrawn 60 times per second) most people notice it. At 65 Hz a few will. Above 70 Hz, you get a rock-solid display.
- Brightness—Does your monitor image appear bright or is it washed out? If you can adjust the brightness (monitors decrease in brightness with age), this can compensate for it.
- Contrast—Do you have a good range between the light and dark areas? With good contrast you have dark blacks and bright whites. Is contrast adjustable? This control along with brightness can also compensate for other ills such as the monitor's physical placement in the room and ambient lighting.
- Color—Do you like the tint or color of the screen? Is it blue-white (pre-

ferred Mac standard), gray, or yellow-white? Are your colors rich and on track and uniform in tint over the entire screen?

Tube

This section is concerned with the overall characteristics of the picture tube that goes into your monitor:

- Focus—How clear is the information appearing on your screen? Do you get crisp readable text? Is the focus uniform over the entire screen area?
- Color alignment—Is the color pattern uniform in all areas of the screen or are there patches where it appears wavy or splotched?
- Pin cushioning—Are the screen edges wavy or distorted? Are the corners cramped or misshapen?
- Phosphor persistence—Is there ghosting, i.e., do movements of your white cursor across a dark screen leave a noticeable afterglow?
- Flatness—Is the tube face flat or curved? Some older tubes made you feel you were looking into a fish bowl. Flatter is better.
- Scanning—How straight are the edges of the electronically scanned area in the display? Are they in physical alignment with the tube or rotated, twisted, or horizontally or vertically skewed?
- Glare coating—Does the tube have one? Does it interfere with the image? Either too much or too little is bad. Too much makes the screen appear unfocused, too little reflects too much ambient light off the screen face.

Interface

This section is concerned with the hardware and software interface of your monitor:

- Compatibility—Can the monitor be used across all Cat Macs? Does it have optional interface adapters, i.e., Mac SE, SE 30, NuBus—so you can take your favorite monitor with you should you change Cat Mac logic boards down the road?
- Software—Does it have the software features you want, such as tear-off menus, tool palettes, or multiscreen features if you are working with a Mac SE or SE 30?

Packaging

This section is concerned with the physical aspects of your monitor:

- General—Is it the right size and weight for your needs? (A 50-pound color monitor is not portable!) Does the case color match your room drapes?
- Ergonomics—Does it come with a tilt-swivel stand and/or other extras?

Price performance
This section is concerned with the value aspects of your monitor:
- *Bigger monitor screens definitely enhance productivity.* Numerous studies have proven it; even a 14" monitor will give you significant benefits over a standard Mac 9" screen, since it cuts down the scrolling time to view information on a page. A 15" full-page display or a 19" two-page display benefits you even more if you can afford one.
- *Match your machine to the monitor you need at the outset.* Yes, you can now add color capability to a 68000-powered Macintosh logic board, but it really is better to start off with a Mac LC or Mac II and up if you need color.
- *Corporate users prefer color despite cost.* Basically this is aesthetics, but many corporate users cite further productivity gains with color.
- *Gray scale is a worthwhile investment if your business justifies it.* For example, corporate publishing departments that work with halftones need gray scale.
- *Avoid obsolescence.* Look for features that let you expand later and don't lock you in. What is the next step you are likely to take with your display?
- *Quality/vendor.* It's worth it to pay more for quality. Buy the best quality you can get from a vendor you can trust.
- *Price.* I put price last because it should be last in your mind when monitor shopping. Only after getting all the features you want should you consider the price and who to buy from. If someone has helped you look at 50 different monitors in the store, it is a nice touch if you buy one from them.

Monitors and video cards I have known
Now let's look at some specific Cat Mac monitor and video card solutions for you. Here are my recommendations for the low, midrange, and high end. I'll begin with the low-end monochrome TTL monitors and work my way upward.

Low-end Cat Mac video solutions
Low-end monitors (in this case I mean those intended for use on other than NuBus Macintosh logic boards) and video cards come and go but a great selection of video options is always available to Cat Mac builders. In the first edition of this book, the combination of the Princeton MAX-15 Multisync monitor and the Power R module gave outstanding performance at a great price. The bad news is the MAX-15 monitor has gone to that big monitor heaven in the sky and technology has passed the Power R module by. The good news is Cat Mac builders now have even better solutions.

The lowest cost solution is to put a relatively inexpensive TTL monitor (identical to those used on DOS PCs) on your Cat Mac, and drive it with an ATS (Atlanta Technical Specialists) video board.

For most Cat Mac builders, using one of the family of Lapis video cards, which you can merely plug into your Macintosh logic board, and then plug your monitor into it, makes the most sense.

The build-your-own video interface to drive your TTL monitor, mentioned in the first edition as a not recommended curiosity, is today a needless exercise in self-flagellation given the fact that you can buy the same capability plus additional features in the inexpensive ATS video board. I strongly recommend you don't build your own.

TTL monitors and cards

Today, 12" to 14" monochrome TTL monitors from Amdek (Wyse Technology), Samsung, Epson, and Hyundai (among others) are available in paperwhite, amber, and green flavors. As you recall from the definitions, TTL is the absolute lowest cost solution in the monitor department. Your investment in this department is in the $70 to $150 range—with paperwhite the most costly and green the least. You might, of course, be able to secure an even better deal depending on the particular monitor you select and your source of supply. As with hard drives, I don't recommend buying a used monitor because you don't know who used them, for how long or how hard. Fortunately, newer monitors all come with a date-of-manufacture stamp on the back (usually next to the serial number). While a one- or two-year shelf life is a definite possibility, you know something is tainted if your "new" monitor has a 1988 date stamp. A Samsung TTL amber monitor is shown on the Cat Mac system of Fig. 6-1. Isn't it cute? And hey, it's inexpensive and it obviously works too!

The simplest and least expensive way to connect your inexpensive TTL monitor to your low-end Macintosh logic board is with the ATS video board—it was used to drive the Samsung TTL amber monitor of Fig. 6-1. This board (it comes bundled with all ATS build-it-yourself Macintosh kits along with all cabling) basically adjusts the levels of the TTL video signals already available on any Macintosh logic board to be compatible with those on standard TTL monitors. Plus it gives you a distribution center for all your other typical Cat Mac project chassis cables: speaker, LEDs, reset/interrupt switches, etc. It is available in two flavors: a model for Mac 128 through Mac Plus logic boards shown in Fig. 6-2, and a model for Mac SE and up (adaptable to the Mac Classic and Classic II) logic boards shown in Fig. 6-3. The good news is it gives you years of trouble-free service, it costs around $40, and it saves you the needless labor of building your own TTL video interface. The bad news is that it might not be initially compatible with all TTL monitor models without tweaking. Call ATS to be sure.

Understand too what you are not getting when you elect to go the ATS route or to build your own (arrgh!). You are basically replicating the image of the smaller internal Macintosh 9" screen on a larger external 12" to 14" TTL

6-1 Samsung TTL video monitor on Cat Mac system.

6-2 ATS video board for Mac Plus and earlier logic boards.

6-3 ATS video board for Mac SE and later logic boards.

monitor—the exact same 512 × 342 pixel image is displayed. If you want to fill more of your 12" screen, you tweak the monitor, but you are only making the pixels larger, not adding more information. At around 10" or so you lose the ability to tweak any more; distortions wipe out your gains.

The Lapis connection

Buying a ready-made video card from Lapis Technologies that you just plug into your Cat Mac logic board is another story. When driving your TTL monitor from the Lapis card, no monitor adjustment is required; you use your TTL monitor right out of the box without any tweaking. The Lapis card also gives you the desirable option of making a number of higher resolution display modes available. A Lapis general-purpose video card costs about $350, but opens up the world of DOS PC monitors to you. In addition, Lapis licenses their technology to numerous other vendors today, so combination cards from other sources quite possibly have Lapis technology "under the hood." Figure 6-4 shows a typical Lapis video card—in this case a Mac SE 30 model—with the ATS adapter at the right for mounting it either in a Cat Mac SE 30 or IIsi project.

Lapis has made connecting any model DOS PC monitor—from among the hundreds available—to virtually any model Macintosh logic board into the easiest process imaginable. Choose the Lapis card that matches the monitor and Macintosh logic board you have; install it in your Cat Mac; load the Lapis software; then boot up your Cat Mac. At the low end, Lapis 1-bit monochrome

6-4 Lapis Mac SE 30-style video card with ATS 90 degree adapter at right.

video cards offer 720 × 350 or 640 × 480 resolution on just about any monochrome TTL or multisync monitor. While I am talking about the low end here, Lapis also has 8-bit color video cards to adapt color monitors to any Macintosh logic board that supports it. Table 6-1 summarizes Lapis video card capabilities for typical Mac SE and Mac II compatible monitors.

Table 6-1. Lapis video options.

Monitor class	Resolution	Horizontal	Vertical
Apple Two-page	1152 × 872	68.5 kHz	75 Hz
Lapis Dual-page	1024 × 828	64.7 kHz	75 Hz
Dual-page	1152 × 910	62.5 kHz	66.7 Hz
Dual-page	1152 × 872	50 – 70 kHz	50 – 75 Hz
Dual-page	1024 × 768	50 – 70 kHz	50 – 80 Hz
Apple Portrait	640 × 872	68.85 kHz	75 Hz
Lapis Full-page	640 × 872	68.85 kHz	75 Hz
Full-page	640 × 872	50 – 70 kHz	50 – 80 Hz
Apple 12" mono	640 × 480	35 kHz	65 Hz
Apple 13" RGB	640 × 480	35 kHz	65 Hz
VGA mono	640 × 480	31.5 kHz	60 Hz
LCD panel (VGA)	640 × 480	31.5 kHz	60 Hz

Lapis also offers bundled Lapis video card plus monitor display subsystems (such as the Lapis DisplayServer full-page display and video card at $899) and has periodically offered special deals and pricing on selected packages. The Amdek TTL paperwhite monitor and Lapis video card especially designed for it shown in Fig. 6-5 are an example of one such offer. Of course, new monitor and Lapis card combinations are constantly being introduced. You can expect something new and different to be available in the future after you read this and contact Lapis for information and current prices.

6-5 Amdek monitor and Lapis 1-bit video card—special promotion from Lapis Technology.

Lapis 1-bit monochrome video card alternatives

Lapis Technologies lists compatibility with Ehman/Cutting Edge, Dotronix, Hyundai, Mirror, Protege, PPL, Real Tech, Samsung, Zenith and VGA-style—among others. I have yet to find a monitor that would not work! But let me tell you about my favorites.

In the first edition, I mentioned the NEC 2GS monochrome monitor as an attractive alternative for Cat Mac builders. I liked it then for its overall clarity, sharpness, and the closeness in color of its 14″ blue-white screen to the hue of the original Apple Macintosh 9″ screen. In 1991, NEC repriced its entire monitor line and lowered the list price of its entry-level NEC 2GS monitor to under $200—making it an even better deal for Cat Mac builders. It is perfectly matched in performance to Lapis video cards available for the Mac SE, SE 30, Classic, or any of the NuBus models.

In the first edition, I also mentioned the Apple high-resolution monochrome monitor (originally offered as the low-end video solution on the Apple Mac II) as an excellent choice for Cat Mac builders. Apple reduced the list price on it from $399 to $299 when the Mac LC was introduced in October 1990. It was an outstanding monochrome monitor choice for the Mac II in 1987. Combined with the appropriate Lapis video card, it is still an outstanding choice for any Cat Mac builder's project requiring a monochrome video monitor today, and delivers a highly readable blue-white screen image.

Princeton MAX-15 monitor and Power R module

The Princeton MAX-15 monitor and Power R module were the featured stars of the first edition and might still be useful to some of today's Cat Mac builders. Although production of the Princeton MAX-15 monitor has been discontinued, you can occasionally find refurbished units. Contact Princeton Graphic Systems directly for current sources. The Power R video module, coupled with the Princeton MAX-15 monitor, produced great results. While you didn't get any more information than was on the Macintosh 9" screen, the MAX-15's oversize mode painted it corner to corner for you on its much larger 14" screen. It was wonderful for writers—very easy on the eyes.

The Power R video module did a great job with the MAX-15, but unfortunately it was the only monochrome multisync monitor around. Also, later Power R modules were built on a vertical circuit board rather than integrated with the cable assembly as in earlier ones. This made them an extremely tight fit in the desirable PS/2-style Cat Mac chassis and totally unusable for newer, even smaller LAN-style Cat Mac chassis without an additional cable adapter. Plus the Power R module costs twice as much as the ATS video board. Contrast the vertically mounted Power R video adapter and its cable, shown on the right in Fig. 6-6, with a typical flat-mount video card and cable assembly shown on the left.

Midrange Cat Mac video solutions

Above the low-end monitor price performance range lie the numerous full-page and two-page monochrome monitor offerings. As I write this, several quality mail order vendors offer full-page and two-page monitors for as low as $499 and $799, respectively, with their Lapis video card interfaces.

My favorite midrange Cat Mac builder offering is the Radius Pivot monitor. Radius, the first Macintosh third-party large-screen vendor has met or exceeded every user need with this exceptional product that switches between the landscape and portrait mode with a gentle hand tug. Even if not equipped with this extremely convenient feature, the monitor itself would place it at the head of its class. Its 78-dpi screen supports 640×864 pixel resolution on a 15" diagonal screen ($8" \times 11"$ full-page size) at 75-Hz vertical refresh (no flicker!) and delivers it with clarity, sharpness, contrast and overall readability—it's a product you really have to see to appreciate. If you are starting with a Mac IIsi, IIci, or Quadra logicboard, you can save a few dollars and use the Radius Pivot without its video card—only $1295 instead of $1695. Just install the Radius Pivot monitor driver software and you receive nearly identical performance to the full-fledged Radius offering when the monitor is connected directly to the logic board video port. Radius also listened to its customers and brought back

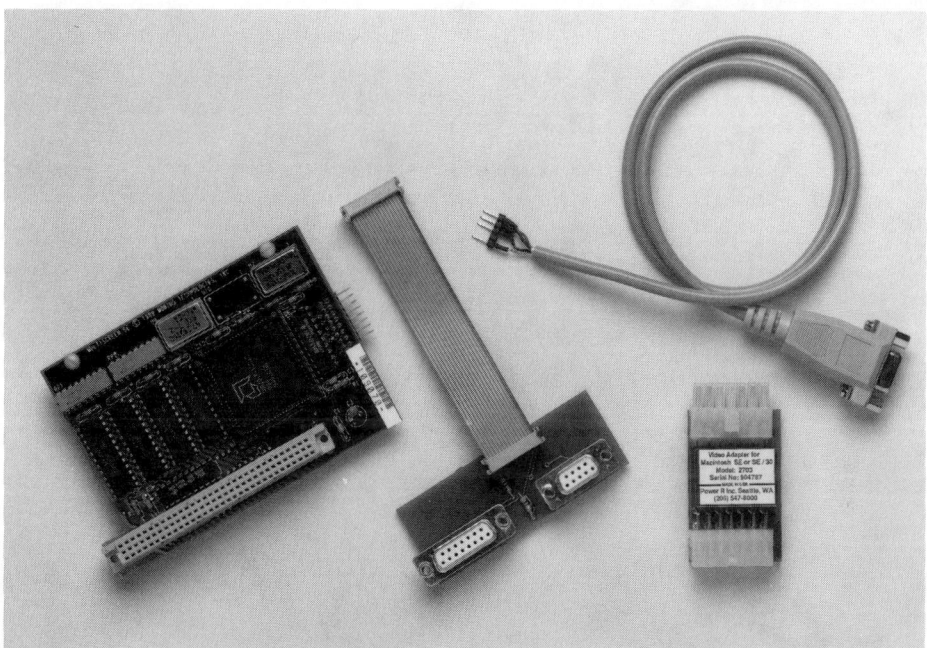

6-6 Contrasting flat-style video card on right with vertical-mount Power R module on left.

its original full-page display which provides nearly as good an image quality minus the pivot feature at an attractive price.

Close behind Radius at the top of the pack are both the full-page and two-page offerings from Apple. While not the first to market with its products, Apple has certainly done its homework and gotten the feature set right. You pay a little extra but your eyeballs will be pleased with your choice over the long haul.

Right behind Radius and Apple is Mobius with its full-page monitor from Zenith. Even if not for the clever combination Mobius accelerator and video card,[1] this monitor would stand by itself near the top of the pack. The accelerator/video card elevates this monitor into its own special category for Cat Mac SE builders because nothing else on the market is quite like it in its price performance range. Figure 6-7 shows the Mobius full-page display and accelerator board combination.

Color Cat Mac video solutions

Monochrome graphics on the Macintosh are great, but color is fantastic. Gray scale is an in-between step (all color monitors automatically deliver gray scale). While color for most word-processing and desktop publishing applications is overkill (especially if you are delivering output in black-and-white printed form), it can improve your productivity under certain circumstances. It can

6-7 Mobius accelerator/video card and Zenith full-page display—bundled package from Mobius Technologies.

also deliver enhanced performance over the entire spectrum: Color gives you another category to sort objects on your desktop; numerous studies have reported productivity gains when database entry screens were painted in color; and no one would question color's contribution to complex CAD/CAM or 3-D rendering programs. What you get is more rapid recognition of patterns, relationships, or graphics data. What you give up is money (color costs more) and speed (color has more bits per pixel so it takes more horsepower to drive at the same speed).

While most Cat Mac builders don't need color today, you might take a look at your future plans. Even if you are just using black and white, can a step up to a gray-scale monitor that displays photographic images better help you? My recommendation to you in the color monitor area is simple—give your eyeballs the best you can afford. While there are numerous low cost DOS PC color monitor vendors hawking their wares, this is one case where you want to buy quality at the best price rather than an inferior cheap imitation. Stick with the quality vendors: Apple, Radius, and SuperMac (selected products from E-Machines, RasterOps, and Sigma Designs would also make the list). Don't buy from another vendor unless you see its color monitor and look at its specifications first. Buy the 13" Apple color monitor for general purpose use, the 12" Apple color if you want color on a budget, the Radius Color Pivot or one of the 16" color monitors if you are doing production color, or 19" or 21" color for high-end specialized needs.

Apple color monitor offerings

The original Apple high-resolution RGB display (introduced with the Apple Mac II in 1987) is still the one to beat in the 13" color monitor category. Based on Sony Trinitron technology, Apple got this one absolutely correct right out of the starting blocks and it has been a best-seller for Apple ever since—as its longevity attests. Regardless of the video card you couple it with, Apple video, Lapis, another third-party, or direct-input into a Mac LC, IIsi, IIci, or Quadra logic board, you will not be disappointed with the color performance you receive. Offering you 640 × 480 resolution, 70 dpi, 67-Hz refresh, and a 0.25-millimeter dot pitch when used with Apple's Mac II video card, it gives an extremely bright, clear, sharp display with true blacks and very reliable color representation for its $999 list price. I strongly endorse this solution for all Cat Mac builders.

If you are on a budget, the Apple Macintosh 12" RGB display introduced with the Macintosh LC in late 1990 at $599 list price might be just the solution for you. It features 512 × 384 resolution at 64 dpi (text can be read more easily when enlarged from the Apple 72-dpi WYSIWYG standard) and a bright, clear, sharp, high-contrast display with true colors that comes very close to the original Apple color display at an economy price.

While Apple set the industry benchmarks for its low- and midrange Macintosh color monitor offerings, it went to school on what features customers preferred at the upper end before making its move. The results are two superior products. You will not hurt yourself with the Apple 16" color display at $1699 or the 21" color display offering 1152 × 870 pixels at 79 dpi for $4599 at the upper end of the performance spectrum.

Other color monitor offerings

If the Radius Pivot monitor was great, the Radius Color Pivot has to be the greatest. It has two color modes: 72-dpi WYSIWYG at 564 × 760 pixel resolution, and 82 dpi at 640 × 870 resolution also on a 15" diagonal screen (8" × 11" full-page size). The monitor lists for $1995 and PDS or NuBus compatible 8-bit video cards for $795—Cat Mac IIsi, IIci, or Quadra owners have the option of using direct plug-in for the 82-dpi mode. It's another product you really have to see to appreciate.

SuperMac went to school on Apple's original high-resolution RGB display but innovated it one step further to come out with the first Macintosh 19" color display—also based on Sony Trinitron technology. SuperMac's original 19" color monitor was for many years superior to virtually any other Macintosh color monitor except Apple's original smaller size RGB display. SuperMac obviously hasn't stopped innovating either. Today's SuperMac 19″ color monitor provides 1024 × 768 resolution at 72 dpi and 75-Hz vertical refresh with a 0.31-millimeter dot pitch for $2800; its dual mode 19″ monitor adds 1152 × 870 resolution at 77 dpi for $4200; and its 21″ color monitor offers the higher resolution at $4400. SuperMac's Spectrum 8 or 24 NuBus cards complement its offerings. Cat Mac builders might spend a little more to get them, but will never be disappointed with or criticized (certainly not by me!) for choosing a SuperMac color monitor solution.

E-Machines (originally known for its Big Picture 17″ full-page monochrome display) simply had a better idea: Take proven Sony Trinitron technology in a 16″ color monitor and offer it in the midrange between Apple's 13″ and SuperMac's 19″ color monitor. In addition to being the right idea at the right time, E-Machines' razor-sharp 16″ monitor has won all the awards in its class and gives you a resolution of 832 × 624 pixels, 72 dpi, 67-Hz vertical refresh and a 0.26-millimeter dot pitch. Its success has spawned a host of competitors (including Apple's $1699 and SuperMac's $1199 16″ color monitors) but E-Machines' blend of outstanding hardware (providing a bright, clear image with good contrast and true colors) and excellent software makes for a product you very rarely find in the used equipment market—users love their T16s.

The SCSI monitor connection

Aura Systems pioneered this entire area several years ago with its Scuzzy Graph interface adapter that attached to the SCSI connector on a Mac Plus, SE, or Classic logic board (even a Mac Portable!) and enabled it to run full-featured color monitors (Apple's SuperMacs, other Sony Trinitron models, Ikegami, etc.). At only $695 list it was an economical option, and the SCSI interface allowed it to be shared or moved as you upgraded to newer Cat Mac models. Quite a nifty, handy device—well worth a look.

Sigma Designs announced the ultimate video toy for Cat Mac builders at the January 1992 MacWorld—a 15″ monochrome display system that plugs into the SCSI port of any low-end Macintosh logic board. With its design, all the video interfacing you need is already inside the monitor itself! The Sigma Designs Power Page display offers 576 × 768 pixels at 72-dpi WYSIWYG, 640 × 870 pixels at 80-dpi full-page, and 704 × 940 dpi at 88 dpi for A4-sized pages for $995 list.

Today, Aura Systems now offers its Scuzzy Graph II model, and the popularity of the Apple PowerBooks has spawned a host of competitive products from Radius, SuperMac, Computer Care, Lapis, RasterOps, and Sigma Designs. The best news for Cat Mac builders is that these options not only offer you more video monitor flexibility to begin with, but they can be repackaged inside your larger Cat Mac chassis for maximum attractiveness and compactness.

Combination accelerator and video cards

These combination cards were a novel idea in the first edition—the Mobius package had just been announced and a few other vendors were beginning to work on a la carte offerings. How things change with time! Today, following the trail blazed by Mobius, numerous vendors offer combination packages and dual-function accelerator/video cards. Virtually all enhancement/accelerator board vendors either provide expansion video cards or suggest compatible video solutions for their boards.

Mobius Technologies clearly leads the packaged crowd, and has extended its offerings to include full-page and two-page monochrome monitors as well as full-fledged and low-cost versions of its 68030-based accelerator card. Packaged solutions start around $1095. You'll see how to build with them in chapter 9. By the way, the same performance boost that makes the Mobius monochrome full-page monitor a pure delight to work with becomes a necessity instead of an option at the upper end of the color monitor line. You see Super-Mac, RasterOps, E-Machines, and even Apple with its 8/24 GC NuBus video card adding acceleration along with video capability, although they might use alternative approaches to the 68030 chip. Don't even think of using these high-performance monitors without them—unless you are the type that wonders how a lawnmower engine would work in your Porsche.

ImagePro Systems, the marketing arm of Novy Systems (the accelerator people), offers a wide assortment of monitors and combo accelerator/video cards in different speed ranges. Think of them as the Lapis of the accelerated video market. Their approach is the exact opposite of Mobius. You can mix and match monitors and accelerator speeds for capabilities above and below Mobius across a broader range of Macintosh logic boards. Boards start at $695, combination packages with monitors around $1295.

Total Systems and NewLife Computer both add special purpose video cards to their accelerator cards to drive a wide assortment of monitors. It's best to contact them first to see if the monitor you want to drive is supported by their cards.

Applied Engineering's TransWarp SE or LC has a special video output connector that is compatible with many of the Radius monitors. Here again, it's best to call first.

Build your own video interface

You can produce a video TTL monitor interface that is inexpensive in terms of parts (the labor cost depends on your skill and your persistence), if you are not afraid of soldering irons and opening up a video monitor to tweak the insides. The lowest priced Cat Mac video solution owes its debt of gratitude to the authors of the *Computer Shopper* "Hackintosh" articles.[2] Grab a reprint if you want the details. However, Fig. 6-8 shows you what you are up against in opening up the inside of the Samsung monitor for modification according to their

6-8 Inside Samsung Amber TTL monitor.

recommendations. The pencil shows the location of resistor R606 which needs to be modified. Don't touch that high-voltage capacitor on the left—oops, sorry! On the Samsung it was easier to add a 10K variable resistor rather than a fixed resistor at location R606—then I just dialed in the value I needed. However, I found every monitor was different, and this process was tedious on most, nearly impossible on some, and only infrequently easy on others. That is why I don't recommend it to Cat Mac builders.

Speaking of tweaking, no matter how I tweaked the intensity and adjusted the contrast of the amber TTL Samsung monitor, I found it harder on my eyes compared to the paper-white Mac screens I have viewed for years. But, it worked great. A green monitor screen was also harder on my eyes and I never could get used to seeing the IBM logo on the case. I know this is heresy to some Mac users, but an original green IBM monochrome monitor worked as well on my original Cat Mac SE with the Lapis card as the Samsung did.

The purpose of *Build Your Own Macintosh and Save a Bundle* is to do it with off-the-shelf catalog parts that make it easy and be up and running in a short time. My experimenting in the area of low cost monitors and do-it-yourself video interfaces has only led me to one conclusion—it doesn't do this. Skip this option unless you are prepared for a substantial investment of your time before you realize the final product of your labors. Besides, the ATS video interface is a low-cost and painless alternative that works, does more, and requires no time investment—plug in your cables and go.

Sources

Monitors and video cards are available new and as upgrade replacements through Apple dealers. New and used Apple monitors and video cards are also available through the Apple used equipment dealers. All other monitors and video cards are available directly from the manufacturer and through the mail order distributors.

Manufacturers—Video monitors and adapters

Atlanta Technical Specialists
3550 Clarkston Indus. Blvd., #F
Clarkston, GA 30021
(404) 292-6655

Aura Systems
P.O. Box 4576
Carlsbad, CA 92008
(800) 365-2872

E-Machines
9305 SW. Gemini Dr.
Beaverton, OR 97005
(503) 646-6699

ImageProSystems
1860 Fern Palm Dr.
Edgewater, FL 32141
(800) 638-4784

Lapis Technologies
1100 Marina Village Pkwy., #101
Alameda, CA 94501
(415) 748-1600

Mobius Technologies
5835 Doyle St.
Emeryville, CA 94608
(415) 654-0556

Power R
1606 Dexter Ave. N.
Seattle, WA 98109
(206) 547-8000

Princeton Graphic Systems
1100 Northmeadow Pkwy., #150
Roswell, GA 30076
(800) 221-1490

Radius
1710 Fortune Dr.
San Jose, CA 95131
(408) 434-1010

SuperMac Technology
485 Potrero Ave.
Sunnyvale, CA 94086
(408) 245-2202

Mail order—Macintosh add-on hardware dealers

Beverly Hills Computer
279 S. Beverly Dr., #1200
Beverly Hills, CA 90212
(800) 426-8166

Dr. Mac
14542 Ventura Blvd., #200
Sherman Oaks, CA 91403
(800) 825-6227

Mac Connection
14 Mill St.
Marlow, NH 03456
(800) 334-4444

MacLand
5006 S. Ash Ave., #101
Tempe, AZ 85282
(800) 333-3353

MacProducts USA
8303 Mopac Expwy, #218
Austin, TX 78759
(800) 622-3475

MacZone
6825 176th St. NE., #100
Redmond, WA 98052
(800) 248-0800

MacWarehouse
1690 Oak St.
Lakewood, NJ 08701
(800) 255-6227

---

[1]Mobius and Lapis share a common heritage from Beck Tech. Mobius passed on TTL compatibility and opted for more powerful combination accelerator/video card/monitor packages for midrange Macintosh logic boards. Lapis went for the broader monitor attachment market, licensing, and TTL.

[2]Max Stax, "Building the Hackintosh," *Computer Shopper*, August 1988, p. 11; Les Hall, "Hackintosh Video Modifications," *Computer Shopper*, March 1989, p. 229; and Les Hall, "Hackintosh Upgrade: A Fourteen Inch Monitor," *Computer Shopper*, August 1989, p. 423.

Chapter 7

Chassis, wiring, keyboard, and mouse

The saying, "the more things change the more they stay the same" is particularly appropriate for this chapter. Cat Mac builders' chassis, wiring, keyboard, and mouse options have changed little from the first edition of the book—there are just more of them. Your first decision in any Cat Mac project is what kind of chassis (case, cabinet, box, etc.) you want to use. Although many alternatives exist, this chapter shows you why you are best served by choosing a DOS PC case and what its benefits are. Next, the wiring of the chassis is covered. You will see how easy it is to wire your Cat Mac project, how the cables for the different Macintosh logic boards all fit into well-defined groups, and how using custom-built cables makes your job even easier. The straightforward keyboard and mouse/pointing device subjects will then be covered. For each topic, I give some background, discuss the pros and cons of alternative choices, and give you my recommendation. Let's start with the chassis.

Chassis

When you build your new Cat Mac, you can exercise your creativity to the fullest. On a practical note, mainframe and minicomputer vendors have been putting their standard products into specialized enclosures for decades. The same has been done with personal computers. The Apple Macintosh is no exception. Usually the reason is to protect them from the harsh and rugged environment of a factory floor (industrial cabinets), shield the electronic emanations coming out of the computer so others can't eavesdrop (security cabinets), or repackage them to fit into a certain space (custom cabinets). Your reasons are more aesthetic and practical. You want to save money, minimize the time it takes you to do it, yet have an attractive result.

Advantages of a DOS PC chassis

You can mount your Macintosh logic board inside anything you can imagine. I have entertained requests for putting it inside an old radio tuner case, a briefcase, a TV set, an old, dusty IBM Selectric typewriter (dastardly!), an old Compaq Portable case (heresy!) and a number of other spots too cute to mention, in addition to the standard industrial, security, and custom requests outlined earlier. On the other hand, if you decide to put it into an inexpensive DOS PC case you can choose from a multitude of cases in all sizes, shapes, and colors, containing internal power supplies which provide the exact voltages you need. I believe most Cat Mac builders will choose this option. The following section outlines the advantages of using a DOS PC case to mount your Cat Mac logic board.

Readily available *Computer Shopper* and numerous other magazines are filled with advertisements from chassis vendors, and several companies specialize in cases already custom tailored for Cat Mac builders (chapter 10 covers them).

Inexpensive Typically from $40 to $100 for PC-XT-, PC-AT-, PS/2-, and LAN-style cases. Larger, tower-style cases cost from $80 to $200 more.

All the power you need Some newer standard Apple Macintosh models have minimum-sized power supplies designed for lowest cost. Cat Mac builders enjoy the luxury of choosing from numerous power supplies designed to fit DOS PC chassis that provide all the different voltages you require, and are capable of providing far more power than you are ever likely to need. Typically from $40 to $100 for power supplies ranging from 135 to 250 watts.

Ease of access mounting Adding memory, accelerator cards, larger displays, and other options to the standard Apple Macintosh Classic and earlier models of the same cabinet style requires that you jam the cards in; sometimes it's even difficult to close the case. The DOS PC case makes it easy to mount components of all kinds: disk drives, logic boards, speakers, accelerators and video boards.

Ease of expansion The DOS PC case gives you room to expand as your needs grow. And if you need more room, just get a larger case.

Components live longer No heat or air flow problems as in a small case because you're putting all of these components into an oversized chassis rather than a small, crowded box, with a higher capacity power supply and an industrial strength fan that dissipates much of the heat generated.

The bottom line is a DOS PC case gives your Cat Mac all kinds of room, all kinds of electrical power, no mounting problems, and a longer life for a relatively low cost. Some pretty good reasons for choosing a DOS PC case, but again, you are limited only by your imagination in terms of what you mount your Macintosh logic board in.

Whatever kind of case you get, you want to be sensitive to emitted Radio Frequency Interference (RFI). The nice people at the Federal Communications Commission (FCC) do not take kindly to those individuals who interfere with their neighbors TV sets and other electronic appliances. This is another reason why putting it in a metal DOS PC case is a natural choice and also why Apple sprays a metalized coating on the inside of its plastic cases.

Five classes of DOS PC cases are available to meet your Cat Mac building needs:

- PC-XT style
- Mini-tower or PC-AT style
- Low-profile PS/2 style
- LAN style
- Tower style

Each of these DOS PC chassis cases has advantages and disadvantages for your Cat Mac project. Let's take a closer look.

PC-XT-style case

For my first Cat Mac project in the first edition, I chose a standard PC-XT case in a flip-top version shown in chapter 8 in Fig. 8-2. This chassis was an excellent choice for that first project. The flip-top case provided easy access to all components (great for prototyping), its size permitted ease of mounting a wide variety of components, and its low price made the decision easy. The down side of the standard PC-XT case is, it is rather bulky on your desk, its power supply fan is noisy, it has only four half-height openings for $5^{1}/_{4}''$ drives, and it doesn't look all that stylish today because the evolution of computers has passed the PC-XT models by.

Mini-tower- or PC-AT-style case

The main advantages of the mini-tower case (shown in Fig. 7-1 with the Apple monochrome monitor) are that it gives you a lot more room inside to mount components, and it comes already equipped with cutouts, faceplates, and mounting hardware for both $3^{1}/_{2}''$ and $5^{1}/_{4}''$ drives. The same is also true of the PC-AT case, which just has a different orientation of the components. Either chassis is an excellent choice for Cat Mac projects requiring a little more room. Numerous vendor and mounting options are available, and both types are still

7-1   Mini tower case.

in vogue as contemporary styles. Current models of these chassis styles also have locking power, turbo, and reset switches easily accessible on the front panel, along with several colored LED lamps. These can be used, removed, or cannibalized by you for other projects as you see fit.

The down side of the mini-tower or PC-AT-style chassis is that many feature "unusual" orientation of internal or rear chassis card mounting brackets that—while OK for DOS PC users—could interfere with a Cat Mac builder's intended use of the chassis. The best policy is to look at, get photographs of, or ask to verify if there is clearance and room to accommodate the specific Macintosh logic board you are contemplating mounting in the chassis.

Low-profile PS/2-style case

This is the case I have found to be the best for all my midsize Cat Mac projects. It comes in many contemporary styles from different vendors—generally it is labeled their mini-AT or PS/2 chassis or something similar. I found two different models of this case that I liked equally well. One version, shown with the Samsung TTL monitor in Fig. 7-2, has room to mount three 3½" disk drives. The other version, shown with the Princeton MAX-15 monitor in Fig. 7-3, has

7-2 Low-profile PS/2-style case—three drive slot model.

7-3 Low-profile PS/2-style case—four drive slot model.

room for two 3½" and two 5¼" disk drives. I prefer this version because the combination of two different sizes of mounting openings gives you more flexibility. It is the one used to build the Cat Mac projects in chapters 8 and 9.

Both low-profile PC cases come already equipped with cutouts, faceplates, and mounting hardware. Even though both are compact chassis styles, there is a lot of room available inside to mount parts. Despite the reduced vertical clearance, the chassis is actually about the same height as a standard Apple Mac IIsi enclosure, so many Macintosh logic boards and option cards are readily accommodated. Unlike certain mini-tower or PC-AT cases, there are no internal obstructions to interfere with easy building. Its low-profile look is slick and contemporary. Also, the 200- or 230-W power supply you receive when ordering either version has a fan only half as loud as the one in the 135-W power supply you get with the PC-XT flip-top chassis. Both chassis also feature all the amenities—power, turbo, and reset switches easily accessible on the front panel along with the appropriate colored LED indicator lamps.

On the down side, I find the pushbutton power switch on the version shown in Fig. 7-3 annoying because your finger has to push it all the way down in its opening to get it to latch on. Since it is a narrow opening and I have large fingers, I have to be right on the button to make it work right. This would not be a problem if I used the eraser end of a pencil as a finger extension—but I haven't yet dedicated a pencil to the task. The flip switch on the other chassis version shown in Fig. 7-2 is much easier to use.

LAN-style case

Still more contemporary are the LAN-style DOS PC cases. One version, shown in Fig. 7-4 with the Princeton MAX-15 monitor, was used to build chapter 9's compact desktop Cat Mac project. Another even lower profile LAN-style case is shown in Fig. 7-5 being trial fitted for a Mac LC logic board, a Quantum LPS 52 hard drive, and an Apple 1.4Mb FDHD floppy drive. The LAN-style cases typically give you two $3^1/2''$ drive mounting spaces—one available externally and one internally. While this is more than enough to accommodate a floppy drive and any capacity $3^1/2''$ hard drive, the chassis size makes them usable only for Mac SE, SE 30, LC, IIsi, and Classic logic boards. I use them as foundations for my transportable Cat Mac projects or those requiring the smallest possible footprint on the desktop. LAN-style cases also feature easily accessible power and reset switches on the front panel (the turbo switch is usually omitted) along with LEDs.

On the down side, LAN chassis have less room and smaller power supplies, so think of using them in dedicated or fixed-function applications rather than as a platform for your expandable, general-purpose Cat Mac.

7-4 LAN-style case.

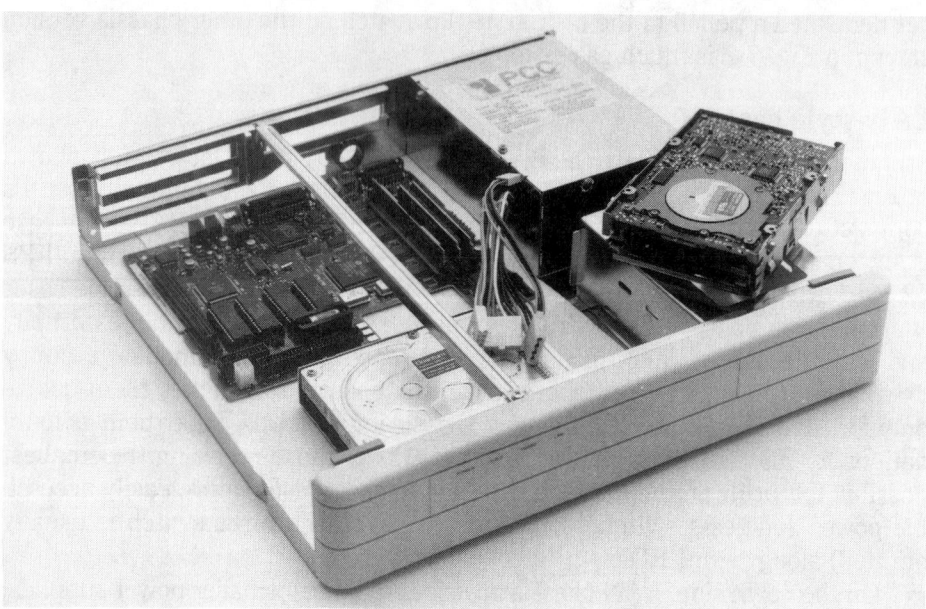

7-5 Lower-profile LAN-style case.

Tower-style case

These are the biggest, most expensive chassis, yet offer you the most flexibility and power and are typically used for your NuBus-based Cat Mac projects. Figure 7-6 shows the ATS tower chassis used to house a Mac IIci logic board. Figure 7-7 shows another, larger ATS tower chassis used to house a Mac II logic board. Both tower chassis models will be revisited further when their kits are assembled in chapter 10. Tower cases are available from just about all chassis vendors to accommodate just about every possible combination of Macintosh logic board, expansion boards, and drives imaginable—all you have to do is let your fingers do the walking through the magazines and order the right one. Tower chassis styles also feature the sportiest of the front panel displays and usually feature an LED speed indicator and separate activity LEDs for each of the drives, in addition to a locking power switch along with reset and turbo switches.

The "right one" is perhaps the only down side. You want to mount your NuBus logic board so its NuBus card openings face the rear and are easily accessible. Even though tower cases have lots of room inside, not all models permit you to do this with all Macintosh logic boards. You need to check out this capability carefully before you buy.

A quick look at the back panel

To finish off your Cat Mac project, you want to do a nice job on the rear panel. This can be an easy or a difficult task depending on the model you have

7-6 Tower case—model to accommodate Mac IIci logic board.

selected. My best counsel is to buy the whole panel if one is available (Fig. 7-8 shows one of the premade panels from Brant Associates), make your own out of aluminum (chapter 8 shows you how), and avoid working on the steel back panels if you can avoid it (use premade connector plates with the holes you want).

Chassis vendors are increasingly spot-welding their rear panels onto the main chassis to save production costs. This is not always so great for Cat Mac builders. While it is no big deal (I show you how to deal with this and add your own premade back panel in chapter 9), the process does consume extra assembly time because you need to work carefully to avoid making a mess.

If you decide to leave your rear panel in place and need more than the few 9-pin and 25-pin cutout holes typically provided, you have few options other than to buy connector plates with the right size holes for your connectors. Globe Manufacturing Sales or Olson Metal Products are excellent sources for the connector plates with premade cutout holes.

Chassis **179**

7-7 Tower case—model to accommodate Mac II logic board.

If you require additional or nonstandard holes, I recommend that you remove the entire rear panel and make whatever you need out of a piece of aluminum (working with steel is definitely not my first choice!).

Also, I recommend that you mount your Macintosh logic board so its connector comes directly out of the rear of the chassis. Try not to mount your Macintosh logic board so that you have to make extra cables for the inside of the case just to bring its connections out to the rear. No big deal—just extra effort, extra time, and extra expense.

Wiring your Cat Mac

Wiring your Cat Mac is easy. You can either make all your cables, have someone else do all the work, or something in between. Cables are definitely not

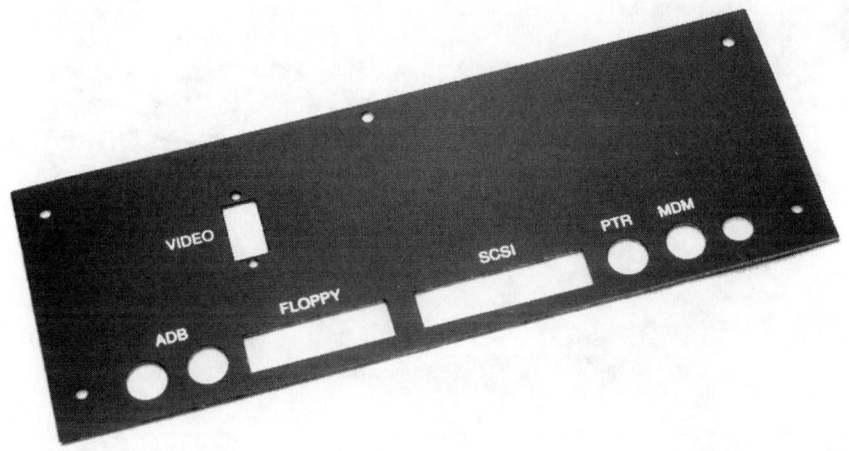

7-8 Premade back panel from Brant Associates.

difficult to make, but buying them ready-made ensures that a small error on your part (like accidentally reversing the power and ground wires!) doesn't wipe out your Macintosh logic board. My best counsel is to buy the whole set if they are available. (Figure 7-9 shows one of the premade three-piece cable sets from Brant Associates.)

Some vendors prefer to utilize an intermediate board (like the ATS video board shown in chapter 6) that serves as a "distribution point" for connecting to your logic board. This is preferred by manufacturers because they can standardize their assembly techniques. For individual Cat Mac builders working on one project, I prefer to utilize the KISS approach (Keep It Simple, etc.) and wire directly. The cables you will need for this technique are listed below.

Power cable This cable directly connects the power supply to the Macintosh logic board. Six different power cable types cover the entire family of Macintosh logic boards. The two connectors at the power supply end are the same for all. Five different connector types are used at the logic board end.

SCSI cable This cable connects the 50-pin male SCSI connector on the back of the drive with the mating 50-pin male SCSI connector on the Macintosh logic board. This is the same for all Macintosh logic boards, differing only in length (and the number of connectors on it if you use more than one internal SCSI device).

Floppy cable This cable connects the 20-pin male connector on the back of the floppy drive to the 20-pin male connector on the Macintosh logic board. This is the same for all Macintosh logic boards, differing only in length (except for those that accommodate more than one floppy drive, i.e., the Mac II, SE, and LC logic boards, which could have two cables).

Wiring your Cat Mac

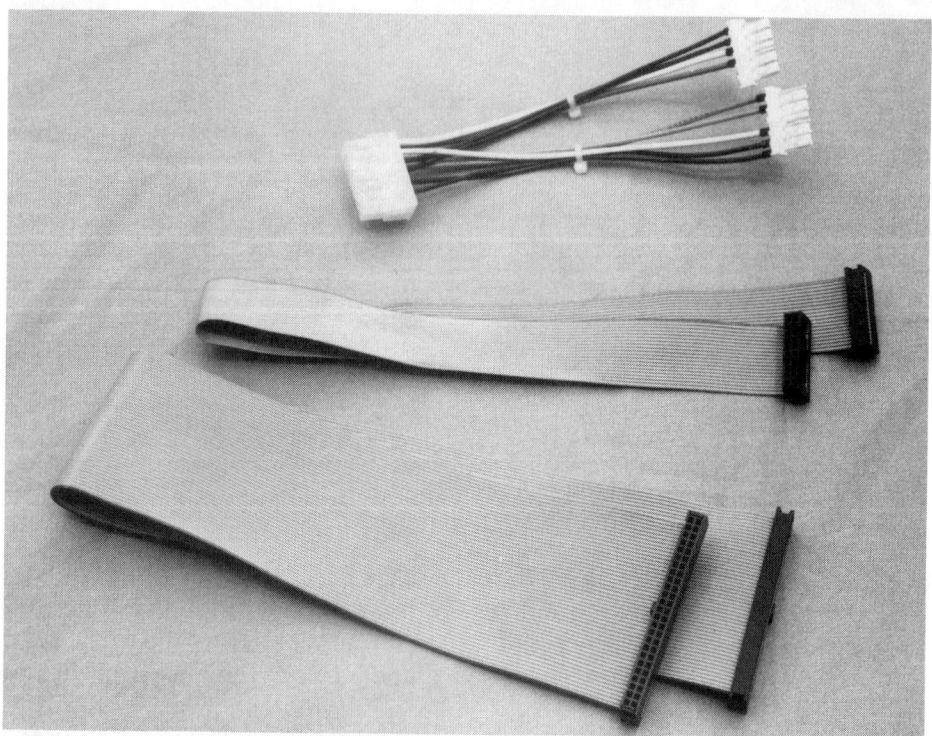

7-9 Premade power, SCSI, floppy cable set from Brant Associates.

Other cables Speaker, reset/interrupt, power-on LED, and drive activity LED cables can be made for all Cat Mac projects from those provided in your DOS PC chassis. The Mac 128, 512, and Plus logic boards also require special keyboard and battery cables. Let's look at all the cables in a little more detail, starting with the power cables.

Power cable

The easy-to-make power cable for your Cat Mac project has only three connectors on it: two at the end that go to mating connectors from the DOS PC power supply (usually labeled "P8" and "P9"), and one at the end that plugs into your Macintosh logic board.

The connectors that mate with the power supply are simple 6-pin 0.156″ center-locking headers with straight square pins (Molex 26-60-4060 or equivalent). The connector requirements for the logic board end are summarized in Table 7-1. Although I mentioned that six different cable types cover all the Macintosh logic boards, only five connectors are shown in Table 7-1 because the Mac SE/SE 30 and Mac Classic/Classic II models utilize the identical 14-pin connector (although they are wired completely differently). I've referenced

Table 7-1. Cat Mac power cable logic board connector options.

Macintosh logic board	Pins	Molex equivalent	Comments
128, 512, Plus	11	09-50-8111	Locking ramp
SE, SE 30, Classic, Classic II	14	39-01-2140	—
LC	7	09-50-8071	Locking ramp
IIcx, IIci, IIsi, Quadra 700	10	39-01-2100	—
II, IIx, IIfx	15	09-50-8150	Amp p/n 1-640251-5

Molex part numbers throughout, but you can also obtain equivalent Amp part numbers for some items.

In every case I recommend you make your power cable about 6″ long (you'll have additional cable length provided by the power supply end). This should be more than enough to accommodate any standard DOS PC chassis. The only exception is the tower models used to mount the Mac II, IIx, IIfx logic boards, for which I recommend that you make your power cable about 12″ long. The extra length is needed because the power connector for these logic boards is usually located in the extreme bottom of the chassis in normal mounting configurations.

Let's start by covering each of the three cable types using a dual-row logic board connector—Molex numbers starting with *39* in Table 7-1. The pins on the dual-row connectors required by these models are keyed; it is not possible to insert them backwards into the logic board unless you have hired a friendly gorilla to do the job.

Mac SE/SE 30 Figure 7-10 shows the construction details if you are making your own cable. The completed cable is shown at the top of Fig. 7-11. Table 7-2 provides the details of the signals required on each pin.

Mac IIcx/IIci/IIsi/Quadra 700 Figure 7-12 shows the construction details if you are making your own cable. The completed cable is shown in the middle of Fig. 7-11. You might have to cut off the connector's locking tab if it protrudes and prevents firmly seating your cable into the mating logic board connector receptacle. Table 7-2 provides the details of the signals required on each pin.

Mac Classic/Classic II Table 7-2 provides the details of the signals required on each pin. Notice it is nearly the mirror image of the Mac SE/SE 30 cable, except that it contains an additional speaker signal. (Don't ask me why Apple decided to make them totally different.)

Now let's cover the remaining three cable types using a single-row logic board connector. The pins on the single-row connectors are all identical; the key is provided by a missing pin telling you how to orient your cable. Even the friendly gorilla can't get this one wrong!

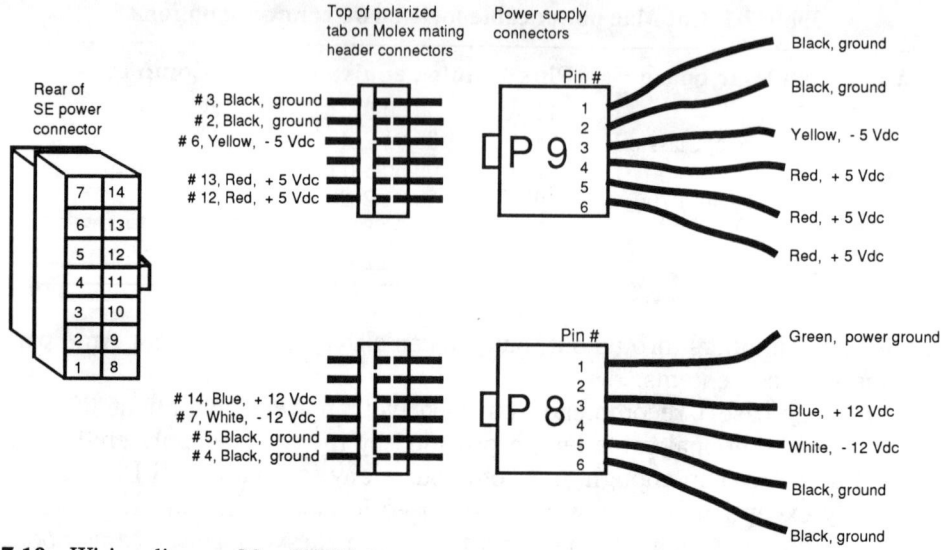

7-10 Wiring diagram Mac SE/SE 30 power cable.

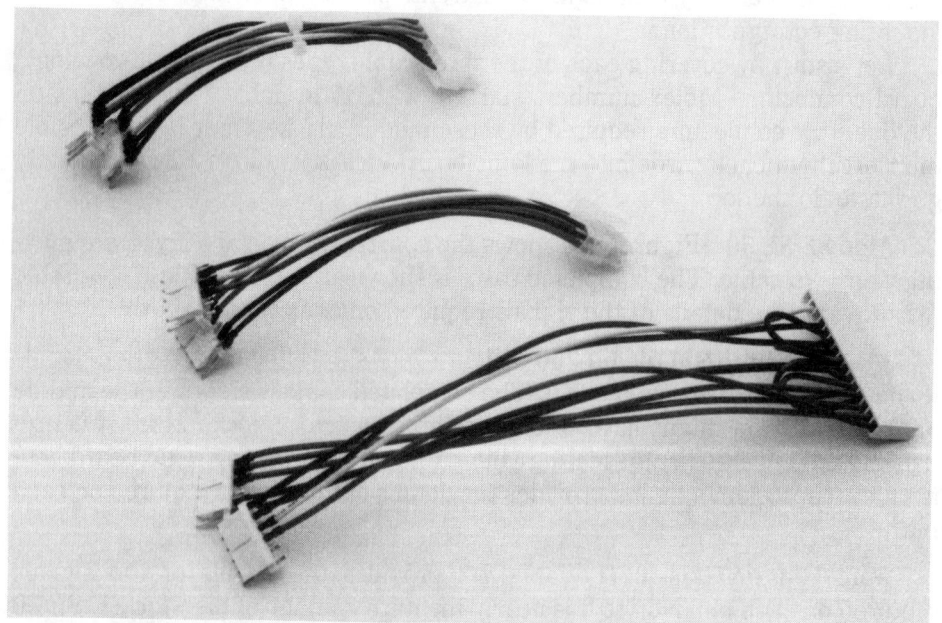

7-11 Power cables for Mac SE/SE 30, IIcx/IIci/IIsi/Quadra 700, II/IIx/IIfx.

Mac II/IIx/IIfx Table 7-3 provides the details of the signals required on each pin. This is the only cable you might want to consider making extra length, depending on your circumstances. The completed cable is shown at the bottom of Fig. 7-11.

184 *Chassis, wiring, keyboard, and mouse*

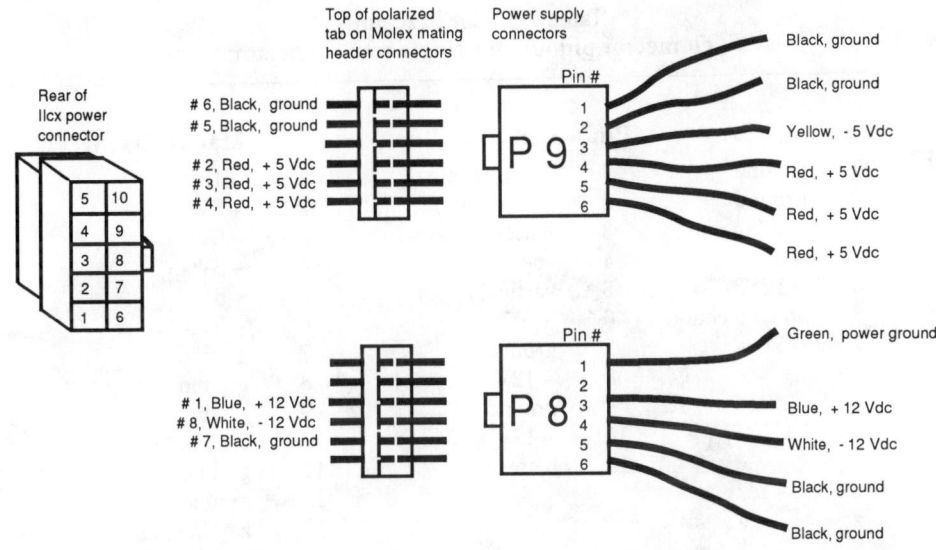

7-12 Wiring diagram Mac IIcx/IIci/IIsi/Quadra 700 power cable.

Table 7-2. Cat Mac power connector pinouts for dual-row connectors.

Pin	Classic, Classic II	Pin	SE, SE 30	Pin	IIcx, IIci, IIsi, Quadra 700
1	+12V	1	ground	1	+12V
2	+5V	2	ground	2	+5V
3	+5V	3	ground	3	+5V
4	vertical sync	4	ground	4	+5V
5	horizontal sync	5	ground	5	ground
6	video out	6	-5V	6	ground
7	speaker	7	-12V	7	ground
8	-12V	8	ground	8	-12V
9	-5V	9	video out	9	power fail warning
10	ground	10	horizontal sync	10	supply voltage for power on circuit (or +5V trickle)
11	ground	11	vertical sync		
12	ground	12	+5V		
13	ground	13	+5V		
14	ground	14	+12V		

Mac LC Table 7-3 provides the details of the signals required on each pin.

Mac 128/512/Plus Table 7-3 provides the details of the signals required on each pin. If you insist on punishing yourself, Fig. 7-13 shows you the magnitude of your task. You need to connect each one of the wires on the "optional video connector." In this case, I strongly advise that you use the ATS video card and accompanying cables because you're less than half done after con-

Wiring your Cat Mac **185**

Table 7-3. Cat Mac power connector pinouts for single row connectors.

Pin	LC	Pin	128/512/Plus	Pin	Mac II, IIx, IIfx
1	ground	1	video output	1	+12V
2	ground	2	key (no pin)	2	+5V
3	key (no pin)	3	horizontal sync	3	+5V
4	+5V	4	speaker	4	+5V
5	+12V	5	vertical sync	5	+5V
6	no connection	6	+5V	6	+5V
7	−5V	7	ground	7	ground
		8	−12V	8	ground
		9	ground	9	ground
		10	+12V	10	ground
		11	battery	11	ground
				12	ground
				13	key (no pin)
				14	−12V
				15	power fail warning

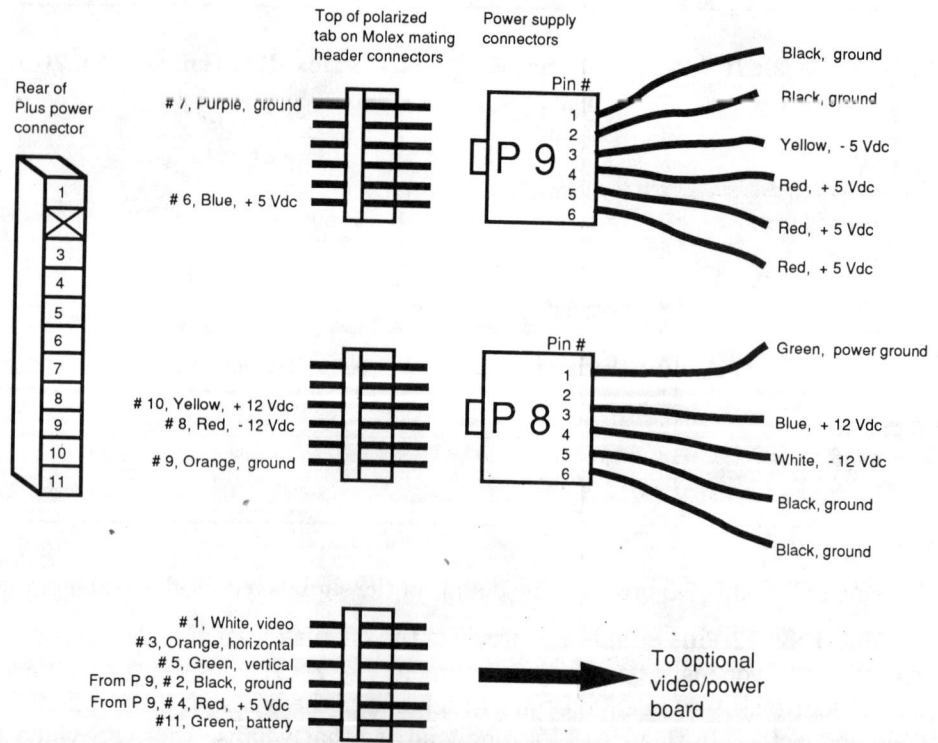

7-13 Wiring diagram Mac 128/512/Plus power cable.

Chassis, wiring, keyboard, and mouse

necting power—you still need to make the "something" that the battery and video signals go to.

SCSI cable

If you are building a Cat Mac based on any logic board except the Mac 128, 512, or Plus, all you need to do is go to your local cable supplier and get an 18" length of 50-conductor ribbon cable plus two 50-pin female IDC ribbon connectors—one for each end. Either have the supplier crimp the connectors on the cable while you wait (both connectors should be on the same side of the cable) or take it home and carefully load it in your vise to accomplish the same results. Not too difficult either way. Or buy the cable ready-made.

If you are building a Cat Mac based on the Mac 128, 512, or Plus logic boards, your problems are a bit more interesting. Both NewLife Computer and Computer Care, the primary daughterboard providers (and virtually everyone else) have elected to bring out their SCSI cables into an external 25-pin subminiature D-type connector. Since all hard drives have a standard 50-pin SCSI connector on them, you need to build a special 25-pin to 50-pin adapter cable. Not my idea of a fun time and just one more reason to not build your Cat Mac project around one of these logic boards. But if you must, use Table 7-4 to help you. Not shown in the table but learned from my own experience, if you are making this cable you need to ground all the unused inputs. Otherwise you could spend days finding out why your cable doesn't work . . ..

The other tidbit I can offer is that Apple standard SCSI cables occasionally come with the /RESET signal line (pin 40 on the SCSI connector or pin 4 on the external 25-pin connector) cut. The ribbon cable just has a notch cut in it, eliminating this wire. I have found it to be helpful in solving certain SCSI problems involving newer disks with older generation logic boards and, conversely, older disks with newer logic boards.

Floppy cable

The floppy cable situation for your Cat Mac is infinitely easier to solve than the SCSI cable. The regimen is identical. Buy the cable ready-made or make it yourself using 20-pin ribbon cable (about 18" long) and two 20-pin IDC ribbon cable connectors. Even here there are wrinkles that you should be aware of, as Table 7-5 shows. Apple has kept the Macintosh external floppy drive interface the same for all models, but if you are using an older floppy drive cable in your Cat Mac SE, or using a newer 800K Mac SE or Mac II Apple floppy drive in a Cat Mac Plus, and things are not working out, cut the cable to pins 9 and 20 and see if that doesn't fix the problem.

Other cables

To finish up your cabling, if you are building a Cat Mac based on any logic board except the Mac 128, 512, or Plus, all you need to do is add the speaker

**Table 7-4. Cat Mac SCSI internal 50-pin
and SCSI external 25-pin connector pinouts.**

Signal	Int 50-pin	Ext 25-pin	Signal	Int 50-pin	Ext 25-pin
ground	1	7	+5V term pwr	26	25
SCSI data bus 0	2	8	ground	27	—
ground	3	9	ground	28	—
SCSI data bus 1	4	21	ground	29	—
ground	5	14	ground	30	—
SCSI data bus 2	6	22	ground	31	—
ground	7	16	/attention	32	17
SCSI data bus 3	8	10	ground	33	—
ground	9	18	ground	34	—
SCSI data bus 4	10	23	ground	35	—
ground	11	24	/busy	36	6
SCSI data bus 5	12	11	ground	37	—
ground	13	—	/acknowledge	38	5
SCSI data bus 6	14	12	ground	39	—
ground	15	—	/reset	40	4
SCSI data bus 7	16	13	ground	41	—
ground	17	—	/message	42	2
SCSI DB parity	18	20	ground	43	—
ground	19	—	/select	44	19
ground	20	—	ground	45	—
ground	21	—	/control/data	46	15
ground	22	—	ground	47	—
ground	23	—	/request	48	1
ground	24	—	ground	49	—
not connected	25	—	/input/output	50	3

and reset/interrupt cables, along with any cosmetic niceties such as LED indicator lamps for power-on and drive activity.

The speaker connector on any Mac SE or newer Macintosh logic board typically uses a mini 2-pin connector (the smallest of those you normally get in any DOS PC chassis kit). Just pick an unused one and connect the other end securely to the speaker terminals.

On the subject of speakers, the message is "32 Ω (or greater) yes, 8 Ω no." You will receive an 8-Ω speaker in any DOS PC chassis kit. Take it out, throw it away. It will not do you any good and it can harm you greatly if you use it in your Cat Mac. Apple specifies 32 Ω or more and they mean it. So march down to your Apple dealer and get yourself a 32-Ω (or 63-Ω) Macintosh speaker and don't worry, or get one of the popular 4" 45-Ω speakers at your local surplus store. Or get a 100-Ω speaker, etc. But do not use the 8-ohm speaker. At worst, it will ruin your logic board and you have a case of a $4 part costing you several hundred dollars. At best, it will create glitches for no apparent reason—especially with accelerator and video cards. So if you have something happening to

Table 7-5. Internal and external floppy connector pinouts for Mac SE and earlier Macs.

Signal	SE int 20-pin	128/512 int 20-pin	Ext 19-pin
ground	1	1	1
control line CA0	2	2	11
ground	3	3	2
control line CA1	4	4	12
ground	5	5	3
control line CA2	6	6	13
ground	7	7	4
register write strobe	8	8	14
$-12V$	not connected	9	5
write data request	10	10	15
$+5V$	11	11	6
control line select	12	12	16
$+12V$	13	13	7
drive enable	14	14	17
$+12V$	15	15	8
read data	16	16	18
$+12V$	17	17	—
write data	18	18	19
$+12V$	19	19	—
motor speed control	not connected	20	10

your setup and you don't know what is causing it, the first thing you should check is to make sure you have a 32-Ω or greater speaker.

The reset/interrupt switches on any Mac SE or newer Macintosh logic board also typically use a 2-pin connector, but in this case the largest of those you normally get in any DOS PC chassis kit. Just transfer a pair (the pins slide out if you lift the plastic retainers) to the ends of the cables coming from the reset (that goes to the reset switch on the logic board) and turbo (that goes to the interrupt switch on the logic board) switches on the front panel of your DOS PC chassis. By the way, because the turbo switch on the DOS PC chassis is a two-position switch (rather than a momentary contact switch as on a standard Apple Macintosh), it is sometimes possible to "accidentally" push it in and totally disable your Cat Mac! If you're not doing programming, don't connect it. Hook up the wire from the drive activity LED (if your chassis has one) to your hard drive, again using a small 2-pin connector. Wire the turbo and power LEDs in series (like Christmas tree lights) and connect them to a convenient source of $+5$ Vdc and ground inside the chassis.

Hey, you're now done with the wiring phase of your Cat Mac project—unless you are building a 128/512/Plus Cat Mac. If you are, the previous procedure is the same for the reset/interrupt switches but the speaker and ground wires, as Table 7-3 and Fig. 7-13 show, now come from pins 4 and 7, respectively, of the logic board connector.

The battery circuit is another wrinkle the Cat Mac 128/512/Plus enthusiast has to tackle. The simple circuitry of Fig. 7-14 keeps the battery from draining when the power is on; or use the ATS video card (it has the circuitry built in) with your own battery holder to save yourself some work.

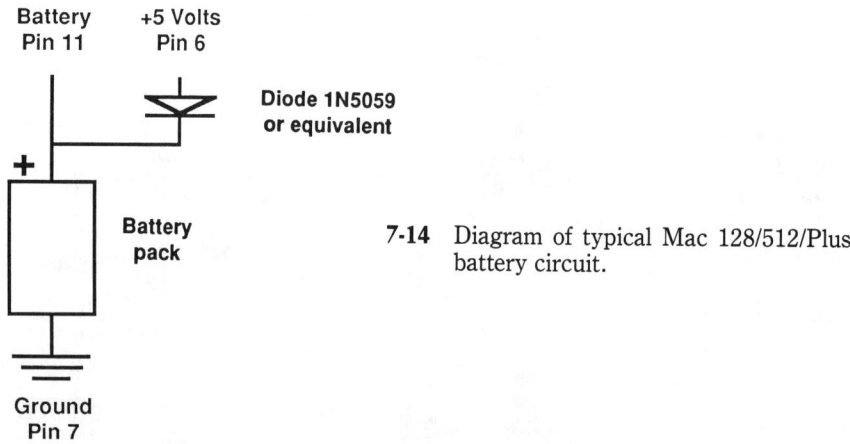

7-14 Diagram of typical Mac 128/512/Plus battery circuit.

Finally, the Cat Mac 128/512/Plus builder has to deal with the keyboard connector. The keyboard connector on the Mac logic board is similar to, but slightly narrower than, a standard RJ11 female connector socket. You can use a straight telephone handset cable as an extension, but you will have to carefully file the ends to fit both the keyboard and logic board receptacles. If you are not making an extension but an original keyboard cable from a telephone handset cable, you should be aware that the connections are reversed. In a handset cable, pins 1-2-3-4 go to pins 4-3-2-1 on the other end. In a Mac cable, pins 1-2-3-4 go to pins 1-2-3-4. The Cat Mac 128/512/Plus builder is now finished with the wiring phase of the project.

Keyboard and mouse

When Apple first introduced the Macintosh your choices were simple. There was one type of keyboard and one type of mouse. Not so today. Apple and third-party keyboard and pointing-device makers offer numerous alternatives. What it all boils down to is your keyboard and mouse are additional areas where a build-your-own Macintosh project can give you superior solutions. As a Cat Mac builder, you can choose exactly the keyboard and mouse you want initially. They become part of your original cost of building your Cat Mac project and there is nothing more to buy later—unless you want to add still more improved devices. Let's look at a few keyboard and mouse solutions for you after a brief detour to see how they are connected to your Macintosh logic board.

ADB versus non-ADB

While a DOS PC chassis can save you money in building your Cat Mac, a DOS PC keyboard and mouse cannot. A DOS PC keyboard and mouse might look the same as a Macintosh one, but that's as far as it goes. They have different wiring and send out different codes. But the good news is the newest Apple Desktop Bus (ADB) keyboards and mouse devices substantially outperform their DOS PC brethren in flexibility and seamless performance with the Macintosh's GUI interface.

There are only two games in town on the keyboard, mouse, and other pointing devices. They are ADB and non-ADB. On the Mac 128, 512, and Plus logic boards, you need to use a non-ADB keyboard and mouse. All other Macintosh logic boards use an ADB keyboard and mouse. Obviously the amount and number of non-ADB choices is declining with time—still another reason not to build a Cat Mac based on one of the older Mac 128, 512, or Plus logic boards.

The Mac 128, 512, and Plus logic boards communicate with the keyboard and mouse over separate interfaces. The keyboard has its own cord, very similar to a coiled telephone handset cord with RJ11 plugs on each end, that plugs into a mating connector at the front of the Macintosh logic board. The mouse has a DB9 connector on the end that plugs into its own connector at the back of the Macintosh logic board.

The Apple Desktop Bus is now the Apple standard serial communication bus that allows you to connect up to 15-ADB input devices such as keyboard, mouse, joystick, puck, other pointing/motion devices, and graphics tablets to Mac SE and all newer Macintosh logic boards. It allows the devices to be connected in daisy chain fashion. Your mouse can be connected to the left or right side of the keyboard, whichever is easiest for you to work. Devices are connected using mini 8-pin connectors. ADB keyboards typically have two; Macintosh logic boards have one or two; and mouse-type pointing devices come with their own single plug.

Once you've enjoyed the flexibility of mixing and matching several ADB devices (e.g., keyboard, trackball, and mouse, or keyboard, tablet, and mouse), it's hard to go back to the non-ADB world or to DOS PC machines. ADB provides you maximum increase in flexibility at minimum increase in cost. The only down side is you don't ever want to disconnect your ADB device from your Mac while the power is on because you run a good chance of zapping it.

Keyboard alternatives

I doubt that anyone reading this book is unfamiliar with a typewriter. Computer keyboards perform the same function as typewriter keyboards and are patterned after them.

For most of us, the keyboard is the main method of getting information into our Cat Mac computer, in addition to controlling what it does. You have to live with your choice of keyboard daily, therefore the keyboard selection process is quite personalized, and aesthetic variables usually enter into the decision process in addition to the normal functional choices. More about that in a moment.

Non-ADB keyboards are available from Key Tronic, Datadesk, and Apple used equipment resellers (or as a spare or replacement part from Apple dealers because Apple no longer sells the Mac 128, 512, and Plus models). Apple Mac Plus keyboards (with the numeric keypad) are typically priced at $99. Used Mac 128 or 512 keyboards (without the numeric keypad) can be found for $50 or so. The increased capability, PC-look-and-feel, extended keyboards from Key Tronic and Datadesk are in the $120 to $150 ballpark via mail order.

Apple offers its standard ADB Keyboard (M0116) and ADB Extended Keyboard II (M0312) at $129 and $229, respectively. Figure 7-15 compares Apple's standard ADB Keyboard (front) with its non-ADB Mac Plus keyboard. Figure 7-16 compares all of Apple's current ADB keyboards: the new keyboard shipped with the Mac Classic, Classic II, and LC (front), standard keyboard (middle), and extended keyboard (rear).

The best third-party ADB extended keyboard solutions are provided by Key Tronic and Datadesk, and cost $100 to $150 via mail order.

Key Tronic manufactures the MacPro Plus, my current keyboard of choice shown in Fig. 7-17. It is a full "extended" version meaning you get typewriter

7-15 Apple's standard ADB keyboard (front) compared with non-ADB Mac Plus keyboard.

192 *Chassis, wiring, keyboard, and mouse*

7-16 Apple's current ADB keyboard models: Mac Classic (front), standard (middle), and extended (rear).

7-17 Key Tronic Mac Pro Plus extended ADB keyboard.

keys, keypad keys, function keys, plus help-delete, forward-home-end-page up-page down keys (great for writers and power word-processing users), and cursor keys, plus it has two ADB ports. It also comes with a non-ADB port for an RJ11 cable which can be ordered from Key Tronic for the price of a phone call. My wife, who is a power typist, found it very comfortable with an amazingly quick key rollover that's like having another gear available in your transmission! As for myself, a two-finger typing specialist, I never found that gear, but this keyboard has a nice touch and feel to it (which you can vary by adding pads under its keycaps) plus my big fingers found the oversized Return key handy. I heartily recommend it.

Datadesk offers a unique product called the Switchboard that has to be the most innovative of the current Mac keyboards. This product offers you the modules, keyboard, keypad, function keys, etc., and lets you "create" your own keyboard. Creation has its price, however, and all this flexibility also makes it the most expensive Macintosh keyboard offering. Its extra features were wasted on me and its feel, key placement, and size were just not in the same league with the Key Tronic offering. But you should check it out for yourself.

The Power Key from Sophisticated Circuits, shown in Fig. 7-18, is another item to put in your "check it out" department. It's not a keyboard at all but a handy little device all Cat Mac builders using ADB keyboards can use to get the same benefits of easy keyboard power turn-on of your Cat Mac—just like standard Apple Mac II NuBus family models. That's what the button at the top center of all Apple's standard ADB keyboards (refer to Fig. 7-16) and top right of every vendor's extended ADB keyboards is for—it's the "power on" key. Plus you get extra switched outlets, surge protection, and software that lets you start up your Mac at specific times or on a regular schedule. It's a useful addition.

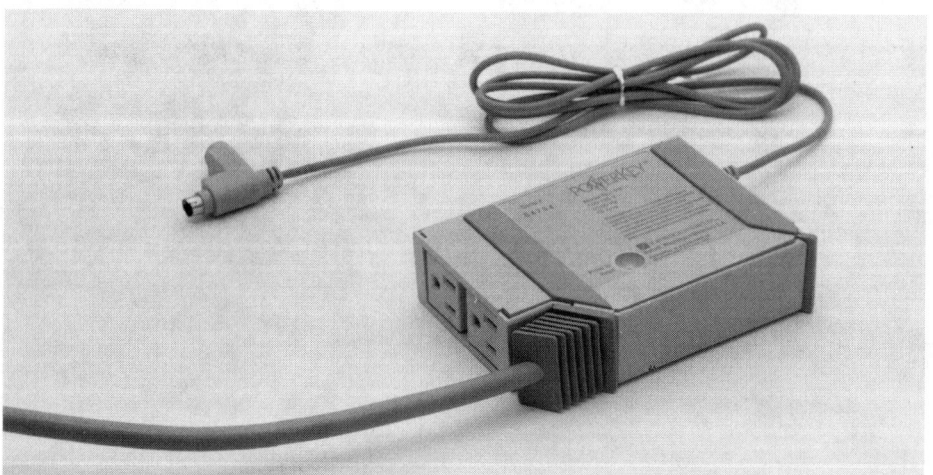

7-18 Sophisticated Circuits PowerKey power turn-on device.

What keyboard should you choose? There is no easy answer. The Apple standard ADB keyboard is the smallest footprint and lowest profile of any of the ADB keyboards. If you intend to mount your Cat Mac in a low-profile PS/2-style case, the Apple standard keyboard will most nicely complement its appearance because of these two factors. It also has the lowest price, typically available for a street price of around $90. On the other hand, it comes without special function keys. If portability or space on your desk are not considerations, then you will definitely find that the extra features and functions of a third-party extended ADB keyboard—like the Key Tronic MacPro Plus—come in handy.

Bottom line, you can read about every keyboard made, but there is no substitute for hands-on experience. I would never buy a keyboard without first trying it. If you live near a city populated with computer stores, your task is somewhat easier. Go into a store and try them. Return policies being offered by most mail order suppliers also make the try-before-you-buy option easy, although if you return every keyboard you order they will probably ask you to shop somewhere else.

Mouse alternatives

Unlike the keyboard, pointing technology (or a mouse) was unfamiliar to most of us until Apple popularized it first with the Lisa computer, and then with the Macintosh in the early 1980s. The mouse is an object about the size of a small bar of soap with one or more buttons on it that you typically hold in your hand and use to control the movement of a cursor arrow on the computer screen. When combined with software featuring pull-down menus and icons, it is the key element that makes the Macintosh easy to learn and easy to use. All you have to do is point and click.

Let's talk about conventional mice first. Apple and Mouse Systems are the main providers for both ADB and non-ADB mouse devices. This includes Apple's mechanical mouse, a product of the early 80s that, with minor improvements, still sells today, and Mouse Systems' optical mouse, whose earliest predecessor was first introduced in 1982 (they've sold more than one million optical mice since). Look at Fig. 7-19—a holdover from the first edition—to get an idea of the relative differences between them. The two Apple mechanical mice are on the left, the two Mouse Systems optical mice are on the right. The upper left model is the non-ADB Apple mouse introduced with the Mac 128 and also used on the Mac 512 and Plus. The Apple ADB mouse is at the lower left. The equivalent Mouse Systems non-ADB and ADB mouse offerings are at the upper and lower right, respectively.

In a mechanical mouse, a rubber coated steel ball turns between two rollers as the mouse is moved and sends x and y electrical direction signals back to a chip on the logic board. It's a relative motion device that communicates the direction and distance it has moved—not its location. It is used on a mouse pad that cushions and protects it and gives it a stable surface to roll on.

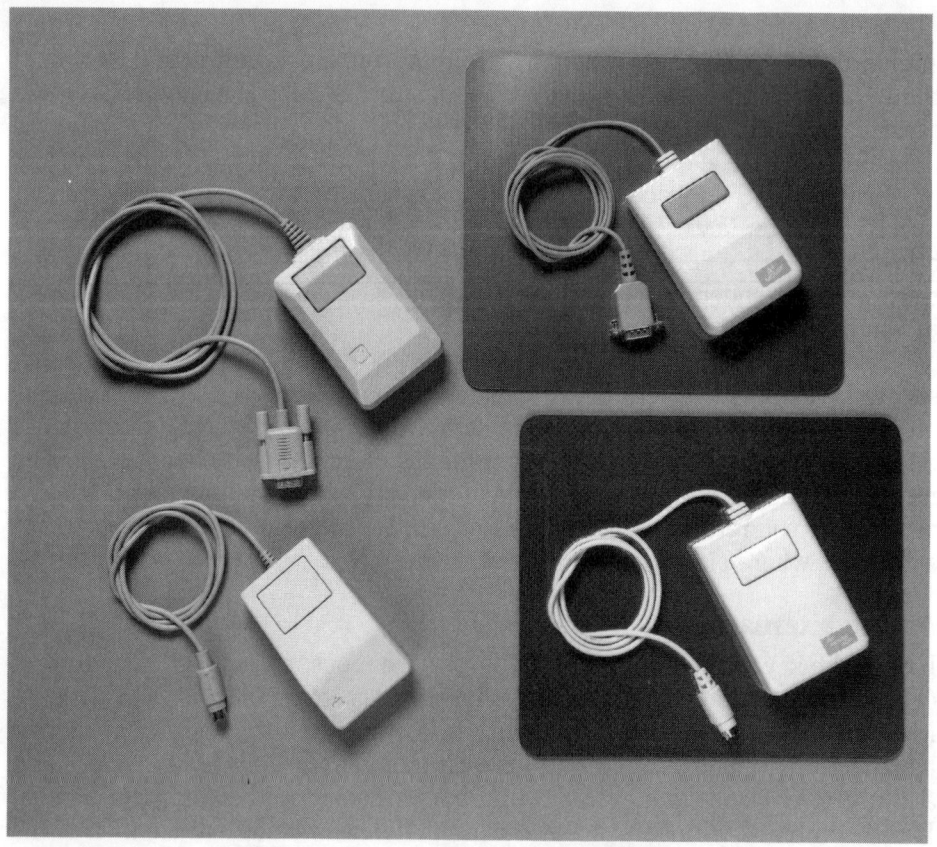

7-19 Older Apple mechanical mouses (left) versus Mouse Systems optical mouses (right).

As shown in Fig. 7-19, an optical mouse comes with its own special mouse pad. The special mouse pad has a nonreflective X-Y grid laid over a highly reflective mirrored surface, both sandwiched together under a layer of optically transparent plastic and bonded to a rubberized backing layer. Inside the mouse, a photodetector senses changes in the light reflected back off the mirror pad from its LED source, and sends relative motion x and y electrical direction signals back to a chip on the logic board. Because there are no moving parts and nothing to wear out or clean, Mouse Systems claims a 30-year MTBF and offers a lifetime warranty.

Today, non-ADB mouse offerings are becoming increasingly hard to find. Apple's mechanical mouse is available through Apple used equipment resellers (or as a spare or replacement part from Apple dealers because Apple no longer sells the Mac 128, 512, and Plus models) for between $50 and $100. Mouse Systems non-ADB optical mouse is available mail order for around $75.

The ADB area is where the action is. Apple's and Mouse Systems' newest offerings are shown in Fig. 7-20. Apple's new Apple Desktop Bus Mouse

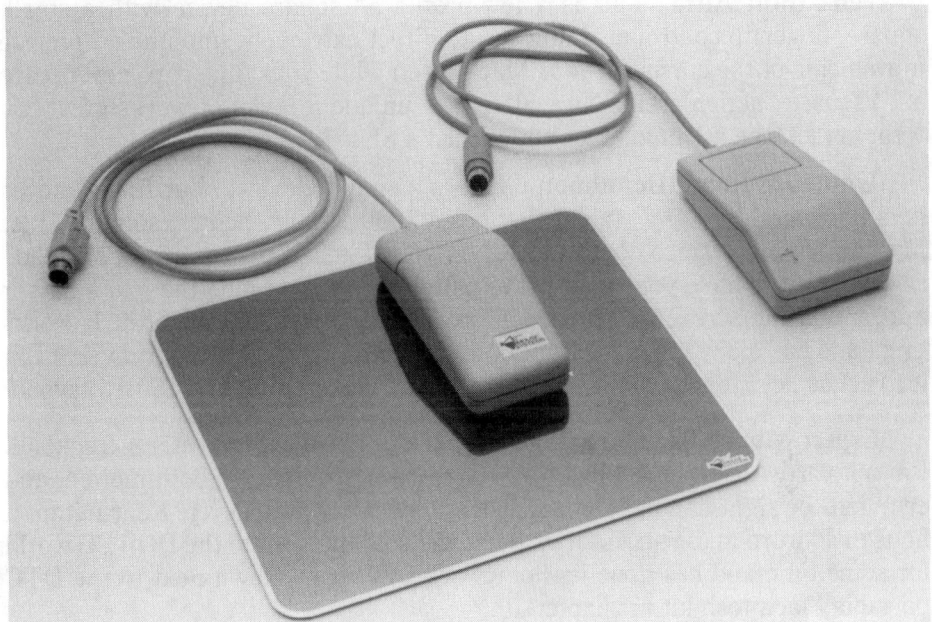

7-20 Current ADB mouse products: Mouse Systems Little Mouse (left), Apple mechanical mouse (right).

(M0142) shown on the right in Fig. 7-20 is a low-power version (you can tell by the open ADB port symbol on its underside) that lists for $99. The new Mouse Systems ADB Little Mouse shown on the right in Fig. 7-20—even smaller, lighter, and more efficient to use than its predecessor—typically goes for about $60 to $80 mail order.

Being a longtime Apple mechanical mouse user, both ADB and pre-ADB, I found the optical mouse extremely gratifying to use, once I got the hang of it. It took a couple of days of getting used to, but after that, the effortless ease of use, the better pointing accuracy, and the thought of no moving parts wearing out and not having to take it apart and clean it periodically, made me a convert. On the other hand, Apple's new ADB mouse sports a new Teflon pad and improved internal design to reduce wear in a new shape that provides a real solid feel.

Eek, a mouse invasion . . .

Or, more correctly, an unconventional pointing device explosion. There has been a dramatic increase in the numbers and types of pointing devices available to attach to your Cat Mac. Numerous articles have been devoted to all sorts of mice, trackballs and graphics tablets you can choose from. More devices appear on publishers' press-release stacks weekly. Listed next are a few that I would recommend you take a further look at.

Felix from Altra This is a low-profile 5″ square device with a small, square, fingertip control enabling you to direct extremely smooth and precise movements of the cursor on your Mac screen while your fingertips never leave a 1″ square "action area." No matter how unique it looks, it works great. So well, in fact, the astronauts took it aboard a Shuttle mission.

Unmouse from Microtouch This is a simple device. Your finger moves on a horizontal 3″ × 4½″ tablet that has a 1000- × -1000-point resolution. Just like the flat electronics control panel on your kitchen microwave, it's capacitance driven. Unlike your microwave panel, when you touch the pad a cursor appears on the screen and moves in precisely the way you guide it. It works great and has many unique features, like its ability to let you program areas on it to act as keys, or the ability to let the entire tablet emulate a 16-key keypad.

Expert Mouse from Kensington This is not a mouse—it's a trackball. I'm not particularly a trackball fan, but the oversize ball, smooth motion, and easy left- or right-handed control at least made me a believer. Kensington, a household word in the accessories field, has sold this unit to the DOS PC world for some time and has done its homework well. It is shown next to the DTC portable Macintosh kit in chapter 10.

What mouse (or pointing device) should you buy? I know Cat Mac builders who can staunchly defend either their mechanical or optical mouse (or trackball, etc.) choices. Only you can make the final decision, but I advise a try-before-you-buy approach.

Sources

DOS PC Cases are available new from numerous sources. Third-party case, cable, and connector suppliers listed below are intended as a starter; there are numerous others.

Manufacturers—Cases, cables, connectors, and other parts

Altex Electronics
10731 Gulfdale
San Antonio, TX 78216
(800) 531-5369

AMTA
Montebello, CA
(213) 724-9480

ASLAN
El Monte, CA
(818) 575-5271

Atlanta Technical Specialists
3550-F Clarkston Blvd., #B
Clarkston, GA 30021
(404) 292-6655

AXION
El Paso, TX
(915) 772-0088
(800) 828-6475

Business Technology Mfg.
42-18 235th St.
Douglaston, NY 11363
(718) 229-8094

Globe Manufacturing Sales, Inc.
1159 Route 22
Mountainside, NJ 07092
(201) 232-7301

Jameco Electronics
1355 Shoreway Rd.
Belmont, CA 94002
(415) 592-8097

JDR Microdevices
110 Knowles Dr.
Los Gatos, CA 95030
(800) 538-5000

IDS Systems, Inc.
2107 N First St., Ste. 280
San Jose, CA 95131

Olson Metal Products Co.
Crossroads Industrial Center
Seguin, TX 78155
(512) 379-7000

Keyboards and mice are available new and as upgrade replacements through Apple dealers. New and used Apple keyboards and mice are also available through the Apple used equipment dealers and, occasionally, through other distribution channels. The third-party equipment mentioned is available directly from the manufacturer and through the mail order distributors.

Manufacturers—Keyboards and pointing devices

Abaton Technology
48431 Milmont Dr.
Fremont, CA 94538
(415) 683-2226

Altra
1200 Skyline Dr.
Laramie, WY 82070
(307) 745-7538

Asher Engineering Corp.
15115 Ramona Blvd.
Baldwin Park, CA 91706
(818) 962-4063

CH Products
1225 Stone Dr.
San Marcos, CA 92069
(619) 744-8546

Cutting Edge Inc.
97 S. Red Willow Rd.
Evanston, WY 82930
(307) 789-0582

DataDesk International
7651 Haskell Ave.
Van Nuys, CA 91406
(800) 826-5398

Ehman Engineering Inc.
P.O. Box 2126
Evanston, WY 82931
(800) 257-1666

Kensington Microware
251 Park Ave. S.
New York, NY 10010
(212) 475-5200

Key Tronic
P.O. Box 14687
Spokane, WA 99214
(509) 927-5515

Micro Touch Systems Inc.
10 State St.
Woburn, MA 01801
(617) 935-0080

Microspeed, Inc.
44000 Old Warm Springs Blvd.
Fremont, CA 94538
(415) 490-1403

Mirror Technologies
2644 Patton Rd.
Roseville, MN 55113
(612) 633-4450

Mobius Technologies Inc.
5835 Doyle St.
Emeryville, CA 94608
(415) 654-0556

Mouse Systems Corp.
47505 Seabridge Dr.
Fremont, CA 94538
(415) 656-1117

Practical Solutions
1135 N. Jones Blvd.
Tucson, AZ 85716
(602) 322-6100

Sophisticated Circuits Inc.
19017 120th Ave. NE., #106
Bothell, WA 98011
(206) 485-7979

Mail order—Macintosh add-on hardware dealers

Beverly Hills Computer
279 S. Beverly Dr., #1200
Beverly Hills, CA 90212
(800) 426-8166

Dr Mac
14542 Ventura Blvd., #200
Sherman Oaks, CA 91403
(800) 825-6227

Mac Connection
14 Mill St.
Marlow, NH
(800) 334-4444

MacLand
5006 S. Ash Ave., #101
Tempe, AZ 85282
(800) 333-3353

MacProducts USA
8303 Mopac Expwy., #218
Austin, TX 78759
(800) 622-3475

MacWarehouse
1690 Oak St.
Lakewood, NJ 08701
(800) 255-6227

MacZone
6825 176th St. NE., #100
Redmond, WA 98052
(800) 248-0800

Chapter 8
Putting together the original Cat Mac

Like a kid with his presents at Christmas, when I received all the parts for my first Cat Mac, an SE version, I could not wait to put it all together. So I chose the simplest route. I started with a flip-top PC/XT chassis and drilled holes in it to mount the logic board. I mounted my Macintosh SE logic board in it on standoff spacers and bolted it down between insulated washers. Then I bolted in my floppy and hard disks.

Next, I used electrical twist connectors to tie the chassis power supply wires to the wires of a standard Apple SE power cable I had cut in half, attached the floppy and hard disks to the SE logic board using standard Apple ribbon cables, plugged the Mobius video card into the SE logic board, and attached its dual-connector mounting panel using the ribbon cable provided. The inside of my project looked like Fig. 8-1.

I then closed the lid on the case and connected my Apple Hi-Res monochrome monitor, hooked up my ADB keyboard and mouse, and I was in busi-

8-1 Inside my first Cat Mac SE.

ness. Elapsed time—under two hours. Figure 8-2 shows the results—my first Cat Mac SE.

It all worked when I turned the power on. Staring back at me was the most beautiful picture of a Macintosh desktop on an Apple Hi-Res monitor screen. I was amazed! The most difficult part was making sure the wires of the power supply went to the right wires on the Molex logic board connector. I took my time and carefully made sure that it was done right the first time, thinking mostly of the money I had just spent for the logic board, not to mention the cost of the other pieces.

Now to be honest, I did do some other things not included in the two hours. I carefully read my Mobius manual and preinstalled the required software driver on the hard disk. I had previously formatted the hard disk itself and installed software on it using my other Macintosh SE before I put it into my Cat Mac. Hey, so I cheated a little. Some of the parts came early and I was anxious.

Of course there was still "cleanup" work to be done: adding the speaker, wiring the reset switch, and making the covers for the front and back panels. All these steps took several hours more. Yet the satisfaction of doing these steps on an already working Mac took all the edge off.

8-2 My first Cat Mac SE with an Apple monochrome monitor, Cutting Edge ADB keyboard and optical mouse.

Putting together the original Cat Mac **203**

Another element of my story is that I was lazy. I didn't want to do any extra wiring. Using the SE logic board was the ideal solution. Not only do you get the fastest platform in the Apple classic Macintosh family, because you have 256K ROMs instead of the 128K ROMs of the Mac Plus, but you also get ADB bus connectors which both the keyboard and mouse plug into, a 96-pin expansion connector (which the Mobius video adapter card plugs into), a 50-pin SCSI connector to the hard drive, two 20-pin floppy drive connectors, and a battery already on the logic board. I just had to plug it in and go.

Now you don't have to copy me. Somehow I doubt that will be a problem because I have yet to find any two Macintosh owners who can exactly agree on anything. Yet there is a certain sequence to the assembly of your Cat Mac which, if followed, will make things a lot easier. Guaranteed that no matter what my experience was, yours will be different.

In terms of any fear of the unknown, there are only three things that can hurt you when you assemble your own Macintosh: Lack of attention or carelessness (e.g., reversing the wiring of the power and ground connections); lack of proper grounding before handling certain sensitive components (e.g., shuffling across the rug and then installing your SIMMs before discharging yourself or using a static guard wrist strap); and lack of cleanliness (e.g., failure to clean up your metal or plastic filings from your work, work area, or hands prior to handling electronic parts such as disk drives or floppy disks). If you pay attention to these three areas and take your time in assembly—go back over a step if you are not sure—you will have no problems.

Once you have your Cat Mac working, you will swell up with a sense of accomplishment. "Hey, look at the computer I just built!" Onlookers will hold you in respect and awe and extend new deferential treatment to you. Heck, all you did was drill a few holes and connect a few wires.

After you get your Cat Mac working comes the best part. If you don't like the results, you can change them. Modify the case, add a new disk drive, change the back mounting panel; you can innovate and experiment to your heart's delight.

Okay! Let's get to it. You are going to look over my shoulder and watch as I put together the Cat Mac SE shown in Fig. 8-3 step by step. After you observe my assembly process, you will have the understanding to go off and undertake an identical, simpler, more complex, or entirely different Cat Mac project of your own choice with a high probability of success.

Assembling the Cat Mac step by step

As with anything in life, it helps if you introduce just a little planning and organization first. This is by no means the only or even the best way to build your Cat Mac—you will discover that for yourself. Let's just say that it was adopted because as Fred Dryer says on the "Hunter" TV series, "It works for me."

8-3 The finished Cat Mac SE.

So the organization is:

Before you build
    Ordering the parts.
    Before you start.
    Tools you will need.
    Receiving your parts.

Assembly
    Make the logic board template.
    Make the rear cover plate template.
    Drill the chassis case.
    Drill the rear cover plate.
    Drill anything else you need to drill.
    Mount the power supply.
    Mount the logic board.
    Mount the accelerator and video cards/modules.
    Mount the hard disk.
    Mount the floppy disk.
    Mount the speaker and cable.

Make the logic board power cable and connect it.
Connect the other cables.
Connect the case to the other parts.
Power On—Phase 1 ("Liftoff and earth orbit").
Connect your hard disk.
Power On—Phase 2 ("Moon orbit and landing").

After you build
Finishing thoughts.
New worlds to conquer.
Troubleshooting.

Before you build

The big difference (to some it might even be a disadvantage) in building your own Cat Mac is that you can't just go out and buy one and bring it home with you today. You have to order the parts, wait for them to arrive, and then put them together. On the other hand, you can custom-design your Cat Mac, there are no friendly salesmen to put detours in your path, all you are working on is how to get exactly what you want at the best price. So you wind up looking through catalogs and magazines and talking to vendors on the phone. It's a real

8-4 Here's all there was to my first Cat Mac SE.

learning and broadening experience and, for me, it was fun. You might enjoy it too.

The parts in my first Cat Mac SE are laid out for you in Fig. 8-4. It was built in the flip-top case shown in Fig. 8-2. However, I recommend you build one with the case shown in Fig. 8-3 because it is more compact (some would say more stylish), you don't have to cut out special bezels, and it comes with a larger power supply and quieter fan. You have two $3^{1}/_{2}"$ and two $5^{1}/_{4}"$ ready-made drive slot bays which should accommodate just about any disk drive or backup option you want to add. The other low-profile PC case shown in chapter 10 (Fig. 10-2) is also suitable if you are going to use only $3^{1}/_{2}"$ floppy and hard disk drives. On the down side, there is less vertical clearance inside either of these cases, and you have to unscrew four screws to get inside, rather than having the luxury of just flipping the lid up. The choice is always yours.

Ordering the parts

Here are the parts I used to build the Cat Mac SE shown in Fig. 8-3. For your Cat Mac project, feel free to substitute parts of your own choice.

- Apple Macintosh SE logic board with 1Mb RAM SIMMS, 256K ROM.
- Hard disk—Seagate ST 296N, 80Mb.
- Floppy drive—Cutting Edge 800K External.
- Keyboard—Cutting Edge Extended ADB.
- Mouse—A+ Optical Mouse ADB.
- Video connector cable—Power R SE video adapter and cable.
- Video monitor—Princeton Max-15 Multisync (comes with cables).
- PC case & power supply—AMTA MTA-304 Mini AT/XT Slim Case.
- Apple SE power cable—Part number 590-0392 (you need only one end).
- Mating PC power supply connectors—GC Electronics part number 41-246 or equivalent (specify locking polarizing, straight header, 6 position with 0.156" centers or just tell them what you need it for).
- SCSI ribbon cable—For a $5^{1}/_{4}"$ hard disk drive you need 18" to 21" of 50-conductor ribbon cable and two standard 50-pin IDC female ribbon connectors. If you are using a $3^{1}/_{2}"$ hard disk drive mounted in the near bay, an Apple SE internal SCSI cable (part number 590-0437) can be used.
- Floppy drive ribbon cable—You need 12" to 15" of 20-conductor ribbon cable and two standard 20-pin IDC female ribbon connectors. An Apple Mac II internal floppy cable (part number 590-0188) works just great.
- Rear cover panel—Aluminum sheet measuring $9^{1}/_{2}" \times 3^{9}/_{16}"$ for the full cover plate. (The partial cover plate measures $9^{1}/_{2}" \times 2^{11}/_{16}"$ but its exact dimensions are determined by the standoffs you use.)
- Apple RFI shroud for logic board—Part number 805-5060. (Comes with logic board or make your own from foil. Not needed if rear panel covers opening completely.)

- Speaker—Do not use the 8-Ω speaker that comes standard with case hardware—you need 32 Ω or greater! I used a 4″ 45-Ω model but you can use any equivalent of Apple SE Speaker (part number 600-0393).
- Software—Apple System Software Kit (part number M0681/A).
- Miscellaneous—Box of floppy disks, standoff spacers, mounting screws, wire, solder, etc. (Most PC cases come with all the mounting hardware you need. You might want to get some cable ties and heat shrink tubing to make your work neater.)

Before you start

After ordering the parts, relax. Be patient. Everything will arrive. Read a book. Reread this book. Believe me, it's less frustrating than getting to a key step and finding out that the critical part you need hasn't arrived yet and you have wet, rapid-setting glue on the two pieces that connect to it. Wait. OK?

Where are you going to build your Cat Mac? A well-lighted 30″ × 60″ desktop or folding table works best because then you have plenty of room to spread out the parts. Pick your spot in a low-traffic area with space around it to accumulate the parts boxes as they arrive. That way no one will be overly inclined to mess with your stuff and you will not accidentally misplace your hard disk in the kitchen cabinet drawer. Everyone has their own idea of how they like their workplace. One word says it all for me—*organized*—because then I can find things.

What about software? With the exception of the system software from Apple, use the same criteria for software decisions that you would use if you were buying a brand new Macintosh from a retail store. No difference. If you already own a Macintosh, use it to prepare a startup disk as described in the "Power On" section—the last step in the Assembly process. If you do not own a Macintosh, have a friend who owns one or the store you purchased your Apple system software from prepare your startup floppy for you from the Apple system software you purchased.

Tools you will need

Two tool kits plus some extras cover the tools you will need. To assemble your Cat Mac you need the Curtis small tool kit, Mac Warehouse ACC 0304 or equivalent at $19. You will also find the static grounding strap, case spreader, and torx driver in the Dove Mac tool kit, Mac Warehouse DRI 0040 or equivalent at $15, will come in handy. A small soldering iron, Radio Shack 64-2051 or equivalent at $7.49, will be needed to make the power cable.

For the bezel, if you elect to go the make-your-own route, a fully equipped machine shop would be nice, but you can get by with an electric drill, a hacksaw, and some small metal files in assorted sizes.

To make the logic board and rear cover panel templates (and floppy cover bezel if your Cat Mac case requires it), you will need some cardboard, plain

20-pound bond copier paper, rubber cement, razor knife, ruler, and straight-edge.

Notice you do not need an oscilloscope, digital voltmeter, signal generator, digital logic probe, dc power supply or other electronic test equipment. If your Cat Mac works, you will know it. If it doesn't, you will know that too. In either event, no test equipment is required. Your eyes and ears will tell you the story, and if you work carefully, your nose won't even get involved—no smoking wires or components!

Receiving your parts

Check what you received against what you ordered. Occasionally, people do make errors. For your Cat Mac project, did you really order that PC-compatible 10Mb full-height hard disk you received yesterday? Check it out before you can no longer return it.

As you receive the parts, check to see that they are not damaged. Familiarize yourself with them, and read the instruction manuals. You might find something of vital importance for later on.

Also, keep all receipts in one place. This makes it a lot easier if you find you need to return or replace a part later on. Most vendors require an RMA (Return Merchandise Authorization) number before they accept returned parts, and that step usually requires your original vendor paperwork for the invoice number, shipping date, etc.

Assembly

The assembly process breaks down into a few basic steps: preliminaries—making templates; drilling steps—the chassis, rear cover plate, and anything else you need to drill; mounting steps—the power supply, logic board, accelerator or video cards, hard disk, floppy disk, and speaker; wiring steps—the logic power cable, everything else, and external chassis connections; "power on" steps—before and after the hard disk is connected; and the "finishing touches" step of tying down the wires inside the case and putting the cover on.

Make the logic board template

The most amazing ideas are sometimes the simplest as the saying goes. A plain piece of cardboard can save you loads of time when laying out your chassis and back panel drill holes. The reinforced cardboard you get from a shipping box works best. The kind you get back from the laundry with your shirts also does the trick.

To make your logic board template, first carefully take your logic board out of its antistatic shipping bag and lay it on your piece of cardboard. Then outline around it with a pencil and mark the location of the two middle and two front board edge holes (closest to the SIMMs) on your cardboard. If you want

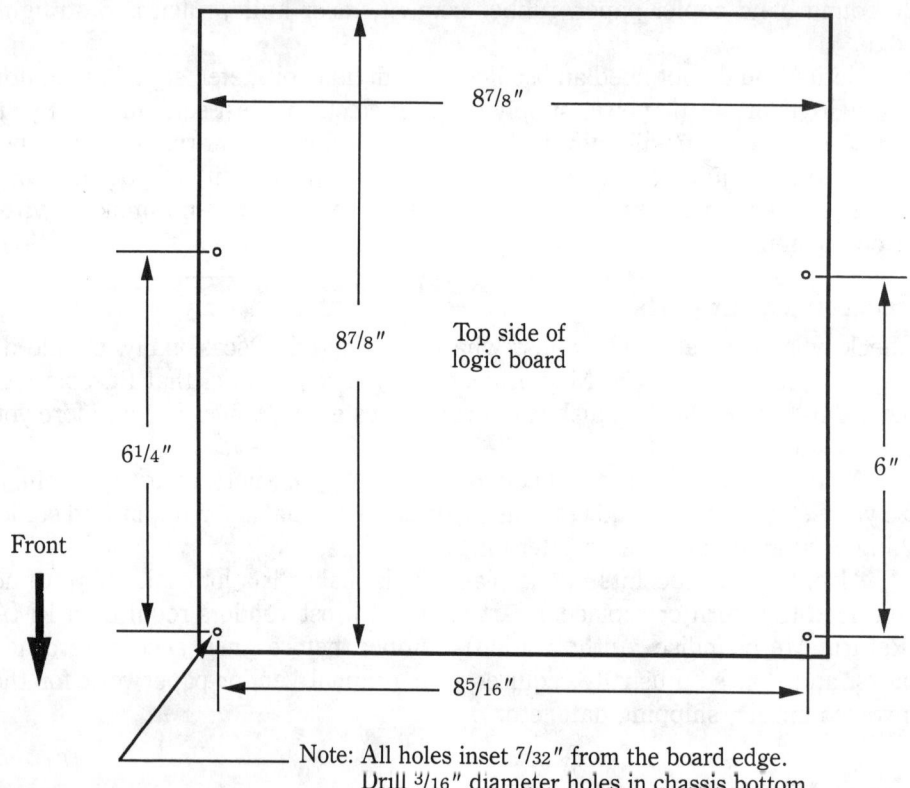

8-5 Logic board mounting template.

to bypass this step, just use the dimensions shown in Fig. 8-5 to make your cardboard logic board template. Mark the holes with crosshairs. You will use these to guide your standard metal centerpunch later on. Cut your cardboard to the correct shape per your measurements or the template shown in Fig. 8-5.

To make your rear cover plate template, rough cut your cardboard to the approximate dimensions by laying the metal card guide you removed from the rear of the chassis over it and marking its overall dimensions as well as its mounting hole locations. Figure 8-6 shows the dimensions for the back panel.

Important: If you are using the Power R Video Adapter Module in the AMTA MTA-304 chassis, the chassis stiffener bar that runs from the front to the back of the case will sit right over the top of your power connector unless you move your logic board from a position that would center it behind the back panel opening to a new position 3/8" to 1/2" closer to the side of the case. Looking at the rear panel from the outside of the case, the SE logic board "sound-out" or speaker jack on the far right of the logic board is now almost next to the edge of the right hand side of the rear case opening. This affects both where you place the logic template to drill the holes in the case and where the logic board holes are located on the back panel.

210 *Putting together the original Cat Mac*

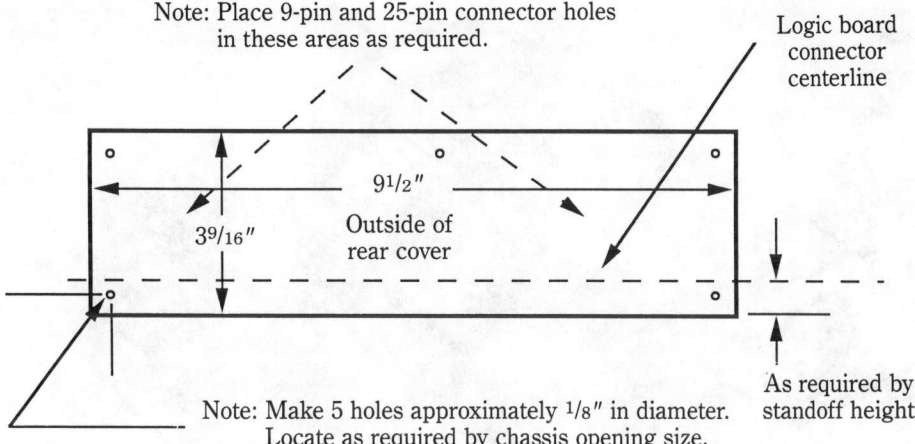

8-6 Rear cover plate template.

In a pinch, I was able to get around this in the photo session by bending the bar slightly, but to do the job right, you just need to shift the location where you mount the logic board and change the placement of your logic board connector holes in the back panel. Other alternatives are bending the bar slightly as I did and drilling a new hole for it in the rear of the case, or having your local sheet metal house fix you up a small angleiron extension with a small U in it to go around the connector that you bolt on to the sawed-off original bar. Neither of these alternatives is as desirable.

The width of the rear cover plate is fixed. It must cover the opening and match the locations of the mounting holes. But you can elect to *partially* or *fully* cover the opening down to the connectors. Either way, the location of the connector holes or the vertical dimension of the cover plate will be determined by the height of the standoff mounts you use. Regardless of the standoff type you select, be sure to allow at least 1/4" clearance between the highest object protruding from the bottom of the board and the chassis. I prefer the plastic or metal standoff with screw threads shown in Fig. 8-7 because it is easier to work with. The clip-type plastic standoffs that come in your chassis mounting kit permit faster initial mounting, but you pay for it later on if you ever want to remove your logic board.

For the MTA-304 Mini AT/XT Slim Case used in Fig. 8-3, the 3/8" plastic standoffs give the partial-cover plate a 2 11/16" vertical dimension. The full-cover plate has a vertical dimension of 3 9/16" and the 3/8" standoffs put the logic board connector mounting bolt centerlines 5/8" from the bottom edge. In either case, a 9 1/2" width leaves enough room to drill the side mounting holes. For your own template, measure the standoff, case, and logic board to be sure of the dimensions.

Put at least one additional hole for the video connector in either style cover plate. A rectangular opening 13/16" × 7/16" with 1/8" holes 1" apart cen-

8-7 Cat Mac chassis with "partial" rear cover plate. Pencil points to metal standoff with plastic insulating washer.

tered on the axis of the larger opening accommodates the 9-pin submin D video connector nicely. If you are using a 128, 512, or Plus logic board and also want to add an SCSI connector, a rectangular opening $1^{21}/_{32}"\times {}^{7}/_{16}"$ with $^{1}/_{8}"$ holes $1^{27}/_{32}"$ apart centered on the axis of the larger opening accommodates the 25-pin submin D SCSI connector. For these logic boards, you might also want to add a small rectangular opening to mount the RJ11 plug for the keyboard connector. I preferred horizontal placement of the opening(s) located high enough away from the logic board so it did not interfere with plugging cables into the board (i.e., I did not put the video connector so close to the floppy drive connector that I had to remove the video connector from the panel every time I wanted to unplug the floppy cable from the logic board!).

Make the rear cover plate template

Like the example of the cardboard, a simple piece of plain 20-pound bond copier paper, a copier machine and some rubber cement can save you a lot of time when you do your rear cover plate and floppy disk bezel.

Want to know the exact dimensions of the holes you should make in your back panel? Put an Apple Mac SE case back flat on the glass of a copy machine and push the copy button. Or trace the outline in pencil if you don't have access to a copier. You get an exact template for the holes you need to cut. For the "full" enclosed option you can either use the neat holes from the paper template or plain rectangular ones. The important thing is that your holes give enough clearance around the connectors to permit the mating connectors to fit snugly to them.

Rectangular holes for the connector openings will work perfectly and are easier to make except for the sound-out jack, which is simply a round hole. I made outline boxes around the openings with a pencil and transferred these outlines to the back panel. Mount your paper template on the back panel with rubber cement using the connector mounting centerline to assist your vertical placement. The result is instant cutting guide template! Figure 8-8 shows both cardboard templates, the "copy paper" Apple SE case back template, some of the tools I used, and the finished rear cover plate already bolted in place in the chassis opening.

If you are using another case style with only 5¼" openings and need to make a floppy disk bezel template, paper and rubber cement can also save you. Draw a 1" × 4" rectangle on the paper and use the rubber cement to attach it to the blank panel plastic bezel that came with your PC case. Measure your

8-8 Cat Mac chassis with finished rear cover plate attached. Notice templates and tools in foreground.

Assembly **213**

floppy drive placement in the opening to make sure you have the exact vertical and horizontal location for the paper rectangle on the plastic bezel.

Drill the chassis case

Now that you have made the templates, you're ready for the first real step in putting your Cat Mac together. Locate your logic board inside your Cat Mac chassis so that its connectors to the outside world on the rear edge of the card barely protrude from the back of the chassis—just like on a real Macintosh. Your cardboard logic board template does all the work for you if you just bring its rear edge in contact with the inside of the rear of the case.

As described earlier, if you are using the Power R video module, offset your template at least 3/8" to 1/2" toward the side of the case (i.e., move it away from the power supply location) to a position which would center it behind the chassis rear opening. Mark the chassis for the logic board mounting holes using a center punch, nail set, or metal scribe. Although my plastic standoffs used 4-40 bolts, I drilled oversize 3/16" holes in the chassis to compensate for any alignment/tolerance errors in my layout.

The MT-304 chassis and most others come predrilled with many holes, but if you are adding a speaker or other options, such as a battery holder, etc., in a special location for which it is necessary to drill holes in the chassis, now is also the time to drill these. **Warning:** *Do not drill any holes in the case with the logic board anywhere near it.* If the power supply comes already mounted in your chassis, you need to remove it as well before drilling the case. Put the logic board in its own foil wrapper or carrying holder, set the power supply aside, and then have a good time with your drill.

After you drill your holes, be sure there are no burrs or rough edges. These can create small metal shavings or particles later on which might wind up floating around the inside of your chassis in the most unwanted places. So take a little extra time now with your file and clean up any rough edges around your newly drilled holes.

Drill the rear cover plate

The rear cover plate is typically a light-gauge (0.050") aluminum sheet that covers the opening in the back of the chassis where the rear connector plate mounting panel used to go. Alternately, you can use the steel connector plate mounting panel that comes with the chassis. The benefit of using the steel panel is that the finished product looks quite attractive, and panel-insert cutouts are available ready-made for just about any connector or combination of connectors. The down side for me was that I found it easier to work with aluminum rather than steel, and I didn't have to make or order special connector cutout plates. Figures 8-15 and 8-16 show how the steel rear connector plate mounting panel was used in another Cat Mac project.

Back to the aluminum plate. When I went by my local sheet-metal supplier and asked him for a 3 9/16" × 9 1/2" light-gauge aluminum sheet, he went over to his scrap bin and cut me a piece. When I asked, "How much?" he laughed and said, "No charge" and sent me on my way. I didn't understand the joke, but my cover plate fits fine, works great, and the price was certainly right. Use your template to mark the cover plate, then drill it out and deburr this piece also, especially the areas around the connector openings. For this Cat Mac SE project, other than the holes for the logic board I already made, I only had to cut a single extra small slot, and drill two small holes for the mounting screws to accommodate the Power R SE video adapter that comes with a cable ending in a 9-pin submin D connector, and my work was completed. I mounted it on the left side of the panel, leaving room on the right side of the panel for other items if I need to expand later. Figure 8-8 shows the finished panel already bolted in place using 4-40 bolts and nuts.

If neatness or resaleability is not important to you, there is no need to cut the slots in the rear cover plate at all. Merely connect the monitor signal cable to the Power R connector module, and tie down or otherwise provide some sort of strain relief for this cable inside the case. Feel free to carve up your chassis cover plate to your heart's delight to accommodate the wires coming out. Just remember to stuff some foil in the openings to minimize interference with your neighbor's cable channels.

Drill anything else you need to drill

If you are mounting speakers, battery holders, reset switches, keyboard connectors, disk drive mounting brackets, special cutouts for keyboard or mouse connectors, or anything that doesn't come already fabricated and predrilled with your chassis kit mounting hardware, now is the time to drill, cut, bend, deburr, make sure everything fits right, and clean up as done in the previous drilling steps before going into the electrical phase. *Resist temptation—do all metal work before you add electronics*. Actually I had a much simpler method. I just thought of the money my SE logic board had set me back, then laid out and worked with all the pieces I needed to mount before I took the logic board out of its shipping pouch. "Works for me" as the man says.

Mount the power supply

Some writers advise you to lay out your parts and apply power outside the chassis first. Although this step is fun and will certainly amaze your friends, it's actually kind of dangerous because you end up handling your logic board quite a bit in the process. Mount your logic board safely in your chassis before applying power to it. Take another look at Fig. 8-4, which shows all the parts laid out for my first Cat Mac SE, to relieve your curiosity and bypass this step.

The power supply is big, bulky, and heavy compared to all the other electronics; you do not want it sliding around and bumping into the delicate electronics. That is why I recommend you always install your power supply first—unless you need extra room to make installing your logic board easier. If it came already mounted in your chassis, you had to remove it before drilling the case. Now is the time for you to put it back.

Some chassis designs, this one included, skimp in certain areas and attach their power supply with screw tips that protrude outside the case. So that you don't mar your family heirloom mahogany writing desktop later, take the time now to fasten the power supply in place from the outside of the chassis with less dangerous round head bolts. After bolting your power supply in place, you are ready for the next step. Figure 8-9 shows the power supply, with its maze of wires protruding, being moved into place.

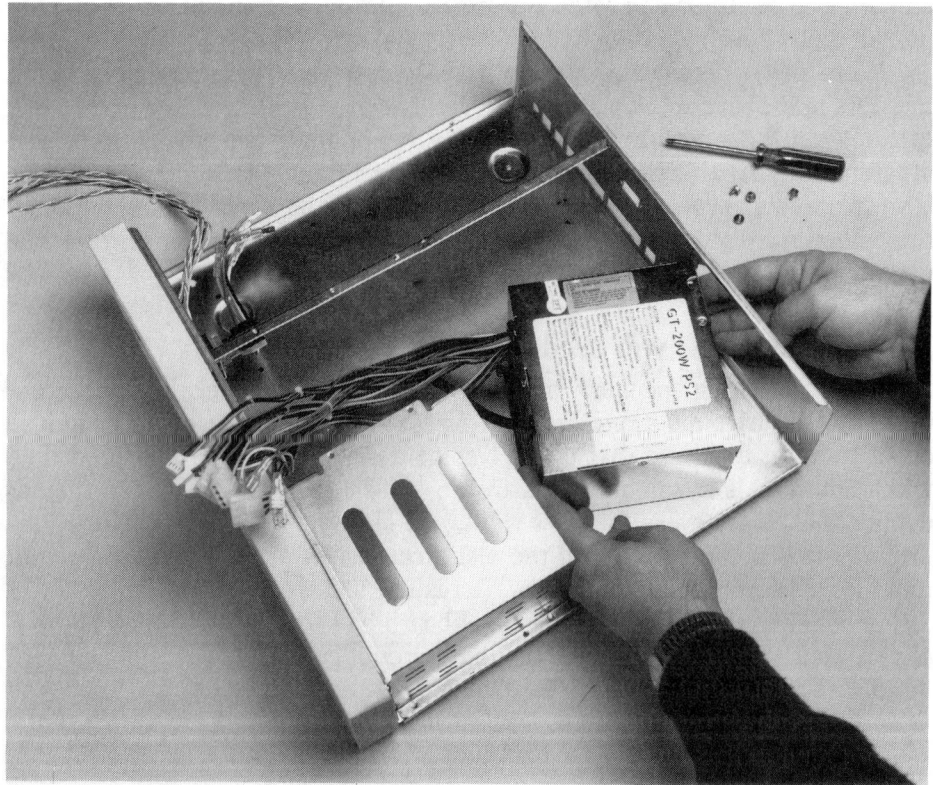

8-9 Moving the power supply into place.

Mount the logic board

Your logic board is the platform for everything else you will be mounting in your case. That is why it usually gets installed right after the power supply. However, if you are attaching anything else (i.e., memory, memory upgrades, accelerator cards, video adapters, etc.) to the 68000 processor chip or 5380 SCSI chip using a Killy clip, this must be done before you mount the logic board in the case. The MacSnap series of memory upgrades from Dove is another good example. The Killy clip and MacSnap require that pressure be applied to snap them into place. To do this you need a clean, static-free, flat surface for the logic board to rest on. If you try to do this with a mounted logic board supported at only four points (three points in the case of the 128/512 boards), you run the risk of damaging it. Working on your logic board outside the case is much easier. You can easily view it from the front and the side to position it for mounting the Killy clip, just by moving your head.

With the SE logic board you don't have any problem because everything just smoothly attaches to the 96-pin connector with no extra pressure (potentially damaging to the board) required.

Even if you are just adding SIMM memory chips to your Mac SE logic board, this is initially done best with the board outside the case on a flat, clean, static-free work surface. As Fig. 8-11 shows, the logic board for this project has two 1Mb SIMMs mounted in the two SIMM slots closest to the front of the logic card. The on-board jumper just behind the left bank of SIMMs is in the "2/4Mb" position (moved to the left when viewed from the front or memory side of the logic board). If you were going to add two more 1Mb SIMMs, a total

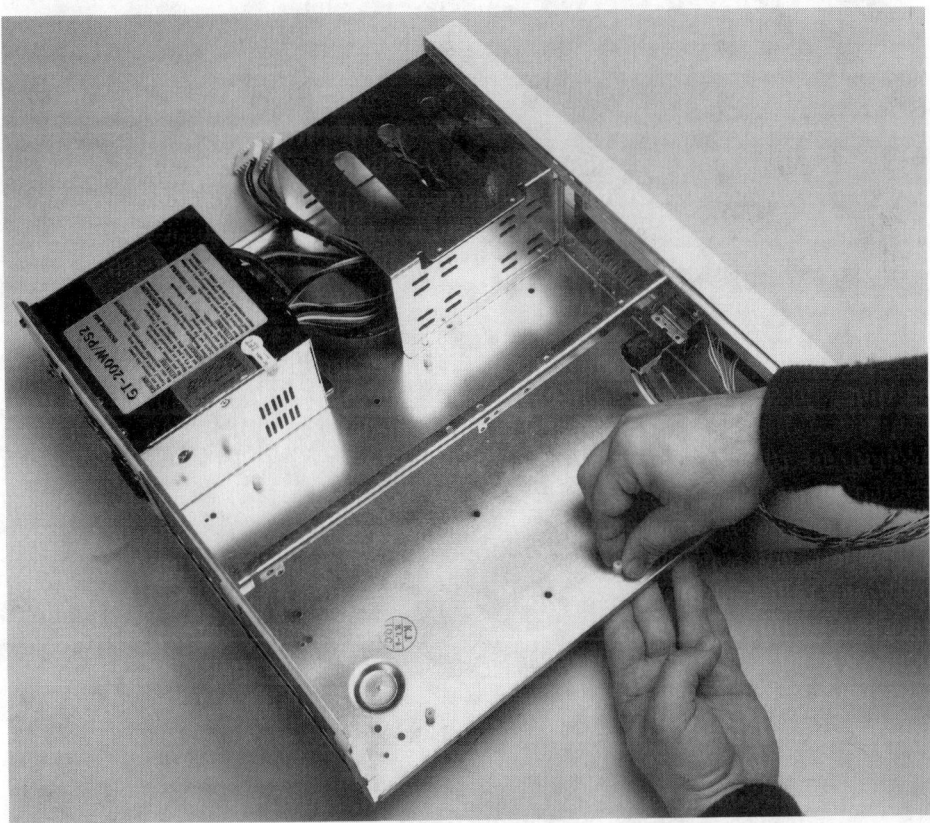

8-10 Installing the plastic standoffs.

Assembly **217**

of 4Mb of memory, you would move this jumper over to the left one more pin (the jumper is now on just one pin), but I recommend you never remove it from the board, in case you want to change something later on.

You have already been introduced to the standoff mounting bolts I prefer in Fig. 8-7. In this project, because of the low-profile case and the Power R module height, I used the 3/8" plastic standoffs shown in Fig. 8-10. Bolt these into the chassis initially only finger tight, then put the SE logic board in place over them and finish up with another insulating washer and bolt. Figure 8-11 shows the logic board installation process with a handy extractor tool being used to maneuver one of the logic board bolts into place. Don't overtighten the bolt; make it just a little more than finger tight to hold the logic board in place. As mentioned in the drilling-the-chassis-case step, the oversize 3/16" holes in the chassis gives you a little room for moving the 4-40 standoff bolts around and makes the logic board mounting process easier.

Many types of alternate standoffs can be used. A simple and effective solution if you cannot find the type I recommend is to use just a plain bolt of the proper length covered with a piece of neoprene tubing sleeve around the bolt,

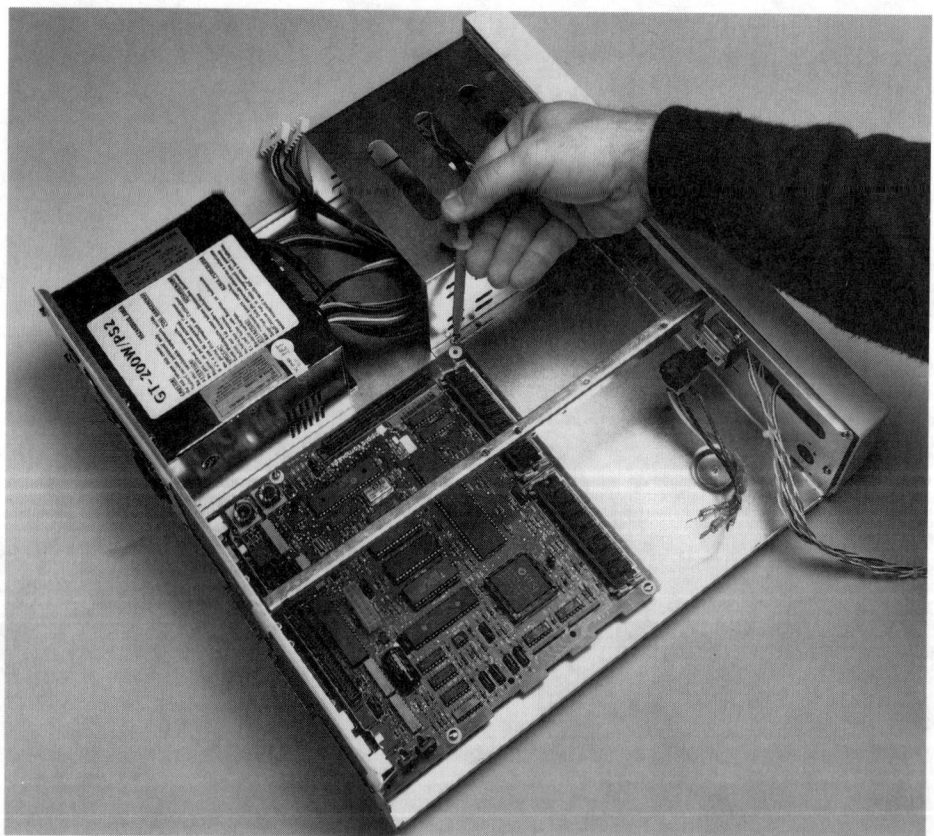

8-11 Bolting down the logic board—extractor tool helps to get bolt started in a tight place.

long enough to leave no more than about 1/8" of thread exposed above the top of the logic board.

To summarize, use whatever standoffs you want, tie down whatever standoff arrangement you are using with plastic insulating washers on both sides of the logic board, and don't overtighten the nuts. And never use lockwashers!

In the wiring steps coming up next, be careful to keep all other boards, disk drives, cables, and wires in the case away from the SIMMs module area in the front of the logic board. During construction you might even consider covering this area temporarily with an antistatic plastic sheet just to keep your fingers out of harm's way while routing other wires, etc. My first Cat Mac in the flip-top PC/XT case allowed the Seagate hard disk almost to rest on the DIP SIMMs when it was installed in the lower inside bay. I had to use a piece of plastic just for sanity in that instance.

A brief but important note here. If something looks too close, do something about it now—not later. Resist the temptation to say, "Don't bother, let's move ahead." Plan to be safe, not sorry. Otherwise, when you least expect it, you'll move your working Cat Mac and the case will flex just enough to short the drive into the logic board or video card or something else. Trust me, do it right now or you leave the door wide open for Murphy's Law to strike you down later.

Mount the accelerator and video cards/modules

You add these cards next because they sit on top of your Cat Mac SE logic board and plug into its 96-pin connector. This allows you to route any video/accelerator cables without extra cables in the way and also to determine cable clearances for your disk cables. This Cat Mac SE project has no extra boards, so this step is easy!

Here are a few examples of other projects that did require extra work due to the additional cables and/or special connectors involved. Figure 8-12 shows a Total Systems Gemini accelerator board mounted on a Plus logic board. The Total Systems board needed an additional SCSI connector slot cut into the back cover plate. Figure 8-13 shows the completed partial back cover plate for this project. Figure 8-14 shows a Mobius video card mounted on an SE logic board using the original steel connector plate back. The Mobius card required special slots for the small PC board with 9-pin and 15-pin submin D connectors to be mounted on the rear cover plate. This was a lot of extra work which the outside view of Fig. 8-15 and inside view of Fig. 8-16 does not show. No external drives are ever going to be used for this project, otherwise the metal reinforcing plate down the middle of the connector opening would have to be removed for access to the logic board connectors.

I used the Power R video module, discussed earlier, which just snaps into place in the logic power plug socket. You see it installed in Fig. 8-18. If you followed the earlier instructions, the top of it should rest just next to the chassis stiffener bar. Bend the cables over at a 90 degree angle and route them

8-12 Total Systems Gemini accelerator board mounted on a Cat Mac Plus logic board.

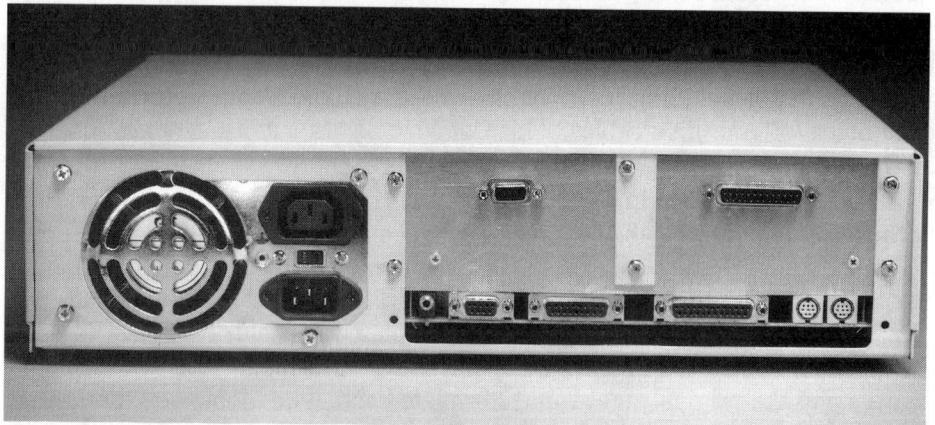

8-13 Finished partial rear cover plate for a Cat Mac Plus. Notice SCSI (right) and video (left) connectors at top.

under the stiffener bar to make it easier to close the case later. It is a very tight fit!

Mount the hard disk

Trial fit your hard disk drive into the chassis at this point to see what you are up against. This chassis can accommodate either $3^{1}/_{2}''$ or $5^{1}/_{4}''$ drives easily. In

220 *Putting together the original Cat Mac*

8-14 Another Cat Mac project with Mobius card mounted on a Mac SE logic board.

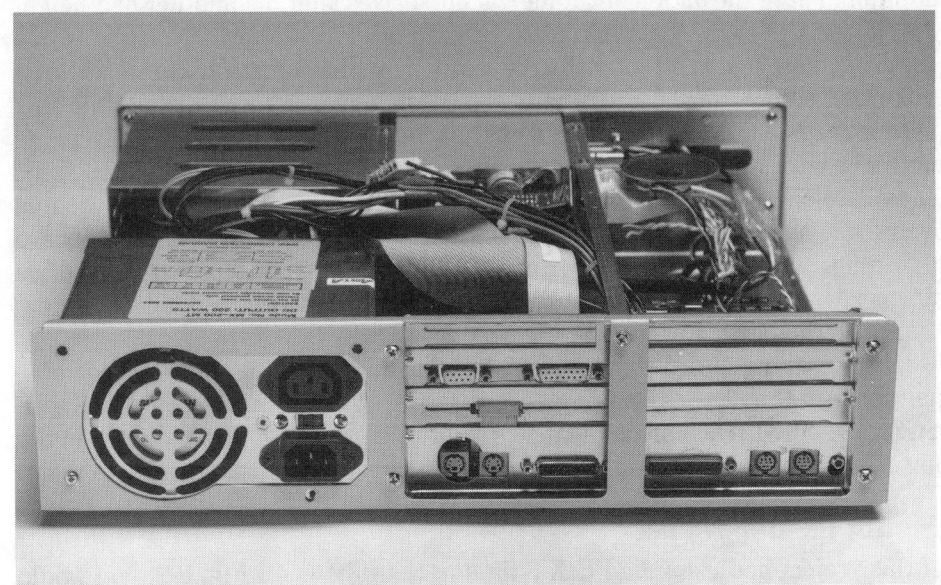

8-15 Rear view of a Cat Mac SE finished with original steel rear cover plate and Mobius video connectors in place.

8-16 Inside view of a Cat Mac SE finished with original steel rear cover plate—pencil points to video connectors.

addition, I have the option of adding backup drives later on: another half height disk drive, CD-ROM, tape/hard disk backup or extra floppy drive.

The floppy bracket next to the hard drive bay obstructs access to its mounting screws so the 5¼" hard disk definitely has to be installed first. I used a Seagate 80Mb 5¼" drive which fit the opening perfectly. I replaced its normal black half-height front bezel with a gray front bezel which matches the chassis color scheme quite closely as shown in Fig. 8-17. Only two screws hold it in place and, once again, the extractor tool came in handy. The cardboard that ships with the drive shown in Fig. 8-17 should be kept with the drive whenever you handle it because it protects the exposed imbedded SCSI controller on the bottom of the drive case.

If everything clears okay, bolt the hard disk into the location you have chosen for it in the chassis, making sure that you have room to get at its power, SCSI, and SCSI ID connectors later on. For this project, it was mounted in the lower 5¼" drive bay as shown in Fig. 8-18. Do not attach any cables to it yet.

Mount the floppy disk

If this project had used the PC/XT flip-top case shown in Fig. 8-2, you would have to mount your 3½" floppy disk drive in a 5¼" chassis opening and, in addition, cut a bezel opening for the floppy. A mounting bracket such as the

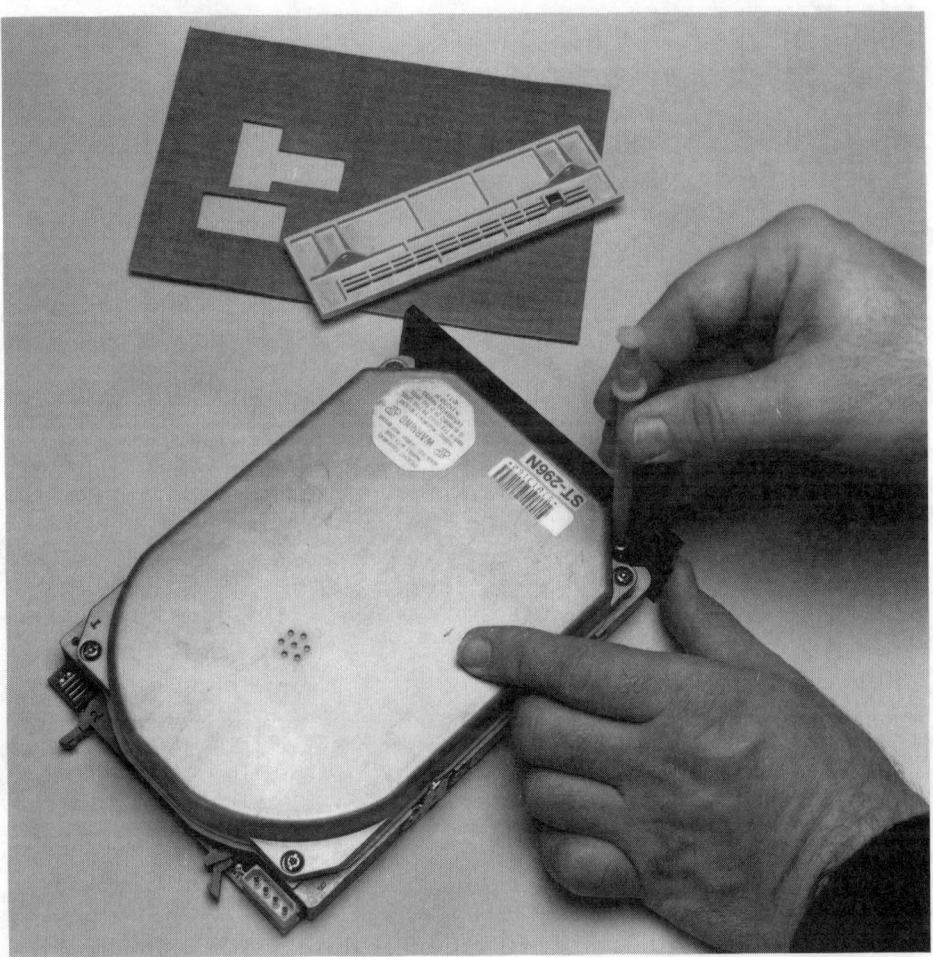

8-17 Changing the Seagate hard drive bezel—again the extractor tool comes in handy.

Toshiba 3½" Universal Floppy Disk Mounting Kit, part number ND 352/356KU, or Citizen's OSDA 3½" mounting kit for their 1.44M IBM PC floppy (each at about $15 or so) makes quick work of the mounting but you are strictly on your own as far as the bezel is concerned.

Using the MTA-304 case bypasses both steps. The 3½" floppy disk mounts in its own bracket next to the hard drive bay and its own bezel protrudes through the case front with nothing extra to add. To mount your floppy disk, first remove it from the external mounting case it came in. Set aside the case, cable, and external case screws for later use, but use the mounting bolts and washers that held the floppy in the external case for this project. Test fit your floppy into the case first until you get the disk to sit in the chassis the way you want it, and hold it in place by tightening one bolt on the bracket. Then

Assembly **223**

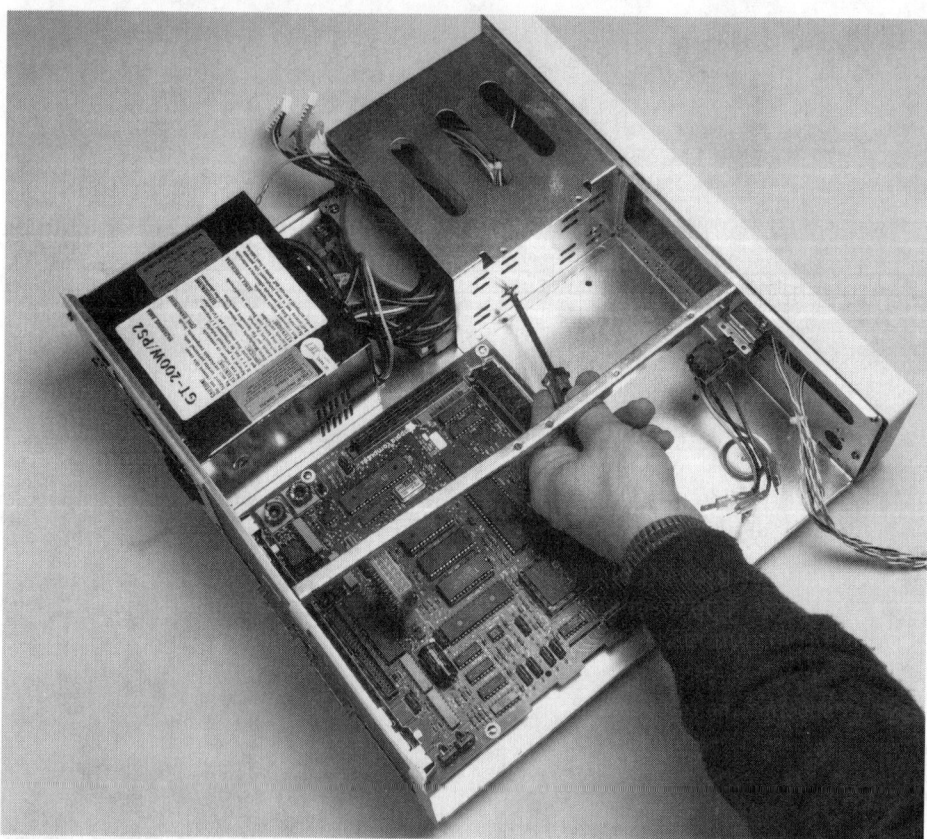

8-18 Bolting the Seagate hard drive into the 5¼" lower drive bay.

remove the bracket, add and tighten the other three bolts, and reinstall the bracket in the case. You will have to angle the drive down into the opening at a 45-degree angle to get the bracket in place, as shown in Fig. 8-19. When in place, the bracket holes align with the chassis mounting holes. Use four flathead bolts to hold it in place; these allow the case top to fit flush with the internal chassis frame parts. The green chassis ground wire from the power supply fits under the front flathead screw closest to the chassis front as shown in Fig. 8-21. Do not attach the ribbon cable to the floppy yet.

Mount the speaker and cable

An 8-Ω speaker comes standard with your PC case mounting hardware. Don't use it! You need to get a 32-Ω or higher impedance speaker of the type Apple uses in its Macintosh SE. No kidding, you do. Otherwise, you risk ruining a perfectly good logic board that you paid money for. For a better sound, you can get a larger speaker, but make sure it's a 32-Ω or higher impedance version. I used the larger of the two speakers shown in Fig. 8-20, the 4" diameter, 45-Ω

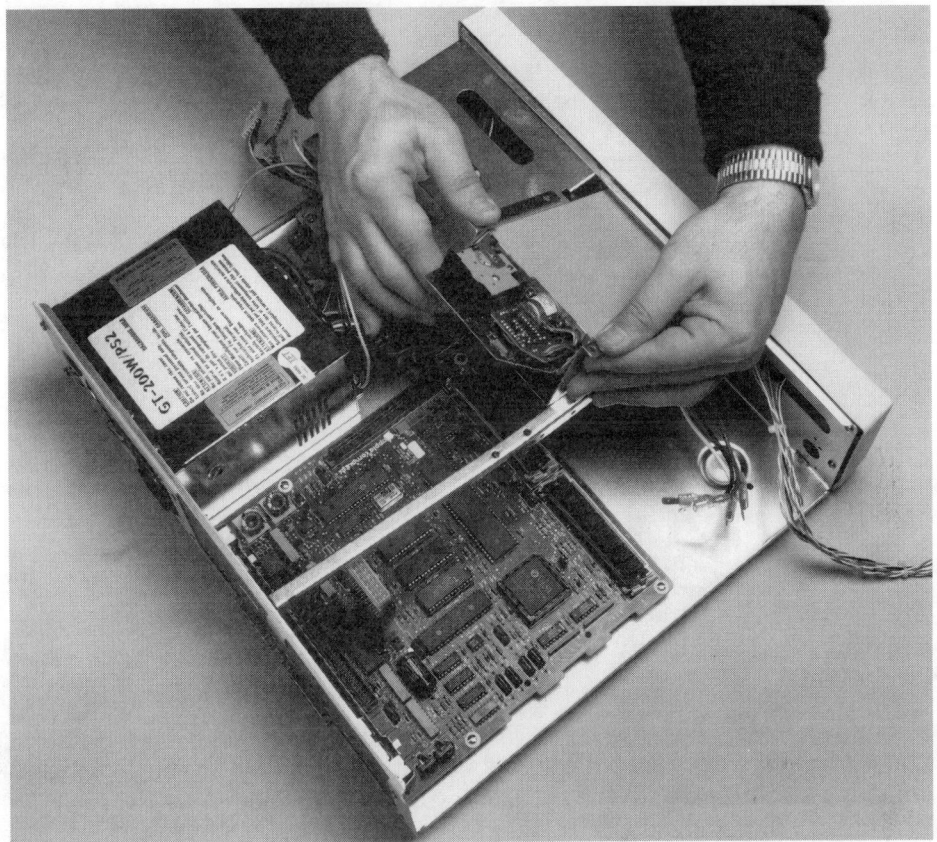
8-19 Installing the floppy drive into its mounting bracket in the chassis.

version that produces a good sound. The other speaker, a smaller 100-Ω unit, will also work. Both are available from local electronics parts houses for a few dollars each. Apple also offers a selection of speakers to choose from. All its Macintosh speakers are 32 Ω or greater impedance, so take your pick from a used Apple parts dealer.

The speaker is the only other area of the Cat Mac project that requires soldering—two minutes worth. Depending on which one of the chassis LEDs you use, if any, you will usually have an extra twisted-pair cable ending in a 2-pin connector. This is excellent for wiring your speaker. Clip it off near the switch, solder the clipped end to the speaker terminals, and plug the connector end into the Mac SE logic board speaker connector pins. As shown in Fig. 8-21, the speaker is attached to the chassis with a single bolt and held in place with two washers and a nut. The bolt passes through an existing hole in the case. Next, add a thick washer, add the speaker using the mounting hole in its frame, another washer, and then the nut. Tighten it up very well. During the installa-

8-20 Two Cat Mac SE speaker candidates: 100-ohm unit (left) and larger 45-ohm 4" unit (right).

tion process be sure to keep the speaker away from the case so you do not accidentally magnetize it with the speaker's voice coil magnet.

You can forget about the speaker entirely if you just plug your earphones or amplifier into the external sound jack on the logic board, or if you fall into the class of users who disable their own standard Apple Macintosh speakers with a dummy audio plug or simply work all the time with the volume on the control panel turned completely off.

After installing the speaker, wire the power supply on/off switch to the thick power cable coming out of the power supply. All the wires are color-coded and end in spade lugs so there is little room for error. If the color codes are not identical, you will receive a card with your chassis showing you how to hook up the on/off switch wires, or there will be a decal on the power supply itself telling you the connection scheme. With the MTA-304 chassis it is simple: blue to blue, white to white, brown to brown, and black to black.

Any other hardware to be mounted (i.e., the battery case if you were building a 128/512 or Plus version, or special custom video cards) should be mounted now before the wiring phase.

Make the logic board power cable and connect it

Figure 7-10 in chapter 7 showed you the construction details for the power cable for this project, and the top of Fig. 7-11 showed the connection details.

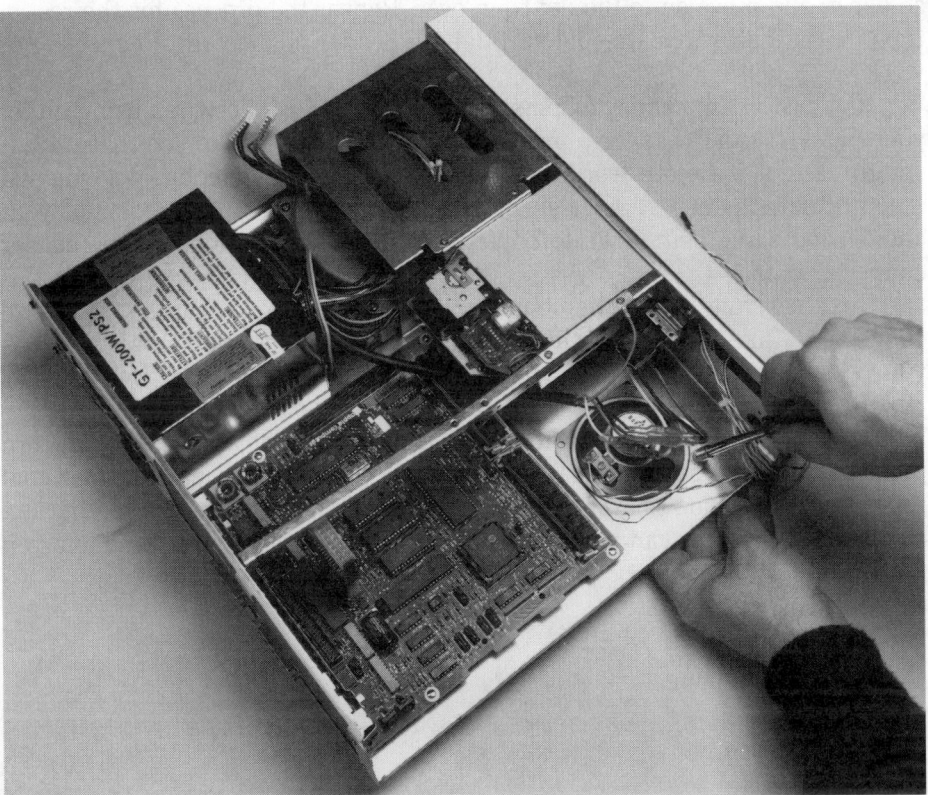

8-21 Installing the speaker—one bolt holds it in place. Notice chassis ground wire attached to floppy drive bracket.

Table 7-2 (the middle column) showed the signals required on each pin. I recommended that you buy it ready-made to avoid any wiring "accidents" that could fry your logic board.

For those of you who elect to make your own, I will now tell you how to do it. It represents the only other time in building your Cat Mac that you will have to go near a soldering iron (the speaker was the other). From a standing start, it should take you or anyone in your family 10 years of age or older less than 30 minutes to make.

Of course, you need to obtain the three connectors and wire. I recommend AWG 18-stranded insulated wire be used in the colors shown (see Fig. 7-10), but you can do it all in one color if you are careful. You will need nine identical lengths of wire about 6" long. Refer closely to Fig. 7-10 as you work. Notice you will have five wires that go to one connector and four that go to the other.

Start by plugging the header connectors into the power supply P8 or P9 connectors to guide you. On each side of the separate wires, start at one end and trim about 1/8" of insulation off the wire that goes to the exposed pin at the back of the header connector. Temporarily hold it in place with a pair of pliers,

Assembly **227**

solder it, and move on to the next pin over. Repeat the process for the rest of the pins until all wires are soldered to both header connectors. Recheck your work.

Now fasten the connector pins to the other end of the wires using either your pliers, a small vise, or a proper crimping tool. Check to see that each is snugly fastened. Before working on the logic board connector, cut yourself nine $1/2''$ lengths of $1/8''$ heat shrinkable tubing pieces (in the color of your choice) and slide them down to cover your solder connections on the header connector pins.

Next, carefully insert the connector pins into the rear of the logic board connector. Make sure that each is fully seated and cannot pull loose. Recheck your work.

After you are done, take your almost completed cable assembly to the kitchen and hold your heat shrink tubing over your hot air electric popcorn popper—turning it so that the tubing shrinks evenly around each header connector pin. If you don't have the hot air popper, a hair dryer, range-top burner, or just plain matches can be used. Recheck your work one final time and you

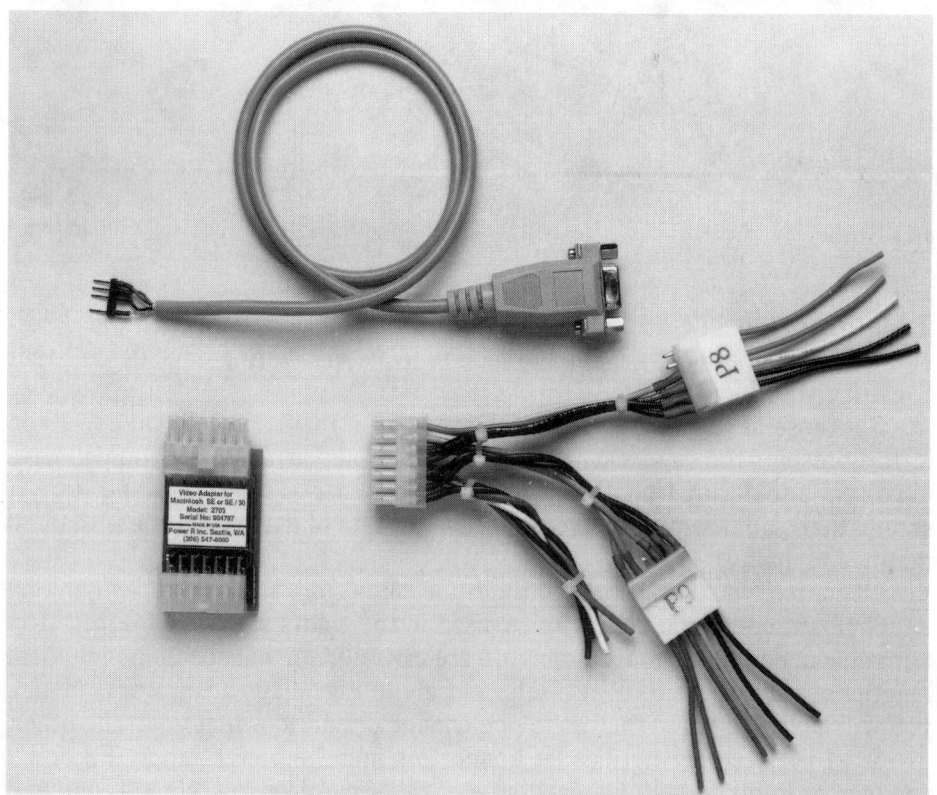

8-22 Finished Cat Mac SE power cable (right). Power R module and cable (left) for size comparison purposes.

are finished with the cable-building step. Fun, wasn't it? Figure 8-22 shows a completed Cat Mac SE power cable on the right.

Now, back at your Cat Mac SE chassis, plug the Power R video adapter module (shown on the left in Fig. 8-22) into the power connector on the logic board and plug the mating connector on the cable you just built into it. Everything is keyed so it is rather difficult to plug things together backwards unless you have a gorilla to assist you. If you notice anything taking an undue amount of effort or force to connect, check your premises. Are you doing it correctly?

Here is the biggest warning of the project, so it gets its own paragraph and bold letters:

Check to be sure you have not switched connectors P8 and P9!

Double check your cable connection before you apply power. Figure 8-23 shows the power connections being carefully rechecked before moving to the next step.

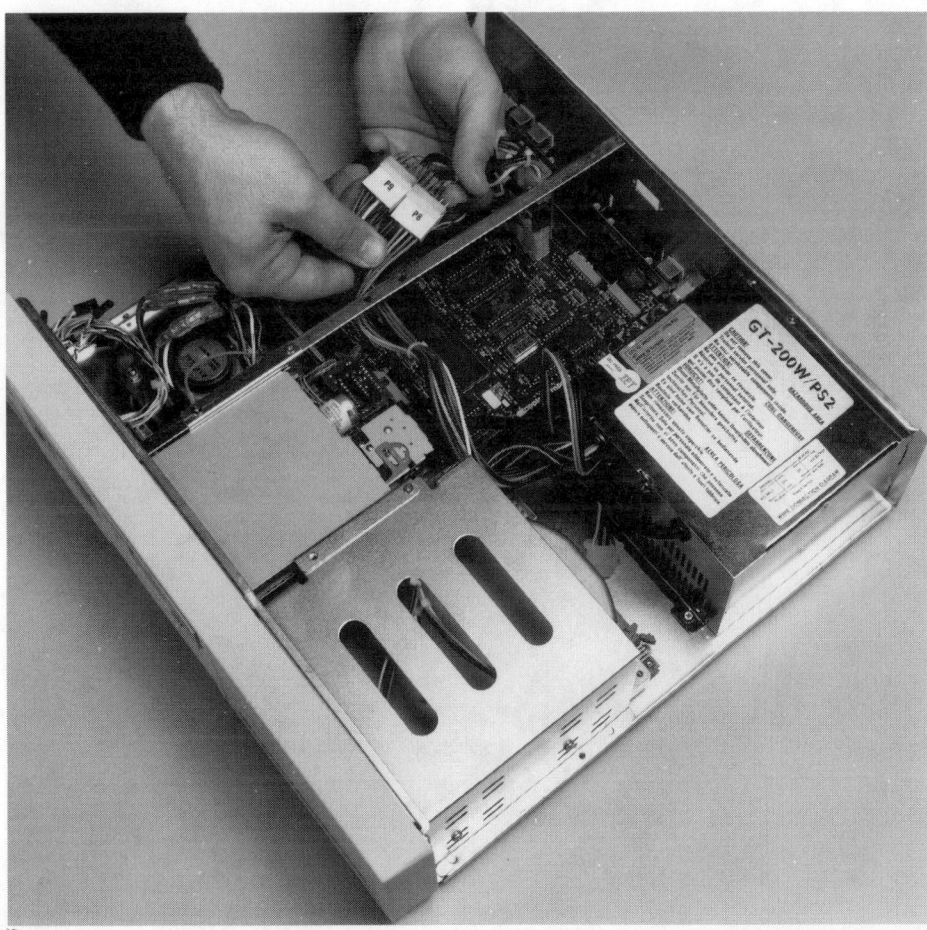

8-23 Installing the power cable. Recheck P8 and P9 and route cable under stiffener bar.

Assembly

While it might not be fatal, depending on the type of power supply you use, it is potentially the only step that can wipe you out completely in the twinkling of an eye and cost you big money for your logic board repairs. Why? Because the ground wires on one connector go to the same pins as the power wires on the other connector. You could possibly emerge unscathed from making a mistake of wiring to the wrong pin on either connector—depending on the pin. But *plugging P8's cable into P9's connector and vice versa is usually fatal. Zap. Kaput.* I believe you get the message. Just think of the money you've saved by being careful. Now onward.

Connect the other cables

Plug the video cable into the Power R module as shown in Fig. 8-24 and bolt the other end to the rear connector plate on the chassis as shown in Fig. 8-25. The pins on this cable that go into the Power R module are small and can

8-24 Connecting the video cable to the Power R module.

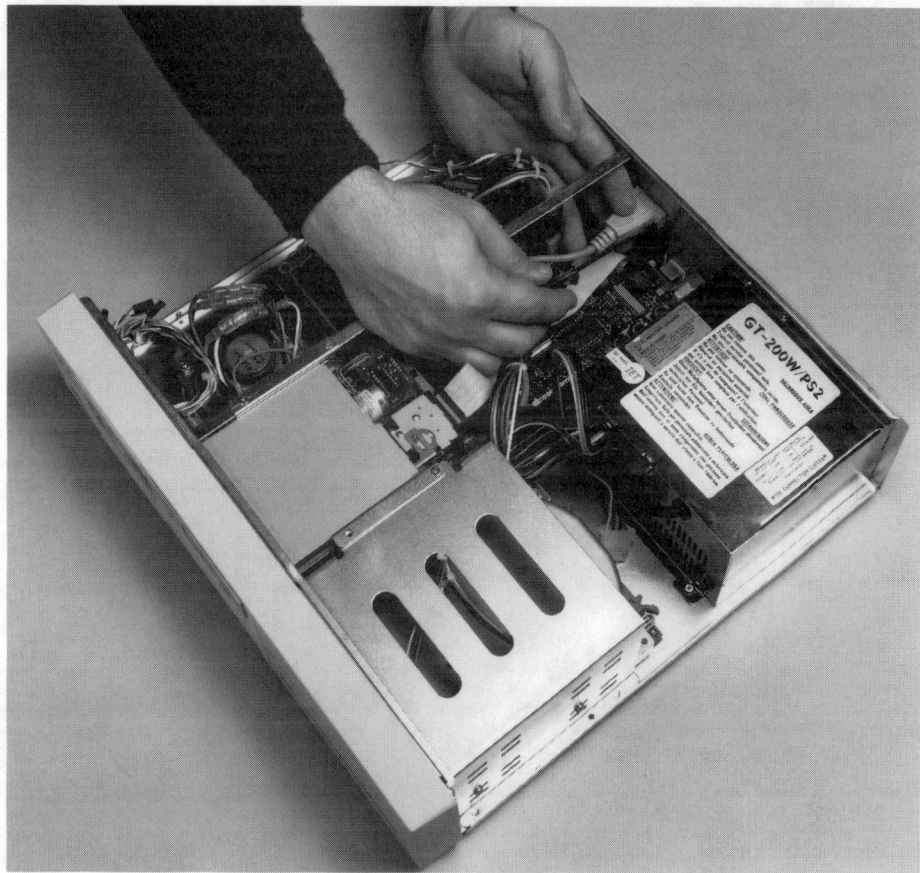

8-25 Attaching the video cable to its rear cover plate connector opening.

sometimes shake loose when moving your Cat Mac around, so tie this end of the cable in place securely with a cable tie to restrict its movement—without connecting it permanently so you cannot remove it again if you have to in the future.

Now connect the floppy cable between the floppy disk drive and the Mac SE logic board as shown in Fig. 8-26. The floppy cable is a 12" to 15" length of 20-pin ribbon cable with a standard 20-pin female IDC connector crimped onto each end. If you use the standard Apple Mac II floppy cable, the connectors are keyed. If you do not, don't worry; just remember there are no twists in the cable (i.e., if the red stripe on one edge of the ribbon is on the left at the back of the floppy disk, it is also on the left at the logic board connector). The cable goes into the "lower drive" connector on the logic board. If you add a second floppy later, it uses the other slower "upper drive" connector.

Next come the reset and interrupt switch cables. Carefully remove the 2-pin connector from the pair of wires coming from the reset switch. Substi-

Assembly **231**

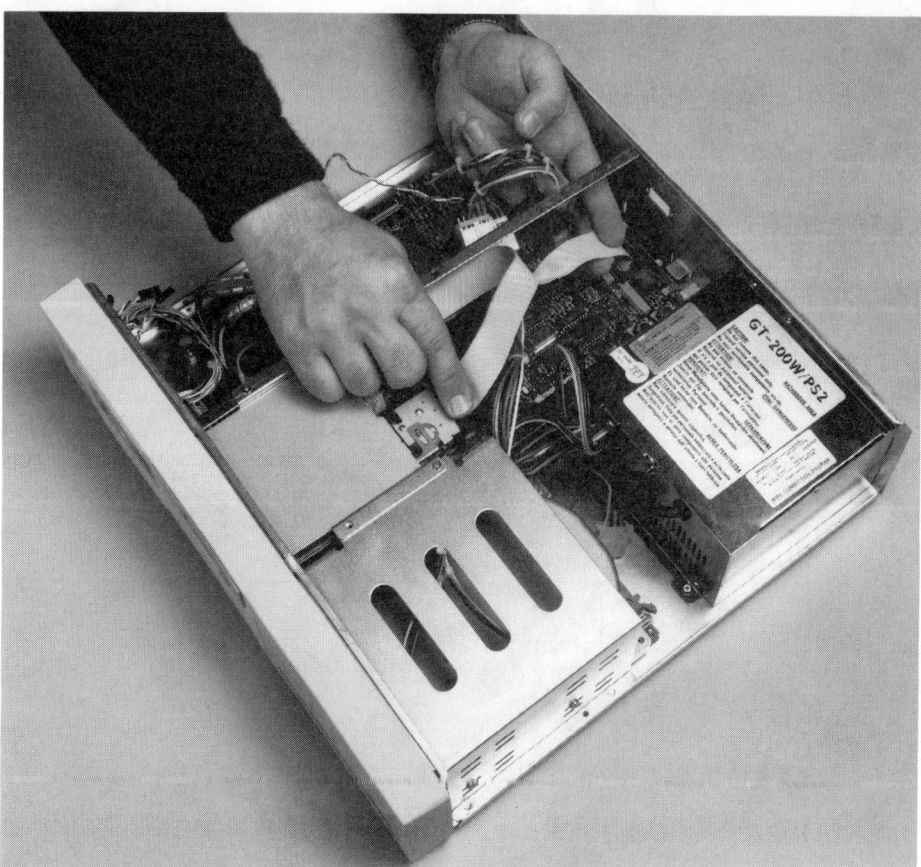

8-26 Connecting the floppy cable.

tute a 3-pin connector you have taken from one of the other unused cables. Locate the reset and interrupt switches at the back right of the logic board (viewed from the rear) near the audio-out jack. Each switch has two pins or tabs at its top. Bend these each 90 degrees so they are standing straight up. Attach the wires from the turbo switch to the rear switch on the logic board. Now attach the wires from the reset switch to the switch right in front of the rear switch on the logic board as shown in Fig. 8-27.

A word of caution here. The reset switch works normally. You push it, and it makes something happen. But the turbo switch on the PC chassis was intended to perform a different function than the interrupt switch on the Mac logic board it is now connected to. Your turbo switch is a push-to-hold type. If you push it once it will definitely perform its function and interrupt the computer. *But you must push the turbo switch again* to release the Mac logic board back into its normal state; in other words, if you do not hit it twice, you will hang your Cat Mac up indefinitely. The only reason for using the switch is to

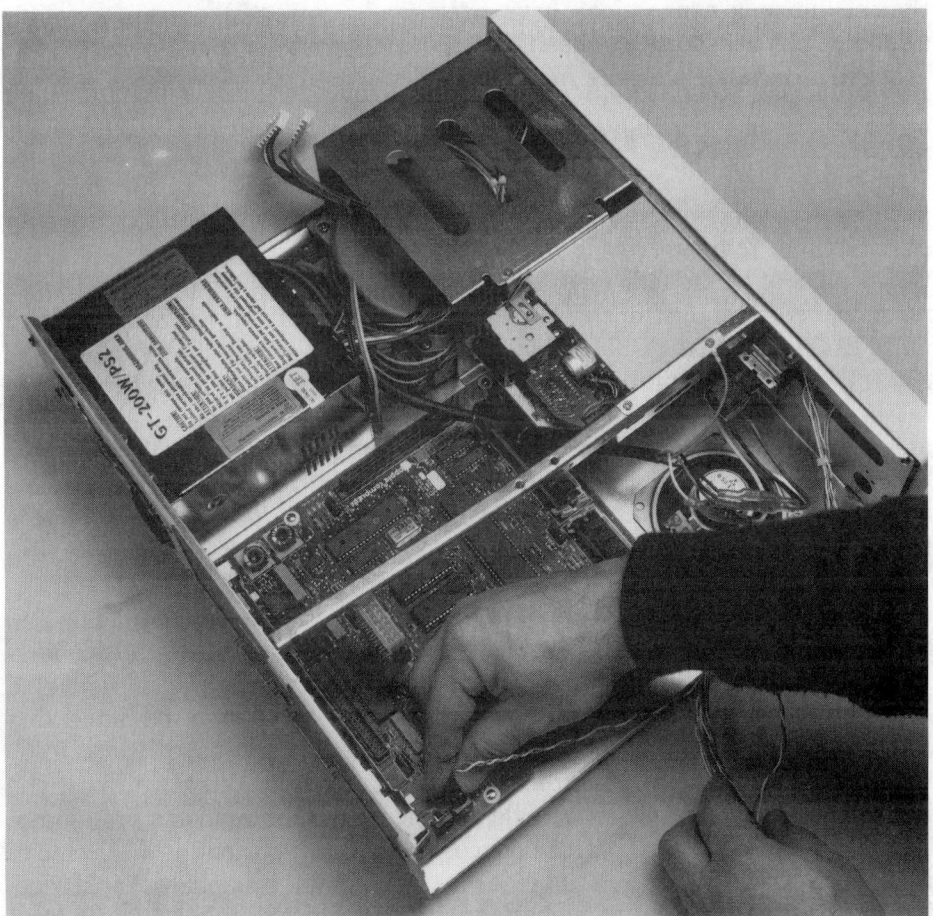

8-27 Connecting the reset switch cable.

assist in programming. *If you are not going to do any programming, don't connect the turbo switch.* The reset switch, on the other hand, is useful and saves having to turn your Cat Mac off and on.

Connect the case to the other parts

Now you are ready to take your first test drive. Hook up the monitor video cable to the Power R video cable connector on the back connector panel. *Make sure this connection is absolutely tight and the connector is fully seated all the way.* Hook up the monitor power cable. Connect the keyboard to either one of the ADB ports on the logic board (the pair of connectors on the left when viewed from outside the rear of the chassis). See Fig. 4-7 in chapter 4 (the SE logic board layout) to verify the connector locations. Connect the ADB mouse to the keyboard if you are right-handed; otherwise use the other ADB port. At this stage you want to put the eyeball on your creation to see

Assembly **233**

that all obvious connections have been made correctly, parts are solidly attached, no part shorts against another, etc. Give it a thorough going over so you will experience pleasure, not pain, when you turn the power on.

Power on—Phase 1 ("Liftoff and earth orbit")

I don't believe the Apollo moon-landing astronauts had a level of apprehension any higher than mine when it was time to power on my Cat Mac SE creation for the first time. Your experience will probably be similar. Okay, are you ready for the moment of truth? Turn on your monitor (the power switch on the right side when viewed from the front). Turn on your Cat Mac (the power switch in front on MTA-304 chassis).

If everything is working properly, which is highly likely with this configuration, you should hear the familiar Mac "bong" sound through the speaker, and also hear the power supply fan come on and the screen toggle through a few steps before stopping with a picture of a floppy disk icon with a blinking question mark in it. If you get this result, great. If not, go to Table 8-1 in the troubleshooting section.

Now you need to use your Startup disk. This is the floppy diskette you format to 800K, label *Startup*, and load a copy of the System, Finder, and Silverlining software onto (just these three icons). The system should be at least version 6.0 and should be a "skinny" version without a lot of fonts and desk accessories in it so it fits easily on your floppy along with the Finder and Silverlining software. Put your floppy into the drive as shown in Fig. 8-28.

Now what do you see and hear? If everything is working, you hear the floppy whirring and see its drive light coming on while it reads its first floppy. After a while the Monitor screen bounces to life with its friendly "Welcome to Macintosh" dialog box. You should now be looking at the standard Apple Macintosh desktop. If you get this result, great. If not, go to Table 8-1 in the troubleshooting section.

Congratulations, you have just passed Phase 1 testing and you are now in orbit around the earth, in Apollo space program parlance. Your Cat Mac and monitor are working along with your floppy disk drive, and you are now ready to activate your hard drive. Shut down your Cat Mac and unplug the power cables, or if you like, stop and play awhile with the icons.

Connect your hard disk

The correct power cable is already provided for you by the power supply—you merely have to hook it up. Actually there are four power connectors available. Two with smaller and two with larger connectors. Just plug in the nearest yellow-black-black-red cable from the power supply into the connector that matches up with it on the disk drive as shown in Fig. 8-29.

The SCSI cable is a 15" to 18" length of 50-pin ribbon cable with a standard 50-pin female IDC connector crimped onto each end for connection between the Mac SE logic board and disk drive. If you are making it yourself

Table 8-1. Cat Mac SE troubleshooting guide.

Problem/symptom	Cause(s)	Corrective action
Cat Mac does not turn on, no power supply fan noise	1. No power 2. Internal short 3. On/off switch 4. Power supply	Check power cord and outlet. Check wiring, reverse plugs P8 and P9. Check that wiring is per enclosed diagram. Possible defective power supply.
No video display	1. No power 2. Monitor	Check that cable is connected, monitor is turned on. Possible defective monitor.
Power but no video display	1. Cable 2. Turbo switch 3. Brightness	Check that monitor cable is tight at both ends. Press turbo switch and reboot Cat Mac. Check brightness level, increase setting.
"Sad Mac" icon on monitor	1. Bad SIMM 2. Logic board	Replace SIMM Replace logic board. This is unlikely, check all connections to logic board first.
Hard disk doesn't come on	1. No power 2. Hard disk	Check if power cable to hard disk is tight. Possible defective hard disk.
Hard disk on but can't talk to it (format software says no connect)	1. SCSI cable	Reverse one end of SCSI cable. Check that SCSI cable is tight at both ends.
After formatting hard disk, reboot gives blinking question mark icon	1. No software	Check that system and finder are installed on hard disk.
Floppy disk doesn't work	1. Cable 2. Floppy	Check that floppy drive cable is not reversed. Possible defective floppy disk.
No keyboard	1. Cable 2. Keyboard	Check that ADB cable is tight at both ends. Possible defective keyboard.
No mouse	1. Cable 2. Mouse	Check that ADB cable is tight. Possible defective mouse.

or having it made, leave a little bit of slack so you can easily attach and detach the cable without having to unbolt the drive. If you are using a Seagate ST 296N hard disk, mounted as shown in Fig. 8-30 with its imbedded controller card facing down or the shiny cover side facing up, then the SCSI ribbon cable has a single 180-degree twist in it after you connect it. (This is shown more clearly in Fig. 8-1.) Notice the red stripe is on the left side at the back of the disk drive, but on the right side when plugged into the logic board.

In the next step, when you turn the power on, if your drive turns on but you are not initially able to communicate with your hard disk, or the hard disk write LED just periodically blinks on and off, don't worry. You have connected your SCSI cable in backwards. Turn the power off, reverse the SCSI cable and try again. *Always turn the power off before changing SCSI connections to your hard disk*! Please.

Assembly

8-28 Loading the startup diskette. Notice question mark icon on screen and disconnected SCSI cable.

Power on—Phase 2 ("Moon orbit and landing")

Turn on your monitor and Cat Mac and insert the Startup disk. Your fan and monitor should come on, you should again hear the "bong" sound from the speaker and the sound of the hard disk winding up to speed, and your floppy drive should begin reading its diskette. The little hitch or delay in the boot up process occurs because the Mac automatically checks out your Cat Mac memory before turning over control of the machine to you. The more memory you have, the longer the delay (I am talking about a few seconds here). You should arrive at a picture of the Macintosh desktop as in Phase 1.

Now double click on the Silverlining icon and you should have the screen shown in Fig. 8-31. If you do not, go to Table 8-1 in the troubleshooting section. Notice the cursor arrow points between "Drive: SCSI Drive (85M)" and "Port: 0." Cancel out of any intermediate dialog boxes that come up until you get the screen shown in Fig. 8-31. In the "SCSI Drive Tests:" dialog box, click on the button called "Tests . . ." and let it take you through the steps of formatting your drive. Choose an interleave factor of 2 for your SE logic board (Plus interleave = 3, Mac II or SE 30 interleave = 1). This should take about 10 to 15 minutes. Name your drive HD85 or whatever you like, mount it (click until you make two check marks appear) and initially don't partition it into smaller vol-

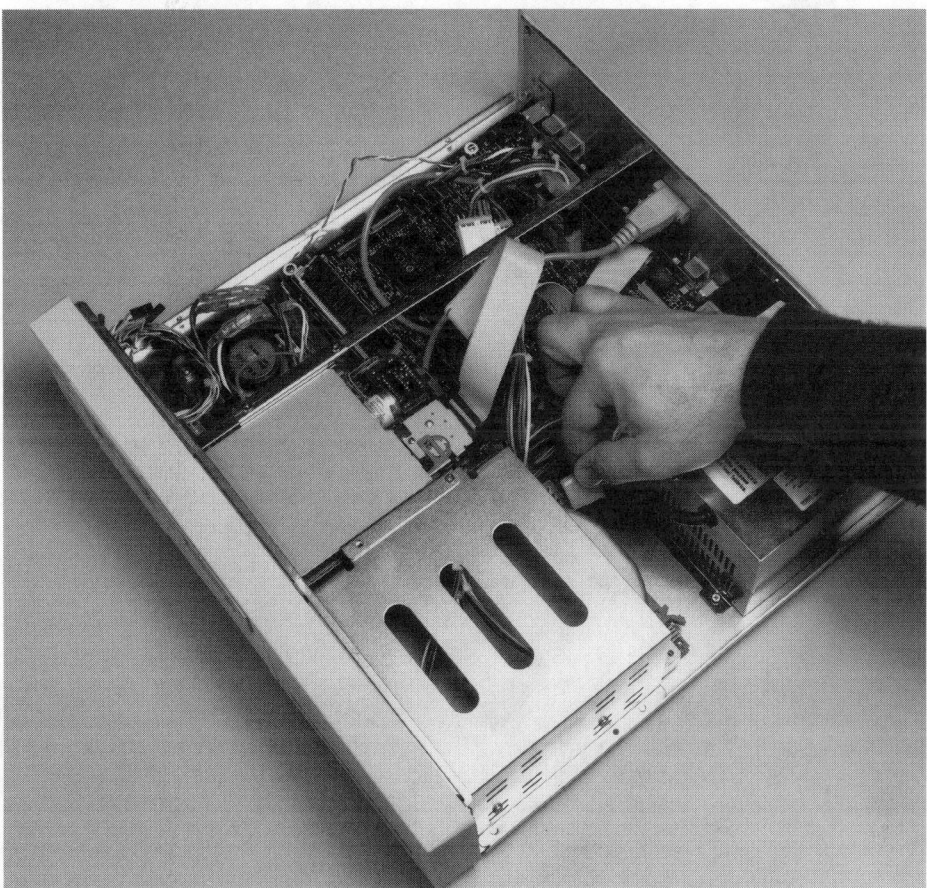

8-29 Connecting the hard drive power cable.

umes: leave it as one volume. Quit the application when you are done. When you return to the desktop, you now have two icons on it in the upper right hand corner: a floppy disk icon called Startup and a hard disk icon called HD85 (or whatever). The hard disk is now ready for you to load software onto it.

Start by loading your system software. The Apple System Software Kit (part number M0681/A) at list price $49.00 has all the tools you need. Follow its instructions, load your system software and you are almost in business. After you have loaded your system software on your hard disk, eject any floppy disk remaining in the drive and reset your system either from the front panel switch or from the menu on your screen. The hard disk now reboots and you return to the desktop, this time with only one icon HD85 on it. You have reached your destination—you've landed on the moon. Your Cat Mac is now ready for you to load your favorite software applications onto it.

At this point, you might want to extend this occasion to include champagne for everyone in the building if you are so inclined. . . .

Assembly

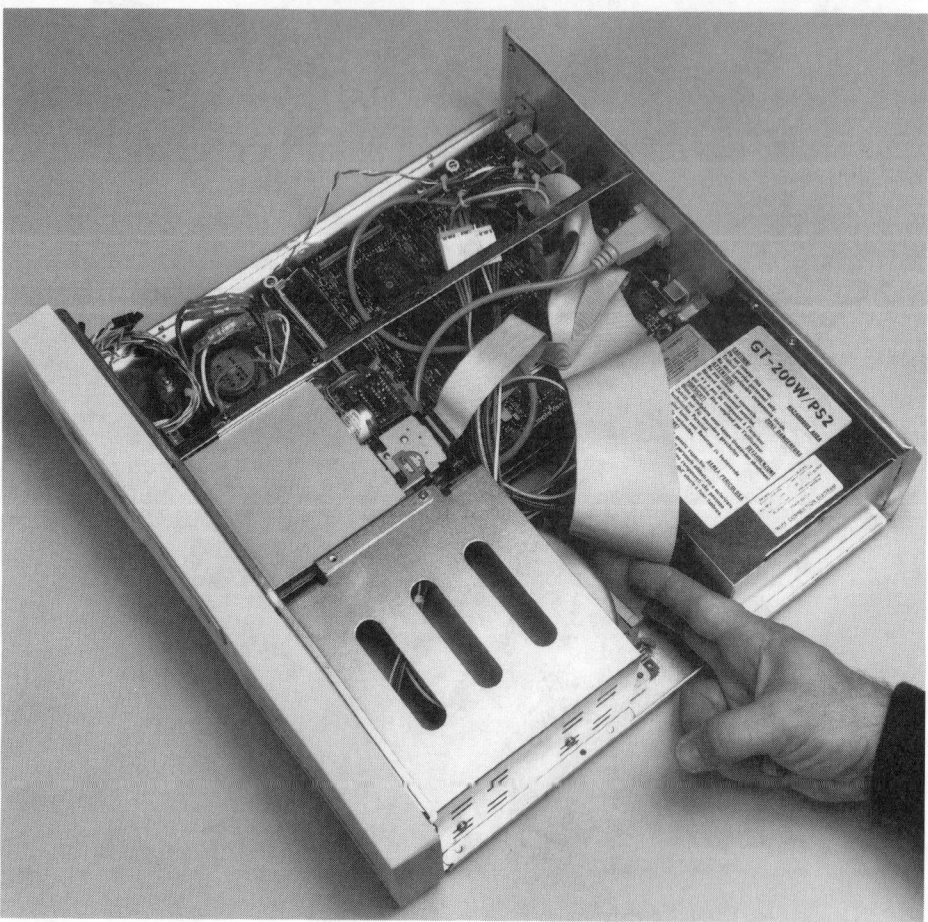

8-30 Connecting the hard drive SCSI cable.

After you build

If you had started your Cat Mac project with an earlier Macintosh 128/512/Plus logic board or were attempting to do the custom video board, you would still be working now while I kick back and sip a tall iced tea. As a Cat Mac SE builder, you have done your finishing touches already while others must fiddle with mounting battery holders (including a diode so that your batteries don't drain when the power is on), keyboard connectors, building all the other necessary cables, and having their heads into their custom video board and probably into a disassembled video monitor, tweaking it to get the display just right. The kit from ATS mentioned earlier makes it easier on them but they still have to do the extra steps. Still thirsty? Ready for a refill on your iced tea yet?

8-31 Using Silverlining software to format your hard drive.

Finishing thoughts

After you have a working Cat Mac, including your hard disk, you can put your cover on as shown in Fig. 8-32. Before you close the cover, double check that all connections are tight, that no wires are loose, and especially that no wires dangle around the area of the SIMMs chips. If you use the Power R video module, it will be a very tight fit to close the cover of the case so make sure nothing gets pinched or comes undone in the process. Use cable ties to make your wiring inside the case neat and secure. This will help prevent the wires from accidentally coming loose if you should move your Cat Mac. When you do a "look what I built" at your local Mac user group and your Cat Mac is suddenly DOA (dead on arrival), the wiring is the first thing to check—before checking the components. You probably wonder how I know this . . .

If you used a Mobius video card or other video board rather than the Power R module, which requires no additional software, you need to add the Mobius Card init software (or other products init software) to your Startup disk. Without this init software, you would only get a blank screen upon startup. Don't forget to put this init software into the system folder on your

After you build **239**

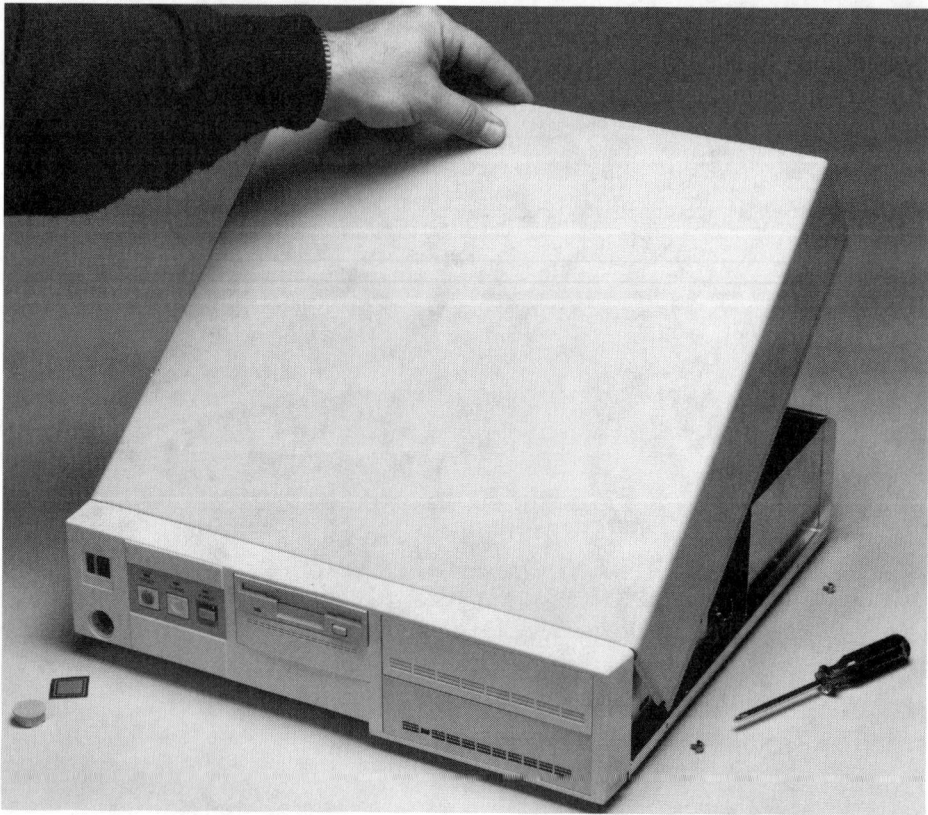

8-32 Putting the cover on your case. Objects at left plug openings in chassis front. Two cover screws at right.

hard disk as well, after you format it. This is also true of accelerator card init software, if you used one of these in your Cat Mac.

You do not need to mount your floppy and hard drives inside the case. The floppy already comes in its external case so you merely wire it into its logic board floppy connector. Connect your hard disk in its external case into the logic board SCSI connector. Yes, you do have a few more chassis boxes around but your assembly time is shortened, you can move your hard disk to another machine if you have to, and your Cat Mac really runs cool because now there is only a logic board in the chassis.

As mentioned at the beginning of this chapter, seeing your first Cat Mac working is really a great experience. You feel like you have really accomplished something. The mystique of what's inside a Macintosh is gone forever and you are probably thinking of new worlds to conquer. You know that if you don't like the results, you can change them—modify the case, add a new disk drive, change the back mounting panel—you can innovate and experiment to your heart's delight.

New worlds to conquer

Now that you have built the Cat Mac SE, nothing prevents you from extending your platform to more powerful logic boards in the Mac family. Upgrading to the SE 30 logic board is easy. You unplug your SE logic board and remove it from the chassis, then bolt in and plug in the SE 30 logic board. You need to reformat your hard disk with a new interleave factor but that's all there is to it. Instant SE 30—everything else works.

Upgrading to a Mac II or Mac IIcx is a little trickier as was discussed in chapter 4. However, now you have the experience and confidence to move on to this as a future project. The power connections are different and you need a more sophisticated and costly power supply if you want to implement the full ADB keyboard power control function, yet the concept is still the same. Put a board in a box and save a bundle.

Troubleshooting

What if your Cat Mac doesn't work the first time? Okay, don't panic. Observe what is or is not happening and match it with the cause(s) in Table 8-1. Then take the corrective action recommended in Table 8-1 to make it happen. It is highly likely with this configuration that everything will work properly, so you only need to keep a cool head while you methodically and logically isolate the problem, using Table 8-1 as a starting guideline.

Chapter 9
New desktop Cat Macs

The techniques you learned in the last chapter on building the original Cat Mac are timeless. Whatever model you build, you will always be able to utilize the same basic techniques. However, the options, peripherals, and accessories you can use to build your Cat Mac (and even the chassis you to select to put it in) change with time. This chapter proves the point, as you will see when you watch me build two new and different Cat Mac models.

First, I'll build a desktop Cat Mac using the DOS PC PS/2-style chassis you saw in the previous chapter, but this time with an Apple 1.4Mb FDHD floppy drive, a Quantum 105Mb 3½" hard drive, a Mobius combination video board/accelerator along with a full-page monitor, a Key Tronic MacPro Plus keyboard, and a Mouse Systems Little Mouse. Along the way I'll also look at optional storage devices that can be incorporated in your design, such as CD-ROM, SyQuest, and tape drives.

Second, you'll see how to build an even more compact desktop Cat Mac. This model uses the LAN-style PC chassis case, which is even smaller than the popular PS/2-style case, and is a design you might want to use if you want to make your Cat Mac a little bit more portable. Both projects will be built around the ageless Mac SE logic board.

Desktop Cat Mac

The completed desktop Cat Mac SE I'll be building in this section is shown in Fig. 9-1 (you already met it in Fig. 1-1 of chapter 1). It represents an overwhelming improvement in the Cat Mac SE project of the first edition. Its full-page display is in itself a tremendous improvement over the 14" display of the first edition's Cat Mac. Adding the Mobius combination video/accelerator card makes it strictly no contest in a performance comparison with its predecessor. The clarity and sharpness of the Zenith display from Mobius, plus near Mac IIci-performance accelerator/video card, combined with the benefits of the highly flexible yet relatively inexpensive Cat Mac DOS PS/2-style chassis, makes for a Cat Mac that can serve many needs. It makes an outstanding tool for a writer, as well as entry-level desktop publishing and light-to-medium business use.

While the big news is the new desktop Cat Mac SE's latest components deliver vastly superior performance, putting it together also requires a few new construction techniques. Let's get started.

A quick course in unwelding

One of the first things you'll notice that is different about the new PS/2-style chassis cases (and all DOS PC chassis in general) from the chassis used in the original Cat Mac project of the same style is that vendors are increasingly going to rear panels that are spot-welded in place. While this is an advantage for chassis manufacturers because it enables them to build at a lower cost, and

9-1 Desktop Cat Mac SE with full-page display and 25-MHz 68030 accelerator.

the difference between spot-welded and bolted-on rear panels is not noticed by DOS PC chassis users, as a Cat Mac builder you might find that the spot-welded rear panel interferes with either Macintosh logic board mounting or the rear panel you want to use.

So the first step in building with the newer chassis is removing the spot-welded rear panel. This can either be hard or easy—it's up to you. You can attack the chassis with your hammer and eventually remove the spot-welded panel, but this will result in needless dents to both your ego and the chassis. As you know from reading previous chapters, I recommend the KISS technique. All you have to do is drill a few well-placed holes over the existing spot-welds

Desktop Cat Mac

and then gently pry the rear panel loose using a putty knife or maybe a putty knife combined with a small hammer.

Figure 9-2 shows a cross-section before and after a spot weld. The secret is always to use a larger drill than the weld area to drill out the spot-weld shown at the top of Fig. 9-2, but not to put a hole in the main chassis when finished, as shown in the lower part of Fig. 9-2. All you are doing is removing the welded material and a little bit of the surrounding area and not penetrating the outer skin of the main chassis. You make a little dimple in its inside only. If you've chosen a large enough drill, there's very little flash-over material left, and your putty knife can make quick work of freeing the two sheets of metal from one another because of the thinness of the residue. If you've used too small a drill, you'll have to exert a little more effort both with your putty knife and with the small hammer you are using to disengage. If you are noticing that it takes too much effort, then it probably means you need to go back and redrill the holes with a larger size drill.

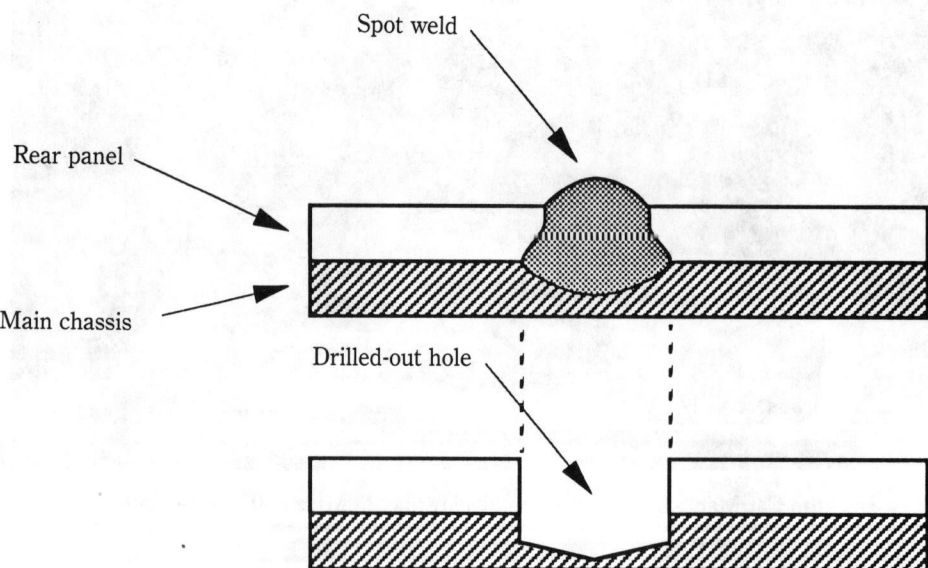

9-2 Simple process for removing spot-welded chassis back.

Mount the rear panel and logic board

The chassis as it comes to you with its spot-welded rear panel is shown in Fig. 9-3. To remove the spot-welded rear panel, you must first completely remove plastic or electrical components. Also during this step you can mark and drill the holes in the bottom of the chassis to accommodate the standoffs for mounting the logic board.

In this case, I used a different standoff mounting technique than I did in

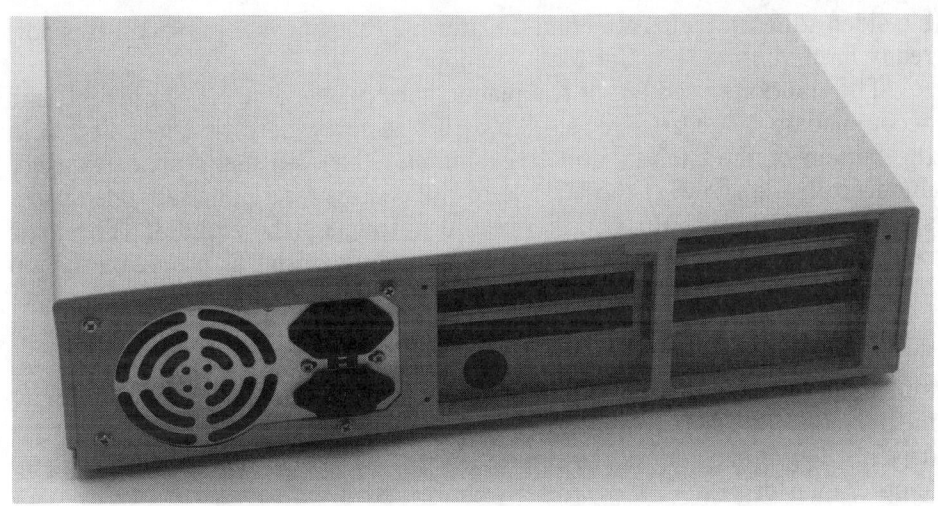

9-3 Original desktop Cat Mac chassis rear panel.

chapter 8 because I am going to use a premade Brant Associates Mac SE rear panel. It's a painted and silk-screened rear panel which already has the connector cutout holes in it and requires the Macintosh logic board be mounted closer to the bottom of the chassis. Figure 9-4 shows the premade panel mounted in place of the original, and all the standoffs mounted, plus four dou-

9-4 Desktop Cat Mac with new rear panel, standoffs, and speaker mounts installed.

ble-sided adhesive strips attached (to later hold the speaker in place). It is now ready for mounting your Cat Mac components.

The standoffs used are of the plastic variety or nylon, 1/4" in height, and accommodate 4-40 size screws. The 4-40 size screws are first installed from the bottom of the chassis, and I recommend that you use a spacer washer underneath the screw at the outside of the chassis (and optionally also use a spacer washer inside the chassis) before putting on the standoff. The logic board then rests on the standoff, and an insulating washer is placed on the top of the logic board prior to the 4-40 screw being tightened snug.

This is important in mounting the logic board: Do not over-tighten any of the mounting screws. This includes both external screws on the chassis bottom and also those that directly attach the logic board to the standoffs. Snug means more than finger tight, but it means that you stop turning your screwdriver when it encounters resistance. Avoid the temptation to ratchet it up another quarter turn.

The Mac SE logic board can now be mounted as shown in Fig. 9-5; the Mac SE logic board connectors line up exactly with the holes in the rear panel. The screwdriver is shown tightening down one of the four 4-40 screws used to hold the logic board in place.

Mount the power supply

Next the power supply is reinstalled in the chassis as shown in Fig. 9-6. The power supply in a PS/2-style chassis is usually held in place by several screws

9-5 Mounting the Mac SE logic board.

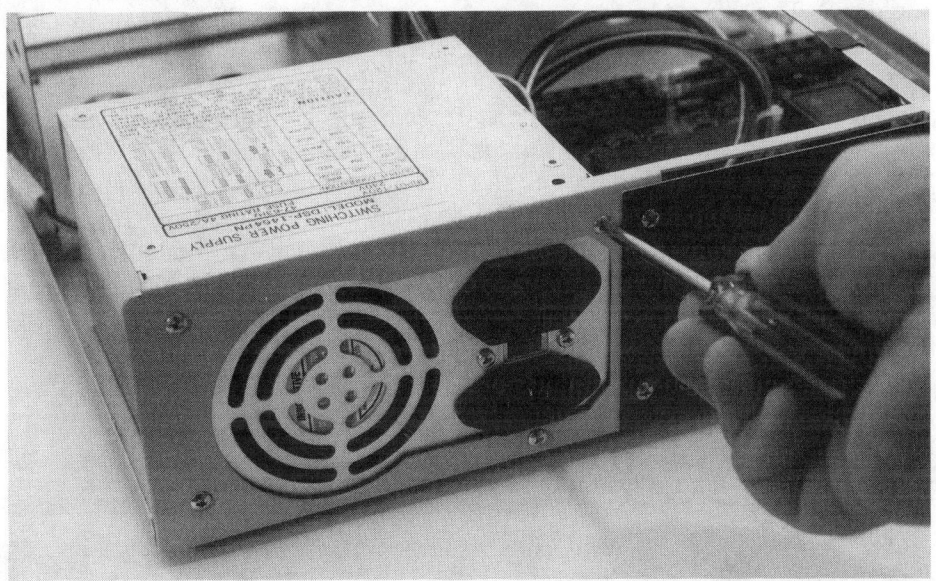

9-6 Reinstalling the power supply.

from the rear and one or two screws on the inside. As in the previous chapter, make sure the inside screws that protrude through the sheet metal don't extend so far beyond the feet as to mar whatever desktop surface you might be using your chassis on. If they are too long, cut them off to make them shorter. In chapter 8, I recommend that you install a power supply before the logic board. In this chapter I reverse the process because the type of standoffs, with two screws in them rather than two protruding bolts, actually makes it easier to install the logic board without the power supply in place first. Depending on your standoff arrangement, you can use either one technique or the other. If your logic board is harder to get at, put it in first. If it's easy to mount, put in the power supply first.

Mount the speaker

Next, mount the internal speaker and connect the reset, interrupt, and speaker wires as shown in Fig. 9-7. The speaker I selected for this project is a 45-ohm 4″ variety. You can use whatever speaker size you want, subject to the 32-ohm restriction I mentioned in chapter 7. Please don't use an 8-ohm speaker, the kind commonly shipped with all DOS PC chassis in your Cat Mac project! Any size speaker (obviously, you don't want a flat 8″ woofer here!) is okay as long as it fits and its impedance is more than 32 ohms.

Mount the speaker in the chassis well away from your floppy and hard drives because it has a magnet in it that you don't want to interfere with their media in any way. Find a convenient, vacant place. In this project, I used the front left of the chassis behind the switch area, and I mounted the speaker facing down. There was already a convenient hole available there for its installation, and I used double-sided sticky-back tape to assist me in mounting the speaker. By using four small strips located around the outside edge of the speaker, it was possible to hold the speaker in place quite securely with only one bolt through the chassis. This is clearly visible in Fig. 9-7. The most important caveat here is to tighten the bolt up securely so that the speaker is not wobbling or flopping around, but don't overtighten it so much that you bend the speaker frame and render it inoperative. It's also a good idea to use a lockwasher so that over time the screw holding the speaker in place does not vibrate loose.

9-7 Mount the speaker and connect the speaker, reset, and interrupt wires.

In attaching the reset and interrupt cables to the switches at the back of the Mac SE logic board, utilize the connectors that came with the chassis wiring harness. Just switch the cable connector ends to the larger 3-pin (with center unused) connector you need. The same is true for the speaker wire. Find one of the unused LED 2-pin receptacle connectors and twisted wire pair from the chassis wiring harness to give you exactly the solution you need for the cable between the speaker terminals and the 2-pin plug on the Mac SE logic board. Bare a longer length of wire from insulation and thread this wire several times through the speaker contact hole to make a good connection or solder it to make an even more secure contact with the speaker terminals.

Mount the accelerator/video card

Next mount your video card or your accelerator cards on the logic board. This is a fairly straightforward step with the Mac SE logic board or any other that has a PDS slot or NuBus slots on it. If, on the other hand, you are using a Macintosh logic board that requires a clip-on connector of any sort, you want to do the clipping on before you mount the logic board. It just makes it that much easier.

The same is also true for installing the SIMM memory modules—it's easier if you do this step when the logic board is out of the chassis. The Mobius accelerator/video card requires that at least 1Mb of memory remain on the logic board, so I installed 1Mb of 256K SIMMS prior to mounting it in the chassis.

The Mobius accelerator/video card, shown in Fig. 9-8, itself has four SIMM sockets that I filled with 1Mb SIMMS (for a total 4Mb). Gently lower the Mobius accelerator/video card's connector over the Mac SE logic board's mating PDS connector and push down firmly to seat it. The Mobius accelerator/video card has its own standoffs at the end opposite from the connector, so that's all there is to installation. All that remains is to hook up the cable to the Mobius accelerator/video card. First, mount the video output connector on the rear chassis panel through the predrilled mounting holes. Then attach the cable to the Mobius accelerator/video card as shown in Fig. 9-9.

9-8 Mobius accelerator/video card prior to mounting.

Mount the hard drive

Next it's time to mount the hard drive. In the original Cat Mac project you were dealing with a 5¼" half-height hard drive. You are unlikely to be using

Desktop Cat Mac **251**

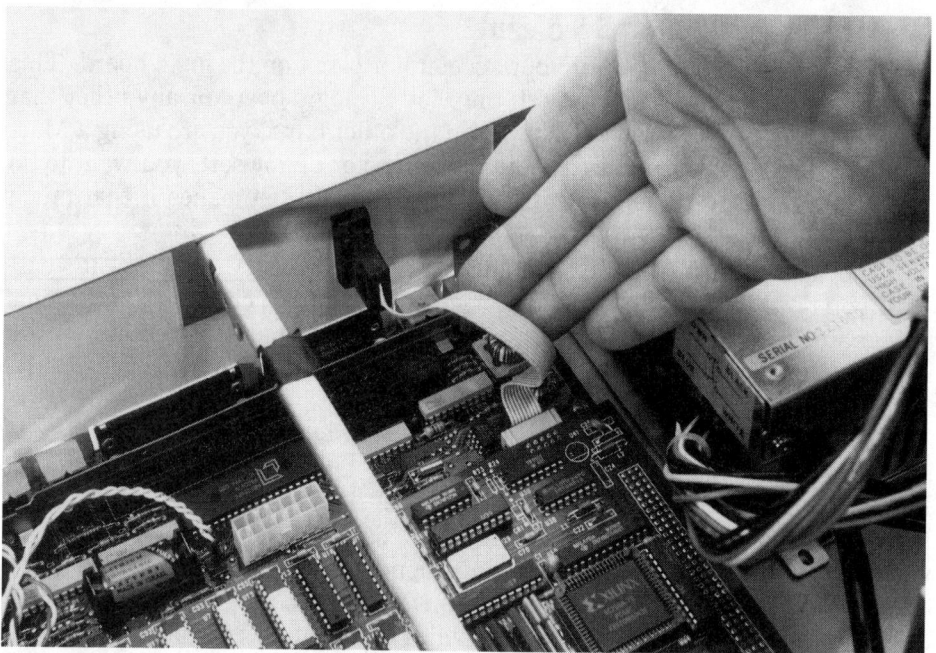

9-9 Connect the Mobius video cable.

this type of hard drive today, unless you go to a very large capacity model, typically a 150Mb and up variety. Even then, it is increasingly likely today that you would be using a 3½" hard drive, either in the half-height variety or the 1" high variety. For this Cat Mac project I used a fast Quantum Pro-Drive 105 (a half-height 3½" drive). This PS/2 chassis design has room to mount two 3½" peripherals. Normally, you would mount a 3½" hard drive in either the lower or upper position in this bay.

However, to show you an alternative approach for this Cat Mac project, I mounted the 3½" hard drive in a 5¼" bracket and put it in the lower 5¼" bay. Figure 9-10 shows the Quantum Pro-Drive 105 model next to its 5¼" mounting frame with the grey plastic bezel attached to the front of it. Depending on the hard drive model you choose and the way it is mounted in the 5¼" bracket adapter, it might be easier to attach the SCSI and power cables to it before you mount it into the adapter. This is something that is totally dependent on the manufacturer and model of the hard drive you choose to use. In this case, it was easier to make the connection before final mounting of the hard drive in the bracket, so I snaked the power cable through the front opening, along with the SCSI cable, attached it to the drive, then mounted the hard drive in the bracket, and finally slid the bracket and hard drive assembly carefully back through the front of the chassis as shown in Fig. 9-11.

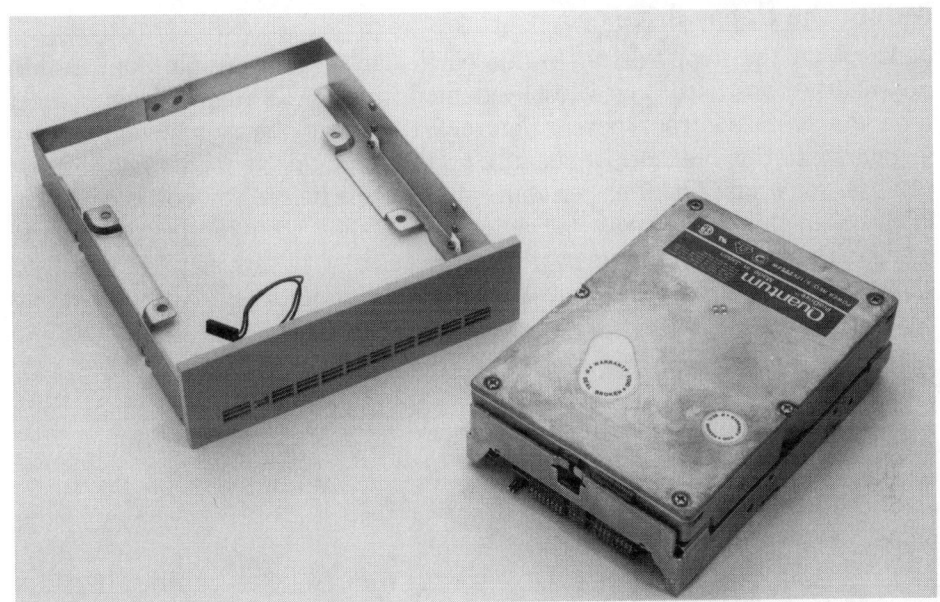

9-10 Quantum 3½" hard drive (right) and 5¼" adapter bracket (left).

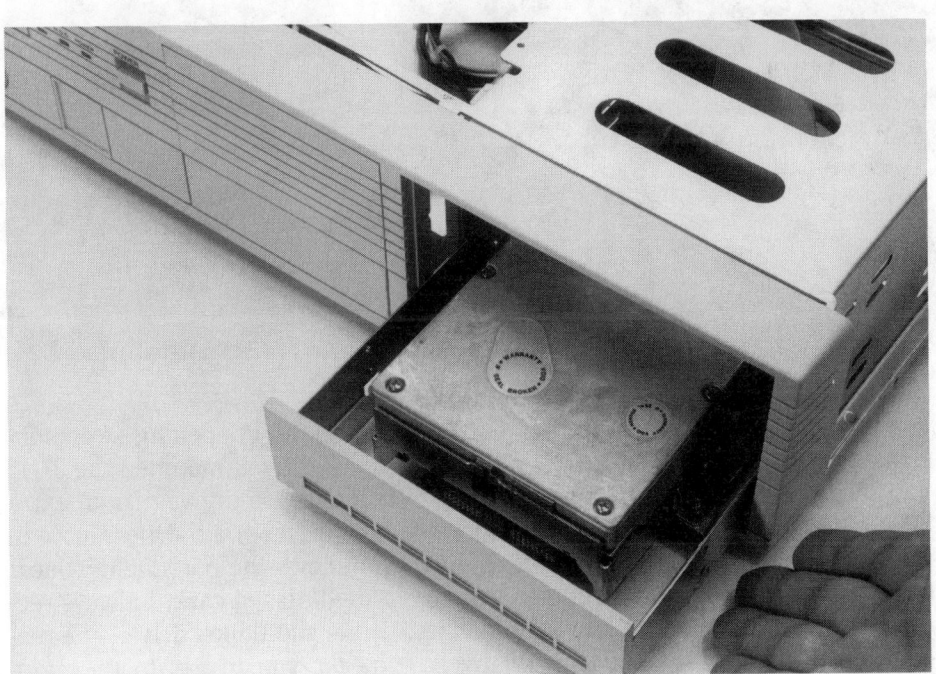

9-11 Installing the Quantum hard drive and bracket assembly into Cat Mac.

Desktop Cat Mac 253

Mount the floppy drive

Next mount the floppy drive. In this particular case the Apple Sony 1.4Mb floppy drive was used, and it was mounted in the ATS floppy drive bracket with the prefitted front bezel. Figure 9-12 shows the floppy drive being installed into this bracket. Depending on the floppy drive model and bracket you use, you might find it easier to install the cable before you bolt the bracket in place. In this case it was just as easily installed after the bracket was in place, so no particular extra work was necessary at this step. Figure 9-13 shows the floppy drive bracket being slid into the upper 5¼" chassis mounting bay.

9-12 Mounting the Apple 1.4Mb floppy drive in ATS 5¼" adapter bracket.

While I chose to mount a 3½" hard drive in the 5¼" opening to demonstrate the flexibility of being able to do so, obviously if you mounted the 3½" hard drive in its normal chassis mounting position it would give you an extra 5¼" slot to mount either a CD-ROM drive, a tape drive, or a SyQuest drive in that position under the floppy drive. Figure 9-14 shows the potential SyQuest (right) and tape drive (left) candidates on top of the finished case. I always recommend that any optional drives be mounted under the floppy drive. The reason you do this is so that it is relatively easy for you to get to the more frequently used floppy drive opening when inserting and removing your diskettes. Its higher mounting position usually allows the diskettes to clear your keyboard easily, no matter what kind you have.

9-13 Installing the floppy drive and bracket assembly into Cat Mac.

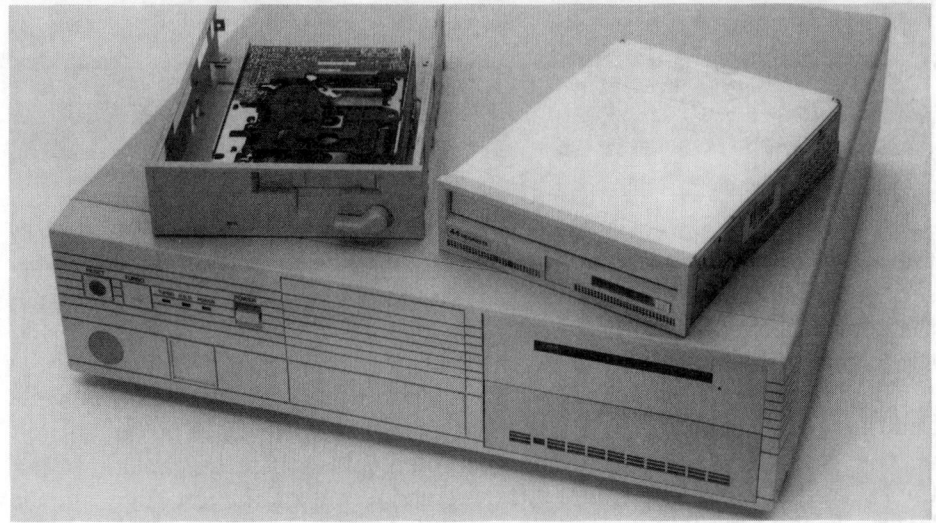

9-14 Alternative SyQuest (right) and tape drive (left) solutions for your Cat Mac.

Cabling your Cat Mac

The cabling process for this Cat Mac project is considerably simplified by using the Cat Mac SE cable set from Brant Associates. It consists of three pre-assembled cables—the power, SCSI, and floppy cables.

Using the preassembled power cable makes hooking up a breeze. One end is connected into the logic board power connector and the other ends go to the power supply P8 and P9 connectors. The wires on the power connector are color-coded, so it's only necessary to match them to the P8 and P9 connectors, the four-wire cable going to P8, and the five-wire cable with the red wires in it going to P9. This is shown in Fig. 9-15.

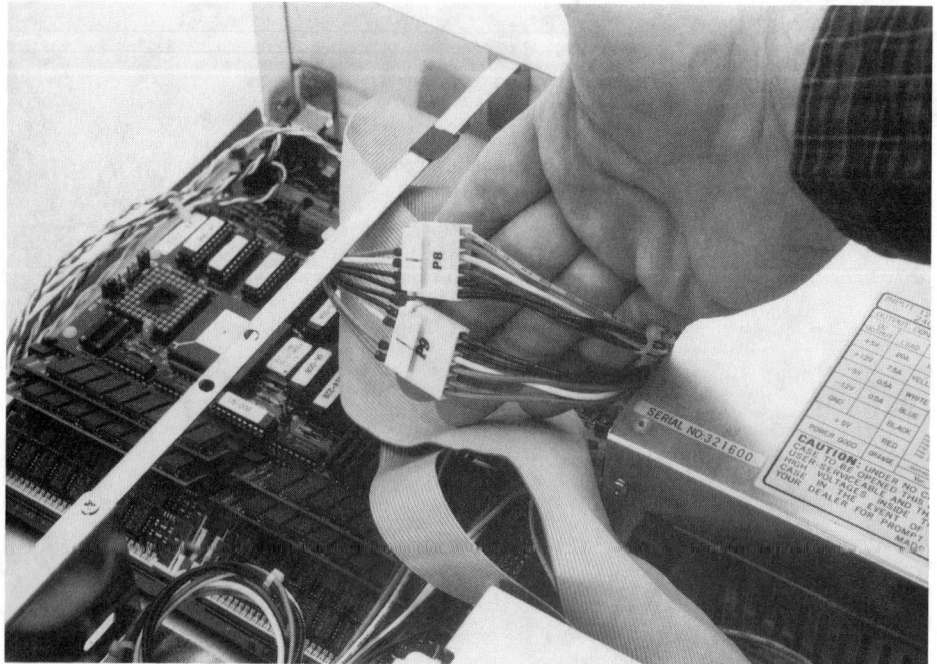

9-15 Connect the power cable.

The SCSI cable previously installed on the back of the hard drive goes to the SCSI 50-pin connector on the Mac SE logic board. The plugs on the preassembled SCSI cable have keys on them so that all you need to do is to match the keys on the plug with the keys on the connector at both the hard drive and the logic board end and all your work is completed.

The floppy cable is connected between the floppy drive rear connector and the floppy connector on the Mac SE logic board. If you've made the connection correctly and used the preassembled cable, then the cable between the two will have no twists, and if the red stripe was on the left edge when it left the back of the floppy drive, it will also be on the left edge entering into the logic board. Completed chassis cabling prior to putting the cover back on is shown in Fig. 9-16.

Mounting more than one SCSI device

If you want to add a second SCSI drive in your Cat Mac's PS/2 chassis (such as the SyQuest drive shown in Fig. 9-14) you must take several additional steps.

9-16 Inside view after all Cat Mac cables have been hooked up.

First, you need to relocate the hard drive to the $3^{1}/_{2}''$ bay to accommodate the SyQuest drive in the lower $5^{1}/_{4}''$ drive bay.

Second, you need to add another connector plug on your 50-pin SCSI ribbon cable; it will then have three plugs on it. One plug will go to the logic board and the other two to the respective drives. Make sure all plugs on the SCSI ribbon cable are on the same side and facing the same direction. That means that pin 1 on any of the connector plugs will be connected to exactly the same wire on the ribbon cable. Look at how the SCSI drives and their connector sockets are laid out inside your chassis, test-fit the cable around to these locations without any drastic folds, and figure out the length of cable that you need to make the run and where on the cable plugs need to be located.

Third, make sure that the jumper settings on all SCSI devices are set differently from one another (go back and review the jumper ID settings in chapter 5). A Mac SE internal hard drive requires an SCSI ID setting of "0." This default setting allows it to boot off the internal hard drive first. All other SCSI devices that you mount internally you can set to higher ID numbers as you wish. This is really not a big deal with a SyQuest, tape, or CD-ROM drive unit. None of these units are typically active bootup devices. Normally, they will not even have media in them so that your Cat Mac will default automatically to your hard drive.

Fourth, make sure that SCSI termination is correct. SCSI rules specify

Desktop Cat Mac 257

that only the last device in the chain should have SCSI terminating resistors in it. Verify that this is the case, and install these terminating resistor packs per the instructions given in chapter 5.

Finally, remember that the drives that you install inside your Cat Mac are going to be on all the time because they are powered from the same on/off switch. If this is creating problems for you (e.g., if you're not able to get them to boot properly), check to see that all hard drives you are using are of the same vintage. When using an older hard drive with a newer one, the older (typically slower) hard drive taking a longer time to come up to speed can create problems at bootup time.

My experience has shown that well over 90% of bootup problems created with two or more hard drives on Mac SE or newer logic boards are created by a mismatch of the speed and types of hard drives used. If all your drives are from the same manufacturer and the same vintage, you very rarely encounter startup problems. It's also rare that you would encounter a startup problem when using a single hard drive with a typical backup device, such as a SyQuest drive or a tape drive, in that both of these units are only typically used after your hard drive is already running and up to speed.

I do not recommend you use a Mac Plus logic board as the foundation for your Cat Mac project if you also anticipate using two or more hard drives. The older design of the SCSI circuitry on the Mac Plus logic board made it a lot more difficult to manage two dissimilar hard drives. Often the only solution is to mount one of the hard drives outside the Cat Mac chassis.

Final assembly and checkout

Now that the assembly and cabling process is complete, all that remains is to connect your external monitor, keyboard, mouse, and ac power supply cable to your Cat Mac. Go ahead and do this, and give all connections a last-minute check for tightness and to see that they are properly made. When you turn on your Cat Mac power supply switch you should be greeted by the familiar bong sound that tells you all is well. You should also hear the SCSI hard drive whirring up to speed. After you have everything working properly, you can replace the top cover on your new Cat Mac creation. All that remains are the initializing and formatting steps.

In this case, using the Mobius accelerator/video card requires that several inits be installed into your hard drive's Apple System software folder to make the process automatic. When booting up your Cat Mac for the first time in this configuration, unless you have previously set up your hard drive on another Macintosh system, it's necessary to do this installation from a separate floppy drive.

What I usually do is make a separate floppy installation diskette with the System folder and the Mobius accelerator and video inits on it, such as shown in Fig. 9-17. Then I use this floppy diskette to boot up my Cat Mac for the first time. After I turn power on, hear the bong, and verify the SCSI hard drive is up

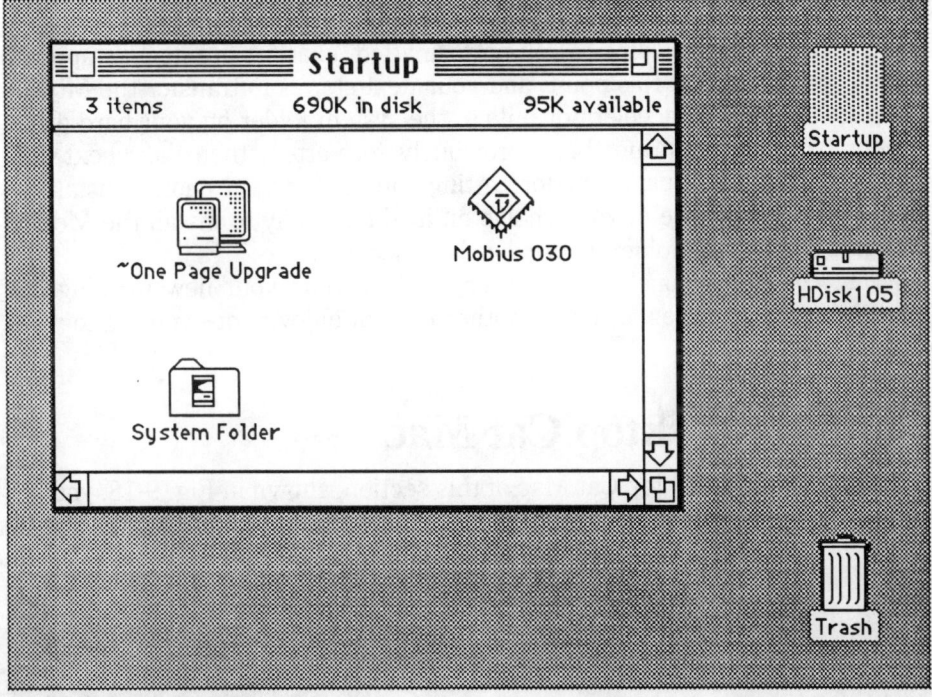

9-17 Startup installation diskette for your desktop Cat Mac.

to speed, I load the bootup floppy diskette. Depending on how much memory is installed, the Cat Mac takes a few seconds and then goes through the launching process where you see in quick succession the Mac icon on the screen and then the screen launching into the Mobius video display. If the video display does not come on at this point, it could mean that either you have not hooked it up correctly or that you have not given the software the correct instructions.

My experience has shown that software is probably the culprit in 98% of the cases. If you've verified all of your connections and you're still not getting an image on the screen, you need to go to another Macintosh to check the contents of your startup diskette. Verify first that your Mobius software is set up for the screen that you have, that both Mobius icons (the accelerator and the full-page display icon) are inside the system folder, and that the system and finder icons are on the diskette.

Verify next on the control panel Mobius screen that it is set to launch onto the larger full-page monitor, not onto the Macintosh 9″ screen, which is the default setting when a Mobius full-page display is used with a standard Apple Macintosh SE.

Having taken these steps and located the problem, rebooting your Cat Mac using the startup diskette ought to result in a normal Macintosh desktop on your Mobius screen. You should be not only pleased by your assembly efforts to this point, but utterly in awe at the beauty and clarity of the image on your Mobius full-page display.

If your hard drive came to you preformatted, chances are its icon appears on the desktop also at this point, and your next step is to transfer the Mobius full-page display and accelerator inits to the system folder on your hard drive. If your hard drive has not been previously formatted, then your next step would be to format it using the formatting software of your choice, install the Apple system software of your choice on it, then finally to install the Mobius inits into this system folder as previously described.

Hey, congratulations! Hope you enjoyed building your new working Cat Mac. Now you get to experience another level of enjoyment—you get to work on it!

Compact desktop Cat Mac

In assembling the desktop Cat Mac of this section, shown in Fig. 9-18, you are taking advantage of the compactness of the new generation of DOS PC LAN-

9-18 Compact desktop Cat Mac SE with Amdek monitor.

style cases now hitting the market to give you a lighter weight and more compact Cat Mac configuration that is readily portable, combined with a 14" monitor. Carrying cases designed to accommodate the Macintosh LC and IIsi with Apple 12" monitor, will also handily accommodate your compact desktop Cat Mac and its 14" monitor, which means you can take it with you and set up anywhere. At the low end you can think of it as a replacement for the Apple Macintosh Classic, except now you have a 14" screen and a much nicer keyboard and mouse. At the high end, you can drop all sorts of accelerator-board options into it, along with larger hard drives and the 14" monitor, and really have a powerful yet relatively portable package. Let's get into the assembly details.

Prepare chassis

You have to take apart all the smaller chassis when you receive them in order to install your logic board and work on the sheet metal. The take-apart sequence for the chassis (usually) dictates the reassembly process. My experience has shown that the reassembly process can vary widely with different chassis. You will have to let your own experience be your guide. Depending on the particular chassis that you select, you might have to substitute one or more steps in the reassembly process due to the way its components are located and mounted.

The compact desktop Cat Mac chassis itself, like the PS/2-style chassis of the previous section, also comes with its rear panel spot-welded in place. You need to use the same techniques to remove the spot-welds prior to removing the rear panel. The logic board mounting holes should also be drilled at the same time as before.

Mount the rear panel and logic board

Again I utilized a premade Brant Associates Mac SE rear panel. In this case, I used a model with the wide video mounting slot—just cut down in size a little bit to fit the smaller chassis. Figure 9-19 shows the premade rear panel mounted, and the chassis standoffs located in place. Standoffs used in this case were even easier—a single long 4-40 bolt goes through the hole in the chassis, the threaded plastic standoff is drawn up snug against it, and the logic board rests on top—held in place by a 4-40 nut sitting on a plastic insulating washer. Simplicity itself. Figure 9-20 shows the Mac SE logic board being installed in the chassis. In this case the logic board must again be installed first because there is absolutely no clearance at all with the power supply in place. You can barely see the four 1Mb SIMMS (total of 4Mb all together) mounted on the SE logic board, but take my word for it!

Mount the power supply and fan

Figure 9-21 shows the power supply being installed. It is held in place by two screws inside and two screws at the rear of the chassis. Figure 9-22 shows the

9-19 Compact desktop Cat Mac chassis after preparation steps with new premade back panel and standoffs mounted.

9-20 Installing the Mac SE logic board.

262 *New desktop Cat Macs*

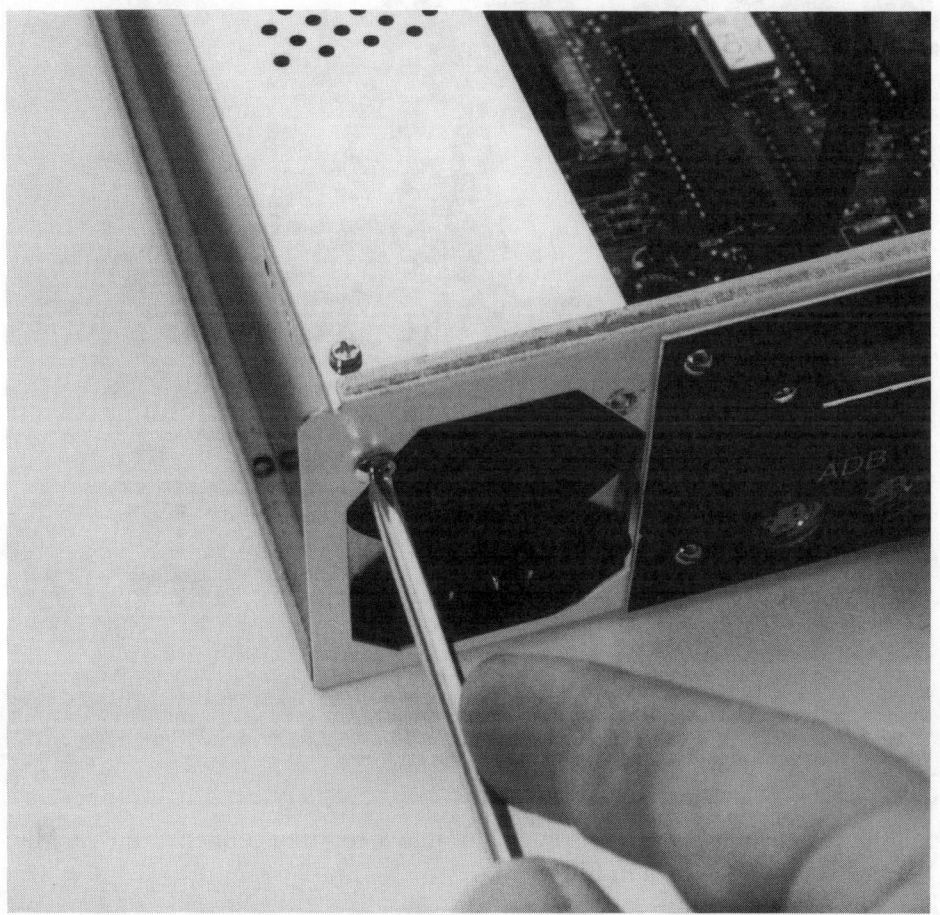

9-21 Installing the power supply.

fan being installed. As a general rule, in all smaller chassis you'll find the fan separate from the power supply, or mounted in a manner uniquely different from how the fan and power supplies are mounted in the larger chassis. This particular one just happens to vent through the right front of the chassis, and it's held in place with four large-diameter screws.

Mount the speaker

Next, mount the internal speaker and connect the speaker wire. In this case I used a standard Apple Macintosh 63-Ω speaker removed from the front panel of a Mac SE. It was approximately the same thickness—the critical factor in its mounting location next to the fan—and only slightly larger in diameter than the original 8-Ω speaker (which I removed and discarded!) so I only had to bend the mounting tabs a little to accommodate it. The Apple Macintosh 63-Ω speaker also came with attached twisted wire pair and 2-pin connector which was per-

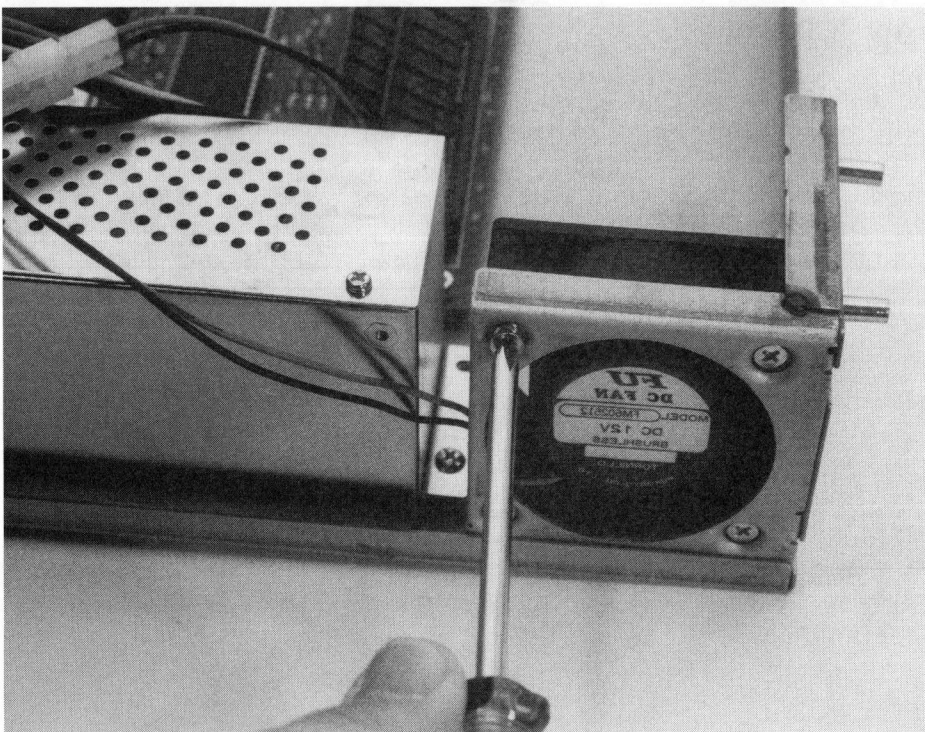

9-22 Installing the fan.

fect for this installation—I just plugged it into its mating connector on the Mac SE logic board as shown in Fig. 9-23.

Mount and connect the LED lamps and reset switch

This particular chassis has a small panel with three LEDs and a reset switch on it (no turbo switch) held in place by two screws. Once you have fastened the panel in place, as shown in Fig. 9-24, route the wire to the reset switch around to the rear of the Mac SE logic board and connect it using the larger 3-pin (with center unused) connector from the chassis wiring harness. There are three LEDs: yellow, green, and red. In this case, I found wiring the yellow and green LEDs in series gave me a nice "power on" indication without necessarily over-stressing the LEDs. I just connected them to a convenient source of +5-V power—one of the unused peripheral power cables inside of the case—with twist tie connectors. I saved the red LED with its 2-pin connector for later attaching to the hard drive as the drive activity indicator.

Mount the video card

The best time to add whatever video card you're going to add to the chassis is after you've mounted your speaker and reset wires, and wired to your front

9-23 Installing the speaker cable—after speaker installation.

9-24 Installing the LED panel.

panel indicator lights. In this case I used the Lapis Amdek display board. First, I attached the Lapis connector panel to the chassis rear panel as shown in Fig. 9-25. The precut rear panel mounting holes accommodate the Lapis connector mounting bracket and screws exactly, so this is a nice, tidy fit. Notice the small square white patch on the logic board chip—it's a small piece of double-sided adhesive rubber Lapis provided to anchor the end of the video card opposite the PDS connector securely in place. The Lapis video card is installed by placing its connector directly over the Mac SE logic board PDS connector and pushing down on it firmly to seat it. After you have mounted both the Lapis card and its connector panel, run the keyed video ribbon cable from the connector panel to the mating connector on the video card as shown in Fig. 9-26.

Mount the floppy and hard drives

This chassis has a metal shelf bracket used for mounting both floppy and hard drives located at the front. In this instance I elected to use a Fujitsu model 800K floppy drive, since it had the preattached bezel and was the correct size to fit the chassis opening exactly. I mounted the floppy drive on the left side of the bracket assembly in a manner which allowed it to emerge properly through the front bezel of the chassis. On the right side of the mounting adapter is space for a $3^1/2''$ hard drive of either the half-height or one-third-height variety. In this particular case I mounted a Quantum 105Mb half-height $3^1/2''$ drive in

9-25 Installing Lapis rear connector panel.

9-26 Installing ribbon cable between Lapis rear connector panel and Lapis video card.

9-27 Compact desktop Cat Mac drive shelf bracket with hard drive (left) and floppy drive (right) installed.

the space. Figure 9-27 shows the underside of the bracket with both the floppy drive and hard drive bolted in place.

Once you've mounted the hard and floppy drive on the bracket which holds them, the bracket must be attached to the chassis. It's held in place by four screws, two from the front and two at either end, facing downward. The front screws are attached first (but not fully tightened) to hold the bracket in place. The screw located adjacent to the floppy drive is attached next, but again not fully tightened. The screw at the hard drive end is located between the power supply and the hard drive. It is least convenient to attach because of all the cabling in this area that has to be kept out of the way while you focus on inserting the screw into the standoff that holds the drive bracket in place. Once it is in place, however, you can tighten it firmly along with all the other bracket screws.

Cabling your Cat Mac

The cabling process for this compact Cat Mac project is also considerably simplified by using the Cat Mac SE cable set with preassembled power, SCSI, and floppy cables from Brant Associates.

The preassembled power cable makes hooking up a breeze. If you are using this cable, the logic board end merely plugs into the logic board receptacle and the P8 and P9 ends match their color-coded counterparts emerging

9-28 Connect the power cable.

9-29 Inside view after all Cat Mac cables have been hooked up.

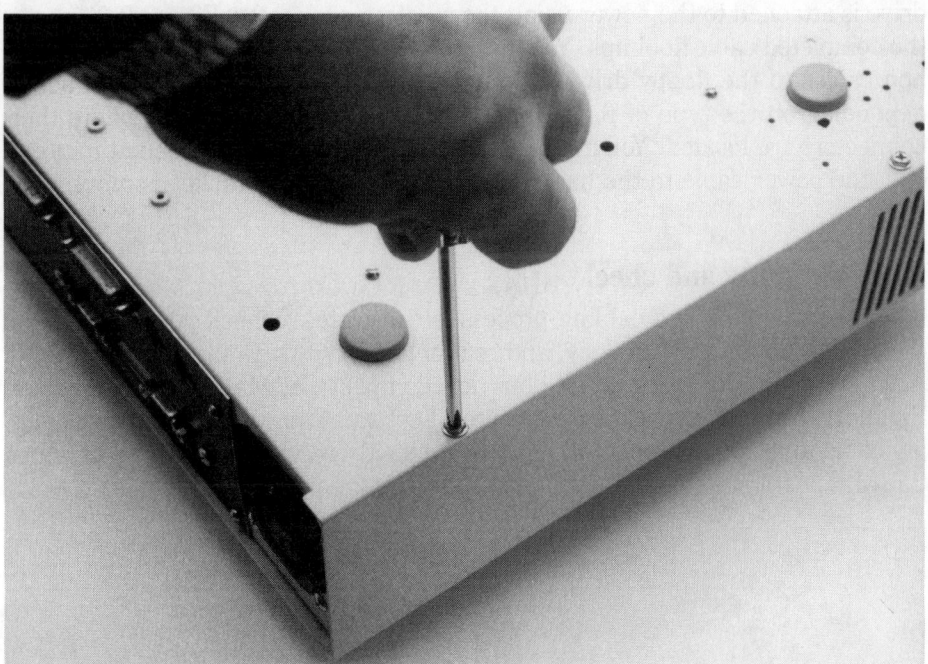

9-30 Reattach four screws underneath case holding top cover in place.

9-31 Front view of completed compact desktop Cat Mac chassis.

from the power supply. This is shown in Fig. 9-28. You might have to preinstall the power cable in your particular chassis. In this case it was not necessary.

The preassembled SCSI and floppy cables go to their receptacles on the back of the hard drive, floppy drive, and on the Mac SE logic board. The hard drive is attached to the power using the existing connector. Figure 9-29 shows the completed cable hookups. You might or might not have to preinstall the ribbon cables to the floppy drive and hard drive before you mount the bracket, depending on the type of floppy and hard drive you've used and where their connectors are located. You might also find it a little more convenient to preinstall the power cable to the hard drive before the drive bracket is moved into place.

Final assembly and checkout

After the assembly and cabling process is complete, recheck your work, slide the chassis cover back in place, and reattach its screws as shown in Fig. 9-30. After stopping briefly to admire your new compact Cat Mac creation shown in Fig. 9-31, connect your external monitor, keyboard, mouse, and ac power supply cable to it and proceed with checkout exactly as was done in the previous Cat Mac section. Then enjoy the fruits of your labors.

Chapter 10

Upgrade kits make building easier

The last two chapters focused on how easy it is to build different Cat Mac models and the flexibility you enjoy when doing it. Wouldn't it be nice if there were a kit you could buy that required no holes to drill, no back panel to fit, no extra cables to purchase, with the chassis decision already made for you? You could assemble it even faster and get right to work. Well, guess what? Kit models are available to meet your every need.

This chapter will focus on kits in three different areas: desktop, tower, and portable. I'll cover each one of these areas in sequence, overview the assembly details, and whet your appetite for these attractive alternatives. Let's get started.

Desktop upgrade kit

MicroMac Technology has built a better mousetrap with its upgrade systems. One glance at the Mac SE 30-powered color Macintosh system enclosed in a MicroMac Technology upgrade chassis shown in Fig. 10-1 tells you why. Its upgrade systems give you a space-saving, low-profile, modern-looking enclosure for your Macintosh that accommodates Mac Plus, SE, and SE 30 logic boards in addition to your choice of floppy drives, hard drives, video options, keyboards, and mouse pointing devices.

MicroMac Technology's small-footprint, slimline chassis enclosure lets you save desktop space while choosing the monitor of your choice, usually a full-page or color display, and delivers it all in a package that is highly transportable. You can readily take it with you to another location—all you need is a second monitor available there.

Assembly is an absolute snap. It takes you under an hour from a standing start and the only tool you need is a Phillips-head screwdriver. MicroMac Technology provides the display, video card, cables, components, software, and documentation. All you need to provide is the logic board, hard drive, floppy drive, keyboard, and mouse or pointing device. Complete monochrome upgrade kits for the Mac Plus or SE start at about $900 for the 14" monitor version. The full-page display is about $100 more. Color upgrade systems for the Mac SE 30, such as the one shown in Fig. 10-1, start at about $900 and the monitor is extra.

Finally, I was tremendously impressed by the attention to detail and precision design of the close-fitting components used inside the MicroMac chassis. Nothing I say here can convey a totally accurate description of the exactness of its construction—you have to experience that aspect for yourself. The assembly process was like putting together a fine Swiss watch.

Let's take a closer look at how easy it is to assemble a Mac SE 30-based MicroMac Technology upgrade system.

10-1 MicroMac Technology SE 30 Upgrade System with color monitor.

Prepare the enclosure

Figure 10-2 shows the front of the enclosure as you get it from MicroMac Technology. You turn it around to the back so that it is facing you, loosen three screws (you don't have to remove them), and the plastic cover lifts off from the rear as shown in Fig. 10-3—leaving you with a totally enclosed metal chassis. This enclosed metal chassis construction minimizes your RFI (radio frequency interference) and actually exceeds even the stringent Apple original equipment specifications. Three screws on either side of this metal chassis hold it in place. Again, all that is needed is to loosen them as shown in Fig. 10-4. Remov-

Desktop upgrade kit **273**

10-2 Front view of MicroMac Technology Upgrade System enclosure.

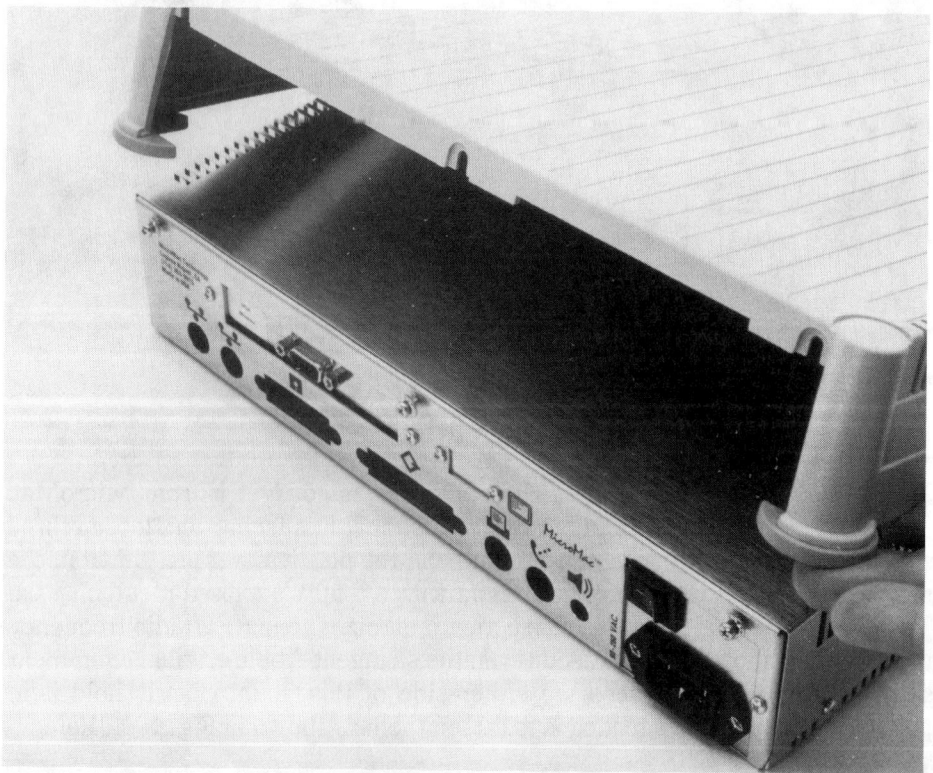

10-3 Loosen three screws to remove plastic cover from rear.

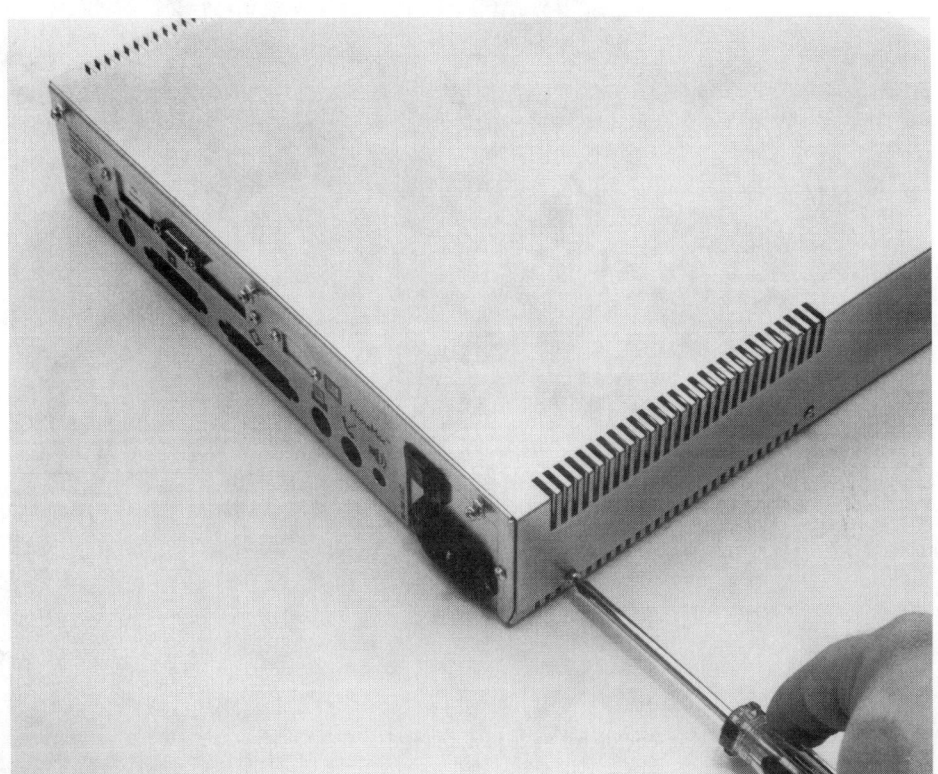

10-4 Loosen six screws to remove RFI cover.

ing the metal RFI chassis cover shows the inside of the upgrade system as it's delivered to you from MicroMac in Fig. 10-5. In this case, the Mac SE 30 system is delivered with the video card that you specified preinstalled in the chassis along with its appropriate matching connector.

Your next tasks are to remove all the other interior parts until you have a bare chassis; then you begin building by first installing your Mac SE 30 logic board. The enclosed documentation thoroughly details how to do this with numerous photographs along the way.

Prepare and install the SE 30 logic board

Before installing your SE 30 logic board, you have a few minor steps to take. MicroMac Technology provides special offset adapters for your ROM and RAM SIMM modules that allow them to be mounted at right angles to the direction they're normally mounted and conserve space inside the chassis. It's much easier to install these on your Mac SE 30 logic board before it's mounted in the chassis. My fingers point to them in Fig. 10-6.

After doing this, you can proceed to mount the Mac SE 30 logic board in the now-bare chassis. Four screws hold it in place. Secure the Mac SE 30 logic

10-5 Inside of MicroMac enclosure as it is delivered.

10-6 Install MicroMac RAM and ROM SIMM offset brackets.

10-7 Install Mac SE 30 logic board.

board in place using the three shorter screws, but don't tighten them down yet. Figure 10-7 shows what things look like at this point.

The fourth screw is a longer one (which you removed earlier) that passes through both the special MicroMac SE 30 adapter that fits over the logic board's PDS mounting slot (it creates a right angle bend to accommodate the video card), and the Mac SE 30 logic board.

Figure 10-8 shows the detail of tightening this single, longer Phillips-head screw. The MicroMac SE 30 adapter is held snugly in place because it's installed over the logic board connector on the socket and retained in place by the Phillips-head screw. At this point you can tighten up all the other logic board screws snugly too.

Reinstall the power supply and drives

After the logic board and adapter bracket are in place, you first reinstall your power supply, then install your Apple 800K or 1.4Mb floppy drive. Prior to installing, mount your floppy drive in its own bracket (using all four screws), then mount the floppy drive bracket assembly in the chassis using the two Phillips-head screws provided, as shown in Fig. 10-9.

Next, mount the hard drive in its drive bracket using all four screws provided. The hard drive in its adapter bracket is then mounted in the chassis very similarly to the way you mounted the floppy drive bracket, but using two much longer Phillips-head screws. The chassis height allows you to accommodate a

10-8 Install MicroMac adapter bracket.

wide variety of the 3½″ one-third height hard drives available today. A Quantum LPS 52 hard drive—already mounted in its bracket—is shown being installed in Fig. 10-10.

Reinstall the video card

The final step in the installation process is the reinstallation (you already did all these steps in reverse to remove it) of the video card, which is first reconnected to its chassis video output connector, and then plugged into the Micro-Mac SE 30 adapter board. Finally, a single Phillips-head screw is reinstalled to hold it in place. Figure 10-11 shows what the completed inside of the Micro-Mac enclosure looks like just prior to replacing the RFI cover.

Notice the hard drive cable folded neatly on top of it, and the floppy drive cable emerging neatly in a flat, straight line from its rear. There's never any rat's nest of wires inside a MicroMac Technology upgrade chassis. Every wire or cable is of the correct length to fit neatly and precisely into its assigned location.

Button up the chassis

After giving your entire assembly job a thorough once-over to make sure you've securely made all connections and attachments, all that remains is for

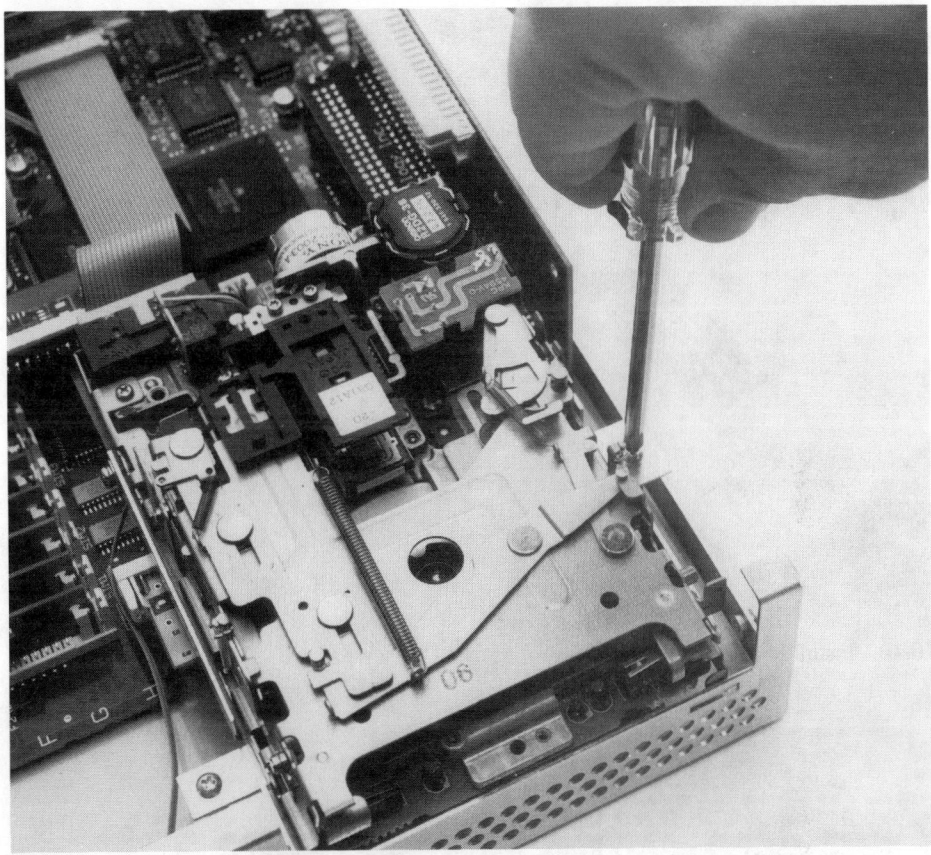

10-9 Install floppy drive bracket assembly.

you to replace the metal RFI cover on the chassis, tighten the six Phillips-head screws as shown in Fig. 10-12, then replace the plastic cover over it, starting from the front as shown in Fig. 10-13. Tighten the three Phillips-head screws, attach the plastic cover to the metal chassis, and you're done.

Connect the external cables and checkout

In the case of the SE 30 color system, all you need to do is attach the power, keyboard, and mouse cables, along with the cable to the video monitor, and turn it on. You get the beautiful results shown in Fig. 10-1. Your friendly Macintosh system greets you and boots directly to the desktop because the software controlling the color monitor is already loaded in ROM. There are no extra diskette or inits to be concerned with. Assembling the Mac Plus or Mac SE MicroMac upgrade systems is nearly as easy: there's only the extra video step required to accommodate loading the monitor init.

The MicroMac upgrade system is the slickest way for Cat Mac builders, starting with Mac Plus, SE, or SE 30 logic boards, to get to a working system

Desktop upgrade kit **279**

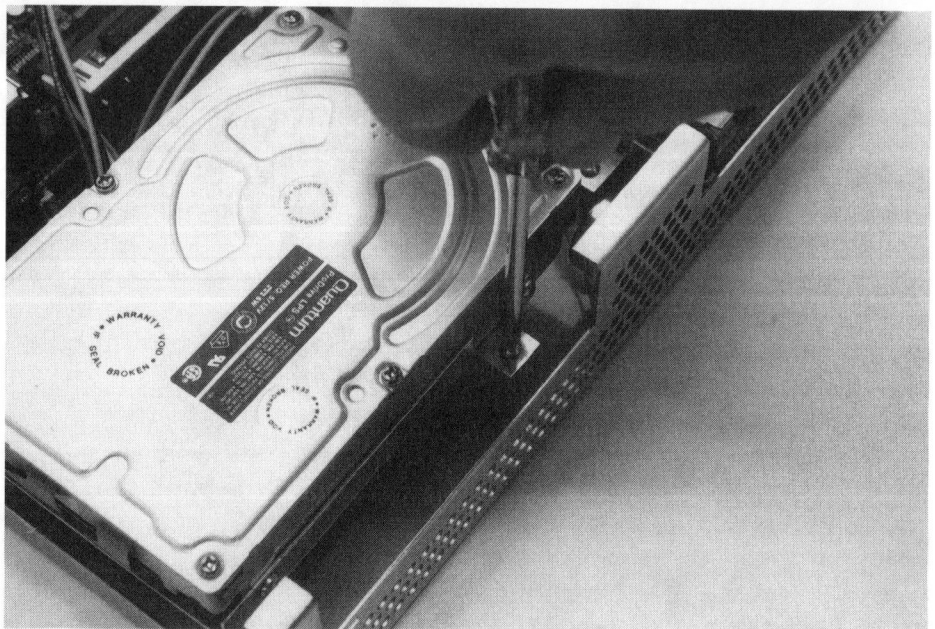

10-10 Install hard drive bracket assembly.

10-11 Inside of MicroMac enclosure after assembly completed.

10-12 Replace RFI cover—tighten six screws.

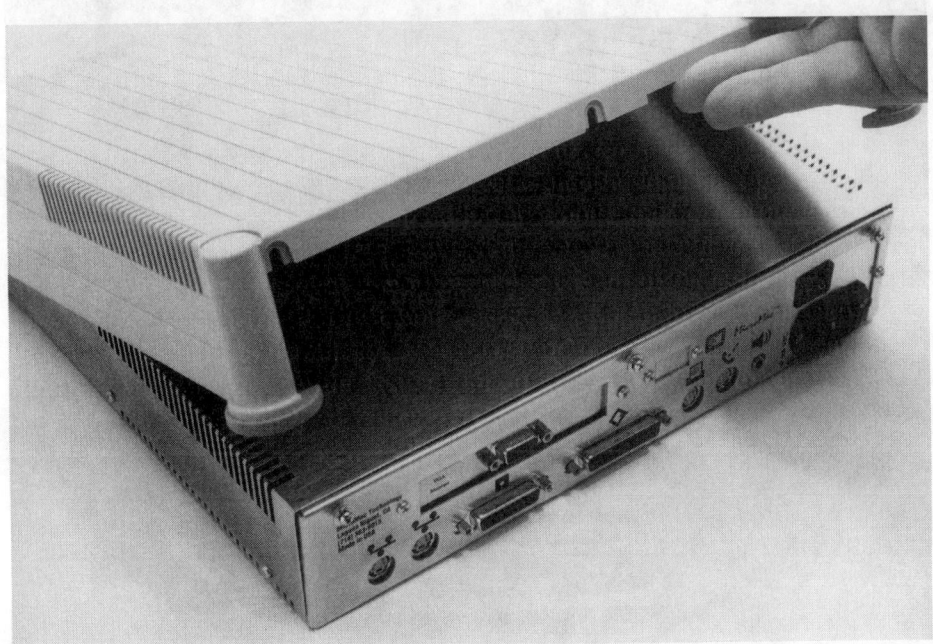

10-13 Replace plastic cover—tighten three screws.

Desktop upgrade kit

in the shortest possible time. And you won't be unhappy with the results. Plus there's a number to call if you get in trouble with any aspect of the assembly process—although this is unlikely. And for those who want all the benefits and don't want to do any assembly themselves, MicroMac Technology also offers preassembled kits as an option for a small additional charge. Needless to say, I highly recommend them.

Tower upgrade kits

Atlanta Technical Specialists (ATS) provides a full line of solutions for Cat Mac builders. While ATS has kits that accommodate projects starting with Mac 128, 512, SE, and SE 30 logic boards, their innovative and well-crafted tower chassis offerings for Mac II-family logic boards really pay dividends. Not only do they save you time and effort in assembly, but they look really attractive and polished in appearance when completed. Most important of all, plug them in and they work. And they continue to work.

In the ATS Mac II "Tower of Power" series kits, two separate chassis styles are offered, one designed to accommodate the three-NuBus-slot Mac

10-14 ATS tower chassis for Mac IIci family logic boards.

282 *Upgrade kits make building easier*

IIcx and IIci logic boards, shown in Fig. 10-14, and another designed to accommodate the much larger six-NuBus-slot Mac II, IIx, and IIfx logic boards. Either tower enclosure allows Cat Mac builders to overcome the space and power limitations of the original Apple Macintosh models. Both of them feature plenty of room for mounting additional expansion hardware, numerous drive bays for mounting full- and half-height hard drives, SyQuest, optical, tape, and CD-ROM drives, plus more than enough power (via 230-watt and optionally larger power supplies) for anything that could be put in the enclosure. These ATS enclosures bring true server flexibility to any Cat Mac builder, starting with a Mac II series NuBus logic board.

Let's get started with a brief look at the construction process for both tower designs. First, the Mac IIci model.

Assembling the ATS Mac IIcx/IIci tower chassis

As you recall from chapter 2, the upper end of the Macintosh logic board line is where maximum performance, gains, and cost-savings are available to Cat Mac builders. The ATS "Tower of Power" chassis kit offerings complement this perfectly by allowing you to minimize any building risks and delivering a working Cat Mac in the shortest possible time.

Figure 10-14 shows the results: A Mac IIci logic board mounted inside the ATS tower chassis with 1.4Mb floppy drive, SyQuest drive, and Teac tape drive, in addition to internal hard drive, all supporting an Apple 13" RGB color monitor, MacPro Plus keyboard, Mouse Systems optical mouse, and allowing you to run Apple System 7 in all its glory, as shown on the monitor's desktop. The ATS tower kits start at about $500, to which you add the logic board, floppy drive, hard drives, monitor, etc. Each of the tower kits gives you the tower chassis with LED display, the high-capacity power supply, front-mounted reset/power switches and key lock switches, floppy drive activity indicator, hard drive activity indicator, and all cables, plus documentation. All you need for installation is a medium Phillips-head screwdriver.

Open the ATS Mac IIcx/IIci tower enclosure

Once again, the assembly process begins with disassembly. In the case of the ATS Mac IIcx/IIci tower chassis, six Phillips-head mounting bolts attach the exterior chassis shell and front bezel to the internal chassis and mounting area. These six bolts are all accessed from the rear chassis panel. As shown in Fig. 10-15, one pair of bolts is located at the top rear, one pair in the middle, and one pair at the bottom rear of the chassis (lower right bolt has already been removed). Once the mounting bolts are taken out, the shell is removed by tilting it up slightly at the rear and sliding it toward the front of the chassis.

Two things become immediately apparent to you after removing the shell and looking at the chassis from the right front, as shown in Fig. 10-16: the large number of wires, and the large number of drive mounting bays.

You can see the wiring is divided into two groups. One group of wires

10-15 Remove six rear panel bolts.

comes from the power supply at the top rear of the chassis. The other group of wires comes from the control panel area at the top front of the chassis. The ATS video board that you were introduced to in chapter 6 provides a distribution panel function for all ATS tower chassis models and is used as a collector point for both sets of cables to tie onto and then to be redistributed to the logic board. The end result is the entire assembly and cable-routing process is considerably simplified, while the maximum amount of useful indicators and switch functions are retained.

The other very apparent item is that there are no fewer than three separate areas for mounting drives (seven half-height mounting spaces in all). The upper and lower drive bays will accommodate a total of two full-height or four half-height 5¼" internal hard drives. The middle bay has room for three half-

10-16 ATS Mac IIci tower chassis interior view.

height 5¼" drives. These can be externally accessed and would typically be used for mounting floppy drives, removable drives, tape drives, and CD-ROM or removable optical drives. Smaller 3½" drives require a mounting bracket to adapt them to either of these bays. A floppy drive is normally mounted in the top position of the middle drive bay. The other two positions are available for whatever you want to use them for. Two blank mounting panels are provided if you have no drives to install in this area. The ATS tower chassis also allows you the optional flexibility of accommodating two internal floppy drives. If you wish to do this it's only necessary to order the additional bracket from ATS for your second floppy.

Mount the Mac IIcx or IIci logic board

The first step is to mount the Mac IIcx or IIci logic board. The eight standoffs that hold it in place are exactly the same as the standoffs used to mount the Cat

Mac logic boards in chapter 9. The eight Phillips-head standoff mounting screws are clearly visible when looking at the chassis from the left front (from the underside of the logic board) as shown in Fig. 10-17. The ATS instructions show you clearly and explicitly how and where to install the standoffs that support your Macintosh logic board. After this step is completed, the logic board is gently placed inside the chassis (be careful to handle it by its edges) and the mounting screws are put in place. Before tightening them down snugly, check the custom ATS tower chassis back panel (a preinstalled, nonremovable item shown in Fig. 10-18), to see that the logic board connectors properly clear its access slot(s).

Mount the drives and connect the cables

After you have securely mounted the logic board, the next step is to mount the floppy and hard drives plus any removable drives you might wish to add. The ATS tower chassis kit comes with a cable for a single floppy drive as well as a single extended-length SCSI cable, and an additional connector. Figure 10-19 shows three drives mounted in the middle bay: floppy, SyQuest, and tape. If you're going to be using more than two SCSI devices and more than one floppy

10-17 ATS Mac IIci tower chassis view from underside of logic board.

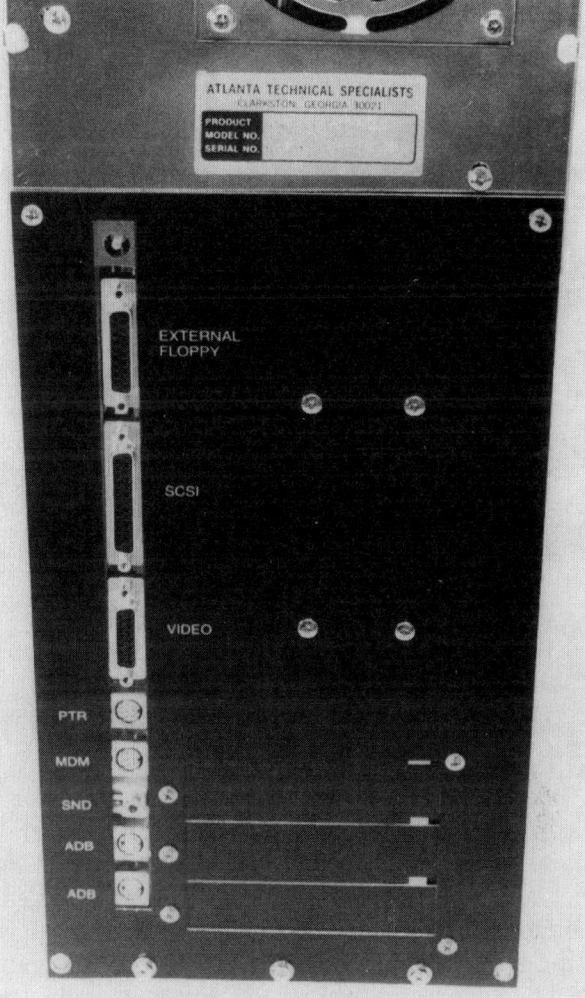

10-18 ATS Mac IIci tower chassis preinstalled custom rear panel.

drive, tell ATS about them, so you can receive the additional required cables with your kit.

Meanwhile, after you have mounted your floppy drive, hard drive, and any other drives, the next step is to connect the cabling inside of the chassis. ATS makes this step rather straightforward and convenient, first by providing all the cables that you need (if you've previously mentioned all the devices you want to mount) and second, providing the ATS video card as a convenient junction to simplify interconnections within the chassis. The ATS video card mounts directly on the back of the chassis case as shown in Fig. 10-20, in an area not occupied by any logic board NuBus cards. The ATS written instructions that accompany the kit tell you in copious detail how to make the specific connections.

10-19 View of floppy, SyQuest and tape drives mounted in tower chassis drive bay.

At the upper part of your tower case you set the LED jumpers shown in Fig. 10-21 for either 16 MHz or 25 MHz, depending on whether you have a Mac IIcx or Mac IIci logic board, respectively. For the Mac IIci logic board shown, it is not necessary to have an extra video card, as the Apple color video monitor to be used plugs directly into the logic board's video slot. If you were using a Mac IIcx logic board instead, at this point you would plug the video card into one of the available NuBus slots and in turn connect the video monitor cable to the card.

Button up the chassis

After giving your entire assembly job a thorough once-over to make sure you've securely made all connections and attachments, you need only replace the metal shell on the chassis, slide it toward the rear until its plastic front bezel clears any drives you might have mounted, tighten the six Phillips-head bolts (starting with the middle pair), and you're done.

Finishing up steps

That about does it for your installation. Connect keyboard, mouse, and power cables to the chassis, and power it on. You should hear the friendly single gong or chime from the Macintosh IIcx or IIci logic board indicating all is well, fol-

10-20 ATS video board—a distribution point for chassis wiring.

10-21 LED jumper panel in upper part of tower chassis.

Tower upgrade kits

lowed by the normal starting up sequence. If you've preformatted your SCSI hard drive(s), then it takes over at this point and you're greeted by your conventional Macintosh desktop running from your drive. If not, you need to do a formatting step (or two). In any event, you're up and running one way or the other.

ATS Mac II, IIx, IIfx tower chassis

If you've opted to base your Cat Mac project on a Mac II, IIx, or IIfx logic board, then the ATS tower solution for these models, shown in Fig. 10-22, uses a different style of chassis because the logic boards are much larger in physical

10-22 ATS tower chassis for Mac II-family logic boards.

290   Upgrade kits make building easier

size—12"×15" versus the 11"×12" for the Mac IIcx and Mac IIci logic boards. The ATS Mac II-family tower case is a thing of beauty. Not only does it easily accommodate your oversized Mac II-family logic board, but it gives you all sorts of room to mount your drives (it has room to mount up to nine half-height devices, six 5¼" wide plus three 3½" wide in all). The room available inside the chassis makes mounting anything an absolute joy and cuts down considerably on the assembly time.

Open the ATS Mac II, IIx, IIfx tower enclosure

Assembly again begins with disassembly. While this ATS tower chassis is a thing of beauty, neither you nor anyone else are likely to be able to get inside it without instructions—the first time! Although ATS didn't intend it as an intelligence test, I have yet to hear of anyone who opened it without instructions on the first try. Yet once you've done it, you'll never forget it—it's that simple. But you can consider all your components to be totally "safe" from casual intruders once mounted inside this baby.

Now watch how easy it is—afterwards you'll be kicking yourself. First lower the smoked charcoal "elegance" panel that hides the drives if it is raised. Next, grab the front bezel by its bottom as shown in Fig. 10-23 and pull straight out. This disengages the bottom pair of metal clips and should expose the next pair above. To help disengage the top pair of clips (they are oriented in the same direction as the bottom pair), use a wide flat-bladed tool (putty knife, etc.), but be careful not to mar the plastic of the bezel.

After removing the front bezel, consider yourself only at the first plateau—you still have to open the sides. The left side panel (viewed from the front) is removed by lifting it about 1" away at the front, as shown in Fig. 10-24, and sliding it straight back to disengage the tabs that hold it. You can then lift it off and set it aside. There now, wasn't that easy? Now go and try it out on your friends!

Mount your Mac II, IIx, or IIfx logic board

Mounting your Mac II-family logic board inside this chassis is literally a snap because ATS decided to go with nylon standoffs instead of the conventional standoffs with screws used on their smaller tower chassis kit. Pop the standoffs through the logic board holes and do the same thing to matching holes in the metal chassis base and you're done. The ATS instructions show you clearly and explicitly where to install the standoffs and what other steps to take. Figure 10-25 shows the result—with a Mac II logic board mounted inside the ATS tower chassis (I had to remove the 3½" drive mounting frame shown in the lower right of the photo to mount the logic board). The ATS video board mounted on the inside chassis back panel once again serves as a convenient distribution point.

The outside view of the preinstalled, nonremovable ATS tower chassis

10-23 Remove front panel by grabbing at bottom front and pulling straight out.

back panel shows that it again provides the dual function of holding the logic board in place and guiding access to its connectors, as shown in Fig. 10-26.

Mount the drives, connect cables, add cards

Mounting the floppy and hard drives proceeds exactly as with the previous tower chassis example except with even greater flexibility. Notice how individual peripherals (such as the tape drive shown in Fig. 10-27) slide in and out on mounting rails, further adding to the convenience. Figure 10-28 illustrates the enormous amount of mounting space available, and shows a typical peripheral complement with room to spare left over. Inform ATS about any special cable requests when you order to make quick and painless work of the cabling step.

The Mac II logic board requires a NuBus video card that typically mounts

10-24 Remove side panel by lifting up about one inch and pulling forward.

in the bottom slot, as shown in Fig. 10-29. Mount any other NuBus card in the available slots above it, working your way up the tower chassis.

Button up the chassis

Check your work to make sure all connections and attachments are secure, and then retrace your disassembly steps—now firmly emblazoned on your mind—to put the chassis back together.

Finishing up steps

You're done with assembly. All that remains is to connect keyboard, mouse, and power cables to your Mac II tower chassis, and then apply power. Once

10-25 ATS Mac II tower chassis interior view.

again, you should hear a friendly chime from your Mac II logic board indicating all is well, followed by the normal starting up sequence. Again, if you've preformatted your SCSI hard drive(s), then it takes over at this point and you're greeted by your conventional Macintosh desktop running from your drive. If not, you need to format it first. In either event, you're up and running pretty darn quickly.

With either one of these custom-made ATS tower chassis, words are truly inadequate to describe the savings in time and labor involved if you've ever done the process yourself. The $500 or so you spend for the ATS solution is a very worthwhile investment—it minimizes your front-end time involvement

10-26 ATS video board—a distribution point for chassis wiring.

and assembly risks, and you have a product that will give you service for years to come as well as a vendor you'll be able to go to later in case you want to do any special expansion (or in the unlikely event that anything goes wrong). Atlanta Technical Specialists has been around for quite a number of years. They also provide custom solutions for DOS PC owners. I recommend you take a look at ATS if you're looking at doing a Cat Mac project based on a Mac II-style logic board with NuBus slots. You will not be disappointed, and you could save yourself lots of time and effort.

10-27 In this tower chassis external peripherals slide in and out on mounting rails.

10-28 This tower chassis provides plenty of room for mounting many peripherals.

296 *Upgrade kits make building easier*

10-29 Mount NuBus video card in bottom slot and others above it.

Portable upgrade kit

The final upgrade kit category to look at is the portable kit available from DTC, the Technology Corporation in Taipei, Taiwan. This one kit is adaptable to Cat Mac builders starting with Mac 512, Plus, SE, or SE 30 logic boards. DTC provides everything else you need: a supertwist backlit flat panel LCD screen, built-in keyboard, 800K floppy drive, attractive enclosure, cabling, adapter boards, durable carrying case along with illustrated instructions. Add the hard drive and pointing device of your choice and you are in business. All you need for assembly is a medium Phillips-head screwdriver. Figure 10-30 shows the finished product with a Kensingston trackball.

Although they advertise their kit as a "laptop," this kit weighs in at about 16 pounds when you're through assembling it and have the hard drive installed (putting it in the same category as the original Apple Macintosh portable, which most people would classify as "transportable"). Unlike the original Apple Macintosh Portable, DTC's portable kit contains no battery—you have to plug it in to AC power. This limitation notwithstanding, you get a highly readable 512 × 348 backlit LCD screen (the exact size as the original 9" Macintosh). Cat Mac builders starting with Mac SE or SE 30 logic boards can obtain

10-30 DTC Macintosh portable upgrade kit.

an expanded 10″ 640×480 display on the LCD screen just by adding an additional card—a relatively inexpensive option which, in my opinion, is well worth obtaining.

Your outlay is about $850 plus shipping for the basic DTC portable upgrade kit, so you're positioned slightly under what you're going to be able to accomplish with any of the current vintage Macintosh PowerBook models in terms of cost (i.e., a Mac SE 30 logic board in the DTC portable kit gives you the equivalent of a PowerBook 140; a Mac SE board gives you slightly less than a PowerBook 100 because of its 8-MHz clock rate versus the PowerBook 100s 16 MHz).

The benefit of the DTC portable kit is that you're able to start with a Mac 512, Mac Plus, Mac SE, Mac SE 30 logic board that you might already have in your possession and emerge with a truly portable unit with a backlit LCD screen that you could take with you on the road and use in your hotel room, etc. DTC's portable kit makes assembly painless, plus you will enjoy the performance of your completed DTC portable system and be able to save a few dollars in the process. What more could one ask?

Open the portable kit

What's involved here is the now-familiar kit twist: taking the kit that is shipped to you, disassembling it down to its bare components, inserting the logic board, floppy drive, and hard drive, making the connections, and buttoning it back up.

The first step is to take the DTC portable kit apart to the point where you can install your Macintosh logic board. Disassembly begins by removing four Phillips-head bolts from its underside as shown in Fig. 10-31—two very long ones from the rear and two shorter ones from the front handle area. Once you remove the four screws you can turn the unit over and remove its top bezel (the LCD panel is removed first—push the button beneath the screen and it slides straight up and off). From this point proceed to remove the floppy drive, keyboard, and power units. Figure 10-32 shows the only units that stay attached inside the lower half of the plastic chassis: the LCD unit (on the right) and rear connector panel (at the top of photo).

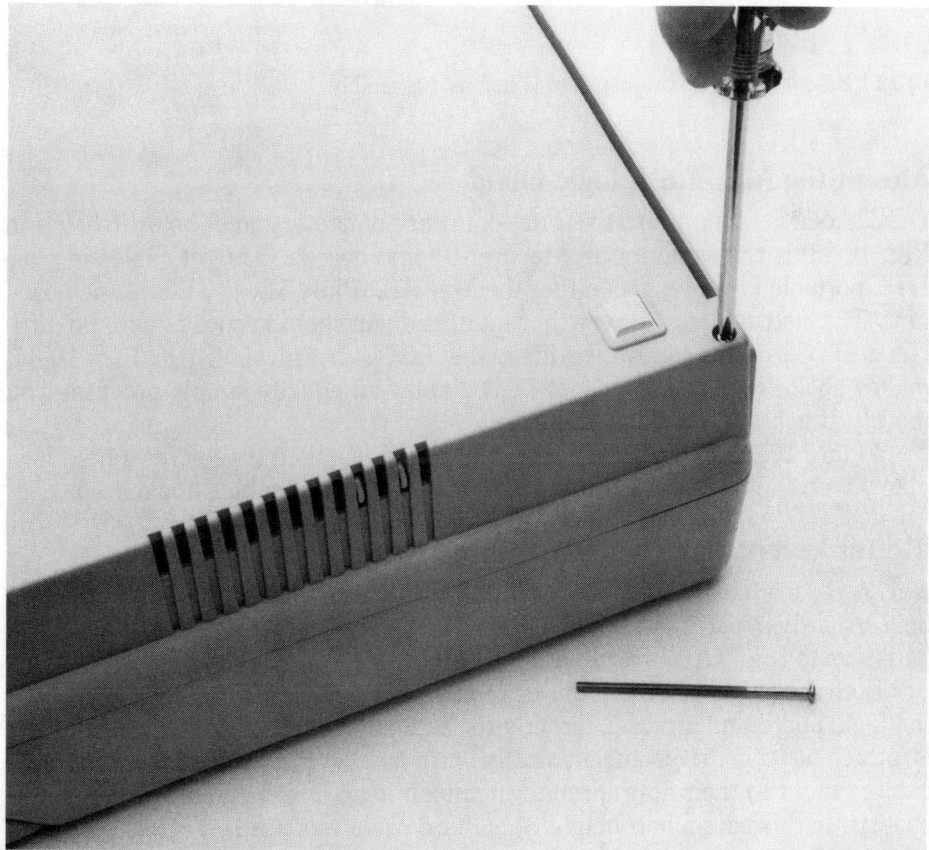

10-31 Remove four bolts from underside to disassemble.

Portable upgrade kit **299**

10-32 Base level DTC portable chassis before reassembly.

Mount the Macintosh logic board

DTC's idea is is an innovative one—its rear connector panel board (shown in Fig. 10-33) is the same for all Macintosh logic boards. You get cables in your DTC portable kit to connect either the Mac 512, Plus, SE, or SE 30 logic board to it. The instructions are very thorough, and you should proceed with no difficulty. DTC's other innovative idea, the LCDC board shown in Fig. 10-34, makes hooking up the flat panel LCD display an equally simple process—you merely attach a few cables.

Figure 10-35 shows a Mac SE logic board installed (two screws hold it in place) with the rear connector panel and LCDC board cables hooked up.

Mount keyboard, drives, power supply

The keyboard panel slips over mounting pins on the plastic chassis frame (it's held securely in place by the two bolts you later install through the handle), and hooks up to the LCDC board with a single cable.

Both the floppy and hard drives mount on a platform or shelf that sits over the logic board and attaches directly to the plastic chassis. All that is involved is attaching the drives mechanically with a few Phillips-head screws and cabling them to their appropriate Macintosh logic board connector inside the chassis. In this case a half-height $3^1/_2$" hard drive was used—Fig. 10-36 shows reinstallation of the shelf into the portable chassis with both the floppy and hard drives mounted.

10-33 DTC's innovative real connector panel card.

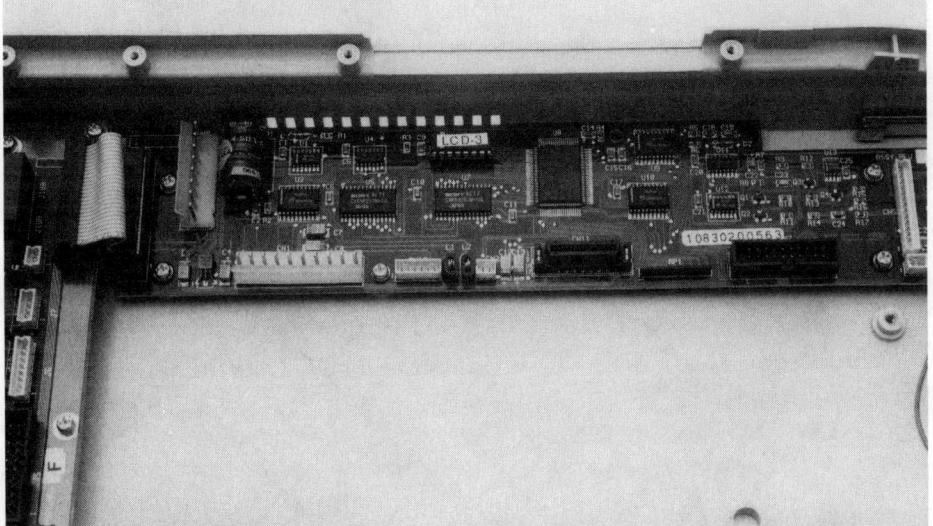

10-34 DTC's innovative LCDC card.

The power supply attaches to the plastic chassis frame using four bolts, and powers the hard drive and LCDC via direct cable attachment as shown in Fig. 10-37.

Replace the top plastic bezel on the chassis panel as shown in Fig. 10-38 and reattach it securely using the four Phillips-head bolts (two long, two short) you removed earlier. Slide the LCD panel back in place until it locks as shown in Fig. 10-39 and you're in business.

10-35 Install Mac SE logic board.

10-36 Reinstall drive shelf with drives on it.

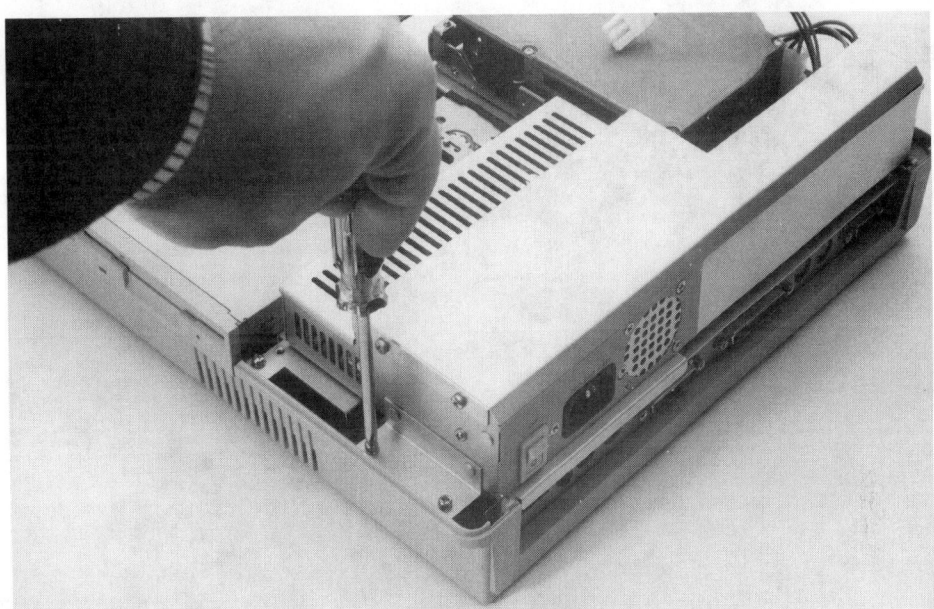

10-37 Reinstall power supply.

10-38 Reinstall top bezel.

Finishing up steps

Turning on your DTC portable kit gives you the familiar "bong" tone (which will vary depending on which Macintosh logic board you have), followed by the

10-39 Reinstall LCD panel display.

familiar desktop display. You might need to make some adjustments on your LCD screen, but that's about all that's involved.

While DTC Technology is somewhat more difficult to work with because of its geographic location, they have manufactured a quality product. Its price is reasonable, and it allows you to make a portable unit out of a number of existing Macintosh logic boards. While this portable unit is not necessarily the latest and greatest in technology and does not compare in lightness with the latest Apple PowerBook offerings, it is a highly functional and working portable unit that should give you years of satisfactory service.

If you already own a Mac 512, Plus, SE, or SE 30 logic board, the DTC portable kit makes a heck of a midlife upgrade for it, and there's no question that the resulting product is more portable and functional. On the down side, it comes with a built-in 800K floppy rather than a 1.4Mb floppy, so if this extra capacity is important to you or if you are going back and forth a lot between the IBM world, you'll need an external Macintosh 1.4Mb floppy. On the up side, there's room inside the chassis to add standard Macintosh accelerator cards and video options, as well as the external video output connector available on the back of the DTC portable kit, as shown in Fig. 10-40.

Inside the DTC portable kit, of course, you're going to have the same flexibility with your hard drive as you would with any of the other Cat Mac models and, in addition, save some money in the process. All in all, it gives you considerable flexibility, and on balance it's probably even easier to expand than any of

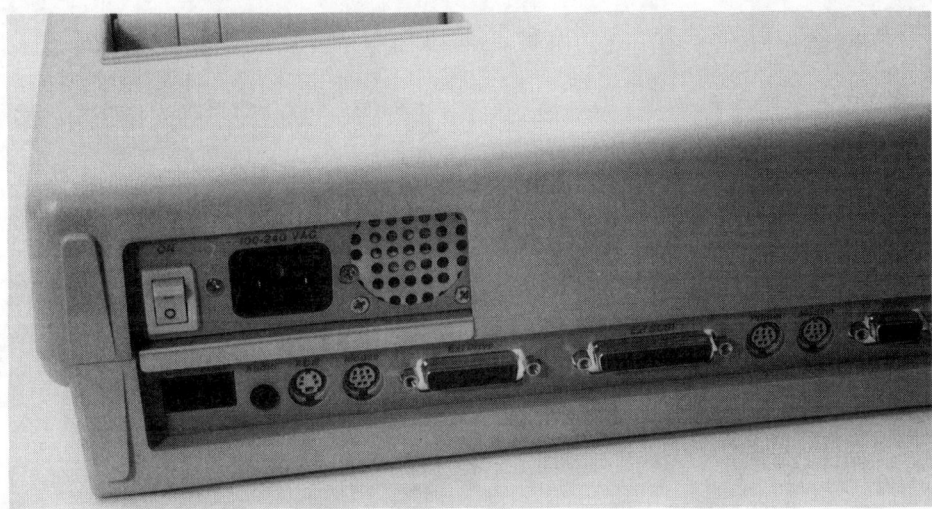

10-40 DTC Macintosh portable kit rear view showing video connector.

the current Apple PowerBook offerings. My only caveat here is not having personally worked with this particular vendor. You might ask them to provide you with the name, address, and phone number of the vendor nearest you that could provide service in the event that your DTC portable goes down (so as not to have to deal with the long umbilical back to Taiwan).

The envelope please

Using any of the three approaches described in this chapter, with kits as your basic building block rather than doing it yourself, only further enhances the Cat Mac builder's benefit. While the kits cost you a little more money than building from the ground up, in most cases they give you a product that you cannot easily obtain anywhere else—at any price—and still result in a lower cost outlay on your part than you would have if you bought the equivalent Apple Macintosh product. Plus you have someone to talk to about the assembly process or if anything goes wrong later on down the road! Once again, Cat Mac builders win.

Sources

MicroMac Technology
9 Sorbonne
Laguna Nigel, CA 92677
(714) 363-9915

Atlanta Technical Specialists
3550-F Clarkston Blvd., #B
Clarkston, GA 30021
(404) 292-6655

DTC Technology
2 Fl, 542-2 Chung Cheng Rd.
Hsin-Tien, Taipei
Taiwan, ROC
02-218-3880

Chapter 11
Cat Mac builder alternatives

This book would not be complete without at least touching on some of the other alternatives available to the Cat Mac builder. Why? Because they might also be able to save you time and money. And even if they don't, reading this chapter will add to your cocktail party vocabulary. Readers of the first edition will recall that the third chapter was titled, "Atari, Mac clones, Mac Portables." I'll revisit those topics in this chapter through a new framework—the broad subject of emulators. There are five that will interest you:

- DOS on Mac
- Mac on DOS
- Mac on Mac (Portable or clone)
- Mac on Atari
- Mac on Unix

DOS on the Macintosh is where the action is today because "connectivity" is probably the most important attribute of any Macintosh computer system—you certainly want your Macintosh data and you'd ideally like your Macintosh application code to operate on the installed base of 60 million DOS PC computers.

Mac on DOS is the flip side of the previous category—it is equally important for some subset of the huge installed DOS PC base to run Macintosh programs as a main part of the job function.

Mac on Mac is the clone area that Apple watches over like a hawk and with good reason—armed with Apple's Macintosh ROM chips, you can build yourself a computer from almost anything in any form factor and make it look like a Macintosh.

Mac on Atari was an area that was visited in depth in the first edition, but has grown little since then for both technical and legal reasons.

Mac on Unix is a recent development that brings the convenience of Macintosh to the power of Unix software and workstation hardware.

Just as there are few free lunches, there are pros and cons to each of these alternatives for Cat Mac builders. This chapter will take a look at each of them from the Cat Mac builder's perspective and offer some guidance. Let's get started.

DOS on Mac

Connectivity is one of the main buzzwords in the Macintosh world today. Your Cat Mac is ideally suited to participate in this arena at reduced cost to you but with no reduction in capability. While your Cat Mac can communicate and share files with virtually all of today's mainframe and minicomputers, most of the attention is centered on its abilities to do the same with the far greater installed base of DOS PC machines. But I have only good news for you. Today, you can instantly import DOS PC files or run DOS PC programs on your Cat Mac, to make it even more useful.

Transfer DOS PC files

Apple File Exchange and Apple DOS Exchange software plus a host of third-party vendor software products make it possible to import DOS PC files and use the data on your Cat Mac. Text data is a piece of cake. You might have to fiddle with it to get the formatting right (remove the carriage returns, spaces, tabs, extra characters, etc.), but here there are numerous utility programs to help you. Graphics data is another story. Programs with their counterparts on DOS PCs (Pagemaker, et al.) come across easily. Other graphics might not come across at all because the way many DOS PC programs handle graphics is fundamentally different from the Macintosh way.

Run DOS PC programs in hardware

Running DOS PC programs in your Cat Mac involves another order of magnitude in complexity. Orange Micro's Orange386 DOS emulator boards—two NuBus cards that you can drop into any Mac II, IIx, IIfx, IIcx or IIci Cat Mac—offers a powerful solution. Basically, you install a DOS PC 80386SX (16 MHz or 20 MHz) computer-on-a-card inside your Cat Mac. The beauty of it is you can share Cat Mac peripherals (video monitor, hard drive, keyboard) and conserve space yet add DOS-specific serial, parallel, and floppy drive ports should your needs require it. You merely go back and forth between the Mac/DOS PC modes as you need.

While you're paying a small premium for the convenience—Orange386 lists for $1999 but many mail order sources offer it for much less—there is no question this beats having two separate computers, monitors, keyboards, etc., on your desk. For Cat Mac builders using tower chassis, the whole question is moot anyway—dropping the Orange386 DOS emulator boards into your Cat Mac tower chassis takes no extra space on your desktop and you hardly notice the difference inside your chassis!

Compatibility is not an issue because it is a genuine 80386SX DOS PC with 1Mb RAM, expandable to 16Mb, that you have under the hood of your Cat Mac—it's just squeezed down in size to fit on two cards. Otherwise it uses your Cat Mac's monitor, $3^1/2''$ 1.4Mb floppy drive (it uses this as drive A) and hard drive (it uses this as drive C)—but it offers two additional PC/AT bus slots and you can add a $5^1/4''$ 1.2Mb DOS PC floppy drive, IDE hard drive, and DOS PC serial/parallel ports to it. Talk about contrasts—it is one thing to talk about Cat Mac versus DOS PC in abstract terms. It is another thing entirely to have Windows 3 and the Macintosh desktop on your monitor screen at the same time. Once you get over the strangeness of the view, however, it's a handy tool to be able to cut and paste Lotus data from DOS or Windows 3 into the Excel spreadsheet on your Cat Mac—if you really need this capability.

Run DOS PC programs in software

If you have a 68030-based Cat Mac with 4Mb or more of RAM and only a casual need to run DOS PC programs—or a low budget—Insignia Solutions offers a program called SoftPC with an EGA/AT module that does it all in software for a street price of under $500. Although it runs at about the same speed as an original IBM PC XT on your 68030-powered Cat Mac, it also gives you a high degree of PC DOS-to-Macintosh compatibility, and again you only have one Cat Mac chassis on your desk.

In its latest incarnation, Insignia Solutions' new Universal SoftPC Version 2.5 not only features improved peripheral support for floppies, hard drives and printers, but enables Cat Mac owners to access DOS PC CD-ROMs, and lets Cat Macs log onto Novell Netware networks with full access to shared applications. Its SoftAT Version 2.5 gives the same capabilities on 68030-class Cat Macs with EGA/80287 coprocessor emulation and LIM Version 4.0 expanded memory support. Neat stuff for Cat Mac builders.

Mac on DOS

Hydra systems has built a better mousetrap for DOS PC users who know that Windows 3 will never be what Apple's System 7 already is (remember the old saying, "if you can't lick 'em, join 'em"?). They offer the Andor One option board that fits inside any DOS PC, lets it run Macintosh software and uses the DOS PC's monitor, hard drive, keyboard and mouse to do it. Think of it as having a Macintosh inside your DOS PC that only costs $995 plus the cost of the Apple ROMs. Figure 11-1 shows it working inside a Compac Deskpro 386/20.

The Andor One option board represents the Cat Mac builder's ultimate tool. For some cross-section of Cat Mac builders who enjoy the freedom to build whatever you want at home yet are constrained to the world of DOS PC machines at work—this is a solid solution to bringing your favorite Macintosh software to your DOS PC machine at the office. Think of it as the "Trojan horse" strategy applied to personal computers. First, you requisition it as an option card for your office DOS PC. After installation, your co-workers will be amazed at your productivity gains, then you can tell them, then they will want Macintoshes, Cat Macs and Andor One boards too. And think of it—you never broke any rules!

While Hydra Systems' Andor One option board (Fig. 11-2 shows it along with cable and software—notice how chock full of custom VLSI circuits it is!) comes at it from the other end of the emulation spectrum from the Orange Micro board, it definitely gives DOS PC owners a taste of the Macintosh and really represents the wave of the future. It requires an XT, AT, 80386 (recommended) or 80486-based DOS PC host and implements a 16-MHz 68000-based

11-1 Hydra Systems Andor One board running on Compaq Deskpro 386/20.

Macintosh that:

- Allows you to add Macintosh compatibility to any DOS PC.
- Runs all popular Macintosh software: Word, Pagemaker, Illustrator, SuperPaint, Photoshop, etc.
- Toggles back and forth between DOS PC and Mac screens by pressing both Shift keys.
- Supports industry standard DOS PC peripherals such as floppy/hard drives, keyboards, mice, monitors, printers.
- Supports standard networks such as Ethernet, Novell, 3Com, Tops, AppleTalk, Phonenet.

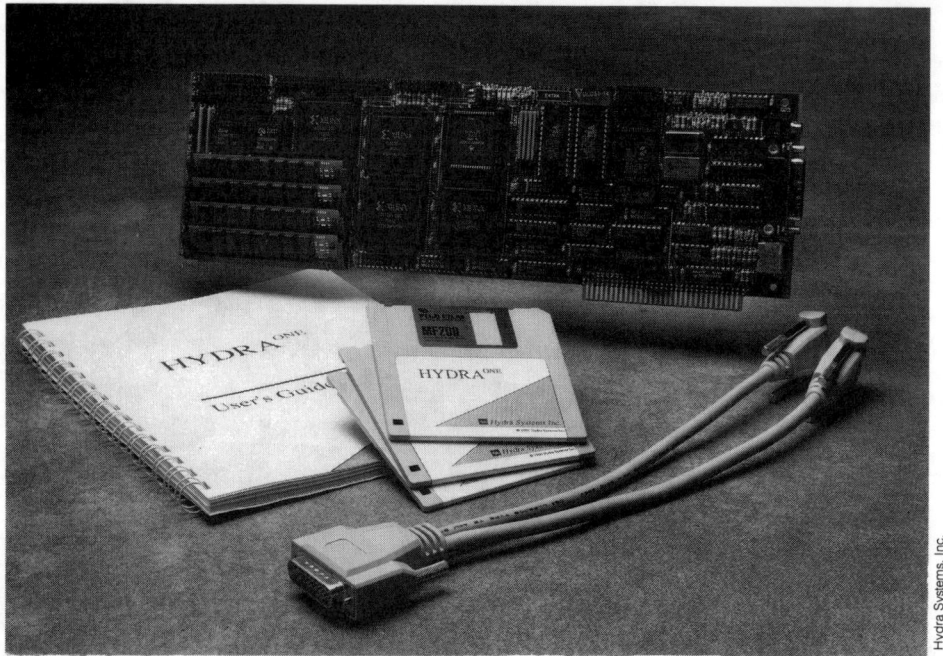

11-2 Hydra Systems Andor One board, cable, software, and instructions.

You get all this for the base list price of only $995. The only other item you have to provide is the Apple Mac 128K ROMs that you used to have to scrounge for when you were upgrading your Mac 512 to a Mac 512KE model. While I haven't actually seen one in operation, the concept and implementation is slick. I can see how Cat Mac builders can add it to a VGA DOS PC clone that you have picked up at a local Superstore or via mail order for $1295 and have a real sweet system that runs both DOS PC and Mac software for under $3000. Very neat stuff for the Cat Mac builders!

Mac on Mac (portable or clone)

Mac on Mac is the area closest to Apple's heart because it is also the area closest to Apple's wallet. This is because you can build yourself a computer from almost anything in any form factor and make it look like a Macintosh—armed with Apple's Macintosh ROM chips. It's the main area clone-makers work in—both Apple and third-party. Yes, you heard right. When Apple makes a PowerBook model, all it is doing is optimizing the Macintosh design to fit in a small space with low power and a flat screen. The same is true of Outbound, the third-party Macintosh portable vendor that has legally licensed the use of Apple ROMs. Other third-party clone-makers might or might not be legally using Apple ROMs. Let's look more closely at the Macintosh portable area—both Apple and third-party—and the subject of clones.

Apple Macintosh Portable

In the first edition I mentioned why the press panned Apple's original Macintosh Portable: it weighed in at 16 pounds and set you back $6499 for a 1Mb RAM, 40Mb hard drive model. I counseled first edition readers that I wanted one "but I'll have to wait until one or two years down the road when they unload the remaining stock at fire sale pricing." Well guess what? Today I own one and am I a happy camper. Apple's improved Mac Portable features a backlit active-matrix LCD display, 4Mb static RAM, 40Mb hard drive, 6-hour battery with clever power management hardware/software, 1.4Mb floppy drive, full-function keyboard, trackball and mouse, plus a sturdy, functional travel case, and it only cost me $1649 mail order brand new with one year warranty.

While its 68000 CPU runs at 16 MHz—the same speed as the Apple PowerBook 100—its backlit active-matrix screen is better, larger and brighter (actually better than a top-of-the-line PowerBook 170's screen), it delivers twice as long a performance on a battery charge (6 hours versus 3 hours), its larger keyboard is easier to use, and you get a trackball and mouse included along with a keypad option as well. It has four extra slots for hooking up internal options (modems, PDS expansion cards, etc.), more direct connections on its larger back panel (external video monitors, SCSI devices—no extra cables required), it accommodates larger capacity 3½" internal hard drives and last—but by no means least—runs any version of Apple System 6 (from 6.04 onward) or System 7 with ease.

I never use my Mac Portable anywhere there isn't a table and chair (definitely not in airports and on airplanes) so I couldn't care less about size and weight issues—it's transportable and then instantly usable, period. I do occasionally use it where there is no power (mountainside and waterfront cabins) and the extra few hours of battery power plus space for a second battery in its travel case comes in handy. All in all—I couldn't be more pleased with my Mac Portable—probably because I fit its original design profile criteria to a tee.

Apple PowerBook

Since the first edition, I've also counseled my Cat Mac newsletter readers to be patient and wait for Apple announcements to legitimize the Macintosh portable marketplace. Apple's three new portables, announced in October 1991, did all that and more. Covering the performance spectrum with 16-MHz 68000 (PowerBook 100), 16-MHz 68030 (PowerBook 140) and 25-MHz 68030 (PowerBook 170) models, these new Macintosh portables accommodated nearly every user's price performance need—as shown in Fig. 1-3 in chapter 1.

The Apple Macintosh PowerBooks lowered the price of the existing Mac Portable model, made a broader selection of portable Macintosh logic boards, cases, and other options available to you to choose from, and did legitimize the whole Macintosh portable area—exactly as predicted by the first edition. Plus technological improvements in DOS PC portables have added still more usable options. But it will be awhile before Cat Mac builders will be able to build your own Cat Mac laptop in much the same way as your desktop-based Cat Mac today. The problem is that the Mac Portable logic board is only now becoming available—you can buy the entire unit for far less than it costs to build, and most DOS PC cases, screens, and keyboards are engineered to fit their offerings—not Macintosh portable-compatible items. So if you're interested in building a portable Cat Mac, you must wait a little longer until the marketplace makes it viable.

Other Mac portables

The same Apple Macintosh PowerBooks that legitimized the whole Macintosh portable area have spelled the death knell for most other third-party Macintosh portable builders who cannot compete with Apple's overwhelming manufacturing economies of scale. While Outbound continues to flourish—thanks to a wisely-forged legal agreement and clever positioning of their Macintosh portable models versus the Apple PowerBooks—I question their long-term staying power. Most other third-party Macintosh portable vendors have either gone out of business entirely or have quietly dropped their portable offerings. I don't see anything for Cat Mac builders here—although there is clearly a need for something like Dynamac's flat-panel LCD display for the Mac LC. Too bad they are no longer in business.

Clones

My position on clones has not changed since the first edition. They are a high-risk proposition because of Apple's legal posture against them. I also made the point that, while Apple is strongly supportive of the used equipment market because it helps sell more new equipment, Apple is not giggly about clones and illegal use of its ROM chips because it amounts to an infringement upon Apple's substantial and ongoing investment in its Macintosh ROM code, which makes the 68000 CPU inside your Cat Mac a Macintosh. It is one thing to "repackage" your Mac—take its logic board, freely available in the used equipment market or out of another Macintosh, and put it inside your Cat Mac housing. No rules broken, no harm done. It is another matter entirely to "clone" it.

I'm sure you understand that you can't go around ripping labels off other people's software diskettes, putting on your own, and reselling them. Yet that is precisely what a number of Macintosh clone-makers have tried to do to Apple. Macintosh clone-makers do away with the Apple logic board entirely—use their own logic board, electronics, and box—but still use Apple's set of Macintosh ROM chips, either real or illegally copied! Either way, it's still a rip-off. Apple's not particularly interested in giving all its technology away for free. And you wouldn't be either.

So I believe a clone manufacturer—any clone manufacturer—is strongly at risk. Apple has a substantial legal process in place to defend its rights, and has shown a history of not hesitating to do so when provoked. All of the clone manufacturers mentioned in the first edition are either out of business or no longer in the Mac clone business. I rest my case. Clones have not yet been successful in the Macintosh world. But it isn't hard to understand why.

Software engineering Apple's System 7 is another nail in the clonemaker coffins. The Mac Plus 128K ROMs enable you to run System 7 but don't really allow you to take advantage of its more powerful features. For that you need the 512K ROMs that come on a Mac IIsi, IIci, or IIfx. The clonemakers have targeted reverse-engineering the 128K ROMs. It is another story entirely to reverse-engineer the 512K ROMs as opposed to the ones that went into the Mac Plus. Just ask anyone in Apple engineering. The clone-makers now have to multiply their labors to get all the benefits out of System 7—just to stay technically even with Apple. But software engineering of the ROM is only part of their problems.

Hardware engineering Look at what Apple has done to the third-party accelerator board vendors by changing its product line: the difficulty they have in keeping up and the great flexibility they have to maintain. This entire scenario is only multiplied for a potential clone-builder because not only do they have to announce "accelerated" products to be compatible with the Apple ROM, but they actually have to develop the ROM to emulate the functions of the increased capabilities of newer Apple systems. It's not a trivial exercise for the clone-builders just to keep up with the Apple innovations, much less to surpass them. But there is still more.

Manufacturing Apple's manufacturing capabilities are legendary—particularly its ability to quickly turn around a product to get it to market, ramp up its manufacturing volumes, and produce it at the lowest cost. Just look at what they have done with the Macintosh Classics, LC, IIsi and PowerBooks. It's going to be extremely difficult for a clone manufacturer to offer a lower-priced solution given Apple's economies of scale and production/manufacturing expertise. I don't see that happening in the near future except with Apple's blessing (as with the licensing and cross-licensing agreements that they are reaching with certain Japanese manufacturers for PowerBooks and other new products).

You must weigh the advantages from your own perspective. Is saving a few dollars worth all the risk—given the many alternate sources and good pricing for the genuine Apple article today? It's doubtful that it is. Why should you risk buying a product that has virtually no resale value from a company that might not be around tomorrow or whose price advantage might be swept away by Apple's next announcement? My advice to you is pass on the clones; just think of better and more innovative ways to use the existing Apple Macintosh logic boards, and package them in a way that best meets your needs. By doing this you'll minimize your risk and maximize your return.

However, the interest in Apple Macintosh clones has remained quite high, and occasionally, the media has been ablaze with new clone companies such as Nutek.[1] Like the efforts of Chips and Technologies and Phoenix Technology who created the IBM compatible chip sets and BIOS, Nutek Computers supposedly engineered a very close approximation of the Apple ROMs from scratch. When used with OSF's Motif interface, it supposedly will look like Apple System 6 software with Finder and Apple System-like files that contain a Nutek version of MultiFinder. You can bet your socks and shorts on Apple's legal department taking a long and hard look at them. Time will tell.

Mac on Atari

In the first edition, I was quite impressed with the ability of the Atari 68000-based machines to run Macintosh software by using a plug-in emulator board that had Apple Mac 128K ROM chips on it. While it is still a clever trick today, quite honestly, the marketplace has passed it by for three reasons.

Technology/market need Several years ago, Apple's low-end models were not as powerful or cost-effective and no high-end models existed. The Atari connection enabled you to bootstrap yourself into a faster, more powerful CPU architecture and still run all your Macintosh software. Plus it was handy for users in the music market—a vertical market niche where Amiga and Apple hardware offerings were equally popular with fledgling software developers.

Today, Apple's Macintosh CPU offerings span the full range of power and it is hard to top Macintosh logic board price performance. Plus a 68000-based Atari model with plug-in emulator board that occasionally hiccuped on Apple System 6 software was OK. A 68030-based Atari model with plug-in emulator board that totally goes out to lunch on Apple System 7 software is not. The emulator—never designed with 68030 models and System 7 software in mind to begin with—just flatly demonstrates it. Finally, both music markets have mature software today—each has its own dedicated following—and there is only occasional need to go between them.

Legal Apple's desire to make life difficult for clone-makers put a real stranglehold on Macintosh ROMs. While this affects Cat Mac builders hardly at all, because almost all Macintosh logic boards are purchased with ROMs, buying the ROM sets by themselves—for use on other boards, etc.—has been made considerably more interesting and expensive. By instructing all Apple dealers not to sell ROMs by themselves, Apple Mac 128K ROMs that could be purchased at one time for $60, now cost $125 or $250 or sometimes as high as $500. What it amounts to is that you are now buying the logic board just to get the ROMs off it and it greatly increases the cost and difficulty of any third-party solution—including the Atari one.

Price Several years ago, Apple's low-end 1Mb Mac Plus cost $1799 without a hard drive, and Mac SE models went for over $3000. The Atari solution simply blew those prices away. Today, the Atari MEGA STE with 2Mb of RAM, an 800K floppy and 48Mb hard drive costs you $1699, a nice SM 147 monochrome 14" monitor costs you $229, the Gadgets by Small emulator costs $299 and the Apple 128K ROMs might cost you $250. The Atari solution is no longer price-competitive with either the standard Apple Macintosh or the Cat Mac solution—not to mention System 7 compatibility issues.

Using the Gadgets by Small Spectre GCR Mac emulator that plugs into the Atari MEGA STE enables you to read and write Macintosh format diskettes with the Atari floppy drive, and is compatible with nearly all Macintosh System 6 software. It delivers the approximate performance of a Mac SE logic board, with a 14" monitor and its own Macintosh partition on the hard drive. You can use either serial or DOS PC-style Centronics parallel connected printers.

The down side is that, first and foremost, it is an Atari computer. You have to learn a second computer just to use your Macintosh, and this does not follow the "KISS" (keep it simple, etc.) principle in my book. Even after you buy your machine and have the dealer configure and partition your disk, when you get it home you still need to have enough Atari skills so that you can initially instruct it in the Atari language to boot up and emulate a Mac. Initially, it is not automatic—someone has to do it for you. Even if the dealer also writes a nice batch setup routine, sooner or later, you are going to have to also learn about the Atari aspects of your Atari Mac clone.

So what is the bottom line for Cat Mac builders? While the Spectre GCR Mac emulator makes a slick low-end unit, it uses 128K ROM chips which don't measure up in performance to a Mac SE logic board (256K ROMs), much less the even larger 512K ROMs of the newer Macintosh logic boards (or the 1Mb ROM of the Quadras!). Let's just say that from a Macintosh purist's point of view, if you didn't have an Atari need, not knowing about its Macintosh capabilities would probably not be a loss to you. But if you were into or were going to need to get into Atari in the future, this technology is certainly worth a look.

Mac on Unix

Many pundits favor the world view that Unix and Windows NT will be the only operating systems left around at the end of the 1990s. As I sit here in 1992, typing on a Macintosh system substantially unchanged from its 1982 core concept and work with other DOS PC clients whose roots go back even further to 1979, I have to take a more pragmatic view. I firmly believe you will be working on Mac System 8.x, DOS and Windows version whatever, and even IBM's OS/2 as the century digits click over. I also believe you will be looking more at Unix—in its many forms.

Regardless of Apple's "vision for the future" rhetoric, it is merely hedging its bet with IBM at the top end, Sony at the low end, and anyone else in between that makes good business sense. What this means to Cat Mac builders is that your upper-end Macintosh might reside on workstation hardware driven by Unix software and your low-end Macintosh might fit in your pocket and be driven by your pen—with everything else in between. So maybe you should start taking a closer look at Unix (and your pens!).

One thing is certain: Unix occupies a position center-stage in Apple's future. Apple's landmark 1991 agreement with IBM featured these four key points—three of which have embedded Unix implications.

Mainstream Apple Unix Apple will integrate the Macintosh more fully into IBM's SAA (System Application Architecture), which is IBM's all-encompassing model for its business computing environment. Mac/IBM connectivity is already quite high; the focus here is to combine Apple's nonstandard A/UX Unix with IBM's nonstandard AIX Unix with the beneficial result in theory being that Apple gets a more mainstream Unix product and IBM gets a Mac interface on top of its AIX. IBM has already moved toward making its AIX compatible with the Open Systems Foundation OSF/1 Unix kernel. At Apple's early 1992 announcement for A/UX 3, it touted A/UX as its server platform for the next decade and mentioned that A/UX 4 (scheduled for 1993–1994) would be based on the new version of IBM's AIX. Voilà! Apple would then have a mainstream OSF/1-compatible Unix product.

Mainstream Apple RISC Apple has seen the future and it is RISC (Reduced Instruction Set Computing). The focus here is (eventually) to produce a single-chip implementation of IBM's RISC System/6000. Interestingly, instead of tossing Motorola (Apple's current 680xx vendor and potential future 88xxx RISC chip vendor) out on its ear, the agreement calls for Motorola to manufacture the chips! In doing this Apple gets immediate access to the RS/6000 five-chip set and a mainstream industry environment on which to base its next-generation products. The beneficial result is that the Mac operating system will run on IBM's new Power PC architecture, featuring products from notebook computers and more powerful desktop PCs, on up through (Unix!) workstations and midrange servers.

Mainstream Apple Multimedia Apple and IBM will develop a joint multimedia standard. This calls for Apple and IBM to develop and cross-license platform-independent software environments for multimedia. Everybody wins. Obviously, true multimedia requires workstation performance—one of the key reasons for points one and two.

Mainstream Apple Software Operating System Apple and IBM will set up a joint venture to develop a new, object-oriented operating system. Apple's code-named Pink operating system gets to run on major industry platforms such as the Intel 80x86, Motorola 680xx, and IBM RS/6000, IBM gets to license some or all of the code, and it gets widely marketed to third-party vendors. Until this new operating system becomes widely adopted—a multiyear process at best—the de facto Unix standard (in its numerous flavors) is the vehicle of choice for all workstation implementations across multiple platforms.

Perhaps the most interesting Macintosh Unix development took place away from center-stage. Quorum Software Systems announced Latitude and Equal in early 1992. Latitude is a developer package compatibility engine that lets Mac applications be converted into native Unix programs. Using it, a Macintosh application retains all its own capabilities and features (menus, etc.) but appears in an Open Look, Motif, or other Unix interface with all its Mac Toolbox calls generating equivalent Unix commands. Equal performs the same function on an unconverted off-the-shelf Macintosh application using a 68000 runtime interpreter in conjunction with the Latitude compatibility engine. The net result of these is rapid availability of a world of low-cost Macintosh software packages on Unix systems with no Apple legal reprisals, because the software replicates the use of the native Unix GUI rather than the Apple Macintosh interface. Can workstation-based Cat Macs be far behind?

Sources

Apple portables are available through Apple dealers. Outbound, at the latest report, announced agreements with a number of resellers to carry its products in the dealer channel. Atari equipment mentioned is available through Atari dealers.

Cat Mac alternatives

Atari Corporation
1196 Borregas Ave.
Sunnyvale, CA 94086
(408) 745-2000

Gadgets by Small, Inc.
40 W. Littleton Blvd., #210-211
Littleton, CO 80120
(303) 791-6098

Hydra Systems Inc.
1340 S. Saratoga-Sunnyvale Rd., #106
San Jose, CA 95129
(408) 253-5800

Insignia Solutions Inc.
526 Clyde Ave.
Mountain View, CA 94043
(800) 848-7677

Orange Micro Inc.
1400 Lakeview Ave.
Anaheim, Ca 92807
(714) 779-2772

Outbound Systems, Inc.
4840 Pearl E. Cr.
Boulder, CO 80301
(800) 444-4607

Quorum Systems
4700 Bohannon Dr.
Menlo Park, CA 94025
(415) 323-3111

---

[1]Kristi Coale, " 'Clean' Mac Compatible To Run Apple's Gauntlet," *Infoworld*, 28 January 1991, p. 1; and Allison Calderbank, "Nutek to Test Macintosh Clone Market," *Computer Reseller News*, 28 January 1991, p. 3.

Chapter 12
The end of the beginning

The famous news commentator Walter Cronkite used to start his broadcasts with the rhetorical question, "Well, what kind of a day has it been?" Now that you have read the book, what do you do next? The next step is up to you. Is the Cat Mac a viable solution for you? You can read all you want and it is just words on paper until you tackle the building step. Then you know. And, as Darwin Gross said in several of his books, "When you know, you know." The only surefire way to reap the benefits of any book is to put its principles into practice. What I am saying here is to bite off a piece of what you have read and try it. If you do, I can almost guarantee that you will find out a different or even a better way to do it and that is all part of the fun. In addition, you will probably have saved yourself some money, and gained some practical experience which can be put to even better use in the future.

On the other hand, maybe you've already followed the advice of this book through the first 11 chapters and you are wondering what to do next. That's why I titled this chapter the end of the beginning. Whether you are an experienced Macintosh user or a brand new one, I can only counsel you as a Cat Mac builder to continue to experiment and "push the outside of the envelope." For myself, I have found it a rewarding experience from which there has been no turning back.

The remainder of this chapter will focus on equipment, software, and some housekeeping items that I have found useful (and newer Macintosh users might also find helpful after you are up and running).

Peripheral equipment you will need

This section presents peripherals that enhance the value of your Cat Mac system. Rather than profile all the available offerings in each category, I'll cut to the chase and give you my best one of two recommendations.

Dot matrix printer Selecting a printer for most people is a very personal decision. Fortunately, this is less of a problem in the Macintosh world. Apple, in its wisdom, has only one low-end dot matrix printer—the Imagewriter II. For many of my clients, it's the best solution I could possibly have recommended to them even if I spent a lot more time searching. It is very reliable, has nice tractor-feed and sheet-feed options, lets you feed single-sheet stationery and #10-size business envelopes through it once you get the hang of it, and does an excellent job on mailing labels. Equipped with the Beverly Hills and Palatino fonts, it does a credible job on business correspondence, though it is obviously not letter-quality output.

Yes, there are many good low-end dot matrix printers but by the time you get the cables, the software, and find out about all their little quirks in working with each individual Macintosh software program, you are better off paying a little more for the Apple Imagewriter II to begin with. It is a rugged, bulletproof workhorse. Just feed it a new ribbon and vacuum it out now and then. "Works for me," as the man says. Your initial hardware investment is in the $400 range.

LaserWriter Notice I didn't say "laser printers." There are many laser printer offerings. Hewlett-Packard owns the market today. But in the Macintosh world there still is only one—the Apple LaserWriter in all its incarnations.

Like the Cat Mac logic board, the original LaserWriter and LaserWriter II declined in price when the new LaserWriter models were introduced, but that didn't make them any less desirable—only more attractive. A dot matrix printer will let you get hard copy output from your Cat Mac, but the LaserWriters will put you on the map and earn you respect in the business world. No one can tell whether you generated your letter on the older, original LaserWriter or the newest top of the line 68030-based LaserWriter IIg. It's laser output—period.

The big reason why all laser printers are not created equal is Postscript. The intelligent CPU and ROM chips inside the LaserWriter that recreate the data after you send it across your serial Appletalk or Localtalk cable make the jagged edges you get on your dot matrix printer typefaces disappear, and your graphics look professionally drawn. Although other laser printers in the DOS PC world do a slick job, and can be tricked into running much faster, and even run Postscript, it is very difficult to replicate the simplicity of working with an Apple LaserWriter across multiple font types, multiple graphics types, and multiple application types—just press the print command and you're there.

Unless you are a printer or in the graphic arts business, it's hard to tell the difference between the 300 dpi resolution that you get from the LaserWriter at $0.05 per page and the 1200 dpi that you get from a typesetter at $5.00 per page. All of it looks better than a dot matrix printer at 72 dpi. For most uses, the lower 300 dpi is perfectly acceptable. When combined with the latest versions of the world-class text processing, graphics, and desktop publishing packages, you are able to output all sorts of slick brochures and newsletters on up to complete ready-to-print books.

Today, your investment is under $1300 for a used Apple LaserWriter Plus (the one with all the fonts), and under $1800 for the LaserWriter II NT (Apple's second generation model that gives you more memory, performance, and paper path options). You are far better off buying either of these used Apple LaserWriter models with Postscript built in than a new, less expensive, non-Postscript laser printer.

LaserWriter Plus and LaserWriter II NT toner cartridges cost about the same—just under $100. These toner cartridges produce 3000 and 5000 copies, respectively. You can typically refill the LaserWriter Plus toner cartridge four times for less than $40 a refill—the LaserWriter II NT's, made with more sensitive drum materials, only go about two refills at roughly the same cost. Bottom line, you are paying about $0.02 per copy for the toner. In my mind, up to this point there was really no viable alternative to the Apple LaserWriter offerings. However, within the last few years, Hewlett-Packard, the worldwide leader in the laser printer market, has taken dead aim at Apple's laser printer market with its LaserJet III featuring Resolution Enhancement print technology and Apple-specific options. Plus, you can pick up a new Hewlett-Packard LaserJet III basic unit, add either HP's Postscript cartridge, Appletalk interface kit and memory, or the equivalent package from Pacific Data Products and spend only about $2500. Compared with the Apple LaserWriter II NT, the Postscript-equipped Hewlett-Packard LaserJet III gives you a superior variable dot print technology that improves print quality, more memory capability (up to 4Mb of HP or 8Mb of third-party memory can be added versus the fixed 2Mb total of Apple), the same number of genuine Adobe typefaces (35) and the identical 8-page-per-minute printer engine and toner cartridge. Take a look.

Networking Although the Macintosh was only available from Apple as a closed box for many years, the beauty of it was you could communicate with it better than any other computer—the networking interface hardware was built right into the box. The epitome of the KISS (keep it simple) principle, you can have an entire Apple five-user network up and running in less time than it takes to remove one popular DOS PC network's hardware from the box and install it onto one computer. Its networking capabilities have only grown with time. Although you really don't see the benefits as a single Cat Mac user connected to a LaserWriter, the minute you add the first additional station to the network the benefits grow. Not only can you easily share the LaserWriter (or Imagewriter II—just add an option board), but easy-to-use software exists, like TOPS, to share files between two or more Macintosh computers. Adding a DOS PC computer to the network is as simple as adding a board to the DOS PC, and its files—text, spreadsheet or database—can be shared on the network via easy-to-use translation software from Dataviz. Your investment here is under $50 per node to share a printer and under $250 per node to share files.

Modem After the printer, a modem is your most important peripheral. It lets you communicate with the outside world. Whether it's your client in Germany, salesperson on the road anywhere in the USA, publisher, typesetter, employee working at home across town, or neighbor across the street, you are equally able to transmit and receive text, graphics, and audio data. Recent versions of traditional Macintosh communications software such as MacTerminal, Red Ryder's Public Version, or Microphone are extremely easy to use and loaded with features. There are many other software packages to choose from that let you access online services and public databases, download stock information automatically, establish your own internal company mail network, or just set up a personal bulletin board. Legendary software packages like Stuffit let you pack your data prior to transmitting it to get the lowest line rates. I would not buy a modem with less than 2400-baud speed capability today or

9600-baud if you want to pass information between sites on a dedicated basis. Your initial hardware investment is under $250.

Scanner A scanner lets you convert printed page data—text and graphics—into electronic form. You can then manipulate this data in your Cat Mac and send the results to a LaserWriter or to another computer over a modem. The primary benefit of this powerful capability to you is time savings. You can scan in graphics (artwork, logos, forms) and modify and improve them in much less time than if you had to perform the entire process from scratch. The text reading process, called OCR (optical character recognition), was originally either very crude or very expensive. Early OCR could hardly keep up with a typist and fell far behind after correction time was factored in. New versions of OCR software packages like Omnipage from Caere adds multiple language (English, Spanish, etc.), dot matrix (read in your Imagewriter output), to multiple font (Times, Helvetica, etc.) reading capability in automated modes at 98% and above recognition rates. Only a bionic typist could keep up with these products today. Apple and Hewlett-Packard provide the best solutions—their scanner hardware is reliable and bundled graphics software packages are easy to use. Your investment is under $1500 for the combination. OCR software is available for under $700.

CD-ROM When it comes to compactly storing and conveniently distributing large volumes of data, nothing beats the CD-ROM (compact disk read only memory). CD-ROMs are identical in appearance and size to their audio counterparts that set a new standard for listening and are now available in music stores everywhere. Standard is the operative word here—lack of standards has blocked more widespread application of this technology to computers. Not to worry, it will happen. If you are a researcher, a single CD-ROM drive puts over 500Mb of text, graphics or sound data at your fingertips. Volumes of niche market data with updates are offered on a subscription basis by some vendors. Manufacturers have already put numerous dictionaries, encyclopedias, and directories on CD-ROM and new products and services are announced daily. Apple set the standard when their CD-ROM player was first announced. Today there are newer products from Toshiba and others which are even faster. Your investment is under $700.

Hardware backup Without background into your setup and application(s), it's difficult to give you specific advice here. A Cat Mac builder with a single system might be completely protected by a floppy-based backup system and an effective backup utility like Fastback from Fifth Generation Systems. But by the time you have three Macintosh systems or a small network you need another storage solution like removable hard drive, SyQuest cartridge drive, removable optical drive or tape drive, plus more powerful backup software like Retrospect from Dantz Development. When you expand your operation, you need to research and investigate better backup storage alternatives—at that particular time. Until that time, enjoy the 800K floppies you are using with the backup utility of your choice—just remember to back up!

Software you will need

This book has focused on hardware—I haven't said much about software. I'll say it here. This section profiles the system software you need with your Cat Mac system.

System 6 software   Much has changed in system software since the early days of Macintosh. Your hardware goal is at least to bring your Cat Mac up to a 2Mb (preferably 4Mb) system with a 40Mb hard drive, so that you can run Apple System 6 software and all its features. Available as an upgrade kit (M0681/C at $49) from your friendly local Apple dealer, this software in its latest 6.08 version simplifies whatever you might want to do, and does so with fewer bugs or hitches than earlier versions.

You have undoubtedly heard of the virtues of Multifinder and its benefits. The Apple's System 6 package brings them to you—just choose Multifinder from the desktop menu and reset. Now you are working in the Multifinder rather than the Finder environment. Your ability to switch back and forth between multiple applications is limited only by the amount of memory you have—my experience has shown you really need at least 4Mb to be happy with its performance. Enjoy.

System 7 software   You have unquestionably heard of the new Apple 7 System software. For this you *must* have a Cat Mac with 4Mb of memory or more and a 40Mb hard drive. Ideally, you want to run it on a 68030-based Cat Mac with an 80Mb or 105Mb hard drive. While nearly all of System 7's (available from your Apple dealer as the M82220LL/A upgrade kit at $99) components and features are available in other products today, System 7 ties everything together into a neat, integrated package that works, introduces a host of nifty new features, and sets the stage for further additions over the next few years. You get neat features like: a more powerful Finder and desktop with Multifinder permanently turned on; powerful file search features; aliases that allow you to open the original "target" file from another location; customizable Apple and tear-off menus with auto-scrolling, auto-sizing windows, but a manual trash can that you have to deliberately empty; True Type (Apple's own technology for outline fonts—smooth representations of characters generated by a "Font Manager") now resident in System software; 32-bit addressing and virtual memory (the feature of System 7 that lets 68030 CPU chips directly address 2^{32} bits or 4Gb of memory and sets aside a portion of your hard drive as a "virtual" extension of your Mac's real memory so program parts are swapped in and out of memory from the hard drive as you need them); IAC or Interapplication Communication (Apple calls this dynamic data-sharing "publish and subscribe"—any user can "publish" information and "subscribers" receive a new version of the data each time the original is updated—as if the clipboard sharing data between applications was a dynamic one instead of a static cut, copy, and paste); Appletalk Fileshare (incorporates the features of Sitka (formerly TOPS) software into every Mac system, so users can share files over a network without a dedicated server); Data Access Manager (allows any user application to access remote databases without having to deal with the particulars of their software query languages—queries to the host database language are done transparently).

These are some—but not all—of the goodies you get. You also get additional utility applications, 32-bit QuickDraw, communications toolbox, sound-system improvements, and the list goes on—all as part of System 7. Having all these capabilities on your Macintosh puts an enormous amount of computer power on your desktop, and the best news is that applications to take full advantage of System 7 won't be available for years yet. If you jump on the System 7 bandwagon today, you can enjoy the best of all worlds: Cat Mac price performance and the slickest operating system in the world. Just remember not to short-change yourself in the CPU, memory, or hard drive areas—System 7 likes the best you can give it in hardware.

Apple A/UX software While Apple developed world class System 6 and System 7 software products for its Macintosh, it astutely covered its bet by developing Unix-based software as well. Called A/UX 2.0.1, the latest version is available from Apple dealers as the M0598LL/A CD-ROM-based upgrade kit at $795. While Apple's highly-touted virtual memory and multiprogramming features of System 7 have always been available on Unix, Apple's A/UX 2.0.1 gives Unix users capabilities they can't get anywhere else. The Apple A/UX software developers had their work cut out for them—it is hard to think of two more opposite environments. Unix is almost all "left-brained" (sequential, logical, text). Macintosh is almost all "right-brained" (random, subjective, graphic). In A/UX 2.0.1, you get the best of both worlds and you give up very little. Unix programmers will be at home with the three flavors of Unix available for the Macintosh on their desktop: Berkeley (default version), System 5, and Network File System. Macintosh users will appreciate the Mac-like Command Shell interface when accessing the power of Unix programs. Here you are looking at a serious Macintosh. My recommendation is to put A/UX on a 68030 Cat Mac with a fast 80Mb hard drive and 4Mb of memory minimum—a 300Mb hard drive and 8Mb is probably a more useful size.

Now that you are up and running

As a new Cat Mac user, let me give you some hints to maximize your enjoyment. If you are already a Macintosh owner, you can empathize with me in some points, and undoubtedly you have learned other hints from your own experience.

Cleanliness Locate your Cat Mac on your desk, stand it on its side, just keep it in a clean environment. Excessive dust, dirt, or smoke will eventually work its way into your Cat Mac and create problems for you. If you have used your Cat Mac for quite a while and one day it quits working, before panic sets in, open the case (remember static!), gently blow or vacuum the accumulated dust layer off your logic board, reseat all the connectors and see if that doesn't solve the problem.

Voltage Power your Cat Mac from an ac voltage source that provides smooth voltages and always use a quality surge protector to prevent damage due to transient overloads, spikes, or a trashy line or, better still, use a UPS (uninterruptible power supply), which has surge protection plus a battery that drives an inverter when ac power goes away. If nothing else, you will sleep better at night. In my case, the UPS paid for itself in only one power outage: I was working at my Cat Mac SE one sunny day, minding my own business, when the power went out. When it came back on, my Cat Mac power supply came on, the screen came on, but I got that sickening feeling in the pit of my stomach as the screen sat there with the dreaded blinking question mark icon. No hard drive. The power hit knocked out my hard drive—it still rotated but some of the data was scrambled. Luckily, the data was backed up, but I still had to go through all the steps to restore it.

Cut to the same scene about six months later, this time at night. The power went out, the UPS came on, and I resumed working in the dark (not exactly—by the light of my Princeton Monitor screen). My next step was to save what I had been doing.

Without a UPS, your safest course of action is to turn off your computer after a power hit. Sometimes the power surges a few times before the power company fixes the problem—none of these surges does your computer any good.

Static Some people are just naturally highly-charged individuals. Seriously. While some have no problems with their computers ever, others are constantly losing the data on their floppies, their hard drives, and encountering strange error messages and system bombs. For these people I recommend a three-step solution. Put an antistatic mat on your desktop under your computer. Put another antistatic mat on the floor under your chair in front of your desk. These antistatic mats are the type that come with a wire that attaches to the ground wire of your wall electrical outlet. Then, make two backups of everything. If this doesn't work, I have more drastic measures to suggest.

Maintenance Maintenance contracts are unnecessary for most people. The pros and cons were well-reviewed in an article by Jim Seymour: for some they are good, for others not. For the Cat Mac project you assemble yourself you don't even have to think about it. But do get a contract if you are using your Cat Mac in a critical application in your business. Remember that fellow Murphy!

As a Cat Mac owner, you have certain safeguards: You already have a beefier power supply to begin with and an industrial strength fan for air flow. Your video is in its own ventilated case with its own power supply. The logic board, the most vulnerable part of your system, is much better ventilated and much better powered, due to the increased space available. Since it is never going to wear out, it should have a long and useful life if you don't mess with it, and failing that, if you take precautions whenever you do work around it (e.g., when adding memory or other options). You have a brand new hard drive, floppy drive, keyboard, mouse, monitor, and case, and have automatically obtained at least a one- or two-year warranty with them.

Disks and Backup Keep one set of your backup diskettes (or other backup media) close to your Cat Mac to remind you to back up regularly. Seriously. The number one thank you I receive from every client sooner or later is "Thank you for telling me to back up my data." There are many good books on the subject, many theories of how to do it best. Take your pick. My counsel is just do it!

A few words about the future

Whatever Macintosh you are now using or plan to use, it is certain that a slicker, faster, cheaper, or lighter one will be developed in the future. The same statement, only more strongly, might be made for Macintosh software. Yet the avalanche of new products coming regularly from Apple and third-party software and hardware manufacturers requires that you adopt some sort of procedure, tailored to your own set of circumstances, ensuring your Macintosh setup is reasonably up-to-date. How do you do it? Easy: read, talk with others, visit shows. Then formulate your own opinions and procedures.

The Macintosh world is unique. The Macintosh user benefits from a combination of dedicated, focused media events, distribution methods, and user groups unlike those found in any other industry. There are a wide variety of information sources to assist you. This is not intended to be an all-inclusive list. I can only touch on the highlights here, so many other excellent sources will not be included—but you will undoubtedly find them in your search.

Mail order

In some geographic areas there is an unusual concentration of good dealers to assist you and whom you assist in return by buying from them. But you can benefit from the mail order channel regardless of where you are located. Virtually anything can be purchased through the mail: books, magazines, software, hardware, accessories, up through complete systems.

How do you deal with this channel? I have found a very simple process works for me. If I am buying a commodity item and I am not already buying that item from a vendor I am familiar with, I'll stick with one of the major mail order suppliers who advertises in the pages of the Macintosh magazines. If it's a new item on the market or a new item for me to buy, I'll go directly to the manufacturer or supplier, large or small, and place a small order for it. If the product, their service, and the price measure up, I'll favor them with a larger order. If not, I'll buy from another source or even return the product.

The mail order sources for the products mentioned in this book have already been listed at the end of each chapter so they will not be repeated here.

Magazines

The Macintosh community is blessed with an amazing selection of outstanding weekly and monthly magazines to suit every palette. They—as much as the enthusiasm of the Macintosh users themselves—are responsible for the spread and absorption of the Macintosh into the mainstream of computer culture.

I have referenced the monthly magazines *MacWorld* and *MacUser* repeatedly in the text. I cannot say enough about them. From the beginning they were a cut above any other computer periodicals I have ever received.

MacWEEK is another outstanding publication, perhaps the best weekly I have ever received. They are legendary in the Mac community for reporting the facts just as they happen straight off the cuff—even if they absorb a little heat in the process from Apple and others for being a little too soon and a little too accurate in their reporting.

As a minimum, you should be subscribing to:

Macworld
P.O. Box 51666
Boulder, CO 80321-1666
(800) 234-1038

MacWEEK
P.O. Box 5821
Cherry Hill, NJ 08034
(609) 428-5000

MacUser
P.O. Box 56986
Boulder, CO 80321-6986
(800) 627-2247

Three other magazines you should subscribe to, although they are not Macintosh-specific (they will make you a well rounded individual), are:

Byte
P.O. Box 555
Hightstown, NJ 08520
(800) 257-9402

InfoWorld
P.O. Box 5994
Pasadena, CA 91107
(818) 577-7233

Computer Shopper
P.O. Box 52568
Boulder, CO 80321
(800) 274-6384

Two shoppers' guides are available to assist you quarterly and annually:

Macintosh Buyer's Guide
5615 W. Cermak Rd.
Cicero, IL 60650-2290
(800) 826-9553

Macintosh Product Registry
660 Beachland Blvd.
Vero Beach, FL 32963-1794
(407) 231-6904

There are many other magazines that you might benefit from, serving niches in the Macintosh market and other aspects of the personal computer field, but the above should get you started.

Computer shows

Again the Macintosh community is blessed. No other industry has a dedicated user event that you can attend once a year and actually see and hear it all. The MacWorld Exposition, held in the spring in San Francisco (serving the West Coast) and in the fall in Boston (serving the East Coast) is the one event every Macintosh user should plan to attend at least once, if not annually. It normally attracts around 50,000 people and, unlike other trade shows, caters specifically to Macintosh products and (except for one industry day) specifically to the Macintosh end user.

To learn more about it, contact:

Mitch Hall Associates
P.O. Box 4010
Dedham, MA 02026
(617) 361-3941

User groups

Although every industry has its user groups, in the Macintosh community this phenomenon has been raised to an art form. There is nothing else that can give you as high a return on, and as much benefit from, your low annual dues investment. Only minutes of networking at a monthly general or special interest group meeting can save you hours, if not days, of time. Later on, when you have established relationships within the group, you can accomplish the same over the telephone.

The User Groups are a marketing force to be reckoned with also. The monthly meetings of the larger User Groups such as Berkeley, Boston, and Portland (Oregon), regularly attract industry leaders who know this fact very well. An auditorium full of experienced, opinionated, and intelligent Macintosh users is also a force to be reckoned with. But it is a two-way street, and the industry leaders go back with much useful marketing feedback.

A simple phone call to Apple Computer gets you the number of the Macintosh User Group nearest to you. Call:

(800) 538-9696 ext. 500

Local dealers

Hey, how about that; even they made the list. This is another resource you might consider and it's right underneath your nose. Where I live (Portland, Oregon) there are five Apple dealers (Alpha Computers, BizMart, CompuAdd, The Computer Store, and Computerland), plus one very Mac-knowledgeable independent dealer (Mac Friends). I hope you are similarly blessed in your area.

Ahhh, but there are rules to obey here. When you use the resources of your local computer store, remember it's a two-way street. The person on the other side of the counter from you is being compensated for his or her time in assisting you. So, use these resources wisely. If someone has just pulled 50 monitors off the shelf for you to take a look at before making your selection, do not go and buy your monitor from a mail order source after giving that person a polite thank you. They will not be excited about working with you again. And you've probably heard, "What goes around comes around."

If you're getting good assistance from a store and from a salesperson, it's just good manners and taste on your part to compensate them for their efforts by bringing them your business. Sure, you might pay more. But it will certainly pay dividends to you over the long haul.

Consultants

Remember the movie, *The Good, the Bad, and the Ugly*? That's the whole book on consultants in short form. My best advice is find one who:

- is trustworthy
- is empathetic to your needs
- knows what he or she is talking about
- is reasonably priced
- is there for you when you need him or her.

And they are out there, believe me. A good Macintosh consultant will make you feel like you have just died and gone to heaven. Treat yourself.

Books

History Books on the history of the Macintosh include:

Jean-Louis Gassee, *The Third Apple*, Harcourt Brace Jovanovich, 1987.
Guy Kawasaki, *The Macintosh Way*, Scott, Foresman and Co., 1990.
Frank Rose, *West of Eden: The End of Innocence at Apple Computer*, Penguin Books, 1989.
John Sculley with John A. Byrne, *Odyssey*, Harper and Row, 1987.
Jeffery S. Young, *Steve Jobs: The Journey Is the Reward*, Scott, Foresman and Co., 1987.

Macintosh In addition to this book, you might find these books helpful:

Sharon Zardetto Aker, et al., *The Macintosh Bible*, 3rd Ed., Goldstein & Blair, 1991.
Apple Computer, *Guide to Macintosh Family Hardware*, 2nd Ed., Addison-Wesley Publishing, 1990.
Bob Brant, *Upgrade Your Macintosh and Save A Bundle*, Windcrest/McGraw-Hill, 1991.
Bob Brant, *Macintosh Hard Disk Management*, Windcrest/McGraw-Hill, 1992.
Craig Danuloff and Deke McClellan, *Encyclopedia Macintosh*, Sybex, 1990.
Jim Heid, *Macworld Complete Mac Handbook*, IDG Books Worldwide, 1991.
Bob LeVitus, *Dr. Macintosh*, Addison-Wesley, 1989.
Robin Williams, *The Little Mac Book*, Peachpit Press, 1990.

Glossary

A/UX Apple's version of Unix, the near industry standard, multiprogramming, virtual memory operating system. Apple's advantage is that their Unix version has a Macintosh interface front end, making it more user friendly while retaining all its powerful features.

access time, average The amount of time it takes the computer to find and read data from a disk or from memory. For a hard disk it is defined as seek time (time to find the track) plus settling time (time to stabilize over the track) plus latency time (time to bring the sector data on the track under the head). Some manufacturers ignore both the average consideration and the latency factor to publish better times.

ADB Apple Desktop Bus is now the Apple standard serial communication bus that allows you to connect up to 15 input devices such as keyboard, mouse, joystick, puck, other pointing/motion devices, and graphics tablets to your SE and newer Macintoshes. It allows the devices to be connected in daisy chain fashion and provides increased flexibility with minimal increase in cost.

alphanumeric Data that has both numerals and letters.

ANSI Abbreviation for American National Standard Institute. A standard adopted by MS-DOS for cursor positioning. It is used in the ANSI.SYS file for device drivers.

ASCII Abbreviation for American Standard Code for Information Interchange. Binary numbers from 0 to 127 that represent the upper- and lowercase letters of the alphabet, the numbers 0 to 9, and the several symbols found on a keyboard. A block of eight 0s and 1s are used to represent all of these characters. The first 32 characters, 0 to 31, are reserved for non-character functions of a keyboard, modem, printer, or other device. Number 32, or 0010 0000, represents the space, which is a character. The numeral 1 is represented by the binary number for 49, which is 00110001. Text written in ASCII is displayed on the computer screen as standard text. Text written in other systems, such as WordStar, has several other characters added and is very difficult to read. Another 128 character representations have been added to the original 128 for graphics and programming purposes.

ASIC Stands for application specific integrated circuit.

assembly language A low-level machine language, made up of 0s and 1s.

asynchronous A serial type of communication where one bit at a time is transmitted. The bits are usually sent in blocks of eight 0s and 1s.

baud A measurement of the speed or data transfer rate of a communications line between the computer and printer, modem, or another computer. Most present day modems operate at 1200 baud. This is 1200 bits per second or about 120 characters per second.

benchmark A standard type program against which similar programs can be compared.

bezel The plastic or metal plate typically covering the front of a floppy or hard disk mounted in a computer case or chassis.

bidirectional Of or relating to both directions. Most printers print in both directions, thereby saving the time it takes to return to the other end of a line.

binary Binary numbers are 1s and 0s.

bit A contraction of the words *binary* and *digit*. One bit is a single binary digit.

boot or bootstrap or reset The startup process wherein the Macintosh is turned on, checks that its memory is OK, checks that its stored parameters are set as they should be, and turns over control to the user. A small amount of the program to do this is stored in ROM. Using this the computer "pulls itself up by its bootstraps." A reset is sometimes necessary to get the computer out of an error message or bomb dialog box if it is hung up for some reason.

buffer A buffer is usually some discrete amount of memory that is used to hold data. A computer can send data thousands of times faster than a printer or modem can utilize it. But in many cases the computer can do nothing else until all of the data has been transferred. By storing data in a buffer, which can then feed the data into the printer/modem as needed, the computer is freed to do other tasks.

bug The early computers were made with high-voltage vacuum tubes. It took rooms full of hot tubes to do the job that a credit card calculator can do today. One of the large systems went down one day. After several hours of troubleshooting, the technicians found a large bug that had crawled into the high voltage wiring. It had been electrocuted, but had shorted out the whole system. Since that time any type of trouble in a piece of software or hardware has been called a bug. To debug it, of course, is to try to find all of the errors or defects.

bulletin boards Usually a computer with a hard disk that can be accessed by modem. Software and programs can be uploaded or left on the bulletin board by a caller, or a caller can scan the software that has been left there by others and download any that he likes. A great source of help for a beginner.

bus Wires or circuits that connect a number of devices together or a path over which signals travel. Typically refers to the input and output paths to the Macintosh such as the NuBus cards in the Mac II family and the expansion bus slot in the Mac SE.

byte The smallest computer word or character is called a byte, and consists of 8 bits, or a block of eight 0s and 1s. These 8 bits can be arranged in 256 different ways. This is $2 \times 2 \times 2 \times 2 \times 2 \times 2 \times 2 \times 2 = 256$, or 2^8. Therefore, one byte can be made to represent any one of the 256 characters in the ASCII character set. It takes one byte to make a single character.

cache memory High speed memory in front of regular processor memory to speed up the computer. When the computer writes data in main memory, it leaves a copy of it in cache memory too. When the computer goes to read data, it looks first in cache memory. If it finds the data there, it doesn't bother to look in main memory. If the cache and program loops are of the right size, the computer hardly ever looks in main memory. The result is that everything runs a lot faster.

capacity This refers to the amount of binary data in 8-bit bytes that can be stored on the hard disk's multiple surfaces. Be aware that not all hard disk capacities are stated equal. It is difficult to state accurately until after the disk is installed in the computer and formatted because different computer types, controllers, formatting software, and disk drives themselves produce different results.

Cat Mac This book is about building your own Macintosh from catalog parts. Catalog Macintosh has been shortened to Cat Mac throughout the book.

CD-ROM Stands for compact disk read-only memory. A convenient and compact way of storing and distributing large volumes of data.

character A letter, a number, or an 8-bit piece of data.

chip An integrated circuit, usually made from a silicon wafer. It is microscopically etched and has thousands of transistors and semiconductors in a very small area. The 80286 CPU used in the AT has an internal main surface of about 1/2" square. It has 120,000 transistors on it.

clipboard A holding place for temporarily storing text or graphics.

clock speed The speed at which the CPU operates. (The operations of a computer are based on very critical timing, so they use a crystal to control their internal clocks.)

clone Computer slang for a copy of another manufacturer's computer. IBM defined the DOS personal computer with their model in 1981. All the copies of it today are clones—they copy its ROM and other features. In contrast, no Apple Macintosh clones exist because Apple has not licensed its ROM, and therefore it is illegal to copy it. The CAT Mac is not a clone, it is a Macintosh—usually mounted in a PC case.

coprocessor Usually an 8087 or 80287 that works in conjunction with the CPU and vastly speeds up some operations.

consultant Someone who is supposed to be an expert who can advise you and help you determine what your computer needs are (similar to an analyst). Because there are no standard requirements or qualifications that must be met, anyone can call themselves an analyst or consultant.

CPU Stands for central processing unit, the engine or chip that drives your Macintosh.

cursor The blinking spot on the screen that indicates where next character will be.

database A collection of data, usually related in some way.

desktop The screen or environment that the Apple Macintosh initially presents to the user—just like working at a real desk.

dialog box A window or full-screen display that pops up in response to a command.

DIP Stands for dual inline package, a type of packaging for a chip.

DMA Stands for direct memory access. Some parts of the computer, such as the disk drives, can exchange data directly with the RAM without having to go through the CPU.

DOS Stands for disk operating system. Also shorthand for MS-DOS and PC-DOS, the software engines that drive the majority of the IBM-compatible clone computers. Totally transparent to the user in the Macintosh environment.

DOS PC Denotes a personal computer which utilizes the IBM DOS operating system as opposed to utilizing the Macintosh operating system, Unix, or something else.

dot matrix printer A printer which represents each character using a series of dots in a closely spaced matrix—the Apple Imagewriter printer is an example.

double density Original Mac diskettes were 400K capacity single-sided diskettes; then 800K double density was introduced. Today's highest density standard is the 1.4Mb capacity drive used by Apple's FDHD Superdrive.

DRAM Stands for dynamic random access memory. A type of memory that must constantly be refreshed, or recharged; the primary type of memory used in PCs.

expansion boards Boards that can be plugged into one of the 8 slots on the motherboard to add memory or other functions.

FDHD Stands for floppy disk high density—Apple's latest floppy drive 1.4Mb standard.

Finder The part of the Apple Macintosh software that creates and maintains the user environment—keeps track of files on the desktop, etc.

fonts The different types of print letters, such as Gothic, Courier, Roman, Italic and others.

formatting The formatting step puts specific track and sector "pockets" into the hard disk—it builds exact locations where you can later find data. To quickly move data on and off the disk, certain tracks are identified as *directory tracks*. These contain information tags, or flags or pointers which point to (identify) the location of data on the disk.

FPU Stands for floating point unit. An additional chip working in parallel that speeds up processing time for numerical calculations.

fragmentation When a diskette or hard disk has data that has been changed several times, pieces of the files are located on different tracks and sectors. This slows down writing and reading of the files because the head has to move back and forth to the various tracks. When these files are copied to a newly formatted diskette, each file is written to clean, contiguous tracks, decreasing the access time to the diskette or hard disk.

Gb, gigabyte One billion bytes.

glitch An unexpected electrical spike or static disturbance that can cause loss of data.

gray market The practice of dealers selling their product to other dealers without adding value in order to meet their manufacturer's delivery quotas and keep their discount levels.

handshaking A protocol between systems, usually the printer and the computer, to indicate readiness to communicate with each other.

hi-res Stands for high resolution (a 640 × 480 or greater resolution monitor as opposed to Apple's standard 9" 512 × 342 display).

IC Stands for integrated circuit. Virtually all components used today will soon be in IC form to improve operating efficiencies and packing density, and achieve lower cost.

icon A graphical representation of an application program, program file, or a file folder (to hold either) on the Apple Macintosh desktop. A mouse can be pointed to an icon and double clicked to open the application or file. A key feature of the easy-to-use Macintosh graphical interface.

interface A piece of hardware or software that follows a distinct set of rules and allows communications between two systems.

interleave Depending on the speed of the computer attached to the hard disk, it might not be fast enough to read all the data from one sector transferred by the disk interface or to write it in one rotation of the disk. To avoid this problem, disks initially being formatted to work with slower Macintoshes have their sectors "interleaved." A "slow" Mac Plus requires a 3:1 interleave. This means the next "logical" sector from which the controller reads or writes data actually skips two sectors over from the last "physical" sector located on the disk. A "faster" Mac SE requires a 2:1 interleave (the next logical sector read or written actually skips one sector over from the last physical sector located on the disk). Mac IIs, Mac SE 30s, and up use a 1:1 interleave (the next logical sector read or written by the controller is identical with the next physical sector located on the disk).

Kb, kilobyte 1024 or 2^{10} bytes.

Killy clip A clip device useful for its special ability to securely attach a ribbon cable to a 68000 or 5380 IC chip.

LAN Stands for local area network; a system in which several computers are tied to each other or to a central server.

Laserwriter The Apple proprietary laser printer with the intelligent 68000-based Postscript engine.

LCD Stands for liquid crystal display.

mainframe A large computer that may serve several users.

Mb, megabyte Stands for one million bytes—1,048,576 bytes to be precise—a measurement of disk or memory storage capacity.

memory A high-speed temporary storage area next to the main computer used to store data and its location information.

menu A list of choices or options. A menu-driven system such as the Apple Macintosh makes it very easy for persons new to computers to learn how to use them.

MHz Stands for one million cycles per second—a measurement of frequency.

microsecond Stands for one millionth of a second (or 10^{-6} seconds in math notation).

modem A device which converts digital signals to analog form for transmission over a phone line, and reverses the process on the other end.

Molex A type of electrical connector useful for its capacity to be keyed, polarized, or locking.

monitor A device that displays a picture, also called a *video monitor*.

mono Single, or one. A *monochrome monitor* has one color capability.

mouse A pointing device that controls the movement of a cursor on the screen.

MTBF Stands for mean time between failures. An average of the time between failures, usually used in describing a hard disk or other components. An MTBF rating of 50,000 hours does not mean each hard disk will last that long before needing repair. It means that in a population of 50,000 hard disks, one will fail every hour, 24 hours per day. This means that about 18% of the drives will have to be repaired before year's end. Over a three-year period, over one half (54%) of the original 50,000 hard disks will require some amount of service.

multisync The ability of a monitor to adjust itself to a wide range of video input signal frequencies and thus be usable for a large variety of applications implemented over numerous computer platforms.

network, networking The ability to connect two or more similar or dissimilar devices, or the product resulting from such a connection.

ns, nanosecond Stands for one thousandth of a microsecond (in math notation 10^{-9} seconds); a very short time. Used to measure speeds of SIMM memory chips, i.e., an 80 ns SIMM is capable of operating faster than a 120 ns SIMM.

PC Stands for personal computer.

PMMU Stands for paged memory management unit. Used with A/UX and Apple system 7.0 software to give multiprogramming and virtual capabilities.

ports Access connections to gain entry to the Macintosh to tell it what to do or to give and receive data to/from it—usually serial, SCSI, or ADB but can be via direct attachment to the CPU chip or a special connector interface.

price performance A measure of efficiency when one factor is divided by the other. Also enables different types of objects to be compared easily by setting up a standard of price and performance.

RAM Stands for random access memory. A volatile memory: data stored in it is lost when the power is turned off.

RGB Stands for red, green, and blue, the three colors that are used in color monitors and TVs. Each color has its own electron gun that shoots streams of electrons to the back of the monitor display and causes it to light up in the various colors.

ribbon cable A flat cable with multiple conductor wires embedded in plastic, such as those used to connect hard and floppy drives to the logic board.

ROM Stands for read only memory. It does not change when the power is turned off.

scanner A device which converts printed information to electronic data. It works like a copier machine except that the information is stored electronically rather than reproduced physically.

SCSI Stands for small computer system interface. A fast parallel hard disk interface system developed by Shugart Associates and adopted by the American National Standards Institute (ANSI). The SCSI system allows multiple drives to be connected. It supports a transfer rate of 1.2Mb per second. Since a byte is 8 bits, this is about the same as the ESDI 10 megabit per second rate.

sector A section of a track on a disk or diskette.

serial The transmission of one bit at a time over a single line.

SIMM Stands for single in-line memory module.

slots Refers to the connectors or connections used for additional boards to be added to a SE, SE 30, or Mac II-family computer.

SOJ Refers to surface mount—a method of attaching chips or components to a circuit board without having to make holes (they are soldered onto the surface of the board).

SRAM Stands for static random access memory, made up of transistors that remain in whatever state they are placed in (either on or off) until changed or power is removed. SRAM can be very fast and does not need to be refreshed.

static Refers to an electrical charge picked up by a user that can be very damaging to delicate electronic computer circuitry and magnetic media. Precautions should be taken against it.

submin D Stands for a connector type typically used with the logic boards of Macintosh computers for SCSI, floppy, and video monitor connections.

SWIM Stands for Super Wozniak Integrated Machine and is the latest in the family of chips (following the IWM) that reduce complex floppy disk controller circuitry onto a single chip.

system, system icon, system software The Apple's Macintosh operating system software, totally transparent to the user, that appears merely as an icon in a folder which resides on a graphical desktop. The user can utilize its features without being aware of its presence.

System 7.0 Stands for the latest in the family of Apple systems and the first one to introduce multiprogramming and virtual capabilities to the Macintosh environment.

throughput Stands for the amount of data input a device is able to handle. It is a measure of capacity.

tracks The pattern of concentric circles or rings on the hard disk's surfaces, established by the formatting software, onto which data is written.

trash icon The icon which is part of the process that allows the Macintosh user to delete a file by pointing to it on the screen and performing a simple operation rather than a command as in the DOS world.

TTL Stands for transistor transistor logic. An electrical interface definition that also applies to the simplest, lowest cost class of monitors.

Unix The industry standard, multiprogramming, virtual operating system developed and supported by AT & T.

user groups Usually a club or a group of people who use computers. Often the club will be devoted to users of a certain type of computer, though anyone is welcome to join.

video Stands for visual or screen or picture-oriented data.

virtual memory A feature that allows certain operating systems to designate a portion of the disk space as a part of memory in a manner transparent to the user, so that larger programs are apparently memory resident all the time.

volatile Refers to memory units that lose stored information when power is lost. Nonvolatile memory would be that of a hard disk or tape.

wait state Slower devices on the bus may not be able to respond at the same speed as the CPU. For instance, if a memory access by the CPU requires more than one clock cycle, then the CPU is slowed down by having the CPU sit idle for one or more cycles while the procedure is accomplished. This is called a wait state.

WYSIWYG Pronounced wizzywig. Stands for what you see is what you get. An inherent feature of the Apple Macintosh graphical interface is that what you see on the screen matches the printed output.

Index

A

Abaton Technology, 199
accelerators, 93-106
  buying, 105-106
  buying checklist, 105-106
  combined with video cards, 167
  CPU/clock, 95
  file compression, 96
  FPU, 95
  full-function, 96-97
  memory/cache, 95-96
  mounting Cat Mac SE, 219-220
  mounting desktop Cat Mac, 251
  quality vendors, 106
  SCSI bus, 96
  software/hardware compatibility, 106
  suppliers, 107-108
  using 25-MHz 68040 CPUs, 104-105
  using 33-MHz 68040 CPUs, 105
  using 68000 CPUs, 97-98
  using up to 40-MHz 68030 CPUs, 98-101
  using up to 50-MHz 68030 CPUs, 101-103
  using up to 55-MHz 68030 CPUs, 103
ADB keyboards, 191-195
ADB mouse, 195-197
  connecting to Cat Mac SE, 233
ADIC, 147
Alliance Peripheral Systems, 142, 145, 147
Altex Electronics, 198
Altra, 199
AMTA, 198
Apple A/UX software, 327
Apple Computer, 143, 147
Apple Desktop Bus (ADB), 191
Apple Macintosh (*see* Macintosh)
Apple PowerBook, 313-314
Applied Engineering, 107, 142
Asher Engineering Corp., 199
ASLAN, 198
Atari Corporation, 319
Atlanta Technical Specialists, 169, 198, 305
Aura Systems, 169
average access time, 112
AXION, 198

B

backing up
  disks, 329
  hardware, 325-326
Bay Microsystems Inc., 143
Bering Industries, 144, 147
Beverly Hills Computer, 169, 200
bibliography, 68-69
binary numbering system, 72
bit, 72
Blackhole Technology Inc., 147
books, 332-333
Boston Computer Exchange, 67
Brier Technology, 142
brightness, 154
Business Technology Mfg., 198
byte, 72
Byte, 330

C

cables (*see* wiring)
cache memory, 74, 94
Cannon USA Inc., 146

capacity, 111-112
case (*see* chassis)
Cat Mac
  advantages, 15
  advantages of building, 3-7
  builder alternatives, 307-319
  builder alternative suppliers, 319
  compact desktop (*see* compact desktop Cat Mac)
  concept, 3-5
  desktop (*see* desktop Cat Mac)
  desktop upgrade kits (*see* desktop upgrade kits)
  flexibility, 6
  logic boards (*see* logic boards)
  portable upgrade kits (*see* portable upgrade kits)
  prices (*see* prices)
  putting together, 201-241
  repairing, 7
  resale value, 6
  system recommendations, 33-36
  systems not recommended, 36-37
  timesavings, 6
  tower upgrade kits (*see* tower upgrade kits)
  upgrade kits, 271-305
  video flexibility, 152
  wiring, 180-190
Cat Mac SE
  assembly, 209-241
  author's first, 202-204
  connecting ADB mouse, 233
  connecting hard disk drive, 234-235
  connecting keyboard, 233
  connecting parts to chassis, 233-234
  drilling chassis case, 214
  drilling rear cover plate, 214-215
  finishing thoughts, 239-241
  making logic board power cable, 226-230
  making logic board template, 209-212
  making rear cover template, 212-214
  mounting accelerator, 219-220
  mounting floppy disk drives, 222-224
  mounting hard disk drive, 220-222
  mounting logic board, 216-219
  mounting power supply, 215-216
  mounting speaker and cable, 224-226
  mounting video cards/modules, 219-220
  ordering parts, 207-208
  power on test, 234, 236-237
  preparation before building, 206-209
  receiving parts, 209
  step-by-step assembly, 204-206
  tools, 208-209
  troubleshooting, 241
Cat Mac SE 30
  mounting logic board, 275-277
CD Technology Inc., 144, 146
CD-ROM, 135, 325
  benefits, 137-139
CH Products, 199
chassis, 22, 172-180
  advantages of DOS PC, 172-174
  assembling ATS Mac IIcx/IIci, 283
  ATS Mac II/IIx/IIfx, 290-291
  back panel, 178-180
  closing cover on upgrade kits, 278-279
  closing cover on tower upgrade kits, 288, 293
  connecting parts, 233-234
  desktop Cat Mac, 244-246
  DOS PC classes, 173
  drilling case, 214
  drilling rear cover plate, 214-215
  enclosed metal, 273-275
  LAN style, 177
  making rear cover template, 212-214
  manufacturers, 198-199
  mini-tower style, 174-175
  mounting rear panel on compact desktop Cat Mac, 261
  mounting rear panel on desktop Cat Mac, 246-248
  opening ATS Mac IIcx/IIci, 283-285
  PC-AT style, 174-175
  PC-XT style, 174
  preparing for compact desktop Cat Mac, 261
  PS/2, 256
  PS/2 low-profile style, 175-177
  tower style, 178
Chip Merchant, 106
clock
  accelerators, 95
  speed, 94
clones, 314-316
  hardware engineering, 315
  manufacturing, 315-316
  software engineering, 315
Club Mac, 142, 145
CMS Enhancements, 143, 147
color, 154-155
color alignment, 155
compact desktop Cat Mac, 260-270
  final assembly/checkout, 270
  installing LED panel, 265
  installing speaker cable, 265
  mounting fan, 261-263
  mounting floppy disk drives, 266-268
  mounting hard disk drive, 266-268

mounting LED lamps, 264
mounting logic board, 261
mounting power supply, 261-263
mounting rear panel, 261
mounting reset switch, 264
mounting speaker, 263-264
mounting video card, 264, 266
prepare chassis, 261
wiring/cabling, 268-270
Compu-D, 67
Computer Shopper, 330
Computer Brokerage Services, 67
Computer Care Inc., 106
computer shows, 331
Connor Peripherals, 143
consultants, 332
contrast, 154
Core International, 143
cost (*see* prices)
CPU accelerators, 95
CPU chip, 93 (*see also* logic boards)
CRA, 67
Cutting Edge Inc., 142, 199
cylinders, 111

D

Data General, 7
DataDesk International, 199
Dayna Communications, 142
Daystar Digital, 107
dealers
  local, 332
Delta Research Labs, 107
Deltaic Systems, 143, 145, 147
desktop Cat Mac, 244-260
  chassis, 244-246
  compact (*see* compact desktop Cat Mac)
  final assembly and testing, 258-260
  mounting accelerator, 251
  mounting floppy disk drive, 254-255
  mounting hard disk drive, 251-253
  mounting logic board, 246-248
  mounting more than one SCSI device, 256-258
  mounting power supply, 248-249
  mounting rear panel, 246-248
  mounting speaker, 249-250
  mounting video card, 251
  PS/2 chassis, 256
  upgrade kits (*see* desktop upgrade kits)
desktop upgrade kits, 272-282
  closing chassis cover, 278-279
  enclosed metal chassis, 273-275
  mounting Cat Mac SE 30 logic board, 275-277

prices, 272
reinstalling disk drives, 277-278
reinstalling power supply, 277-278
reinstalling video card, 278
wiring, 279, 282
DGR Technologies, 146
Digi Graphics, 107
Digital Equipment Corp (DEC), 7-8
disk drives (*see* drives)
DOS compatibility, 17
DOS on Mac, 308-310
  running DOS PC programs in hardware, 309
  running DOS PC programs in software, 310
  transferring DOS PC files, 309
DOS PC chassis
  advantages, 172-174
  classes, 173
dot matrix printers, 322-323
Dove Computer Corp, 107
Dr. Mac, 169, 200
drives, 111
  CD-ROM, 135, 137
  EO, 134
  floppy disk, 21, 114-120, 254-255, 266-268, 277-278, 292-293, 300
  hard disk, 21, 120-131, 234-235, 251, 266-268, 277-278, 292-293
  MO, 134
  optical, 133-140
  removable, 131-133
  suppliers, 141-148
  tape, 140-141
  WORM, 134-135, 139
DTC Technology, 305
dynamic RAM (DRAM), 73

E

E-Machines, 169
Ehman Engineering Inc., 144, 199
80486 CPU chip family, 41
EMAC Div. Everex, 144, 145, 147
embedded controller, 112
Erasable Optical (EO) drives, 134
ESD Electro Rent Division, 67
ETC Peripherals, 145
Exabyte Corp., 147
expansion, options, 94
Exsel Inc., 67

F

fan, mounting compact desktop Cat Mac, 261-263
file compression accelerators, 96

flatness, 155
flicker, 154
floating-point unit (FPU), 94
floppy disk drives, 21, 114-120
   800K, 114
   800K vs. 1.4Mb, 119-120
   400K, 114
   mounting Cat Mac SE, 222-224
   mounting compact desktop Cat Mac, 266-268
   mounting desktop Cat Mac, 254-255
   mounting portable upgrade kits, 300
   mounting tower, 286-288, 292-293
   1.4Mb, 114-117
   reinstalling from upgrade kit, 277-278
   suppliers, 142
   2.8Mb, 117
   20.8Mb floptical, 117-118
   upgrades, 119
focus, 155
formatting, 111, 129-131
FPU accelerators, 95
fragmentation, 112
Fujitsu America Inc., 142, 143
full height, 112
full-function accelerators, 96-97
Fusion Data Systems, 107
FWB Inc., 144, 146, 147

G

Gadgets by Small Inc., 319
GCC Technologies Inc., 144
gigabyte, 73
glare coating, 155
Globe Manufacturing Sales Inc., 199
glossary, 335-343
graphics tablet, 198
gray scale, 153-154

H

half height, 112
hard disk drives, 21, 120-131
   connecting Cat Mac SE, 234-235
   formatting, 129-131
   mounting Cat Mac SE, 220-222
   mounting compact desktop Cat Mac, 266-268
   mounting/connecting, 127-129
   mounting desktop Cat Mac, 251-253
   mounting portable upgrade kits, 300
   mounting tower, 286-288, 292-293
   physical mounting, 128
   power connector, 128-129
   pricing, 124-126
   reasons for buying, 123-124
   reinstalling from upgrade kit, 277-278
   removable, 131
   SCSI cable, 129
   SCSI ID jumpers, 129
   SCSI termination, 129
   suppliers, 142-144
   used, 126
   vendors, 127
Hard Drives International, 143
hardware
   mail order dealers, 200
   suppliers, 169-170
Harris Laboratories, 107
heads, 111
Hewlett-Packard, 143
Hitachi America Ltd., 143, 146
Hydra Systems Inc., 319

I

IBM, 7-8, 318
IBM/OEM, 143
IDS Systems Inc., 144, 199
ImageProSystems, 169
Impulse Technology Sales, 107
InfoWorld, 330
Insignia Solutions Inc., 319
Intel 80486 CPU chip family, 41
interleave, 112
Interstate Computer Bank, 67
Iomega Corp., 145, 146
Irwin Magnetic Systems Inc., 147

J

Jameco Electronics, 199
JDR Microdevices, 199
Jobs, Steve, 46

K

Kennect Technology, 142
Kensington Microwave, 199
Key Tronic, 199
keyboards, 21, 190-195
   ADB, 191-195
   alternatives, 191-195
   connecting to Cat Mac SE, 233
   connecting tower upgrade kits, 288, 293
   manufacturers, 199-200
   mounting portable upgrade kits, 300
Killy clip, 77, 108
kilobyte, 73

L

LaCie Ltd., 144
Lapis Technologies, 169
LaserWriter printers, 323-324

LED, mounting compact desktop Cat Mac, 264-265
Liberty Systems Inc., 144, 146
LLB Company, 107
logic boards, 21, 39-69 (*see also* memory upgrades; upgrades)
   author's advice, 46
   categories, 43
   choosing, 42-46
   entry-level, 42, 44
   high-end, 45
   Intel 80486 CPU chip family, 41
   Mac 128, 42, 46-49
   Mac 512, 42, 46-49
   Mac Classic, 44, 52-53
   Mac Classic II, 44, 54-55
   Mac Hex, 45
   Mac II, 44, 58-60
   Mac IIci, 45, 61-63
   Mac IIcx, 60-61
   Mac IIfx, 45, 63-64
   Mac IIsi, 44, 57-58
   Mac IIx, 45, 60
   Mac LC, 44, 55-57
   Mac Plus, 42, 46-49
   Mac Quadra 700, 45, 64-66
   Mac Quadra 900, 45, 66-67
   Mac SE, 25, 44, 49-50
   Mac SE 30, 44, 50-52
   making template, 209-212
   midrange, 44-45
   Motorola 68000 CPU chip family, 40-42
   mounting ATS Mac II/IIx/IIfx, 291-292
   mounting compact desktop Cat Mac, 261
   mounting desktop Cat Mac, 246-248
   mounting Mac IIcx/IIci, 285-286
   mounting Mac SE, 216-219, 300
   mounting Mac SE 30, 275-277
   obsolete, 42
   portable, 45
   pricing, 25-26
   suppliers, 67-68
   to system cost ratio, 26-27
   upgrading, 40
long-term storage, 113-114

M

Mac Connection, 169, 200
MacDirect, 142
MacHeaven, 67
Macintosh
   Cat Mac (*see* Cat Mac)
   clones, 314-316
   cost overview, 22-33
   future, 18, 329-333
   general information, 2-3
   logic boards (*see* logic boards)
   modules, 20-22
   price performance, 8-10
   prices (*see* prices)
   SIMM rules (*see* SIMM rules)
   vs. DOS PC, 15-18
   why build your own, 1-18
Macintosh Buyer's Guide, 331
Macintosh Product Registry, 331
Macintosh portables
   Apple, 313
   miscellaneous, 314
MacLand, 169, 200
Mac on Atari, 316-317
   legal, 316
   price, 317
   technology/market need, 316
Mac on DOS, 310-316
Mac on Mac, portable or clone, 312
Mac on Unix, 317-319
   mainstream Apple multimedia, 318
   mainstream Apple RISC, 318
   mainstream Apple software operating system, 318-319
   mainstream Apple Unix, 318
MacProducts USA, 107, 146, 170, 200
Mac Sale International, 68
MacUser, 330
MacWarehouse, 170, 200
MacWEEK, 330
Macworld, 330
MacWorld Exposition, 331
MacZone, 170, 200
magazines, 330-331
Magneto Optical (MO) drives, 134
   benefits, 136-137
mail order, 329-330
   hardware dealers, 200
   suppliers, 169-170
   vendors, 12, 14
maintenance, 328-329
Mass Microsystems, 145, 146
Maxoptix Corp., 146
Maxtor Corp., 143
Maya Computer, 68
Maynard Electronics, 147
mean time between failure (MTBF), 113
media, 110
media cartridge, removable, 131-133
megabyte, 73
memory, 21, 71-75
   cache, 74, 94
   cache accelerators, 95-96
   CD-ROM, 325

memory (cont.)
  DRAM, 73
  options, 94
  RAM, 73-74
  ROM, 73
  static RAM (SRAM), 73
  suppliers, 106-107
  upgrades (see memory upgrades)
Memory Masters, 107
memory upgrades, 75-90
  Apple Mac Plus, 76
  daughterboards, 77-79
  Mac 128, 76-79
  Mac 512, 76-79
  Mac Classic, 79
  Mac fixed, 76
  SIMM, 80-90
Micro Exchange, 68
MicroMac Technology, 305
MicroNet Technology Inc., 144, 146, 147
Micropolis Corp., 143
Microspeed Inc., 199
Microtech International Inc., 107, 144, 145, 146, 147
Micro Touch Systems Inc., 199
Mirror Technologies Inc., 142, 144, 148, 199
Mitch Hall Associates, 331
Mitsubishi Electronics America Inc., 146
Mobius Technologies Inc., 169, 200
modems, 324-325
money, saving, 19-37 (see also prices)
monitors, 21, 150-169
  color, 163-166
  full-page, 153
  graphics, 151
  interface, 155
  landscape, 153
  low-end, 156-157
  midrange, 162-163
  overview/history, 150-152
  packaging, 155
  physical viewing screen, 154-155
  picture tube, 155
  portrait, 153
  price performance, 156-157
  Princeton MAX-15, 162
  SCSI connection, 166
  simplicity, 151
  size, 153
  size vs. resolution, 153
  specifications, 154-156
  suppliers, 169
  TTL, 157-159
  two-page, 153

video cards (see video cards)
MOST Inc., 146
Motorola 68000 CPU chip family, 40-42
mouse, 21, 190-191
  ADB, 195-197
  alternatives, 195-198
  connecting ADB to Cat Mac SE, 233
  connecting tower upgrade kits, 288, 293
  Felix from Altra, 198
  manufacturers, 199-200
Mouse Systems Corp., 200
multisync, 153

N

National Inventory Exchange, 68
NEC Technologies Inc., 143
networking, 324
New Life Computer Corp., 107
Newer Technology, 107
North Shore Computers, 68
Novy Systems, 108

O

O.C.E.A.N. Microsystems Inc., 146
Olson Metal Products Co., 199
Optical Access International, 146
optical character recognition (OCR), 325
optical drives, 133-140
  benefits, 135
  suppliers, 146-147
Optima Technology Inc., 144, 148
Optimem div. Archive Co., 146
Orange Micro Inc., 319
Outbound Systems Inc., 319

P

paged memory management unit (PMMU), 94
Panasonic Communications & Systems Co., 146
PCPC, 144
Peripheral Land Inc., 142, 144, 146, 148
Peripheral Outlet, 68, 107
peripherals, 322-326
  prices, 323-326
Personal Computer Peripherals Corp., 148
phosphor persistence, 155
pin cushioning, 155
Pinnacle Micro, 146
Pioneer Communications, 147
pixel, 152
pixel density (dpi), 152, 154
pixel dimensions, 153
platters, 110
portable upgrade kits, 297-305

finishing steps, 303-305
mounting disk drives, 300
mounting keyboard, 300
mounting Mac SE logic board, 300
mounting power supply, 301-302
opening, 299
Power R, 169
power supply, 21
   mounting Cat Mac SE, 215-216
   mounting compact desktop Cat Mac, 261-263
   mounting desktop Cat Mac, 248-249
   mounting portable upgrade kits, 301-302
   reinstalling from upgrade kit, 277-278
Practical Solutions, 200
Pre-Owned Electronics, 68
prices
   accelerators, 105
   Apple Mac SE 20 list, 23
   Apple Mac SE 20 street, 23-24
   Apple Mac SE 20 used, 24
   Cat Mac, 6
   Cat Mac Classic vs. Apple Mac Classic, 30-31
   Cat Mac cost savings, 34
   Cat Mac IIci vs. Apple Mac IIci, 32-33
   Cat Mac IIfx vs. Apple Mac IIfx, 33
   Cat Mac IIsi vs. Apple Mac IIsi, 31
   Cat Mac LC vs. Apple Mac LC, 31
   Cat Mac overview, 29
   Cat Mac SE, 24
   Cat Mac vs. Apple Macintosh, 29-30
   computer vendor vs. performance trend, 8
   desktop upgrade kits, 272
   floppy disk drives, 114-118
   hard disk drives, 124-126
   keyboards, 192
   logic board, 25-26
   logic board to system cost ratio, 26-27
   Mac on Atari, 317
   Mac System vs. logic board, 4
   Macintosh vs. DOS PC, 17-18
   monitors, 156-157, 161, 162, 165-166
   mouse, 196-197
   new vs. new equipment, 13
   optical drives, 135
   overview, 22-33
   peripherals, 323-326
   printers, 323
   real world, 23
   saving money, 19-37
   SIMM, 74-75, 82
   third-party computer vendor vs. performance trend, 11
   tool kit, 208

trends, 23
upgrade, 28
video cards, 159, 162
Princeton Graphic Systems, 169
printers
   dot matrix, 322-323
   LaserWriter, 323-324
Procom Technology Inc., 144, 147, 148
PSI, 107

Q

Quadmation Inc., 142
Quadram, 142
Qualstar Corp., 148
Quantum Corp., 143, 145
Quorum Systems, 319

R

Radio Frequency Interference (RFI), 173, 273
Radius, 108, 169
RAM chips, 74
random access memory (RAM), 73-74
read only memory (ROM), 73
read/write heads, 111
refresh rate, 154
Relax Technology Inc., 144, 147, 148
removable disk drives, 131-133
   suppliers, 144-145
reset switch, mounting compact desktop Cat Mac, 264
resolution, 153, 154
Ricoh Corp., 147
Ruby Systems Inc., 144

S

scanners, 325
scanning, 155
SCSI
   bus accelerators, 96
   mounting more than one, 256-258
Seagate Technology, 143
Second Wave Inc., 108
sectors, 111
short-term storage, 113
Shreve Systems, 68
SIMM, 74
   buying, 80
   installating/removing, 82-85
   memory size, 82
   memory upgrade, 80-90
   price history/trends, 74-75
   prices, 82
   rules—Mac Classic II, 89-90
   rules—Mac Classic, 89-90

SIMM (cont.)
  rules—Mac IIfx, 90
  rules—Mac IIsi, 89-90
  rules—Mac LC, 89-90
  rules—Mac NuBus, 86-88
  rules—Mac Plus, 85-86
  rules—Mac Quadra 700, 89-90
  rules—Mac SE 30, 86-88
  rules—Mac SE, 85-86
  sizes, 81
  speeds, 81-82
  types of, 80-81
single inline memory module (see SIMM)
68000 CPU chip family, 40-42
small computer system interface (SCSI), 112
software, 326-327
  Apple A/UX, 327
  control, 94
  System 6, 326
  System 7, 326-327
Sony Corp. of America, 143, 147
Sophisticated Circuits Inc., 200
speaker
  mounting Cat Mac SE, 224-226
  mounting compact desktop Cat Mac, 263-264
  mounting desktop Cat Mac, 249-250
speed, 17
Startup disk, 234
static electricity, 328
static RAM (SRAM), 73
storage, 109-148
  definitions, 110-113
  overview, 113-114
  types of, 113-114
Storage Dimensions, 144, 147
Sun Remarketing, 68
SuperMac Technology, 169
System 6 software, 326
System 7 software, 326-327

T

tape drives, 140-141
  suppliers, 147-148
Techmar Inc., 148
TechNoir, 108
Technology Works, 107
third-party vendors, 10
throughput, 94
Toshiba America Information Systems Inc., 143
Total Systems Integration, 108
tower upgrade kits, 282-297
  assembling ATS Mac IIcx/IIci chassis, 283

ATS Mac II/IIx/IIfx chassis, 290-291
closing chassis, 288, 293
connecting cables, 286-288, 292-293
connecting keyboard/mouse, 288, 293
finishing steps, 288-290, 293-295
mounting ATS Mac II/IIx/IIfx logic board, 291-292
mounting disk drives, 286-288, 292-293
mounting Mac IIcx/IIci logic board, 285-286
mounting video card, 292-293
opening ATS Mac II/IIx/IIfx, 291
opening ATS Mac IIcx/IIci enclosure, 283-285
trackball, 198
tracks, 111
Tradewinds Peripherals Inc., 145
transistor transistor logic (TTL), 153
troubleshooting, 241
Tulin Corp., 144

U

upgrade kits, 271-305
  Cat Mac portable, 297-305
  Cat Mac tower, 282-297
  desktop Cat Mac, 272-282
  suppliers, 305
upgrades
  accelerators (see accelerators)
  Apple, 91-92
  Macintosh, 90-106
  memory, 75-90
  prices (see prices)
  process, 91
  suppliers, 106-107
used equipment, 11-12
user groups, 331

V

video cards, 156-169
  ATS, 157-159
  color, 163-165
  combined with accelerator, 167
  Lapis Technologies, 159-160
  Lapis Technologies 1-bit monochrome, 161-162
  midrange, 162-163
  mounting Cat Mac SE, 219-220
  mounting compact desktop Cat Mac, 264, 266
  mounting desktop Cat Mac, 251
  mounting tower, 292-293
  Power R module, 162
  reinstalling from upgrade kit, 278
video interface, building your own, 167-169

finishing steps, 303-305
mounting disk drives, 300
mounting keyboard, 300
mounting Mac SE logic board, 300
mounting power supply, 301-302
opening, 299
Power R, 169
power supply, 21
   mounting Cat Mac SE, 215-216
   mounting compact desktop Cat Mac, 261-263
   mounting desktop Cat Mac, 248-249
   mounting portable upgrade kits, 301-302
   reinstalling from upgrade kit, 277-278
Practical Solutions, 200
Pre-Owned Electronics, 68
prices
   accelerators, 105
   Apple Mac SE 20 list, 23
   Apple Mac SE 20 street, 23-24
   Apple Mac SE 20 used, 24
   Cat Mac, 6
   Cat Mac Classic vs. Apple Mac Classic, 30-31
   Cat Mac cost savings, 34
   Cat Mac IIci vs. Apple Mac IIci, 32-33
   Cat Mac IIfx vs. Apple Mac IIfx, 33
   Cat Mac IIsi vs. Apple Mac IIsi, 31
   Cat Mac LC vs. Apple Mac LC, 31
   Cat Mac overview, 29
   Cat Mac SE, 24
   Cat Mac vs. Apple Macintosh, 29-30
   computer vendor vs. performance trend, 8
   desktop upgrade kits, 272
   floppy disk drives, 114-118
   hard disk drives, 124-126
   keyboards, 192
   logic board, 25-26
   logic board to system cost ratio, 26-27
   Mac on Atari, 317
   Mac System vs. logic board, 4
   Macintosh vs. DOS PC, 17-18
   monitors, 156-157, 161, 162, 165-166
   mouse, 196-197
   new vs. new equipment, 13
   optical drives, 135
   overview, 22-33
   peripherals, 323-326
   printers, 323
   real world, 23
   saving money, 19-37
   SIMM, 74-75, 82
   third-party computer vendor vs. performance trend, 11
   tool kit, 208
   trends, 23
   upgrade, 28
   video cards, 159, 162
Princeton Graphic Systems, 169
printers
   dot matrix, 322-323
   LaserWriter, 323-324
Procom Technology Inc., 144, 147, 148
PSI, 107

Q

Quadmation Inc., 142
Quadram, 142
Qualstar Corp., 148
Quantum Corp., 143, 145
Quorum Systems, 319

R

Radio Frequency Interference (RFI), 173, 273
Radius, 108, 169
RAM chips, 74
random access memory (RAM), 73-74
read only memory (ROM), 73
read/write heads, 111
refresh rate, 154
Relax Technology Inc., 144, 147, 148
removable disk drives, 131-133
   suppliers, 144-145
reset switch, mounting compact desktop Cat Mac, 264
resolution, 153, 154
Ricoh Corp., 147
Ruby Systems Inc., 144

S

scanners, 325
scanning, 155
SCSI
   bus accelerators, 96
   mounting more than one, 256-258
Seagate Technology, 143
Second Wave Inc., 108
sectors, 111
short-term storage, 113
Shreve Systems, 68
SIMM, 74
   buying, 80
   installating/removing, 82-85
   memory size, 82
   memory upgrade, 80-90
   price history/trends, 74-75
   prices, 82
   rules—Mac Classic II, 89-90
   rules—Mac Classic, 89-90

SIMM (cont.)
  rules—Mac IIfx, 90
  rules—Mac IIsi, 89-90
  rules—Mac LC, 89-90
  rules—Mac NuBus, 86-88
  rules—Mac Plus, 85-86
  rules—Mac Quadra 700, 89-90
  rules—Mac SE 30, 86-88
  rules—Mac SE, 85-86
  sizes, 81
  speeds, 81-82
  types of, 80-81
single inline memory module (see SIMM)
68000 CPU chip family, 40-42
small computer system interface (SCSI), 112
software, 326-327
  Apple A/UX, 327
  control, 94
  System 6, 326
  System 7, 326-327
Sony Corp. of America, 143, 147
Sophisticated Circuits Inc., 200
speaker
  mounting Cat Mac SE, 224-226
  mounting compact desktop Cat Mac, 263-264
  mounting desktop Cat Mac, 249-250
speed, 17
Startup disk, 234
static electricity, 328
static RAM (SRAM), 73
storage, 109-148
  definitions, 110-113
  overview, 113-114
  types of, 113-114
Storage Dimensions, 144, 147
Sun Remarketing, 68
SuperMac Technology, 169
System 6 software, 326
System 7 software, 326-327

T

tape drives, 140-141
  suppliers, 147-148
Techmar Inc., 148
TechNoir, 108
Technology Works, 107
third-party vendors, 10
throughput, 94
Toshiba America Information Systems Inc., 143
Total Systems Integration, 108
tower upgrade kits, 282-297
  assembling ATS Mac IIcx/IIci chassis, 283
  ATS Mac II/IIx/IIfx chassis, 290-291
  closing chassis, 288, 293
  connecting cables, 286-288, 292-293
  connecting keyboard/mouse, 288, 293
  finishing steps, 288-290, 293-295
  mounting ATS Mac II/IIx/IIfx logic board, 291-292
  mounting disk drives, 286-288, 292-293
  mounting Mac IIcx/IIci logic board, 285-286
  mounting video card, 292-293
  opening ATS Mac II/IIx/IIfx, 291
  opening ATS Mac IIcx/IIci enclosure, 283-285
trackball, 198
tracks, 111
Tradewinds Peripherals Inc., 145
transistor transistor logic (TTL), 153
troubleshooting, 241
Tulin Corp., 144

U

upgrade kits, 271-305
  Cat Mac portable, 297-305
  Cat Mac tower, 282-297
  desktop Cat Mac, 272-282
  suppliers, 305
upgrades
  accelerators (see accelerators)
  Apple, 91-92
  Macintosh, 90-106
  memory, 75-90
  prices (see prices)
  process, 91
  suppliers, 106-107
used equipment, 11-12
user groups, 331

V

video cards, 156-169
  ATS, 157-159
  color, 163-165
  combined with accelerator, 167
  Lapis Technologies, 159-160
  Lapis Technologies 1-bit monochrome, 161-162
  midrange, 162-163
  mounting Cat Mac SE, 219-220
  mounting compact desktop Cat Mac, 264, 266
  mounting desktop Cat Mac, 251
  mounting tower, 292-293
  Power R module, 162
  reinstalling from upgrade kit, 278
video interface, building your own, 167-169

video monitors (*see* monitors)
voltage, 328

W

Western Digital, 143
Wetex International Corp., 145
Wholesale 54, 143, 145
wiring
  building your own video interface, 167-169
  cabling Cat Mac, 255-256
  Cat Mac, 180-190
  compact desktop Cat Mac, 268-270
  connecting hard disk drives, 128-129
  floppy cable, 181, 187
  installing speaker cable on compact desktop Cat Mac, 265
  Mac 128/512/Plus, 185-187
  Mac Classic/Classic II, 183
  Mac II/IIx/IIfx, 184
  Mac IIcx/IIci/IIsi/Quadra 700, 183
  Mac LC, 185
  Mac SE/SE30, 183
  making logic board power cable for Cat Mac SE, 226-230
  manufacturers, 198-199
  miscellaneous cables, 182, 187-190
  mounting speaker cable on Cat Mac SE, 224-226
  P8/P9 connectors, 229-230
  power cable, 181-183
  SCSI cable, 181, 187
  SCSI monitor connection, 166
  tower upgrade kits, 286-288, 292-293
  upgrade kit, 279, 282
word length, 73
working storage, 113
Write Once Read Many (WORM) drives, 134-135
  benefits, 137-140
WYSIWYG, 152-153

Other Bestsellers of Related Interest

BUILD YOUR OWN 386/386SX COMPATIBLE AND SAVE A BUNDLE—2nd Edition
—Aubrey Pilgrim

Assemble an 80386 microcomputer at home using mail-order parts that cost a lot less today than they did several years ago. Absolutely no special technical know-how is required—only a pair of pliers, a couple of screwdrivers, and this detailed, easy-to-follow guide. 248 pages, 79 illustrations. Book No. 4089, $18.95 paperback, $29.95 hardcover

BIT-MAPPED GRAPHICS—Steve Rimmer

This is one of the first books to cover the specific graphic file formats used by popular paint and desktop publishing packages. It shows you how to pack and unpack bit-map image files so you can import and export them to other applications. And, it helps you sort through available file formats, standards, patches, and revision levels, using commercial-quality C code to explore bit-mapped graphics and effectively deal with image files. 504 pages, 131 illustrations. Book No. 3558, $26.95 paperback, $38.95 hardcover

MACINTOSH SYSTEM 7: The Complete Sourcebook—Gordon M. Campbell

Campbell shows off some of the exciting new features of System 7 and offers tips for upgrading your hardware and software. This is your best guide to the first major development in the Macintosh since its introduction in 1984. With this book by your keyboard, you can count on clear skies and smooth sailing, for either upgrade or installation. 320 pages, illustrated. Book No. 4074, $32.95 paperback only

THE CONCISE PC NOTEBOOK AND LAPTOP USER'S GUIDE—Dan Gookin

Here, you'll find complete information on computers designed to leave the office and follow you on the road. Useful tips are furnished throughout to help make laptop computing easier and more productive for you, no matter what your technical skill. With this book in hand, your initiation to laptop computing will be virtually painless! 304 pages, 40 illustrations. Book No. 3921, $22.95 paperback only

MS-DOS® BATCH FILE PROGRAMMING
—3rd Edition—Ronny Richardson

Now updated to cover DOS 5.0, this book explores the power of .BAT—the PC user's key to total system control. Richardson shows how to boost productivity dramatically with simple step-saving programs. He discusses two of the most often customized system batch files, AUTOEXEC.BAT and CONFIG.SYS. You can then progress to creating your own batch files in order to make your computer run more smoothly and do exactly what you want it to do. 440 pages, 186 illustrations. Book No. 3916, $26.95 paperback, $36.95 hardcover

MS-DOS® BATCH FILE UTILITIES
—Ronny Richardson

Featuring more than 200 of the best batch file programs available for the PC, this is the most complete source of documentation available for batch file utilities currently offered as shareware or in the public domain. Arranged alphabetically and meticulously cross-referenced by category, this valuable reference features detailed descriptions and instructions for ALL commercial batch files on the DOS market today. 368 pages, 275 illustrations. Book No. 3915, $29.95 paperback, $36.95 hardcover

FOXPRO® : The Master Reference
—2nd Edition
—Robin Stark and Shelley Satonin

Design and run powerful, customized databases in no time using all the exciting new features of FoxPro. This alphabetical guide to every FoxPro command and function covers all versions through 2.0—more than 350 entries in all. Its innovative three-part indexing system leads you quickly to all commands, functions, and examples found in the book. 512 pages, 135 illustrations. Book No. 4056, $24.95 paperback only

NORTON UTILITIES® 6.0: An Illustrated Tutorial
—Richard Evans

Richard Evans shows you how to painlessly perform the most dazzling Norton functions using the all-new features of Norton Utilities 6.0. He also reviews the best from previous releases, providing clear, easy-to follow instructions and screen illustrations reflecting Norton's new developments. You'll also learn about NDOS, a new configuration and shell program that replaces COMMAND.COM. 464 pages, 277 illustrations. Book No. 4132, $19.95 paperback, $29.95 hardcover

101+ FOXPRO® AND dBASE® IV USER-DEFINED FUNCTIONS—Philip Steele

Whether you've already written many lines of database code and just want to improve your code or you want to develop more complex applications for distribution in the corporate marketplace, this book's for you. It contains professional guidelines for writing and developing UDFs that will eliminate repetitive database programming tasks. A companion disk, offered on an order form at the end of the book, contains all the UDFs used in the book. 368 pages, 159 illustrations. Book No. 3951, $22.95 paperback only

GRAPHICAL USER INTERFACE PROGRAMMING—Steve Rimmer

Graphical user interfaces are one of the hottest topics in PC software technology today. Creating and using GUIs requires a delicate combination of graphics programming skill and an ability to organize multiple graphic objects. This book shows you how to combine these skills to create images through bit-mapping graphics. Rimmer shows you how to write tight code menus, screen fonts, mouse interfaces, icons, and more. 440 pages, 176 illustrations. Book No. 3875, $24.95 paperback, $36.95 hardcover

THE RELATIONAL DATABASE ADVISOR: Elements of PC Database Design
—Kimberly Maughan Saunders

Kimberly Saunders gives you easy-to-follow guidelines for every phase in the database design process, providing specific suggestions for building databases that fit a variety of business needs and software environments. You'll soon create sophisticated libraries of database files with common informational links. 248 pages, 128 illustrations. Book No. 3944, $16.95 paperback only

SQL: Structured Query Language—2nd Edition
—Dr. Carolyn J. Hursch and
Dr. Jack L. Hursch

Carolyn J. Hursch and Jack L. Hursch present a complete overview of SQL, tracing its mathematical structure from its basis in first-order logic to its present-day role and the efforts of the American National Standards Institute (ANSI) to develop a standard SQL language. They cover all the components of conventional SQL language; SQL commands, keywords, and data types; and value expressions supported by SQL. 216 pages, illustrated. Book No. 3803, $21.95 paperback, $32.95 hardcover

DOS 5 DEMYSTIFIED—James S. Forney

This book provides a frank appraisal of the strengths, weaknesses, and peculiarities of this new release, offering insider tips to help you get the most from DOS 5's new features. It emphasizes compatibility and productivity to help you take full advantage of the power of DOS 5. Some of the new and enhanced features covered include: HIMEM.SYS, DIS SERVICES, QBASIC, and EDIT. 440 pages, illustrated. Book No. 3860, $24.95 paperback, $34.95 hardcover

THE ENTREPRENEURIAL PC
—Bernard J. David

Put that expensive home PC to work for you. You will learn about the profit-making potential of computers in typing, word processing, desktop publishing, database programming, hardware installation, electronic mail, and much more. David uses detailed, real-life examples to describe some of the more popular avenues of entrepreneurship for the home PC owner. 336 pages, 50 illustrations. Book No. 3823, $19.95 paperback, $29.95 hardcover

UPGRADE YOUR IBM® COMPATIBLE AND SAVE A BUNDLE—2nd Edition—Aubrey Pilgrim
Praise for the first edition . . .
"Every aspect is covered . . . liberally and clearly illustrated . . . invaluable."
—*PC Magazine*

Find valuable advice on adding the newest high-quality, low-cost hardware to your PC with this book. It offers informative how-to's for replacing motherboards with 80286, 80386, and 80486 boards; adding new floppy and hard disk drives; replacing old BIOS chips, installing chips and memory boards; and plugging in internal modems and VGA, fax, and network boards. 264 pages, 60 illustrations. Book No. 3828, $19.95 paperback, $29.95 hardcover

COMPUTER SECURITY HANDBOOK
—2nd Edition—Richard H. Baker

This edition emphasizes practical, affordable measures that protect networks and database servers, featuring all-new coverage of virus control methods, the 1986 Computer Fraud and Abuse Act, and recent case studies of security problems. You'll find complete information on prevention and cure of viruses, electronic eavesdropping, personnel controls, identifying your most vulnerable points, password perils, security planning, and how a computer can protect itself. 432 pages, 70 illustrations. Book No. 3592, $24.95 paperback, $34.95 hardcover

Prices Subject to Change Without Notice.

Look for These and Other TAB Books at Your Local Bookstore

To Order Call Toll Free 1-800-822-8158
or write to TAB BOOKS, Blue Ridge Summit, PA 17294-0840.

Title	Product No.	Quantity	Price

☐ Check or money order made payable to TAB BOOKS

Charge my ☐ VISA ☐ MasterCard ☐ American Express

Acct. No. _____ Exp. _____

Signature: _____

Name: _____

Address: _____

City: _____

State: _____ Zip: _____

Subtotal $ _____

Postage and Handling
($3.00 in U.S., $5.00 outside U.S.) $ _____

Add applicable state and local sales tax $ _____

TOTAL $ _____

TAB BOOKS catalog free with purchase; otherwise send $1.00 in check or money order and receive $1.00 credit on your next purchase.

Orders outside U.S. must pay with international money order in U.S. dollars.

TAB Guarantee: If for any reason you are not satisfied with the book(s) you order, simply return it (them) within 15 days and receive a full refund.
BC